EUROPEAN RUSSIA

Archangel

NORTH

Vologda

Perm

stroma

Viatka

URALS

Nizhnii
Novgorod

Kazan

Ufa

S I B E R I A

Orenburg

MIDDLE VOLGA

Simbirsk

Penza

Samara

EASTERN STEPPE

Saratov

Astrakhan

Caspian Sea

BUS

US

0   100   200   300
Miles

NOBILITY AND PRIVILEGE IN LATE IMPERIAL RUSSIA

NOBILITY AND PRIVILEGE IN LATE IMPERIAL RUSSIA

SEYMOUR BECKER

NORTHERN ILLINOIS UNIVERSITY PRESS

DEKALB, ILLINOIS

1985

Publication of this book was assisted by a grant from the Publications Program of the National Endowment for the Humanities, an independent federal agency.

Library of Congress Cataloging in Publication Data

Becker, Seymour.
  Nobility and privilege in late Imperial Russia.

  Bibliography: p.
  Includes index.
  1. Soviet Union—Nobility—History—19th century.
2. Land tenure—Soviet Union—History—19th century.
I. Title.
HT653.S65B43   1985   305.5'223'0947   84—27230

ISBN 0–87580–133–1

FOR ALLA

CONTENTS

TABLES

PREFACE

THIS study contains much that would be part of a general and comprehensive history of the Russian nobility from 1861 to 1914, but it does not pretend to be such a history. It is rather an examination of several crucial aspects of the history of the nobility during that period of rapid social change: the changing relationships of the nobility to the land and to traditional occupational roles, the significance of the campaign waged by the self-appointed traditionalist defenders of noble interests and of the response they evoked from both the nobility and the state, and the emergence of a *class* of substantial landed proprietors out of the noble *estate*.

Between the emancipation of the serfs and the fall of the old regime the Russian nobility underwent very dramatic changes, usually characterized as "the decline of the nobility." By this is meant the forcible divorce of the nobility from their landed properties and consequently from their traditional way of life, as well as their loss of political influence as they yielded their places in the civil and military service to commoners. Contemporary observers were virtually unanimous in their perception of these phenomena but divided as to whether they considered these developments to be positive or negative. Some observers welcomed the changes as part of Russia's inevitable transition from a traditional society based on legal privilege to a modern society based on legal equality. Others deplored what they saw happening to the nobility as a disaster not just for nobles but for the Russian state and society as a whole. The latter group offered a program designed to halt or at least slow down an evolution they believed was neither desirable nor inevitable.

After a quarter century during which reforms initiated by the state had gone a long way toward undermining the traditional structures of Russian life, the autocracy at the beginning of the 1880s publicly assumed, and never thereafter abandoned, a position in support of the traditional order in general and of the nobility in particular. In the last two decades of the century, the state even implemented some of the proposals of the nobility's traditionalist defenders. And still the economic and social transformation of the nobility continued. Neither the desires of the nobles themselves nor the larger and more concrete interests of the state proved consonant with the ideas and proposals of the traditionalists. By the early twentieth century the noble estate had virtually vanished from the Russian social scene, its members having been absorbed into more modern social groupings. The most visible of these, because it came closest to the traditional image of the nobility and because it was very largely noble in composition, was a class or interest group of intermediate and large landowners seriously devoted to agriculture.

Issues relating to noble landowning were at the heart of the "noble question," discussion of which filled many pages in the newspapers and serious journals of the late nineteenth and early twentieth centuries. Although it was never legally defined as a landed estate, the nobility was widely perceived as such. Thus, after a discussion in chapter 1 of the dimensions of the problem of the nobility's "decline," I shall turn in chapter 2 to a reappraisal of the question of noble landownership. This reappraisal is based on original analyses and correlations of data on purchases and sales of land, size of holdings, land prices and rents, and mortgage debt, by *guberniia* and region as well as in aggregate terms for European Russia. By far the greater part of the evidence introduced in chapter 2, as well as in chapter 6, is derived from (rather than simply reproduces) raw data in published and archival sources and is therefore not elsewhere available.

Chapter 3 deals with the traditionalist ideology, the subscribers to which were encouraged by the state's new course from 1881 to think they could solve the noble question to their satisfaction. Chapters 4 through 7 treat the efforts of these traditionalists to halt "the decline of the nobility," as well as the nobles' own search for new identities in agriculture, state service, the professions, commerce and industry, and so on. Chapters 7 and 8 focus on the emerging class of substantial, and largely noble, landowners. Finally, the conclusion offers some revisionist thoughts on the nobility's share of responsibility for the political intransigence that finally brought down Russia's old regime in 1917.

I should like to express my gratitude to the former Inter-University Committee on Travel Grants for the opportunity to spend an academic year in Moscow and Leningrad and to the American Council of Learned Societies and the Research Council and Faculty Academic Study Program of Rutgers University for the financial support and time away from the classroom that were necessary for the research and writing of this study.

All translations from Russian sources are my own. The Library of Congress system without diacritical marks and ligatures has been followed in the transliteration of Russian words, with the exception of familiar names and terms, which appear in their Anglicized forms.

NOBILITY AND PRIVILEGE IN LATE IMPERIAL RUSSIA

"THE DECLINE OF THE NOBILITY"

FROM PRIVILEGE TO LEGAL EQUALITY

RUSSIA'S history since the eighteenth century has been part of the history of the West, and the transformation that the Russian nobility underwent between 1861 and 1914 was part of a pan-European phenomenon. This phenomenon has recently been approached from contrasting points of view by Jerome Blum and Arno Mayer. Blum has explored the process of peasant emancipation on the European continent between the 1770s and the 1860s—a process he sees as the watershed between traditional and modern society. Traditional society, both in the West and in Russia, was "divided into orders, or estates, that were arranged in a descending scale of status and privilege. Law and custom defined the orders, and law and custom established the hierarchy of privileges and obligations that characterized the society."[1] Each estate was assigned a specific social function, and the hierarchical arrangement of the orders was determined by the importance the society accorded to each function. The individual's rights, privileges, and obligations depended upon the estate to which he belonged, membership normally being hereditary.[2]

In modern society, by contrast, "there [is] one law for all citizens, and (at least nominally) everyone [is] equal before the law." As a consequence of legal equality, "power follows upon the possession of wealth"—in contrast to estate society, where the reverse was true.[3]

The crucial moment in the transformation of a society based on status and privilege into one based on legal equality, according to Blum, was the emancipation of the peasant masses. Although the implementation of legal equality for all was neither immediate nor total, and "peasants often were still subjected to restraints and handicaps not imposed upon other citizens," while "nobles still enjoyed status and privilege not accorded to others," these were "lingering relics of times past destined to disappear as the years went by." By 1914 "classes determined by common interests and economic roles" had replaced "orders determined by birth," and it was left for World War I only to sweep away "the last meaningful vestiges of the old order."[4]

After peasant emancipation, Blum recognizes, "agriculture continued to be the leading sector of economic life," land was still "the principal form of wealth," and

> up to 1914 noblemen remained the principal owners of estates. Instead of being privileged seigniors, however, the noble proprietors had been reduced to the status of mere landowners, possessed of no more rights and privileges than any other landowner. The loss of their role as seigniors [responsible for the peasants living on their estates] stripped the concept of nobility of its essential meaning.[5]

In fact, Blum admits, custom was not so easily overthrown. Europe was still a "deference society," and the nobility retained its superior status, even without legal sanction. Because of their superior status, noblemen were able to hold onto "an importance in government that was out of all proportion to their numbers, their abilities, and their contributions to their societies." Even so, in Blum's view, the wealthy and titled "high nobility" were the "beautiful people" of their era, and, for the most part, were as uninteresting and as superfluous as their modern counterparts.[6]

As the notion of equality gained wider acceptance and the bourgeoisie gained in self-assurance, even the nobility's political preeminence and superior status came increasingly to be shared with commoners who had risen through education and merit in the civil service or who had made distinguished careers in business or the professions. In civil society "there was interpenetration of high nobility and high bourgeoisie, in which noble became bourgeoisified and bourgeois became feudalized."[7]

In contrast to Blum, Mayer emphasizes continuity rather than change in postemancipation Europe. Right down to 1914 the premodern, preindustrial, and prebourgeois elements were not "the decaying and fragile remnants of an all but vanished past" but rather the still vital features of European life. Traditional elites—"the public service nobilities, both civil and military," as well as "the landed magnates"—successfully adjusted to changing times, the former by assimilating nonnoble recruits to the ethos of the old order, the latter by absorbing and practicing "the principles of capitalism and interest politics." Noble landowners became agricultural entrepreneurs and learned "to resort to lobbying and logrolling as well as pressure and partisan politics to protect or promote their interests. Increasingly, the landed estate assumed the attributes of class and class consciousness, and acted accordingly." This does not, however, in Mayer's mind, signify their *embourgeoisement*, for "the old elites excelled at selectively ingesting, adapting, and assimilating new ideas and practices without seriously endangering their traditional status, temperament, and outlook."[8]

The old regime, which Mayer terms "feudalism," "outlived its juridical disappearance" in several respects. "The interwoven landed and service nobilities" retained a dominant position in the still largely agricultural economy, continued to enjoy their superior status, continued to impose their values upon Europe's cultural life, and translated their power in these areas into political power. They then used their political power to strengthen the old order and their place in it against the threats posed by a rising but still weak bourgeoisie and by the relative decline of the agrarian sector of the economy and with it their "material base."[9]

From the 1870s the old elites allegedly mounted a successful counteroffensive against both the commercial-industrial market economy and constitutional government—a counteroffensive Mayer labels "the remobilization of the old order." Nor was the vitality of the "feudal" elite played out with the passing of the century. After 1900 Europe again experienced an "aristocratic reaction" in defense of the old order, not only against "radical labor, peasant, and nationalist movements" but even against "moderate reformism."[10]

In Russia the moderate reformer Peter Stolypin was one of many European victims of "this conservative intransigence" in the face of efforts at "prudent forward change." The aristocratic reaction was led by landed elites who, because they "feared that an accelerated deterioration of their economic fortunes would be certain to undermine their status, . . . became obsessed with preserving or even bolstering their hold on political society."[11]

It was this intransigence of the old elites in every major power, according to Mayer, that created a general crisis of the old order in 1907–1914, a crisis resolved only in the pan-European war of 1914–1918.[12]

Thus we have two very different portrayals of the period between the substitution of legal equality for legal privilege and the start of World War I. In Blum's view the major battle had been won, the new elements were already dominant, and the remnants of inequality which still favored the nobility were secondary and vanishing features of European life. Mayer, on the other hand, sees the old elites as successfully adapting to legal equality, continuing to dominate all aspects of life, and using their considerable ingenuity to postpone until the Greek calends the relaxation of their hold on power.

Both Blum and Mayer treat Russia as an integral part of Europe in the nineteenth century. The problem is whether to agree with Blum that the emerging elements of modern class society or with Mayer that the surviving features of a still vigorous "feudal" order dominated Russian life. Since the substitution of legal equality for legal privilege did not even *begin* in Russia until 1861, it would seem improbable that the substitution of classes for estates could have proceeded very far by the time the country went to war only fifty-three years later. Recent studies by Terence Emmons and Alfred Rieber, in fact, take exactly that position. Emmons begins with the assumption that by 1900 "the transition from a society of orders to a class society . . . was far from completed, and in some important respects not far advanced."[13] Rieber not only agrees but expresses doubt as to the possibility that the transition could ever have been completed in Russia: by 1914, "the soslovie [estate] system was crumbling away, but socially cohesive and politically unified classes were not emerging to take its place."[14] This was allegedly because "the fragmentation and isolation of social groups" characteristic of imperial Russia reflected something much more fundamental than that society's late (as compared with the West) historical development: "sosloviia [estates] in Russia lacked the essential ingredients for the development of corporate rights and self-consciousness. Unlike Western Europe, Russia had not properly laid the foundations upon which to construct a genuine class society."[15]

Rieber's argument raises a number of questions. May not a class society be "genuine" even though it differs from the Western model? And what is that model—the Third Republic? Wilhelmine Prussia? Victorian England? Did Rieber's "socially cohesive and politically unified classes" ever exist, even in the West? Are not classes rather groupings of related but nonetheless distinct economic interest groups? These questions aside, it is clear that, in Rieber's view, the old order was disintegrating but no new order was emerging. The reason was not, as Mayer would have it, because the old order was still vigorous enough to co-opt the elements of the new but rather because the new elements were so weak that they were unable to mount a serious challenge to the old order— "decaying," "crumbling," and "bankrupt" though it was.[16]

This study proceeds from assumptions and arrives at conclusions different from those summarized in the preceding pages. First, *pace* Emmons and Rieber, Russia's estate society, although clearly different from that of the West, was not only in theory capable of developing into some variant of a modern class society but was in fact evolving in that direction at a fairly rapid pace between 1861 and 1914. Second, although Blum's insistence on the crucial importance of the establishment of legal equality is entirely correct, his characterization of the remnants of the old order as "lingering relics of times past," and of the traditional elites as merely "beautiful people," is far from accurate with respect to Russia. Third, although Mayer has performed a valuable service in emphasizing the resilience of the old elites, it must be noted that in Russia their success in defending and strengthening the old order through the exercise of political power was very limited. The formerly "interwoven landed and service nobilities" came unraveled by the end of the century; the first of these lacked sufficient political power before 1906 to prevent the state from following policies injurious to their interests, and their eroding "material base" received little effective protection (apart from easy mortgage money) from the government. And to the extent that there was a crisis of the old order in Russia in 1907–1914, it was due in the first place to the intransigence of the monarchy rather than to any "aristocratic reaction."

THE MYTH OF THE DECLINING NOBILITY

DESPITE differences as to the nature of Russian society and the extent of the changes occurring within it, there is an all but universal consensus on one point—the nobility was declining, and its plight was due to its inability to adapt to changing times. Accustomed to relying on unpaid servile labor, landed nobles were doomed to extinction in a world where they had to compete freely with enterprising members of the lower social orders. This image of the declining nobility is most familiar from the many unforgettable portraits of inept and passive nobles in the nineteenth-century Russian literary classics.

Two vivid examples from the theater, although separated by the generation in which the social transformation of the nobility took place, are remarkably similar. Both Gurmyzhskaia in Ostrovskii's *The Forest* (1870) and Ranevskaia in Chekhov's *The Cherry Orchard* (1904) are improvident widowed landowners who do not know the value of a ruble. In her vain struggle to make ends meet, Gurmyzhskaia sells her land piecemeal to an enterprising peasant-turned-timber merchant but refuses to part entirely with her forest, romantically insisting that "an estate just isn't an estate without a forest." Ranevskaia's mismanagement has brought her estate to the verge of a forced sale to pay her debts. She and her brother nevertheless indignantly reject the advice of the merchant Lopakhin, son of a former serf of the family, that she raze the manor house and the cherry orchard, subdivide the property, build dachas, and lease them for a handsome income. The cherry orchard is a well-known feature of the district, while dachas and their renters are "vulgar." Lopakhin consequently buys the estate at auction for development along the lines he has proposed to Ranevskaia. Similarly, Ranevskaia's neighbor and fellow noble is uninterested in exploiting the kaolin deposits on his land and leases them instead to some Englishmen.

Even when a noble applies himself diligently to estate management, as does the title character in Chekhov's *Uncle Vania* (1897), he proves lacking in the business sense necessary for success in Russia's new society.

Vania has devoted his life to running the estate his father purchased as a dowry for his now deceased sister. His brother-in-law, a retired professor of nonnoble birth, suggests selling the property and investing the capital thus realized in securities which would yield an annual income more than double that from the estate. Vania reacts by going berserk; to him the estate is not just capital but his life's work, a link with the past and the future. He is as much a romantic as Gurmyzhskaia and Ranevskaia.

If Russian nobles in fiction are temporarily saved from their inevitable fate, it is through no effort of their own. Ranevskaia's neighbor, Simeonov-Pishchik, is as financially irresponsible as she, cheerfully living on the edge of bankruptcy in the conviction that "something or other will turn up, if not today, then tomorrow." And so it does, in the form of the kaolin deposits.

Conventional wisdom has it that the stages on the nobility's road to ruin were marked by uninformed and unbusinesslike estate management, profligate spending and borrowing habits, a rising burden of debt, forced sale of the property to a commoner, and the foolish investment or rapid squandering of such share of the sale price as might remain after the creditors had been satisfied. The classic portrayal of this process is that presented by S. N. Terpigorev, writing under the pseudonym S. Atava, in a series of sketches published in 1880 and entitled *Oskudenie (Impoverishment)*. *Oskudenie* quickly became and long remained the standard term for referring to the changes the landed nobility was undergoing. Terpigorev's landowners lack the knowledge and training necessary to manage their estates without serf labor; all their efforts are consequently bound to fail. Some nobles sell the redemption certificates with which they have been compensated by the government for the peasants' allotments; they live off the capital thus realized until it is exhausted, and then they sell off their forests and/or put out their lands on long-term leases. The next step is to begin the fatal process of borrowing on mortgages and promissory notes. Other nobles engage in misguided attempts to introduce "rational farming" on their estates, wasting their capital on foreign techniques and machines ill suited to Russian conditions. Efforts to invest in nonagricultural enterprises are depicted by Terpigorev most unsympathetically as foolish get-rich-quick schemes in which naive nobles get taken by clever confidence men. Landowners who sell out and migrate to the cities with their capital are portrayed in demeaning roles, such as owner-operator of a dress shop, or in morally censurable ones, such as proprietor of a gambling house or brothel.[17]

It was not only Russia's playwrights and novelists who described the transformation of the nobility in terms of decline, resulting from the nobility's own inadequacies. Social commentators, economic analysts, and polemicists of the period used the same frame of reference, regardless of whether they approved or deplored the phenomenon (see chapter 3). And modern scholarship accepts and even reinforces the conventional image. A forceful presentation of this view is the following passage from a study by one of the most respected of current Soviet historians, A. M. Anfimov:

> the data [on decreases in noble landownership] indirectly testify to the natural incompatibility of the traditional patterns of consumption and parasitical behavior, inherited by this class from the centuries of serfdom, with the demands of capitalist management. . . . The characteristic trait of the majority of nobles was entrepreneurial weakness, the inability to manage their estates rationally.[18]

Western scholarship yields nothing to Soviet in its willingness to subscribe to the conventional wisdom. Roberta Manning's recent study contains the most detailed exposition and explanation to date of the nobility's transformation. Her exposition is couched in terms of "decline and disintegration," and of the "economic crisis of unprecedented magnitude [that] overwhelmed the landowning gentry in the wake of Emancipation."[19] As a result of this crisis, many noble landowners were "compelled . . . to liquidate their holdings," or, put somewhat differently, "were forced to leave their land."[20]

The belief that nobles were being driven from the land is an essential element in the conventional image of the nobility's decline. Manning's explanation of the phenomenon is more complex than most. She begins with the standard interpretation that the responsibility for their decline lies in the first instance with the nobles themselves, and she accepts the portrayals in fiction of "gentry indolence."[21] Accustomed to a style of estate management that "involved little more than extracting revenue from a legally servile and defenseless labor force . . . illiterate, unpaid laborers using their own undernourished livestock and primitive methods and equipment," nobles could not break their old habits. As a result, "much of the vast capital—perhaps as much as four billion roubles—that flowed into gentry coffers in the second half of the nineteenth century from government purchase payments, mortgages, loans, and the sale of gentry lands went to meet daily living expenses, was squandered, or increasingly frequently, was unwisely invested."[22]

Finding, nevertheless, that "the standard interpretation of the gentry's decline is much too harsh and simple," Manning focuses on the "unfavorable conditions" that diminished even further the chances for the nobility's successful adaptation to farming without serfs.[23] These conditions were three: the high price of land, unsympathetic government policies, and falling revenues from the sale of grain. Manning fails to distinguish between the first of these conditions and the remaining two. The high price of land, unlike the other conditions, cannot be held responsible for driving the nobility from the land; the prospect of a capital gain was a lure, not a shove, for a nobleman contemplating selling out. Manning rightly distinguishes two categories of unsympathetic government policies: those favoring industry at the expense of agriculture and those promoting hard money and tight credit. The latter policies, according to her, worked a particular hardship on noble landowners by starving them of capital they urgently needed on the morrow of serf emancipation to hire the workers and buy the equipment and livestock required to farm their estates in the absence of serf labor.[24]

In fact, there was no such urgent need, for nobles not only could, but overwhelmingly did, continue to use their peasant neighbors—as renters or sharecroppers under a variety of arrangements—to exploit their landholdings. Nor were noble proprietors nearly so starved for cash as Manning asserts. She claims that of the half-billion rubles the state owed the former serfowners as compensation for land bestowed on their ex-serfs, one-half was deducted in settlement of old debts and the certificates received in payment of the other half could be sold only at a 30 percent discount.[25] Again, the truth is quite different. Out of the 890 million rubles owed to them by the state, the nobles actually received 575 million after their debts were deducted, and the discount on certificates sold on the market fell from 33 percent in 1862–1866 to only 5 percent two decades later. Nor is it a fact that "the banking system in Russia was poorly developed and long-term credit was generally unavailable in any quantity until the foundation of the State Nobles' Land Bank in 1885."[26] By 1883 the landed nobility had managed to run up a sizable mortgage debt to the banks, totaling 400 million rubles. (For a detailed exploration of these points and those raised in the following two paragraphs, see chapter 2.)

We come now to the third condition that, according to Manning, contributed to the plight of the landed nobility. Like another recent student of the nobility, Gary Hamburg, Manning claims that the 1876–1896 world depression in grain prices lowered "the gross revenues of most Russian estates."[27] In fact, the landowning nobility's income came overwhelmingly from rents (and increasingly from money rents, as opposed to payment in kind) rather than from the marketing of grain, and this was especially true in the 1870s and 1880s; nor were their peasant-tenants major sellers of grain. The price of grain, therefore, could have had little impact upon nobles' incomes.

Faced with their own debilitating "idiosyncrasies and traditions" and a hostile economic and political environment, Manning argues, many of the landed nobility tried to cope (1) "by borrowing heavily to tide them over the period of economic adjustment and the Long Depression," and (2) by abandoning attempts to farm their land themselves, turning increasingly to renting it out to peasants. In fact, borrowing by noble landowners is a more complex problem than meets the eye, and renting was favored over farming right from the 1860s. In any case, these efforts were simply fruitless attempts "to ward off the inevitable," for "in the end, none of the palliatives available to the gentry after Emancipation could stem their inexorable economic decline."[28]

Manning does much more than provide the most comprehensive statement available of the conventional view of the nobility's decline. She also offers a wholly original thesis about the nobility's "turn to the land," apparently beginning soon after serf emancipation (although the timing is not clearly stated) and accelerating over the following decades until its cumulative effect allegedly "resulted in a noticeable tempering of the gentry's economic decline" from the late 1890s to 1914.[29] This provocative thesis has been warmly endorsed in a number of recent scholarly studies (e.g., by Leopold Haimson and Robert Edelman)[30] which question neither its plausibility nor the evidence on which it rests.

According to Manning, the nobility's "turn to the land" was the product of three distinct factors: economic necessity, the diminishing attractiveness of state service, and new opportunities for elective local service.[31] The first factor allegedly operated as follows: "While the economic conditions of the late nineteenth century compelled many Russian landowners to liquidate their holdings or seek outside sources of income, increasing numbers responded to the crisis by moving to the countryside and taking the management of their family estates into their own hands."[32] While this is a plausible enough assumption, there is no convincing evidence to indicate that absentee landlordism was decreasing or that, in general, the phenomenon Manning describes was actually occurring. Her sources are confined to the memoirs of a dozen or so political activists at the beginning of the twentieth century—hardly a broad enough sample to warrant such a sweeping generalization.

The diminishing attractiveness of state service, in Manning's scheme of things, resulted from a number of forces at work in the decades after serf emancipation. Among these were the increasing professionalization of both the bureaucracy and the officer corps, the shift in emphasis in the army from cavalry to the artillery, the rising expenses connected with serving as a cavalry or guards officer, and the takeover of both the civil and the military service by commoners and by the landless descendants of commoners ennobled in the past for service to the state.[33] In short, state service was no longer the gentlemen's club it had once been, and nobles found the new atmosphere uncongenial. Changes in child-rearing practices among the nobility, Manning claims, also worked in the same direction, by making young noblemen feel uncomfortable in the authoritarian environment of the civil and military service.[34] All of these forces combined to produce an ever-growing exodus from state service of landed nobles who went home to their estates.

There are numerous difficulties in reconciling this picture with what actually happened in the relationship between the nobility and state service. To choose but one: rather than decreasing in the second half of the nineteenth century, the number of noble landowners in the civil service approximately *doubled* (see chapter 6). Mass resignations could conceivably have been outweighed by an even more massive influx of landed nobles into the bureaucracy, but there is no indication that this happened, nor could such a phenomenon easily be embraced by Manning's hypothesis.

Manning's third factor behind the "turn to the land" is the new opportunities for elective local service (in the *zemstvo* institutions, as arbiters and justices of the peace, and later as *zemskie nachalniki*) and the new vogue she claims for the old noble assemblies among the landed nobility. The assemblies, Manning alleges, were revitalized through their involvement in serf emancipation and, together with the *zemstvo* institutions, became a "surrogate" for the careers in government the nobles had abandoned.[35] Unfortunately, her only examples are taken from the early 1860s, and the weight of the evidence is overwhelmingly on the side of the continuation of the nobles' long-established apathy toward their corporate institutions. Manning's belief in the revitalization of the *guberniia* noble assemblies is crucial to her interpretation of the landed nobility's behavior in 1905, but that behavior can be perfectly well, and probably more correctly, understood without resorting to such a dubious hypothesis.[36]

Seemingly the most convincing evidence Manning marshals in support of her thesis that the nobility turned to the land in increasing numbers from the 1860s on is in her statistics on the contraction of noble acreage. As nobles returned from their government jobs to their estates and began to take a serious interest in running them, they presumably were able to save more and more of them from forced sale and thereby to stem the flow of noble land into the hands of commoners. According to Manning, this is precisely what happened. During 1895–1905 the annual decrease in noble acreage was allegedly a full 30 percent lower than the levels prevailing during the Long Depression of 1876–1896, and this slowdown in the rate at which nobles were losing their land continued, with the exception of the period 1906–1908, until the fall of the old regime. As further proof that the "turn to the land" was beginning to tell, Manning offers the fact that by the turn of the century, 53–54 percent of all noble acreage sold was being purchased by other nobles.[37]

Actually, a thorough and careful investigation of the statistical data on noble landownership reveals a different picture. There was in fact no slowdown in the pace at which noble acreage was contracting, except for the atypical years 1903–1905 and 1914. Otherwise, from 1895 through 1913 (and not just during the stormy years 1906–1908) the annual decrease in noble acreage was considerably *higher* than it had been during the Long

Depression (except for 1878–1882). As for Manning's second point, while it is indeed true that nobles were buying up 53 percent of the acreage sold by their peers at the turn of the century, this was by no means a new phenomenon. In fact, that percentage had been gradually *declining* ever since 1863–1872, when it stood at 64 percent (see chapter 2).

While it is undoubtedly the case that by the turn of the century a growing percentage of noble landowners were seriously occupied with managing their own estates on more or less rational lines, sometimes including farming them on their own account and dealing with the prosaic details of planting, livestock-breeding, and so on, this development is in no way dependent upon a hypothetical "turn to the land." A much more likely causative factor is the withdrawal over a period of a generation of those landowners most vulnerable economically and those least committed to agriculture and rural life.

Manning's thesis raises a further question. If the "turn to the land" were yielding such striking results by the second half of the 1890s, should not this trend and its impact have been noticed by those who anxiously awaited and hoped for just such a reversal in the landed nobility's "decline"? Not a hint of any awareness of a "turn to the land" is reflected in the works of turn-of-the-century polemicists on the noble question, in the deliberations of the national conferences of *guberniia* marshals of nobility from 1896 on, in the petitions from the *guberniia* noble assemblies to the central government, or in the proceedings of the government's Special Conference on the Affairs of the Noble Estate, which sat from 1897 to 1902. The weight of the evidence would seem to be on the side of the conclusion that the nobility's "turn to the land" never occurred.

Moreover, "the decline of the nobility"—a notion which has behind it a much longer history than does the "turn to the land"—is also a misleading concept. What happened to the nobility, and in particular to noble landowners, after serf emancipation would more usefully be viewed as the adaptation of the nobility to significant economic and social change. "Decline" conjures up images of debility and illness—the nobility as "the sick man of Russia." And so the nobility was, in the conventional portrayal. But what if the nobility was not the passive victim of its own pathology and of external forces beyond its control but rather, to a significant extent at least, an active participant in a process of adjustment to changed conditions? Admittedly, in adjusting, it was transformed into something other than its former self, but change is not normally identified with decline except in the minds of diehard traditionalists. Again, a provocative thesis, but how does it accord with the available evidence? The reader will have to judge for himself on the basis of the following chapters—in particular, chapters 2 and 6, which penetrate behind the statistics that have in the past been used to substantiate the notion of decline. While keeping always in mind the adage about "lies, damned lies, and statistics," I believe that a cautious and questioning use of numbers, in particular of the mass of data underlying the relatively few figures that have been quoted time and time again, is crucial to a study of this sort.

But, the reader is entitled to object, if the nobility was not in truth declining in the half century after emancipation but was rather making a healthy adjustment to a changed economic and social reality, why has this gone so completely unnoticed both by contemporaries and by modern scholars? For the same reason that man has clung to many other, much more important, myths. Myths are useful in apparently explaining phenomena that man wants or needs to understand, and they are comforting in that they explain these phenomena in ways that conform to man's preconceived notions. The decline of the Russian nobility is just such a myth. The perception of the nobility as the helpless victims of their anachronistic attitudes and spendthrift behavior—in short, as totally incapable of competing in a world dominated by *homo oeconomicus* (who usually took the form of a social upstart or a grasping foreigner)—has had a continuing appeal primarily because of a highly ambivalent attitude toward the nobility on the part of many of its contemporaries as well as many of those more removed in time or place or both.

On the one hand, the privileged beneficiaries of an extremely unjust social order get their comeuppance at the hands of the very social inferiors they have always despised. Thus is satisfied the desire to see justice done. On the other hand, the nobles are doomed to extinction precisely because they remain loyal to values, both aesthetic and human, that ill equip them for success in a world suddenly conquered by a countinghouse mentality. On this score nobles enjoy a certain degree of sympathy from those who find something of worth in the traditional values to which the nobility is wedded. The myth of the doomed nobility is thus doubly satisfying. Like most myths, however, it does not offer to rational minds the most convincing interpretation of the available data.

Marxist historians are, of course, a special case. No ambivalence here, just a commitment to a worldview that identifies the nobility with a certain stage of social development. When the historically ordained hour arrives, the angel of death in the guise of a revolutionary class executes the sentence. No sense pitying the victim; the old and worse must make way for the new and better.

SOCIAL ESTATES IN RUSSIA

THE nobility was a social estate, and social estates are juridical structures, their composition, privileges, and obligations being legally defined. Before proceeding further, then, let us briefly survey the juridical context in which the Russian nobility existed.

Muscovite Russia's hierarchical arrangement of orders placed those who served the state in a personal capacity at the top, and this ranking was preserved in imperial Russia. The 1649 legal code grouped the preexisting two dozen *chiny* (ranks), defined in terms of obligations to the state (which in turn were based upon economic condition and occupational roles), into the three estates of servicemen, townsmen, and peasants. At the same time the code drastically reduced social mobility by making membership in each estate hereditary and nonrenounceable and also endowed the first two estates with "exclusive juridical privileges."[38] Peter the Great abolished the old *chiny* altogether, thereby making the estates the unchallenged source of social and legal identity and leveling the distinctions among the members of each estate. Peter also extended the bounds of the estate system by incorporating the peripheral elements (slaves, indentured servants, vagrants, and others) who had stood outside the system of *chiny*. Catherine the Great gave the estate system its definitive form by confirming her late husband's emancipation of the nobility from compulsory state service and by issuing charters in 1785 defining in detail the legal rights and privileges of nobles and townsmen and conferring corporate institutions upon both estates.

Western scholars frequently either deny the existence of true estates in Russia or concede their appearance only after 1785.[39] By true estates these scholars mean social orders identical to those of the medieval and early modern West, with guaranteed rights against the monarchy and also a corporate political role. The fact that estates in the West enjoyed such rights and were the component elements not only of the social structure but of the political system as well (being represented *qua* estates in the parliaments and diets of every Western state from the Atlantic to the Vistula) was the result of a unique historical conjuncture in the formative centuries of the life of the society. Neither this conjuncture nor the phenomena to which it gave rise was duplicated in other estate societies. The Western pattern, instead of being taken as the standard for all estate societies, should be seen as a deviation from the norm.

Another product of ethnocentrism among modern Western historians—this one confined to the Anglophones among them—is the translation of *dvorianstvo*, the term that became common in the last quarter of the eighteenth century for Russia's service estate, as "gentry."[40] The intention behind the use of this term is understandable—to indicate that the great majority of *dvoriane*, with respect to wealth, style of life, and closeness to the centers of power, much more closely resembled those rural landowners known in England as gentry than they did the aristocratic elite who alone bear the title of noble in that country. The application of the term "gentry" to the *dvorianstvo* is nevertheless misleading, for the English gentry had no parallel in Russia. Although the gentry together with the titled nobility in England formed an informal status group of "gentlemen," who constituted the political and social elite well into the nineteenth century, neither this larger group nor the gentry alone formed an estate. The nobility by itself did constitute an estate and sat in Parliament (in the House of Lords) as such. The gentry in juridical terms was simply one component of the middle estate, the commons, along with merchants, yeoman farmers, and the like, and did not share even such limited legal privileges as the nobility enjoyed.[41] In Russia and other Continental lands, by contrast, social strata equivalent to the English peerage and gentry combined, plus impoverished and landless nobles who would not have qualified even as gentry in England, constituted the noble estate.[42]

That the membership of the Russian *dvorianstvo*, like that of other Continental nobilities, exhibited a much broader range of power, status, and wealth than did the English nobility is not to the point, for such internal differentiation was normal in a social estate. Among the members of a given estate there was always a considerable range of power, status, and especially wealth. Even among the members of those estates held in highest esteem, the poor and relatively powerless were usually numerically preponderant. The defining characteristic of an estate was the common and distinctive legal status of its members. In this respect the *dvorianstvo* was the precise equivalent not of the English gentry but of other Continental nobilities.

The hierarchy of estates in Russia is the subject, in exhaustive detail, of the ninth volume of the Code of Laws compiled in 1833 by Mikhail Speranskii and revised periodically thereafter.[43] The estate system embraced all of the Christian peoples of European Russia, Poland, and the Caucasus, plus the Jews of the western borderlands and the Muslims of the Crimea and the Volga-Ural region; the Grand Duchy of Finland retained its own historical estates. By law all members of the above communities were assigned to one of four estates—in descending hierarchical order, the nobility, Christian clergy, townsmen, and peasantry. The precedence of the nobility over the clergy, in contrast to the West where the order was reversed, can be explained both by the preeminence accorded to state service as the most valued social function from the Muscovite period on and by the nature of the Russian clergy.[44] The four estates were in turn subdivided as follows: (1) hereditary and personal nobles, the latter enjoying noble status for the lifetime of the recipient only;[45] (2) Orthodox, Roman Catholic, Protestant, and Armenian clergy; (3) hereditary distinguished citizens, personal (for the lifetime of the recipient only) distinguished citizens, merchants (further subdivided into three guilds until 1863, two thereafter), and *meshchane* (artisans and laborers); and (4) serfs belonging to private individuals, peasants attached to lands in the possession of the state or of the ruling dynasty, and peasants attached to factories or mines.

Before the 1860s and 1870s the nobility, clergy, and distinguished citizenry were privileged (*nepodatnye*) groups in that their members were exempt from the poll tax (*podat*), compulsory labor service, military conscription, and corporal punishment. The merchantry were only semi-privileged, in that they substituted various cash payments for the poll tax, labor service, and military conscription, and membership in the third guild of merchants carried no exemption from corporal punishment. The *meshchanstvo* and peasantry were unprivileged (*podatnye*) estates, subject to all the above onerous obligations and marks of social inferiority.

Although membership could be acquired in each of the estates and subestates under conditions prescribed in the Code of Laws, it was hereditary in only four: the hereditary nobility, the hereditary distinguished citizenry, the *meshchanstvo*, and the peasantry. Upon attaining their majority, sons of members of all other groups automatically became members of either the hereditary distinguished citizenry (in the case of sons of personal nobles and higher clergy) or the *meshchanstvo* (in the case of sons of lower clergy, personal distinguished citizens, and merchants) unless they could personally meet the qualifications for membership in a higher legal category. A merchant, in fact, retained his status not even for life but only as long as he maintained his guild membership by payment of the requisite annual fees; failure to do so meant reversion to the *meshchanstvo*. Until 1874 conscripts into the army, while on active service and after retirement, constituted a separate hereditary estate, intermediate between the merchants and the *meshchane* with respect to their status and rights; after the 1874 army reform, conscripts reverted to their previous estate membership upon the completion of their term of service.[46] The legal status of women was determined by that of their fathers or husbands.

Corporate estate institutions existed from the reign of Catherine II at the *guberniia* (province) and *uezd* (district) levels for hereditary nobles, from the same period at the municipal level for merchants and for *meshchane*, and from the 1860s at the *volost* (township) and *selskoe obshchestvo* (commune) levels for peasants. The only estate organized at the national level was the clergy. Personal nobles and distinguished citizens, both hereditary and personal, lacked any corporate organization.

The slight decrease in the relative weight of the hereditary nobility in the total population between 1858 and 1897 (see table 1), to the extent that it reflects more than the crudity of the 1858 estimates, was the result of the purge of Polish nobles in the western *gubernii* after the unsuccessful rebellion of 1863. There had been no significant change in this percentage since the 1830s, when the moderate rise that began in the reign of Peter I came to an end.[47] The relative weight of the nobility in Russia was less, in some cases very much less, than that in many Western societies at a comparable period in their social development. In

TABLE 1. POPULATION DISTRIBUTION BY SOCIAL ESTATE IN
EUROPEAN RUSSIA, 1858 AND 1897 (PERCENT)

	1858		1897	
	SUBESTATE	ESTATE	SUBESTATE	ESTATE
First estate		1.5		1.4
Hereditary nobles	1.0		0.9	
Personal nobles				
and *chinovniki*	0.5		0.5	
Christian clergy		1.0		0.5
Urban estate		7.3		11.2
Distinguished citizens	—		0.3	
Merchants	—		0.2	
Meshchane	—		10.6	
Military estate		6.4		
Rural estate		82.6		85.7
Peasants	—		84.2	
Cossacks	—		1.5	
Others		1.3		1.2
Total		100.0		100.0

Source: Data are from *Statisticheskiia tablitsy Rossiiskoi imperii. No. 2. Nalichnoe naselenie imperii za 1858 god* (St. Petersburg, 1863), pp. 267, 292–93; *Obshchii svod po imperii rezultatov razrabotki dannykh pervoi vseobshchei perepisi naseleniia, proizvedennoi 28 ianvaria 1897 goda* (St. Petersburg, 1905), 1:xiii.

Note: European Russia consisted of the fifty *gubernii* (forty-nine before 1865) situated west of the Ural Mountains, excluding the viceroyalty of the Caucasus, the Grand Duchy of Finland, and the ten *gubernii* (five before 1866) that had formerly constituted the kingdom of Poland. The term *chinovnik* here refers to a holder of class rank in state service who is neither a hereditary nor a personal noble. After 1873 military conscripts no longer formed a separate estate. Dashes indicate that data are unavailable. Discrepancies between totals and subtotals are the result of rounding off the latter.

France on the eve of the 1789 revolution the nobility had constituted 1.5 percent of the total population, in Spain at the same time over 5 percent, in Hungary over 6 percent, and in Poland over 8 percent.[48]

THE PRIVILEGES OF THE NOBILITY

THE privileged legal status attained by the Russian nobility in the second half of the eighteenth century consisted of both civil rights, enjoyed by the individual noble, and political rights, exercised by the nobility in their corporate capacity.[49] The first estate's civil rights may be divided into personal rights, both useful and honorific, and property rights. Useful personal rights which the nobility shared with the other privileged estates included trial by a jury of their peers and exemptions from personal taxation, compulsory labor service, military conscription, and corporal punishment. For hereditary nobles alone the last exemption extended even to men serving in noncommissioned ranks in the army who were convicted of breaches of discipline normally punished by flogging. The right to enter the civil service was shared with only a few other groups. Useful personal rights exclusive to the nobility included exemption from the billeting of troops in their homes; preferential treatment in state service with respect to initial assignment, promotion, and retirement benefits; the right to travel abroad and enter the service of an allied foreign power with government permission; a guarantee against deprivation of noble status except upon conviction of a major crime such as treason, perjury, brigandage, theft, or forgery; and the right to appeal a sentence of death or deprivation of noble status to the Senate and the emperor.[50]

Exclusive to the nobility were its honorific personal rights, such as the use of a family coat of arms and the addition of the name of an inherited family property to a noble's legal signature—Western customs promoted by Peter I. To prevent the extinction of the family name (and coat of arms and title, if any), a noble could adopt a relative by blood or marriage.[51] Nobles also enjoyed the right to wear the uniforms of their respective *guberniia* noble societies, but in fact these uniforms were worn only at the triennial assemblies of the societies, and then generally only by those who were not entitled, by virtue of present or past service in the military, the bureaucracy, or elective local office, to wear a more prestigious uniform.[52]

The most important of the property rights (indeed, of all the rights) of the first estate was that, shared only with the state and the imperial family, of owning land to which serfs were attached—the principal form of wealth in preindustrial Russia. A nobleman's other property rights included that of trading in the agricultural produce of his estates, as well as in the products of any industries established on them, without joining a merchant guild. Noble landowners enjoyed the exclusive right to distill alcoholic spirits until 1863. Should a noble wish to acquire urban real estate for the purpose of operating an industrial establishment, he was permitted to join a guild in order to enjoy the commercial privileges of the merchantry without forfeiting his membership in the nobility. Nobles alone had the right to entail their estates. And if a noble was convicted of a crime carrying the penalty of capital punishment or deprivation of noble status, his patrimonial property went to his legal heirs instead of being confiscated by the state.

The nobility's civil rights were in each case the gift of an autocratic state intent upon providing its servants with the necessary material support and moral authority to perform their roles. Stemming from the needs of the state and existing in the context of the unequal power relationship between the nobility and the monarchy, these rights proved none too secure. The emperor Paul revoked the charter of 1785 after little more than a decade and ended the nobility's exemption from corporal punishment and compulsory state service. Although the charter was reconfirmed in 1801 after Paul's assassination and never again revoked, the autocracy continued unilaterally to regulate, amend, and eliminate the privileges of the nobility as it deemed necessary in pursuit of broader interests of state. Nicholas I severely curtailed the right of foreign travel and reimposed compulsory state service upon Polish nobles in the Western *gubernii* who owned fewer than one hundred serfs each. And by emancipating the serfs, Alexander II abolished the nobility's most valued privilege. Estate rights in Russia clearly had no solid juridical foundation, only a political one: "The supreme authority granted one right and took away another, depending on the needs of the state."[53]

Raison d'état was equally the source of the nobility's corporate organization and rights. Lacking the trained personnel and the financial resources to perform the manifold tasks of local government, the Catherinian state followed the example of its Western contemporaries in calling upon the corporate institutions of the nobility and the bourgeoisie. In the West, however, in the seventeenth and eighteenth centuries long-established corporate estate institutions were reduced to instruments of the absolutist state; in Russia such institutions had first to be created by the state.[54]

Summoned as an ad hoc body in 1766 to elect representatives to Catherine's Legislative Commission, the *uezd* assembly of nobility was established as a permanent institution by the 1775 Statute on Provincial Government and charged with electing local nobles for three-year terms to carry out judicial and police functions in rural areas. The official leader and spokesman of the nobility in its new corporate role was the *uezd* marshal of nobility, an office also created in 1766 on an ad hoc basis. A parallel system was established at the same time to place responsibility for municipal government upon the merchants and *meshchane*. With the passage of time the list of elected rural officials expanded beyond judges and police chiefs to include those responsible for apportioning land taxes, inspecting schools, maintaining reserve grain stores, conducting land surveys, and constructing buildings and roads. Although chosen by the nobility and accountable to their constituents when they stood for reelection, all such officials (but not the marshals) were in fact agents of the state rather than representatives of the nobility. They were confirmed in office by the provincial governor, they were responsible to superior officials in the civil bureaucracy, and their offices conferred upon the holders regular civil service ranks, salaries, and uniforms.[55]

The 1785 Charter of the Nobility shifted the focus from the *uezd* to the *guberniia* by vesting the corporate rights and powers of the nobility in a new corporate person, the *guberniia* noble society, and by formally recognizing the office of *guberniia* marshal of nobility, which had existed de facto since the latter 1770s. Henceforth the *uezd* assemblies were reduced to performing housekeeping chores such as verifying the lists of nobles eligible to vote in the *guberniia* assemblies; for these purposes the *uezd* assemblies met three months in advance of the triennial meetings of the *guberniia* assemblies. At the latter, held usually in December or January, substantive matters were discussed, elective local offices filled, the *uezd* marshals chosen (the nobles of each *uezd* voting separately for their respective marshals), and candidates nominated for the post of *guberniia* marshal. The *guberniia* assembly also elected a noble deputy assembly, consisting of one member from each *uezd*. Chaired by the *guberniia* marshal, the deputy assembly maintained the genealogical register (*rodoslovnaia kniga*) which served as the membership roll for the society. New families were enrolled by a two-thirds vote of the deputy assembly upon giving proof of noble status and of the ownership of land in the *guberniia*. Families were eligible for membership in the society of each *guberniia* in which they owned land. All male members of an enrolled family who were twenty-five or over could attend the triennial assembly, but only those could vote who personally owned land in the *guberniia* and who had attained commissioned officer rank or its bureaucratic equivalent, that is, class fourteen or above in the Table of Ranks.[56]

Noble societies were established wherever a critical mass of noble landowners existed. By 1860 there were societies in forty-five of the forty-nine *gubernii* of European Russia, although in Vologda and Astrakhan the societies functioned in only a few of the *uezdy*. Viatka, Perm, and Archangel lacked sufficient numbers of noble landowners to support corporate institutions; Olonets held noble elections only until 1811 and had an appointed *guberniia* marshal at intervals thereafter until 1858. When Orenburg *guberniia* was separated from Ufa in 1865, the Orenburg nobility received their own society, bringing the total to forty-six. Outside of European Russia, noble societies were formed in 1847–1852 in Tiflis and Kutais in the Transcaucasus, Stavropol in the North Caucasus, and the five *gubernii* of the former kingdom of Poland.[57]

Unlike the elective local officials, who were government agents pure and simple, the assemblies and marshals of nobility were hybrid institutions. On the one hand they were intended to serve the interests and needs of the first estate. The assemblies could discuss matters of common interest, tax their members for common purposes, and petition the governor, the Senate, and the emperor concerning their needs. In the intervals between the triennial elections the *guberniia* assembly could be called into extraordinary session to discuss and act upon matters of interest to the society. The marshals presided over the assemblies and in general acted as the representatives of and spokesmen for their constituents. On the other hand, from the point of view of the government which had created them, the principal function of the assemblies was to supply loyal personnel for local offices. Any other activities were secondary and were not to interfere with the execution of this responsibility. The government's intention of keeping the noble societies on a short rein was evident in the 1785 charter, which charged the appointed provincial governor with convening the *guberniia* assembly, laying proposals before it, selecting one of the assembly's two nominees to serve as *guberniia* marshal, and certifying the results of all noble elections in the absence of any "clear defect" in those elected. The assembly was liable to a fine if it adopted resolutions "contrary to the laws." And over the years the *uezd* and *guberniia* marshals, whose primary responsibility was to their constituents, were made to assume an increasingly heavy burden of governmental duties. By 1861 they were involved in apportioning army recruits among serfowners and taxes among landowners, periodically revising the census of male serfs, maintaining buildings and roads, inspecting post stations, supervising local grain reserves, supplying horses to the army from stud farms, implementing public health measures, and supervising prisons and children's shelters.[58] Unlike the elective local officials, the marshals received no salaries.

At the hands of the emperor Paul the first estate discovered that its corporate privileges were as insecure as its civil rights. First the nobility's right to petition the government was eliminated, then the *guberniia* assemblies were abolished and the election of those local officials who were not replaced by government appointees was returned to the *uezd* assemblies.[59] After the full restoration of its privileges by Alexander I, the nobility remained ambivalent about its corporate rights, viewing them rather as corporate obligations—compulsory service in a new form. The triennial assemblies were poorly attended. Wealthy aristocrats preferred the attractions of Petersburg, Moscow, or foreign lands to an often long and arduous journey in the dead of winter to a rustic *guberniia* town in order to rub shoulders with their legal peers but social inferiors. Even the intermediate and petty landowners resident in the *guberniia* often yielded a sparse turnout, despite the attraction of the social whirl attendant upon a meeting of the assembly. An exasperated Speranskii complained in 1818 that "the nobles run away from their elections, and soon it will be necessary to convoke them using gendarmes in order to compel the nobles to take advantage of their rights."[60] The quality of officials elected by the nobility also left something to be desired. Able and ambitious men desirous of a career in service were much more apt to seek it in the central bureaucracy than in elective local posts far from the centers of power. These posts were frequently filled by less talented men to whom the salary was attractive or else went begging and had to be filled by appointment.[61]

A thoroughgoing reform of the nobility's corporate institutions in 1831 attempted to correct these deficiencies.[62] To make officeholding more attractive, *guberniia* marshals were henceforth appointed directly by the emperor, the civil service ranks of all elective local offices were raised by one class, and their holders were for the first time made full members of the civil service and given six-year terms of office. At the same time the pool of nobles eligible for office was enlarged by eliminating the previous service and property qualifications—class fourteen rank or above and an annual income from land of at least one hundred rubles. To give the *guberniia* assembly more stature, its right to petition the government was broadened to cover all local administrative abuses and faults, whether or not the nobility was the sole or primary victim. And to make attendance at the assemblies more attractive to the wealthier nobles, especially to nonresident aristocrats, voting was made conditional upon the amount of property owned. Large landowners retained a personal vote in the election of estate and local officials, intermediate landowners were henceforth represented by electors, and petty proprietors were disenfranchised.[63] All landowners who held class ranks retained a personal vote on matters other than elections.

So ineffective was the 1831 reform in satisfying the state's requirements for local officials that before the decade was out further measures were adopted. In case fewer than twelve nobles from any one *uezd* showed up at the assembly, the *guberniia* marshal was empowered to combine the nobles of two or more contiguous *uezdy* for election purposes. A personal vote in elections was given to any intermediate landowner who held a rank no lower than class six in the army (colonel) or four in the civil service (actual state councillor) and to any noble, landowner or not, who had served a full three-year term as a marshal. The continuing reluctance of nobles to stand for election led the government to sanction in certain cases the holding of two elective offices by a single person and to make personal nobles eligible for election to *uezd* police posts.[64]

The government's efforts availed little. Complaints about the poor quality of elective officials continued unabated down to the abolition of these positions in the 1860s, when Boris Chicherin voiced a widely acknowledged truth—that Russian nobles had always valued their property rights over their human chattels much more highly than their right to influence local affairs by electing and serving as officials.[65] Given the tight rein of the autocracy over both its own appointed agents and those chosen by the nobility, and considering the narrow confines within which the noble societies were expected to operate, the first estate's perception of the relative value of their property rights and political rights was undoubtedly not far from the mark.

The very legislation that attempted in 1831 to stimulate the nobility's interest in participating in the assemblies and holding local office also made even clearer than before that the state regarded these functions as duties rather than privileges. Fines were prescribed for nobles who failed either to attend the assemblies (unless they presented a valid excuse in advance) or to assume the duties of an office to which they had been elected, the governor's supervisory role vis-à-vis the *guberniia* assembly was strengthened,[66] and it was emphasized that enrollment in the genealogical register and electoral list of the appropriate *guberniia* was not only a right but was "required" of every noble who came into possession of land.[67] In the same vein, the distinctive uniforms for each noble society that had been adopted in the 1780s were replaced in 1832 by a modified version, standard for nobles of all *gubernii*, of the dark green uniform of the Ministry of Internal Affairs. While Catherine's uniforms had expressed the corporate unity of the nobility of each *guberniia*, Nicholas's emphasized the nobility's role as agents of the state.[68]

THE IMPACT OF THE GREAT REFORMS

FROM Peter I to Nicholas II the Russian state set for itself the double challenge of minimizing the power disparity between Russia and the West through selective borrowing from the latter and of absorbing into the existing autocratic political system and hierarchical social structure the changes which such borrowing inevitably brought in its wake. In the eighteenth century the challenge was met successfully, with the state energetically promoting technological, administrative, and cultural Westernization while strengthening the traditional political and social structures. In the nineteenth century the challenge became infinitely more difficult as the estate societies of the West one after another were transformed into class societies, and the dynastic states into nation-states based on the principle of popular sovereignty. Viewing this trend with intense disapproval, the leaders of Russia's old regime developed an acute sensitivity to the connection between intellectual and economic change on the one hand and fundamental social and political transformations on the other, and they adopted a correspondingly cautious attitude toward the further penetration of Western ideas and techniques. The price of this excess of caution was Russia's humiliating defeat in the Crimean War at the hands of Britain and France, two societies whose power, relative to Russia's, had been enhanced in a spectacular manner by continuing modernization of their economies, social structures, and political systems.

In the six decades following the Crimean defeat the old regime took a renewed interest in military and economic modernization for the sake of increasing the power and security of the state, without, however, intending to abandon either the traditional estate society or the autocratic political system. In fact, the political system was maintained intact—in form until 1906 and, to a considerable extent, in substance until 1917, when the bill for such inflexibility was finally presented. The estate system was preserved in form until 1917; the only structural changes were minor ones in the 1860s—the reorganization of the three merchant guilds into two and the fusion of the various subestates of serfs and peasants into a legally homogeneous peasantry.[69] By 1917, however, most of the substance of the estate system had long since been sacrificed by the regime to the demands of modernization.

First, both in time and in significance, among the developments that reduced the estate system to a hollow structure was the emancipation of the serfs in 1861. This radical reform both raised the legal status of the peasantry and deprived the nobility of their most valued privilege—the exclusive right to own populated land and to profit from the uncompensated labor of their serfs. Serf emancipation also deprived nobles of their individual roles as wielders of the state's police, judicial, and tax powers vis-à-vis their own serfs. Most of the personal privileges which the nobility shared with the other privileged estates did not long survive the emancipation of the serfs. The exemption from the poll tax was extended to the *meshchanstvo* in 1863,[70] and the tax itself was abolished twenty years later. Other fiscal impositions, primarily real estate and excise taxes, had always applied equally to members of all estates. Corporal punishment in its more severe forms was abolished in 1863, although in certain cases peasants were still subject to beating with birch rods.[71] Based on "the principles of the blindness of justice toward estate distinctions, of the equality of all citizens before the law,"[72] the judicial reform of 1864 was a most serious blow against privilege. The right of nobles to a trial by their peers now took on a radically different aspect: in the most famous trial of the postreform period in Russian fiction, Dmitrii Karamazov, a hereditary noble, was convicted by a jury consisting of four low-ranking bureaucrats, two merchants, and six *meshchane* and peasants.[73] The judicial reform transformed into the common rights of all Russians not only the right to a trial by one's peers but also other former estate privileges, such as guarantees against deprivation of life, status, or property without due process and the right to carry a judicial appeal all the way to the emperor. The right to a passport for travel abroad and the right to engage in trade and industry were also made universal in the 1860s.[74] The exemption of the privileged estates from military recruitment was a casualty of the army reform of 1874, which introduced universal military conscription and recognized distinctions based on education but no longer on estate membership. And with the abandonment of the practice of billeting troops on the civilian population, the nobility's exemption from that obligation ceased to have any significance.

State service was the last area in which meaningful distinctions among the estates continued to exist. Until 1906 the nobility enjoyed a certain degree of preferential treatment in entering service and in being promoted from rank to rank, while the *meshchanstvo* and peasantry, officially referred to after the abolition of the poll tax as "the former *podatnye* estates," continued to be barred from the civil service.[75] Apart from this case, the only significant division along estate lines after the great reforms was that between peasants and others, the former remaining subject to their own special courts, to corporal punishment, to compulsory labor on public works in case of natural disaster, and to restrictions on their freedom of movement and of residence.[76]

Reforms affecting the local police and other government services at the *uezd* and *guberniia* levels, including the judicial system, had long been under consideration. When they were implemented, under the stimulus of serf emancipation, in the early 1860s, the corporate role of the nobility in local administration was all but eliminated. In 1862 the rural police officials at the *uezd* and sub-*uezd* levels elected by the nobility were abolished, and police powers in both the rural and urban areas of the *uezd* were transferred to government appointees. The *zemstvo* assemblies and boards established in rural areas in 1864 were intended to provide more effectively the social services for which responsibility had rested since 1775 (not often to their credit) on a number of commissions and officials elected in whole or in part by the first estate.[77] In another drastic blow to the principle of privilege, the *uezd zemstvo* assemblies, the only popularly elected bodies created under the *zemstvo* act, were chosen on a property basis rather than by social estates, noble landowners being grouped together as equals with all other individual landowners in the first curia of voters. The judicial reform of 1864 both replaced the separate courts of first instance for the several estates which had existed since 1775 and abrogated the right of the estates to elect judicial officials. The new courts had jurisdiction over persons of all estates (although separate *volost* courts were established to handle minor civil and criminal cases involving peasants alone) and were staffed either by professional jurists appointed by the Ministry of Justice or by justices of the peace elected by the *uezd zemstvo* assemblies.

After the reforms the only local official still chosen by the *guberniia* assembly of nobility was one of four assessors of the *uezd* police bureau.[78] For several other posts, including the arbiters of the peace and representatives of the first estate to the *guberniia* and *uezd* bureaus for peasant affairs, the noble assembly composed short lists of nominees from which the governor, in consultation with the *guberniia* marshal, made his appointments.[79] Although the noble societies remained unaltered, their role in supplying local officials had been drastically curtailed. Their competence was now confined pretty much to the area of purely estate concerns, where they continued to operate within the narrow limits and under the forms of supervision and control devised by an autocracy jealous in the extreme of its political monopoly.

Thus, within a decade or two after the proclamation of serf emancipation, the nobility had seen itself deprived by the state of the overwhelming majority of its legal privileges, both civil (including personal and property) and political. The weight of custom and tradition; the continued deference of the lower orders; the dominant position still held by nobles in agriculture, at the policy-making levels of the bureaucracy, and in the highest echelons of the officer corps all guaranteed that Russia's first estate would for some time to come still wield influence out of all proportion to its numbers, but it would have to manage without the protection of legal privilege.

Since the ownership of serfs had been the nobility's most valuable privilege, the abolition of this right was bound to be the most serious of all the losses suffered by the first estate in the great reforms. From 1801, members of other estates had enjoyed the right to own uninhabited land, that is, land to which no peasants were attached, but only nobles could own inhabited land. Serf emancipation and the land settlement of 1863–1883 eliminated the category of inhabited land, thereby transforming privately owned land into a commodity which could be freely traded like any other. In contrast to such Western countries as France and Prussia, in Russian law there was no concept of noble land per se, independent of the social estate of the owner; all privilege had pertained to the landowner rather than to the land. Once the landowner and his former serfs had reached an agreement on the terms of redemption for the peasant allotments that were carved out of each property—a process completed under government prodding by the late 1880s—his remaining land was for the first time eligible for purchase by members of all social estates.[80] A necessary condition had been established for the divorce of the nobility from their lands; nobles lost no time in beginning the process.

THE NOBILITY AND THE LAND: A REAPPRAISAL

THE HISTORICAL CONTEXT

I N the half-century following serf emancipation there was a continuing process of separation between those who enjoyed noble status
and those who owned rural land—two groups which had formerly
overlapped to a striking degree. The pace and extent of that separation
are indicated in table 2. The nobility's decreasing identification with
landowning is reflected also in the rapid urbanization of the first estate.
By 1897, 47.2 percent of the nobility in European Russia was urban,
compared with only 15–20 percent in 1858.[1] The data on internal mi-
gration tell a similar story: of all urban nobles in European Russia in
1897, 64.2 percent were living in *uezdy* other than those in which they
had been born, and 49.1 percent had not even remained in their native
gubernii.[2] Thus a major social upheaval had taken place within the first
estate. On the eve of serf emancipation, four-fifths of all nobles belonged
to landowning families and only one-fifth or fewer were urban; on the
eve of World War I, fewer than two-fifths still belonged to landowning
families, while between three-fifths and four-fifths were towndwellers.[3]

The decline by slightly more than half in the percentage of nobles
belonging to landowning families between 1861 and 1912 was accompanied by a similar decline in the amount of land owned by hereditary
nobles. In the land settlement that followed serf emancipation, the first
estate surrendered 28 percent of its acreage to its former serfs.[4] The 87.2
million *desiatiny* that remained in the hands of the nobility in European
Russia minus the Baltic region in 1862 diminished to only 41.1 million
over the next fifty-two years—a decrease of 53 percent (see the following
section, "Sales and Purchases of Noble Land").

TABLE 2.   NOBLE LANDOWNERS, 1861–1912

YEAR	NUMBER OF NOBLE LANDOWNING FAMILIES	% OF NOBLES BELONGING TO LANDOWNING FAMILIES
1861	114,500–115,500	78–81
1877	98,000–100,000	69–74
1895	103,000–104,500	54–55
1905	86,500–88,000	38–39
1912	94,500–96,500	36–37

Note: Figures are approximate; see appendix C for their derivation.

The reduction of the landed nobility to a minority of the first estate, the loss of over half the noble acreage held on the morrow of serf emancipation, and the transformation of the nobility from an overwhelmingly rural to a predominantly urban group—such are the indications of the dramatic changes the nobility experienced in the half century after the great reforms. In order to understand the meaning of these changes, we must start with the historical context of the nobility's relationship to the land in Russia.

By origin and tradition a service estate, even after its emancipation from compulsory state service in 1762 the nobility continued to be drawn toward the court and the towns. Urban life, if only for the winter "season," was the ideal for a nineteenth-century noble. He regarded his rural estates primarily as the source of the provisions and income that made his urban existence possible and secondarily as a pleasant summer retreat. That the majority of nobles found this ideal beyond their material means before 1861 did not dissuade them from subscribing to the cultural values of their betters and treating estate management as an unworthy occupation fit only for peasant bailiffs. Western visitors were very much struck by the weakness of the Russian nobility's ties to the land. In the 1840s Baron von Haxthausen dwelt on this phenomenon, noting in particular that the typical manor house had much more of the aspect of a temporary retreat—simply built, rudely finished even on the interior, and plainly furnished—than of a permanent dwelling, even when the owner was a person of consequence.[5] An English resident in Russia at the end of the century described the rural homes of the nobility in much the same terms,[6] and the Frenchman Leroy-Beaulieu also emphasized this point in the 1880s:

Between the *dvorianstvo* and the soil there never has been the same bond, the same association as in the West. The nobility is not identified with the soil as [it is] in the rest of Europe, nor with the region in which it resides. The nobles do not bear the name of their estate or their township, as indicated by the French *de* and the German *von*. . . . Nothing [in Russia] recalls the proud dwellings of the Western aristocracies, the inheritors of feudalism; nothing resembles those mediaeval castles, so solidly squatting on the soil, so haughtily pervaded with the might of the families whose strongholds they were. Russian nature herself seems to repudiate these domestic fortresses, by providing neither the sites nor the materials for them—the rocky steeps whose brow they should crown, the stone of which they should be built. The wooden house, so often burned down, so quickly worm-eaten, so easy to transport or to reconstruct, is a meet emblem of Russian life; the very dwellings aptly represent the precariousness of the aristocracy's destinies.[7]

Even the more substantial Palladian manor houses of the eighteenth and early nineteenth centuries were rarely family seats in the Western sense, for estates did not often remain in the same family longer than a couple of generations.[8]

The nobility's weak attachment to its estates was in part the result of its traditional service orientation and of Russia's lack of a feudal past. In the West nobles were the spiritual heirs, if not often the lineal descendants, of the medieval warrior-landholders who, secure behind their castle walls, had been de facto sovereigns over their fiefs, wielding political power and influence in proportion to the extent and wealth of their lands. Land was the historical basis of the Western nobles' position and power. By contrast, the first estate in Russia was the heir of the Muscovite service *chiny* and owed its lands, as it owed its privileges and indeed its very existence, to the state. State service and not land was the historical basis of the Russian nobility's position in society.

The nobility's relatively weak attachment to its estates was also in part the product of the cultural divide between the nobility and the other social estates, especially the peasantry and the clergy. In every estate society, style of life, as well as legal status, has distinguished one estate from another, but in Russia the usual social distance between the first estate and the others was multiplied many times over. Having shaved off their beards, donned Western costume, and acquired at least a rudimentary Western education—all at Peter the Great's command—the nobility rapidly developed into a group whose style of life and thought, indeed whose very spoken language in the latter eighteenth and early nineteenth centuries, was totally alien to the traditional values and manners of the other estates. For almost two centuries membership in the nobility involved, in addition to the status superiority that was intrinsic to it, an assertion of cultural superiority that was unparalleled in the West. The cultural distance separating the Westernized nobles from the traditional country folk, coupled with the relatively vast geographic distances in rural Russia, posed a problem of cultural and social deprivation for noble landowners that was qualitatively different from anything experienced by their comparable numbers in the cultural backwaters of the

Western countryside. To the end of the nineteenth century, attention was repeatedly called to the sacrifices that residence on their estates imposed on cultured and energetic nobles by depriving them of the company of educated people and of access to schools, libraries, and theaters.[9]

A no less important factor in shaping the nobility's traditional attitude to the land was the unprofitability of agriculture in much of European Russia and especially in the *gubernii* that were the historic homeland of the Great Russian nobility—from Olonets and Vologda in the north to Kursk and Voronezh in the south, and from Pskov and Smolensk in the west to Simbirsk in the east. Infertile soil and a short growing season in the north and center and unreliable precipitation in the south made for low productivity, and the urban market—small and growing only too slowly—provided little economic stimulus. Under these circumstances it made little sense to sink capital into estate improvements. Instead the nobility attempted to get "the most out of the land with the least possible investment of time, effort and money," regarding the land with some justice "as a means of subsistence, not of enrichment."[10] The typical noble landowner, even if resident on his estates, lived as a parasite off the peasant economy, contributing to the latter simply the use of his land and taking in return his serfs' payments of quitrent (*obrok*) in money or in kind and their labor (*barshchina*) on his demesne, if he maintained one.

The impact of serf emancipation on the nobility must be viewed against this background. Emancipation created a free market in agricultural land and thereby gave nobles the option of converting their estates into other, potentially more rewarding, forms of capital and of exchanging the role of landowner for perhaps more congenial occupations. Their traditionally pragmatic attitude toward landownership and lack of emotional attachment to the land facilitated for many the exercise of this option.

SALES AND PURCHASES OF NOBLE LAND

OVER the half century following serf emancipation, the rate at which the acreage owned by the nobility diminished varied considerably, as is clear from table 3. The early peak in the rate of decrease during 1878–1882 probably represents the impact of the decisions of those nobles who had least interest in farming to divest themselves of their land once they had come to terms with their former serfs (the conclusion of redemption agreements was 78 percent complete by 1876 and 86 percent complete by 1881, measured by the state's gross compensation to the former serfowners for the land taken from them; see table 13 below). The figures for 1878–1882 may also reflect the impact on the economically most vulnerable noble proprietors of the world depression in grain prices that had recently begun, although this is much

TABLE 3.   DECREASE IN ACREAGE OWNED BY NOBLES, 1862–1914

| | ACREAGE AT END OF YEAR | | AVERAGE ANNUAL DECREASE | |
YEAR	NO. OF DESIATINY (millions)	% OF 1862 ACREAGE	PERIOD	NO. OF DESIATINY (000's)
1862	87.2	100.0	–	–
1867	83.9	96.3	1863–1867	638
1872	80.7	92.6	1868–1872	652
1877	77.0	88.4	1873–1877	736
1882	71.2	81.7	1878–1882	1,146
1887	66.8	76.7	1883–1887	880
1892	62.9	72.2	1888–1892	781
1897	58.4	67.1	1893–1897	896
1902	53.2	61.0	1898–1902	1,061
1905	51.3	58.8	1903–1905	630
1909	45.6	52.3	1906–1909	1,418
1913	41.5	47.6	1910–1913	1,036
1914	41.1	47.1	1914	400

Sources: Derived from data covering forty-seven *gubernii* of European Russia (only the Baltic region is missing) through 1905 in *MSDZ* 21 (1912):xxiii, and for 1906–1909 in ibid. 24 (1915):63, 66–67. The latter volume contains very minor corrections to data in the earlier volume for the years through 1905 but gives figures for ten-year periods only. The data for 1862, 1872, 1902, and 1905 have been corrected accordingly; in each case the revised figure is 0.1 million *desiatiny* higher than that published in the earlier volume. Data for 1910–1914 are derived from A. M. Anfimov and I. F. Makarov. "Novye dannye o zemlevladenii Evropeiskoi Rossii," *Istoriia SSSR*, no. 1 (1974), pp. 86–87. The statistics in Anfimov and Makarov are taken from the same official tax records that were used in *MSDZ*, but the end-of-year acreage figures are consistently about two million *desiatiny* higher than those for the period through 1909 published in *MSDZ*. I have therefore subtracted the annual decreases for 1910–1914 (from Anfimov and Makarov) from the figure in *MSDZ* for the end of 1909.

Note: The data in *MSDZ* and in Anfimov and Makarov comprise the sole available uniform set of statistics covering the period from serf emancipation to World War I; according to V. V. Sviatlovskii, *Mobilizatsiia zemelnoi sobstvennosti v Rossii (1861–1908 g.)*, 2d ed. (St. Petersburg, 1911), pp. 27–47, these statistics contain fewer inaccuracies than either the 1877 or the 1905 land censuses. The figures for noble acreage in *MSDZ* are somewhat higher than those in the two land censuses because the former include not only usable but also waste land. See A. P. Korelin, "Dvorianstvo v poreformennoi Rossii (1861–1904 gg.)," *Istoricheskie zapiski* 87 (1971):142. For a comparison of my figures with those presented in Manning, *Crisis*, see appendix D.

less likely (see discussion in "Stratification of Noble Landowners" below). Any further effects of the agricultural depression on noble land-ownership would appear to have been minimal (see chapter 1 above). During 1883–1897 the average annual decrease in noble acreage fell back to levels only moderately above those of 1863–1877 and never again even approached those of 1878–1882 until 1898–1902—several years *after* the depression ended.

Nor does table 3 offer any support for the notion of the nobility's "turn to the land." The decrease in noble acreage was in fact accelerating during the 1890s (precisely when Manning claims it was slowing down as the "turn to the land" began to reach full stride) and actually peaked in 1898–1902 at a point not far below that of twenty years earlier. The much slower decrease in the brief period 1903–1905 probably represents a pause for breath after the heavy selling of the previous five years rather than the beginning of a new trend. The peasant revolts of 1905–1907 are reflected in the unprecedented rate of decrease in noble landownership for 1906–1909, after which the rate returned to a level only slightly below that of 1898–1902. The outbreak of war in the summer of 1914 accounts for the sudden drop in that year.[11]

Behind the statistics depicting the dramatic and uninterrupted contraction of noble acreage stand other figures that have never attracted the same attention. Nobles were indeed the major sellers of agricultural land—although noble acreage as a proportion of all acreage sold declined steadily from 80.4 percent in 1863–1872 to 49.5 percent in 1903–1905 and then rose only to 51.4 percent in 1906–1909.[12] But nobles were also major *purchasers* of agricultural land—in fact, until almost the end of the nineteenth century, *the* major purchasers (see table 4). From 1863 through 1897 nobles were the largest purchasers of land, followed by merchants in 1863–1882 and by peasants in 1883–1897. During the period 1898–1905, nobles were still the second largest purchasers, yielding only to peasants. In 1906–1909 the State Peasant Land Bank (included in the category "juridical persons") for the first time acted as a major purchaser of land for resale to peasants.

The nobility's interest in buying land held remarkably steady for most of the period between serf emancipation and the 1905 revolution. Aver-

TABLE 4.   AGRICULTURAL ACREAGE PURCHASED, BY SOCIAL
ESTATE OF THE PURCHASER, 1863–1909 (PERCENT)

YEARS	NOBLES	MERCHANTS	PEASANTS	JURIDICAL PERSONS
1863–1872	51.6	22.6	12.7	4.1
1873–1882	42.9	24.2	17.7	4.8
1883–1892	34.6	20.8	29.2	4.6
1893–1897	33.2	18.2	27.0	8.8
1898–1902	27.0	17.8	36.7	6.4
1903–1905	26.2	13.7	40.4	7.3
1906–1909	15.2	7.0	37.4	32.0

Source: MSDZ 21 (1912):xiv; ibid., 24 (1915):xi.

Note: "Nobles" here includes hereditary and personal nobles and nonnoble *chinovniki;* "merchants" includes also distinguished citizens; "peasants" includes individuals, communes, and various types of cooperatives and associations; "juridical persons" is composed primarily of banks. I was unable to find exact data for juridical persons after 1909.

age annual purchases by nobles varied only slightly (between 938,000 and 967,000 *desiatiny*) during three of the four decades between 1863 and 1902; the exception was 1873–1882, when, taking advantage of a sharp rise in land sales by members of their own estate, nobles raised their purchases to an annual average of 1,293,000 *desiatiny*. Only during 1903–1905, when the "turn to the land" was supposedly in full swing, did noble land purchases drop to a new low of 705,000 *desiatiny* per annum. As a result of the 1905–1907 peasant revolts, the average annual rate fell even further in 1906–1909—to 597,000 *desiatiny*. With the return of normal conditions to the countryside, however, the nobility's confidence was restored, and their purchases of land recovered slowly but steadily from a low of 461,000 *desiatiny* in 1906 to 758,000 in 1909. By 1911–1914 the first estate's land purchases had staged an amazing comeback, averaging 1,025,000 *desiatiny* annually—higher than at any time since 1873–1882.[13]

Although nobles were net sellers of land, the ratio of their purchases to their sales maintained an impressive level (see table 5). The sharp but temporary drop in the wake of the 1905 revolution was the result much more of curtailed *purchases* than of higher *sales* of noble land; in fact, 1907 was the only year in which noble land sales were unusually high. During 1911–1914, with the restoration of peace in the countryside and of noble confidence, the ratio regained the level it had held during 1883–1905.

TABLE 5.   RATIO OF PURCHASES TO SALES OF LAND BY NOBLES, 1863–1914

YEARS	ACREAGE PURCHASED AS A % OF ACREAGE SOLD
1863–1872	64.2
1873–1882	60.1
1883–1892	53.1
1893–1902	52.0
1903–1905	53.0
1906–1909	29.6
1911–1914	52.9

Source: Derived from data in *MSDZ* 21 (1912):xiii–xiv; ibid., 24(1915):xi; and Anfimov and Makarov, p. 86.

Note: Figures for 1910 are missing because *MSDZ* 25 (1916) was unavailable to me.

The desire and ability of nobles to recoup through purchase a substantial portion of their losses in acreage was most marked in the western borderlands. From 1892 to 1896 the ratio of purchases to sales for nobles was 61 percent in the six Lithuanian and Belorussian *gubernii* and 70 percent in the three southwestern *gubernii*; the ratio for European Russia as a whole from 1893 to 1897 was only 54.5 percent.[14] As the preceding data clearly demonstrate, some nobles not only viewed land, at least in certain regions, as a good investment, they also competed successfully with commoners for its purchase. A more complete picture of the relationship between nobles and others in the land market is presented in table 6.

If it was nobles who kept the Russian land market active by putting their acreage up for sale, it was nobles and peasants together who bought up 80 percent of that same acreage over the entire period 1863–1905—and, in fact, in an ever increasing share, from 74 percent in the first decade after serf emancipation to 95 percent in the years immediately preceding the 1905 revolution. In 1906–1909 the enormous expansion in the activity of the Peasant Land Bank, purchasing land for later resale to peasants, compensated for the diminished role of the nobility as buyers of land. In the last years before World War I, the nobility came back into the market as purchasers, while the Peasant Bank resumed its former minor role: in 1911–1914 nobles and peasants together bought 93 percent of the aggregate of land sold by nobles and the excess of merchants' sales over purchases.

These data suggest that there is very little truth in the conventional image of nobles as victims of their own inability to compete with com-

TABLE 6. NOBLE LAND PURCHASES AND INCREASES IN ACREAGE OF OTHER SOCIAL CATEGORIES AS A PERCENTAGE OF NOBLE LAND SALES, 1863–1914

| | | NET INCREASES IN ACREAGE | | |
YEARS	NOBLES' PURCHASES	MERCHANTS	PEASANTS	JURIDICAL PERSONS
1863–1872	64.2	22.8	10.0	1.1
1873–1882	60.1	20.7	14.8	1.2
1883–1892	53.1	14.0	29.2	3.6
1893–1902	52.0	6.5	34.7	4.8
1903–1905	50.8	—	44.3	3.2
1863–1905	56.8	15.1	23.6	2.5
1906–1909	27.1	—	44.6	28.8
1911–1914	48.5	—	44.5	<2.0

Source: Derived from data in MSDZ 21 (1912):xiii–xiv; ibid., 24 (1915):xiii; and Anfimov and Makarov, pp. 85–86.

Note: In 1898–1902 the landholdings of juridical persons (including banks, and most notably the Peasant Land Bank) registered a net decrease of 7,000 desiatiny, most of which was sold to peasants. The increase in peasant acreage for 1893–1902 has consequently been lowered by that amount before being divided by the acreage sold by nobles. For the periods after 1902, all percentages were calculated on the basis of noble land sales plus the decrease in merchants' acreage. Noble land sales alone account for the following shares of the aggregate of noble land sales and the net decrease in merchants' acreage: 95.7 percent in 1903–1905; 99.8 percent in 1863–1905; 91.3 percent in 1906–1909; and 91.8 percent in 1911–1914.

moners who were more adept at meeting "the demands of capitalist management, based on commercial accounting, on the continuous growth of investment to expand production."[15] Some of the peasant purchasers of noble land were doubtless entrepreneurs—men like the merchant Lopakhin in *The Cherry Orchard* but who, unlike him, retained membership in the social estate into which they had been born. The overwhelming majority, however, clearly had no idea of utilizing commercial accounting and capital investment to expand production along capitalist lines. They were peasants of the traditional type who were seeking simply to make ends meet by supplementing the meager land allotments they had received at the time of emancipation, often banding together with their neighbors in order to buy the additional acreage they needed. In 1863–1902, 70 percent of the peasantry's net increase in acreage went to communes and to associations (*tovarishchestva*) that were, in fact, usually communes or parts of communes seeking additional land to be farmed communally; this percentage rose steadily from 45 percent in 1863–1872 to 83 percent in 1893–1902. The share going to these collective forms of ownership peaked at 87 percent in 1905–1908, declining thereafter under the impact of the government's new policy of encouraging individual peasant proprietors; even so, for the period 1905–1914, 63 percent of the net increase in peasant acreage went to communes and associations.[16]

STRATIFICATION OF NOBLE LANDOWNERS

THE landowning nobility's losses in numbers and in acreage had a varied effect upon the several strata of noble landowners. The government's land censuses of 1877 and 1905 divided landowners according to the size of their holdings as follows: petty, 100 or fewer *desiatiny*; intermediate, from 101 to 1,000; and large, over 1,000. Although these limits were more appropriate to the fertile left-bank Ukraine and the Black Soil center than to the less fertile non–Black Soil *gubernii* or to the southern and eastern steppe region where extensive farming was practiced, the government's definitions will be used here.[17]

Among the petty proprietors were two very different types—the impoverished backwoods nobleman (akin to the *hobereau* of old-regime France) whose style of life differed but minimally from that of his peasant neighbors, and the urbanized absentee landowner. A vivid portrayal of the first type on the eve of serf emancipation is offered by Terpigorev in a fictionalized childhood memory:

> we had to pass through the large village of Vsesviatskoe, which consisted entirely of petty landed nobles—small farmsteads with cottages and outbuildings roofed with thatch. . . . These

farmsteads were very numerous, and almost all of them were identical—small, half tumbled down, with overgrown garden plots. . . . As we passed through, we used to see some of the landowners walking about their courtyards in red shirts, just like coachmen, or in wide, dirty canvas coats, like old cooks, retired butlers, and other domestic servants out of work. We would also see their wives nearby, seated inside the farmstead or on the threshold, surrounded by children who were poorly and dirtily dressed.

They nevertheless felt very strongly that they were nobles, for, as we noticed from our carriage, their peasants—generally their serfs—would stand before them cap in hand, while they, by contrast, would stroll about and sit with an air of importance, conscious of their quality.[18]

Serf emancipation made little difference to this type of petty landowner, since he rarely owned more than a few souls. In the late 1890s the presence was reported in Kursk *guberniia*, among others, of entire villages of hereditary nobles, all sharing a common surname and inhabiting what had once been a large estate but which had been divided and subdivided over many generations, just like the village described by Terpigorev. The nobles of such villages lived like peasants and even hired themselves out as agricultural laborers to more substantial landowners of the district, including some commoners.[19] The Special Conference on the Affairs of the Noble Estate confirmed the existence, especially in the west and the Black Soil center, of "hundreds of families of illiterate nobles who have turned into simple plowmen."[20]

The urbanized petty proprietor was a noble who had abandoned the land, or whose father or grandfather had done so before him, to pursue a career in government service or, increasingly in the late nineteenth century, in one of the free professions or in business. He retained his small holding merely as a rural retreat and/or as a secondary source of income. Petty landowners of either type took little active part in the affairs of their *guberniia* noble societies, because the majority of them were disqualified from exercising even an indirect vote in the elections of noble officials, and of those who were qualified, many were kept away by their careers. All were barred from exercising a direct vote unless they had achieved high rank in government service or were former marshals of nobility.

In contrast to the petty landowners, proprietors of intermediate and large estates constituted the true landed nobility, that is, those who were able to live nobly on the income from their estates. Intermediate proprietors were the ones most likely to be resident on their estates and to take an active part in the affairs of both the nobility and the local community. Large landowners, especially the magnates owning 10,000 *desiatiny* or more, tended to be absentees with permanent homes in St. Petersburg or Moscow who devoted themselves to high society or high politics or both, or else lived a life of fashionable indolence in western Europe. In the uppermost range of large landowners in 1905 there were 155 individuals, virtually all of them nobles, belonging to 102 families, who owned more than 50,000 *desiatiny* each. By no means the wealthiest members of this select group were Count A. D. Sheremetev, who owned twenty-nine estates in twenty-five *uezdy*, totaling 226,000 *desiatiny;* his brother, Count S. D. Sheremetev, who was the proprietor of twenty-six estates in twenty-two *uezdy*, comprising 151,000 *desiatiny;* and Princess Z. N. Iusupova, the mother of Rasputin's assassin, who owned twenty-one properties in as many *uezdy*, with a total area of 216,000 *desiatiny*.[21]

Data are available on the number of petty, intermediate, and large noble landowners and on the acreage owned by each group both for 1877 (forty-nine *gubernii*) and 1905 (fifty *gubernii*). In 1877 all land belonging to a single proprietor within any one *uezd* was counted as one estate, whether or not it actually formed such, while in 1905 each property was counted separately, and in both years the lands of personal nobles were not differentiated from those of the hereditary nobility. Despite these problems, the two censuses present a sufficiently clear picture of the distribution of noble landowners and acreage among the three strata in European Russia (see table 7). The number of intermediate holdings, and the area they comprised, each declined by 22–23 percent between 1877 and 1905; the number of large estates, and also the acreage they contained, declined by 31 percent. Like the large proprietors, the intermediate proprietors lost members and acreage both through the sale of

TABLE 7. DISTRIBUTION OF NOBLE LANDOWNERS AND ACREAGE BY SIZE OF HOLDINGS, 1877 AND 1905

	1877				1905			
SIZE OF HOLDING (DES.)	PROPRIETORS (NO.)	(%)	DESIATINY (000's)	(%)	ESTATES (NO.)	(%)	DESIATINY (000's)	(%)
1–100	56,551	49.3	1,924	2.6	60,283	57.8	1,622	3.1
101–1,000	44,827	39.1	16,265	22.2	34,795	33.4	12,589	24.1
Over 1,000	13,338	11.6	54,975	75.2	9,180	8.8	37,953	72.8
Total	114,716	100.0	73,164	100.0	104,258	100.0	52,164	100.0

Source: G. Ershov, ed., *Raspredelenie pozemelnoi sobstvennosti v 49–ti guberniiakh Evropeiskoi Rossii v 1877–78 gg. (Statisticheskii vremennik Rossiiskoi imperii*, 3d ser., vol. 10) (St. Petersburg, 1886), pp. 32–43; *Statistika zemlevladeniia 1905 g. Svod dannykh po 50–ti guberniiam Evropeiskoi Rossii* (St. Petersburg, 1907), pp. 64, 78.

Note: Figures are for European Russia excluding the Don Army Oblast. Including the Don Army Oblast, 1905 percentages for petty, intermediate, and large holdings for estates are 56.8, 34.5, and 8.7, respectively, and for acreage are 3.1, 24.9, and 72.0, respectively.

land and through the division of estates by inheritance. Unlike the large landowners, however, the intermediate group saw its losses partially offset by the entrance into its ranks of proprietors formerly belonging to the group above it. The petty proprietors, on the other hand, grew 7 percent in number, more than compensating for their losses to the landless nobility by an influx from the intermediate group and by the increase resulting from the division of already small holdings between two or more heirs. The petty proprietors also registered the smallest decrease in acreage, only 16 percent. Although this group contained a majority of all noble landowners by the late nineteenth century and was holding up better than either intermediate or large proprietors, petty proprietors were clearly an insignificant factor in terms of acreage. They held a sizable share (3.6–12.0 percent in 1877, 5.3–15.7 percent in 1905) of all noble land only in Chernigov, Poltava, Kursk, Riazan, Kovno, Vilno, Grodno, and Smolensk.[22]

Combining estimates of the proportion of nobles who were landless with the data on the distribution of landed nobles by size of holdings, we arrive at a fuller picture of the first estate's changing relationship to the land (see table 8).

TABLE 8. DISTRIBUTION OF NOBLES AMONG LANDLESS AND LANDOWNERS, AND OF LATTER BY SIZE OF HOLDINGS, 1861–1905 (APPROXIMATE PERCENT)

	1861	1877	1905
Landless nobles	19–22	26–31	61–62
Owners of 1–100 *des.*	33–34	34–36	22–23
Owners of 101–1,000 *des.*	45–47	27–29	13
Owners of over 1,000 *des.*		8–9	3

Sources: For the distribution of landowners in 1861, A. G. Troinitskii, ed., *Krepostnoe naselenie v Rossii, po 10-i narodnoi perepisi* (St. Petersburg, 1861), p. 45; for all other data, tables 2 and 7.

Note: For 1861, the upper limit defining petty proprietors was twenty male serfs instead of one hundred *desiatiny*, following the practice of the 1858 revision. In 1858, 58 percent of all landed serfowners owned more than twenty souls each.

The position of the nobility relative to that of the other social estates was very different in petty landholding from what it was in holdings of over one hundred *desiatiny* (see table 9). The peasantry established a dominant position in petty landholding in the years immediately after emancipation and continued to strengthen their position, at the nobility's expense, over the next quarter century. The properties in question were individually owned, as distinct both from the communally owned allotments carved out of noble estates at the time of emancipation and from private land owned by peasant communes and associations. In holdings of over one hundred *desiatiny*, by contrast, the nobility retained its dominant position right into the twentieth

TABLE 9.   DISTRIBUTION OF INDIVIDUALLY OWNED LANDHOLDINGS
BY SOCIAL ESTATE, 1877 AND 1905

SIZE OF HOLDING (DES.)	1877				1905			
	OWNERS (NO.)	(%)	DESIATINY (ooo's)	(%)	HOLDINGS (NO.)	(%)	DESIATINY (ooo's)	(%)
1–100								
Nobles	56,551	14.0	1,924	30.6	60,283	9.1	1,622	16.9
Merchants	6,080	1.5	177	2.8	12,375	1.9	292	3.1
Meshchane	54,802	13.5	779	12.5	77,108	11.7	1,147	12.0
Peasants	266,635	65.9	3,022	48.1	466,587	70.7	5,764	60.2
Others	20,813	5.1	378	6.0	43,873	6.6	745	7.8
Total	404,881	100.0	6,281	100.0	660,226	100.0	9,569	100.0
Over 100								
Nobles	58,165	76.1	71,239	83.5	43,975	51.9	50,542	68.0
Merchants	6,550	8.6	9,617	11.3	10,331	12.2	12,443	16.7
Meshchane	3,202	4.2	1,130	1.3	6,996	8.3	2,484	3.3
Peasants	6,439	8.4	1,984	2.3	20,051	23.7	6,907	9.3
Others	2,121	2.8	1,354	1.6	3,350	4.0	2,000	2.7
Total	76,477	100.1	85,325	100.0	84,703	100.1	74,377	100.0
All Sizes								
Nobles	114,716	23.8	73,164	79.9	104,258	14.0	52,164	62.1
Merchants	12,630	2.6	9,794	10.7	22,706	3.0	12,735	15.2
Meshchane	58,004	12.1	1,910	2.1	84,104	11.3	3,632	4.3
Peasants	273,074	56.7	5,006	5.5	486,638	65.3	12,671	15.1
Others	22,934	4.8	1,733	1.9	47,223	6.3	2,745	3.3
Total	481,358	100.0	91,606	100.1	744,929	99.9	83,946	100.0

Source: Based on data in Ershov, pp. 30–43, and in *Statistika zemlevladeniia 1905 g.*, pp. 12–13, 64, 78.

Note: Figures for both 1877 and 1905 are for the forty-nine *gubernii*, without the Don Army Oblast. Totals of 99.9 and 100.1 are the result of rounding off percentages.

century. In this category the major gains at the nobility's expense were made by merchants in the 1860s and 1870s and by peasants thereafter.

The dominance of the first estate in holdings of over one hundred *desiatiny* varied greatly by *guberniia*. Those in which nobles owned the greatest share (75 percent and over) of all private acreage in holdings of this size in 1905 were the three Baltic *gubernii*; eight of the nine western *gubernii* (Vitebsk was the exception); Kursk, Tula, and Voronezh in the Black Soil center; and Perm, Penza, and Poltava. Those in which the nobility's share was the smallest (17–50 percent) were Olonets, Vologda, Viatka, Kostroma, Vladimir, Novgorod, and Pskov in the non–Black Soil north and center, and Kherson, Tauride, Samara, and Orenburg in the southern and eastern steppe zone. There had been relatively little turnover in the membership of either group since 1877.

Regional variations in the relative weight of the nobility in private landownership vis-à-vis the other social estates directly reflected the differential rates of decrease in noble acreage between 1862 and 1905 (see table 10).

TABLE 10. DECREASE AND DISTRIBUTION OF NOBLE ACREAGE BY REGION, 1862–1905 (PERCENT)

	DECREASE	DISTRIBUTION	
REGION	1862–1905	1862	1905
Non–Black Soil center and north[a]	60	24.1	16.4
Southern and eastern steppes[b]	52	18.7	15.1
Left-bank Ukraine and middle Volga[c]	41	11.1	11.2
Black Soil center and Urals[d]	33	22.6	25.7
West[e]	17	23.5	31.6
Total		100.0	100.0

Source: Calculated from provincial statistics in MSDZ 24 (1915):66–67.

Note: The regions comprise forty-seven gubernii; comparable data are not available for the entire period for the three Baltic gubernii, where serfs had been emancipated without land in 1816–1819, but between 1877 and 1905 the Baltic region experienced a smaller percentage decrease in noble acreage than any other. Regions with similar rates of decrease in noble acreage have been combined.

[a]Archangel, Olonets, Vologda, Viatka, St. Petersburg, Novgorod, Pskov, Tver, Iaroslavl, Kostroma, Vladimir, Moscow, Smolensk, Kaluga. Archangel contained an insignificant number of noble properties.

[b]Kherson, Tauride, Ekaterinoslav, Don Army Oblast, Astrakhan, Saratov, Samara, Orenburg. Astrakhan contained an insignificant number of noble properties.

[c]Left-bank Ukraine: Chernigov, Poltava, Kharkov; Middle Volga: Penza, Simbirsk, Nizhegorod, Kazan.

[d]Black Soil center: Kursk, Orel, Tula, Riazan, Tambov, Voronezh; Urals: Perm and Ufa.

[e]Kovno, Vilno, Grodno, Minsk, Mogilev, Vitebsk, Volynia, Kiev, Podolia, Bessarabia.

The evidence adduced above as to the identity of the purchasers of noble lands has already cast doubt on the accuracy of the conventional image of nobles who were psychologically crippled by the loss of their serfs being forced to sell their estates to commoners who were capable of farming with hired labor, investing capital to raise productivity, and producing for the market. Correlations on a regional basis of the decrease in noble acreage with the methods by which nobles managed their lands only raise further doubts as to the validity of the conventional wisdom. The regions where capitalist practices were most widespread among the landowning nobility were the Baltic and western gubernii and the southern steppes. In the Baltic and western regions farming on the landowner's own account, as opposed to turning over the greater part of the estate to peasant lessees, was traditional among the German and Polish nobles who dominated private landowning in these areas. These landowners were more likely than those in other regions to react to the world agricultural depression of the last quarter of the nineteenth century by shifting from grains to more profitable crops and by investing capital to raise productivity. The depression sharply lowered both export and domestic prices of grains, in which 95.5 percent of the sown area of European Russia was planted in the first half of the 1870s.[23] Modern farming with hired labor combined with fertile soil gained for the Black Sea steppe and lower Volga, recently colonized areas with a sparse peasant population, the lead over the Black Soil center as Russia's leading grain producing region from the mid-1880s.[24] In the Baltic and western *gubernii* capitalist farming was indeed accompanied by the lowest rates of decrease in noble acreage anywhere in European Russia. On the southern steppes, however, where capitalist farming was even more prevalent, the decline in noble acreage was well *above* the average for the fifty *gubernii*. And in the Black Soil center, where traditional patterns of land use persisted (the peasants farming by age-old methods and the nobles contenting themselves with collecting their rents), the first estate sustained acreage losses well *below* the national average. Again, the picture of rational farmers and improving landowners driving out the parasitical traditionalist landlords does not hold up.

In most regions of European Russia the nobles who remained landowners, some even purchasing additional acreage, maintained their traditional parasitic relationship to the peasant economy. With certain local exceptions, agriculture continued to offer little hope for profitable investment of the landowner's capital. The domestic market for agricultural produce was growing only slowly, and grain prices continued to fall until the late 1890s. Moreover, the land settlement that followed serf emancipation left the peasants short of arable land, virtually deprived of pasture and forest, and kept relatively immobile by the structure of communal responsibility, while their numbers increased at a very rapid pace (58 percent between 1860 and 1897).[25] The result was (1) the maintenance of a pool of cheap peasant labor, which discouraged the introduction of capital-intensive, labor-saving improvements that would have raised the productivity, but not necessarily the profitability, of agriculture,[26] and (2) the creation of an intense and growing demand on the part of peasants for both the lease and purchase of noble land. For most noble landowners there was more profit to be gained in leasing than in farming their lands, and toward the end of the century close to three-quarters of total noble acreage, and an even larger share of the nobility's arable and meadows, was leased to peasants.[27] On the estates of the 155 largest landowners, less than one-quarter of the arable was farmed by the owners with their own tools and livestock and hired labor.[28] Hired workers, both full- and part-time, constituted only 10 percent of the adult agricultural labor force at the turn of the century.[29] A government commission of 1901 articulated what had long been a guiding principle among noble landowners when it noted "the unprofitability of money expenditures on agriculture."[30]

Leasing arrangements took various forms—money rental, sharecropping (*ispolu*), and the working of the landlord's farm by peasants using their own tools and livestock in exchange for the use of some other part of the landlord's estate (*otrabotki*). Money rental became increasingly common, and by 1901 in the fifty *gubernii* of European Russia over 83 percent of all acreage leased by peasants from private landlords was paid for in money.[31]

Some nobles who remained landowners were able to profit from Russia's economic growth by putting their land to nonagricultural uses. A number of nobles in the Donets basin opened coal mines on their estates in the 1860s and 1870s, and a considerably larger group took advantage of its ownership of property in or near a growing urban area, especially one of the two capitals. The princes Beloselskii-Belozerskii put up more than sixty houses on St. Petersburg's Krestovskii Island, a large part of which they owned. Count Alexander Dmitrievich Sheremetev inherited two parcels of land totaling over eighty-eight *desiatiny* on the northern edge of Moscow at Ostankino and the neighboring Marina Grove, which he subdivided into 584 building lots and leased out for a total annual rent of 38,000 rubles in 1899. His older brother Sergei rented his large house at the corner of Nikolskaia Street and Bolshoi Cherkasskii Lane, just off Red Square in Moscow, for shops and offices, netting a profit of 127,000 rubles in 1900 and 250,000 rubles in 1910, more than the income he received from any one of his numerous rural estates. Sergei Dmitrievich also collected over 27,000 rubles in 1909 from the lease of 363 building lots at his Kuskovo estate in the eastern suburbs of Moscow. Prince Felix Iusupov and his parents owned five large rental properties in St. Petersburg and several more in Moscow from which, during the years 1910–1914, they averaged an annual net profit of over 122,000 rubles— roughly one-third their total net income.[32] Although such windfalls were available only to a lucky few, all landowners stood to profit from the steep rise in the value of agricultural land.

LAND VALUES

THE average price per *desiatina* of rural land sold in forty-four *gubernii* of European Russia (excluding the Baltic region, Archangel, Astrakhan, and Perm) for the period 1854–1858 was 13 rubles. It rose sharply during the first decade after serf emancipation, reaching 20 rubles for the years 1868–1872. After holding fairly level in the first half of the 1870s, the average price rose steadily for two decades, reaching 47 rubles during 1893–1897. An even steeper increase over the next ten years brought the price of a *desiatina* to over 93 rubles for the period 1903–1905—a rise of 615 percent in half a century, or 12–13 percent per annum.[33] In fact, prices rose so sharply that noble land increased in value faster than it decreased in extent. The value of all rural land owned by the hereditary nobility in the same forty-four *gubernii* rose by 282 percent between the end of 1862 and the end of 1905, from 1.278 billion rubles to 4.879 billion.[34] Since inflation averaged well under 1 percent per annum between 1867 and 1905,[35] the rise in land values was a very real one. Between 1905 and 1912 the average price of a *desiatina* of rural land continued to climb at about the same rate as previously, reaching 163 rubles in the latter year. Nobles who held onto their land saw its aggregate market value soar to 6.939 billion rubles in 1912, despite an 18 percent decrease in area since 1905. Between 1862 and 1912 noble land had increased in value by 443 percent even while diminishing in extent by more than one-half.[36]

The dramatic rise in land prices did not reflect any increase in the profitability of Russian agriculture, for productivity remained low, and the last third of the nineteenth century was a period of falling grain prices. Rising land prices reflected, rather, strong and growing peasant demand for noble land. For the first two decades after emancipation, land-hungry peasants found it easier to lease than to buy and drove up land rents faster than land prices. In many areas rents reached a point where a tenant could not cover his own labor cost out of the income produced by the land he leased.[37] By 1887/88 rents on short-term, usually one-year, leases, which were most common, represented an annual return on the market value of the land of 13.7 percent in twenty-three Black Soil *gubernii*, and 25.2 percent in twenty non–Black Soil *gubernii*. During the following two decades rents rose only moderately in the great majority of Black Soil *gubernii* and actually fell in almost all of the non–Black Soil *gubernii*. Land prices meanwhile were driven ever more steeply upward by the rising number of peasant purchasers, assisted beginning in 1883 by the State Peasant Land Bank. Peasants normally bought land in much smaller lots than did nobles or merchants, and small lots sold at a much higher price per *desiatina*. By 1901, thanks largely to the rise in land prices, rents yielded a return of 7–8 percent per annum on the land's market value.[38]

There is a positive correlation between the level of land prices in various *gubernii* and the ability, or desire, of the nobility to hold onto their land—low prices being generally associated with very large decreases in noble acreage, and high prices with relatively small decreases. Of the sixteen *gubernii* in which prices were low in at least two of the three periods selected (see table 11), eleven registered very large decreases in acreage (53–70 percent) between 1862 and 1905: Olonets, Vologda, Viatka, Novgorod, Pskov, Smolensk, Tver, Iaroslavl, Kostroma, Samara, and Orenburg. All but Samara and Orenburg were located in the

TABLE 11. LEVELS OF AVERAGE LAND PRICES, 1854–1858 TO 1903–1905

	1854–1858		1878–1882		1903–1905	
LEVEL	PRICE IN R.	NO. OF GUBERNII	PRICE IN R.	NO. OF GUBERNII	PRICE IN R.	NO. OF GUBERNII
Low	3–10	13	3–20	16	9–70	16
Medium	11–20	17	21–40	15	71–120	14
High	21–33	13	41–71	14	121–203	15

Source: MSDZ 13 (1907): table 4; ibid. 21 (1912):xxxii.

Note: The data for 1854–1858 cover 43 gubernii of European Russia, excluding the three Baltic provinces, Archangel, Astrakhan, Bessarabia, and the Don Army Oblast; the data for the other periods cover 45 gubernii, excluding only the Baltic region, Archangel, and Astrakhan.

non–Black Soil center and north, where natural conditions were least favorable to agriculture and rents were both low and falling from the mid-1880s. Here land was a relatively poor investment compared with the alternative possibilities for investment of capital opening up as a result of Russia's economic development, and the decrease in noble acreage was consequently steepest. Of the fourteen gubernii in which prices were high in at least two of the three periods, three experienced very small decreases of 4–23 percent in noble acreage (Kovno, Kiev, and Podolia), and eight experienced moderate decreases of 26–38 percent (Bessarabia, Poltava, Kursk, Orel, Tula, Voronezh, Tambov, and Penza). These eleven gubernii were located in the west, the left-bank Ukraine, the Black Soil center, or on the middle Volga—all regions where either agriculture itself was more profitable or rents were high and continued to rise. Here land was a relatively better investment, and the decline in noble acreage was accordingly less severe.

In all regions rising land prices were a tempting inducement to sell, even in the 1860s and 1870s when land rents produced an extremely high yield on the capital investment which an estate represented. For nobles who sold out during the first two decades after serf emancipation such noneconomic considerations as the greater attractiveness of urban life may often have played a determining role. From the mid-1880s an even steeper rise in land prices and a falling percentage return from rents provided yet stronger inducements to sell land (see table 12). Everywhere the market value of a noble's estate often rose out of all proportion to the annual income he could realize by farming it himself. Under these circumstances the decision to sell one's estate, rather than invest capital in its improvement, was frequently a wise choice—and at the very least an understandable one for landowners having no deep commitment to the land.[39] An improving landlord, on the other hand, often had to buck social pressure, and not only from tradition-bound peasants. No less an

TABLE 12.   AMOUNT OF MONEY REALIZED BY NOBLES FROM LAND
SALES, 1863–1914

YEARS	INCOME FROM LAND SALES (MILLIONS OF RUBLES)
1863–1872	122
1873–1882	217
1883–1892	302
1893–1902	598
1903–1905	175
1906–1914	1,597
Total	3,011

Source: Calculated from data on decreases in noble acreage in *MSDZ* 24 (1915):66–67, and price data in ibid. 13 (1907); table 4; 21 (1912):xxxii; 23 (1914):xxi–xxii; 24 (1915):xxi; A.M. Anfimov, *Krupnoe pomeshchiche khoziaistvo Europeiskoi Rossii* (Moscow, 1969), p. 358.

Note: Figures are based on net decreases in noble acreage in forty-five *gubernii*, excluding the Baltic region, Archangel, and Astrakhan.

authority than Alexander III advised a noble landowner who was drain-
ing a marsh on his property: "Do not invest all the money you make in
your estates, because you will ruin yourself."[40]

In the period 1863–1892 nobles also received as compensation for the
land taken from them and allotted to their former serfs a sum equal to
85–90 percent of the amount they realized from sales of land during the
same years. The government's compensation covered 80 percent of the
value of the peasant allotments; in some cases landowners received supplementary payments from their former serfs to cover at least part of the
remaining 20 percent. In compensating the nobility, the state subtracted
the unpaid balance owed to it on mortgages contracted before emancipation. The net sum was paid in special bank notes exchangeable at par at
state credit institutions and in nonregistered redemption certificates
which were not convertible into money. Each landowner received bank
notes in an amount equivalent to 100 percent of the first 1,000 rubles
owed to him by the state; 20 percent of the next 9,000 rubles; 10 percent
of the next 40,000 rubles; and 5 percent of any balance above 40,000
rubles. He was given redemption certificates to cover the remainder of
the state's debt to him.[41] Both the special bank notes and the redemption
certificates paid 5 percent annual interest. The certificates were to be
replaced in installments by additional issues of the special bank notes
over a period of fifteen years; the bank notes were scheduled for retirement in lots over forty-nine years. With each passing quinquennium the
nobles who concluded redemption agreements with their former serfs
were less heavily in debt to the state and were more likely to hold onto
their redemption certificates than to sell them at a discount (see table 13).
Assuming that not over 90 percent of the state's compensation was paid

TABLE 13. COMPENSATION BY THE STATE TO FORMER
SERFOWNERS, 1862–1891

YEARS	GROSS SUM OWED BY STATE (MILS. OF RUBLES)	NET SUM PAID TO NOBLES (MILS. OF RUBLES)	NET AS % OF GROSS	MARKET VALUE OF REDEMPTION CERT. AS % OF PAR
1862–1866	329	173	52	67
1867–1871	259	152	59	75
1872–1876	105	77	73	85
1877–1881	71	56	79	90
1882–1886	108	99	92	95
1887–1891	19	18	96	—
1862–1891	890	575	65	

Source: The market value of the redemption certificates is from *O zadolzhennosti zemlevladeniia v sviazi s statisticheskimi dannymi o pritoke kapitalov k pomestnomu zemlevladeniiu so vremeni osvobozhdeniia krestian (Vremennik tsentralnago statisticheskago komiteta,* no. 2 [1888], pp. vi, x; all other data are from V. Ionov, "Fakty i illiuzii v vo prose dvizheniia chastnoi zemelnoi sobstvennosti," *Zhizn,* April 1900, p. 205.

Note: If no more than 10 percent of their former serfs came up with supplementary payments covering the value of the land not compensated by the state (222.5 million rubles), noble landowners would have received an additional 22 million rubles. The figures in column 1 add up to 891 because of rounding off

in the form of certificates, and that at least half of the certificates were held until the state converted them into bank notes, we arrive at a conservative figure of 525 million rubles for the cash sum received by the nobility from the state and from purchasers of unmatured certificates— in addition to the peasants' supplementary payments.

MORTGAGE DEBT

BEFORE looking at the uses to which the nobility put the capital realized from the sale or expropriation of their land, we must turn to the question of mortgage debt. If, as the conventional wisdom has it, sale was ordinarily the result of hopeless indebtedness, then the greater part of the sale proceeds would have gone to liquidate the debt. In fact, as we shall see, this was very far from being the case.

From the mid-eighteenth to the mid-nineteenth century long-term credit had been available to noble landowners, using their serfs as collateral, from a variety of government sources.[42] Under Nicholas I, especially, the landed nobility had borrowed freely, taking advantage of the government's policy of extending credit to the first estate "primarily for reasons of social policy without regard to strict economic calculations."[43] By 1859, when loans from government sources were terminated in anticipation of serf emancipation, two-thirds of all male proprietary serfs had been mortgaged to state institutions, and the total mortgage debt of the landed nobility stood at 425.5 million rubles, an increase of 372 percent since 1823.[44] After emancipation new sources of mortgage credit were gradually established: the Kherson Land Bank, a mutual credit society serving the *gubernii* of New Russia from 1864; the Mutual Land Credit Society in St. Petersburg, organized by and for nobles in 1866; and eleven joint-stock land banks, each of purely regional significance, founded in 1871–1872. These were all private institutions, offering credit in limited amounts at competitive commercial rates of interest, from 7 to 8.5 percent. For a quarter of a century after serf emancipation, the government took no responsibility for providing cheap long-term credit to the landed nobility; the new State Bank established in 1860 did not give mortgage loans.[45]

The scarcity and high cost of long-term loans, at least in comparison with the previous reign, in part account for the fact that the landed nobility borrowed relatively little money in this manner during the first decade or two after serf emancipation. Of probably greater importance is the fact that few nobles had much need or desire to mortgage their estates in the 1860s and early 1870s, for this was the period during which the nobility received the greater part of the compensation for the peasant allotments. As the redemption process liquidated old debts and few new ones were contracted, the nobility's mortgage debt fell to 250.5 million rubles by the beginning of 1873. Over the next decade it rose again to 400.2 million—a reflection of both the renewed interest in borrowing and the greater availability of loans after the founding of the private land banks (see table 14).

From the second half of the 1870s the nobility's demand for more and cheaper mortgage credit grew until it was satisfied by the government's creation in 1885 of the State Noble Land Bank, which quickly became the principal source of mortgage loans for members of the first estate. By 1896 the Noble Land Bank and its Special Department (the restructured Society for Mutual Land Credit from 1890) held the mortgages on 63 percent of all mortgaged noble acreage in forty-three *gubernii*.[46] With the establishment of the Noble Land Bank the first estate's mortgage debt increased immensely, reaching a total of 1,299.8 million rubles at the beginning of 1906 and 1,401.5 million on the eve of World War I. By 1896, 42 percent of all noble acreage was mortgaged either to the Noble Land Bank or to one of the private credit institutions; in eighteen Black Soil *gubernii*, from Podolia and Kherson in the west to Ufa and Orenburg in the east, more than half the acreage owned by nobles was mortgaged to one or another bank.[47]

These data on the size and growth of the nobility's mortgage debt would seem to confirm the conventional wisdom about the inexorable slide of noble landholdings through mounting debt toward liquidation.

TABLE 14.   MORTGAGE DEBT OF NOBLES AND VALUE OF NOBLE
LAND, 1863–1914

YEAR	MORTGAGE DEBT (MILS. OF RUBLES)	VALUE OF NOBLE LAND (MILS. OF RUBLES)	MORTGAGE DEBT AS % OF LAND VALUES
1863	425.5	1,277.6	33
1873	250.5	1,816.6	14
1883	400.2	2,156.4	19
1893	748.1	2,902.0	26
1906	1,299.8	4,879.3	27
1914	1,401.5	6,939.4	20

Sources: O zadolzhennosti zemlevladeniia v sviazi s statisticheskimi dannymi o pritoke kapitalov k pomestnomu zemlevladeniiu so vremeni osvobozhdeniia krestian (Vremennik tsentralnago statisticheskago komiteta, no. 2 [1888]), pp. v–vi, x; Ezhegodnik Rossii 1908 g., pp. xcii–xciii; and Ezhegodnik Rossii 1914 g., p. 39.

Note: Values are as of January 1 of each year. Data are for forty-five gubernii; excluded are the Baltic region, Archangel, and Astrakhan. The value of noble land in the several years was calculated by the method outlined in n. 34 above; for the way in which mortgage debt was estimated, see Appendix E.

Of much greater significance, however (as any modern homeowner will recognize), than the ruble amount of the debt or the share of noble acreage that was mortgaged, is the relationship between indebtedness and the total value of noble land. The latter figure, as is evident from table 14, was rising as fast as the first estate's debt after 1893, and even faster than the debt after 1906. At no time in the postemancipation half century could mortgage debt be considered a very heavy burden on the land. Despite both the rapid increase in the nobility's mortgage debt and the rapid shrinkage in the acreage they owned, rising land prices meant that mortgage indebtedness as a percentage of total capital value never again reached the level of the last days of serfdom. In fact this ratio did not rise significantly after the early 1890s and experienced an impressive decline after the 1905 revolution. In 1914 the burden of mortgage debt was no heavier than it had been on the eve of the establishment of the Noble Land Bank, despite the nobility's heavy use of the bank. The statistical evidence supports Count Witte's caustic remark in 1898 to the Special Conference on the Affairs of the Noble Estate that the landed nobility were not nearly so heavily in debt as their champions believed.[48]

While the nobility's mortgage debt as a percentage of the value of the land in their possession declined in European Russia as a whole, it rose in a number of gubernii — most notably in the southern and eastern steppes, from Kherson to Saratov, Ufa, and Orenburg, and also in Kovno and Vilno. In 1906 the regions where this percentage was above average were the west (except for Minsk), the Black Soil center, the left-bank

Ukraine (except for Chernigov), and the middle Volga.[49] The Baltic region should probably be included in this group, although it is not possible to establish a ratio between the size of the nobility's mortgage debt and the value of its lands in Estonia, Livonia, and Courland. In this region, where the nobility owned more than 90 percent of all privately held acreage in estates of over one hundred *desiatiny* in 1905, 86.5 percent of total private acreage was mortgaged at the beginning of 1914—a higher percentage than that for any other region and far above the average of 51.6 percent for European Russia.[50] The five regions in which the nobility's burden of mortgage debt was heaviest were precisely those in which the acreage owned by the first estate had decreased by the smallest percentages since serf emancipation.

By contrast, in the non–Black Soil center and north and in Samara,[51] where the percentage decrease in noble land had been the highest, the mortgage debt of the nobility relative to the value of their lands was the lowest in 1906. Coincidentally, interest in a state land bank for nobles in the early 1880s had been strongest in the Black Soil *gubernii*, whereas in the non–Black Soil center and north the first estate had been more interested in the establishment in 1883 of the State Peasant Land Bank, which by financing purchases of land by peasants was seen as raising effective demand for noble land.[52]

The positive correlation between the nobility's willingness to borrow money on the security of its land and its desire and ability to hold onto that land casts into doubt the conventional belief that the mortgaging of a noble estate was the prelude to its sale. On the contrary, the mortgaging of an estate would appear to have been an alternative to sale as a means of raising capital.

The establishment of new credit institutions, especially the Noble Land Bank with its low interest rates and sixty-seven-year mortgages, made the alternative of borrowing very attractive. During its first decade the Noble Land Bank served largely to enable noble landowners to pay off the mortgage money they had borrowed at higher rates in the previous quarter century from the private banks; as of the beginning of 1893, 65 percent of the outstanding loan balance of the Noble Land Bank had been used for this purpose.[53] The Society for Mutual Land Credit was reorganized as the Special Department of the Noble Land Bank in 1890 and saw its outstanding loan balance decline from a high of 143.9 million rubles in mid-1888 to only 45.8 million at the end of 1905,[54] primarily as the result of refinancing through the Noble Land Bank proper. During its second and third decades the bank used its capital increasingly to refinance the mortgage loans of its existing borrowers and to provide them with additional funds as the value of their land continued to increase (see tables 15 and 16). The uncertain conditions prevailing during the first half of the period 1906–1909 explain the temporary decrease in borrowing from the Noble Land Bank, while the sharp rise in the percentage of noble acreage bought by commoners in the same period is undoubtedly a major part of the reason for the quantum leap in the amount repaid to the bank.[55]

TABLE 15. OPERATIONS OF THE STATE NOBLE LAND BANK, 1886–1913 (MILLIONS OF RUBLES)

YEAR	ALL LOANS	NEW LOANS	ADDITIONS TO EXISTING LOANS	REFINANCING OF EXISTING LOANS	AMOUNT REPAID	OUTSTANDING LOAN BALANCE AT END OF PERIOD
1886–1890	271.9	259.9	7.6	4.4	0.0	267.5
1891–1895	254.8	147.8	31.8	75.2	50.5	396.6
1896–1900	455.3	231.1	69.9	154.3	63.9	633.7
1901–1905	331.2	98.6	75.1	157.5	80.1	727.3
1906–1909	140.1	24.8	39.0	76.3 ⎱	246.4	791.8
1910–1913	431.4	114.7	132.3	184.4 ⎰		
1886–1913	1,884.7	876.9	355.7	652.1	440.9	791.8

Source: Based on data in Ezhegodnik Rossii 1908 g., pp. xcii–xciii, and in Ezhegodnik Rossii 1914 g., pp. 39, 48–49.

Note: Virtually all of the Noble Bank's loans (98.4 percent by value as of January 1, 1914) were on lands in forty-seven gubernii of European Russia (excluding the Baltic region); the remaining loans were on lands in the North Caucasus and Transcaucasus (Ezhegodnik Rossii 1914 g., pp. 52–53).

TABLE 16. DISTRIBUTION OF NOBLE LAND BANK'S LOANS BY VALUE, 1886–1913 (PERCENT)

YEARS	NEW LOANS	ADDITIONS TO EXISTING LOANS	REFINANCING OF EXISTING LOANS
1886–1890	95.6	2.8	1.6
1891–1895	58.0	12.5	29.5
1896–1900	50.8	15.4	33.9
1901–1905	29.8	22.7	47.6
1906–1909	17.7	27.8	54.5
1910–1913	26.6	30.7	42.7
1886–1913	46.5	18.9	34.6

Source: Table 15.

USE OF CAPITAL

THERE is no reason to doubt the accuracy of the general conviction among contemporaries that very little of the nobility's mortgage money was invested in the improvement of their estates,[56] for such investments did not often make much economic sense. It is also probably true, as has often been alleged,[57] that a share of the borrowed money went to cover ordinary living expenses or extraordinary expenditures occasioned by the marriage of a daughter, illness, and the like. Such behavior was the product not so much of waste and extravagance as of the gap between the modest incomes of the great majority of landed nobles and the cost of maintaining the style of life expected of even lesser members of the first estate. That style included, for example, at least a secondary education for a nobleman's sons.[58] As land values rose, nobles borrowed against their increasing equity in their estates to finance their budget deficits. In a seller's and lessor's market for land this was an unsound practice only if indulged in to excess. By no means all mortgage money, however, was used in economically nonproductive ways. The minority of noble landowners who farmed their estates with hired labor and their own tools and livestock used mortgage loans to expand their working capital. Many more nobles, regardless of how they exploited their estates, discovered that it made good sense to borrow at low rates of interest on the security of their lands and invest the borrowed sums in stocks, bonds, and bank accounts paying higher rates.[59]

Much of the same pattern governed the use of the more than 3.5 billion rubles realized by the nobility from the sale or expropriation of their land between 1863 and 1914. One-eighth of the total (441 million) went to pay off mortgages to the Noble Land Bank, and a lesser amount can be presumed to have been employed in the liquidation of other debts. A good deal was no doubt spent on consumption—foolish or otherwise. But a significant amount was invested, and (apart from the conventional image of nobles as financial *naifs*) there is no reason to assume that all or even most of the capital so disposed of was invested "unwisely."[60]

A small number of nobles used the proceeds from the sale of their estates to purchase businesses. As early as 1882 in Moscow approximately 500 hereditary nobles owned industrial enterprises, and 234 more owned commercial establishments. Between 70 and 85 percent of these were middling to small in size, and some were family operated.[61] Much more common was the nobleman who invested in government bonds and in securities issued by railroads, banks, and other private firms, either as an alternative or a supplement to investment in land. As of 1882 many Moscow nobles were reported to be deriving the major part of their income from dividends and interest on such investments. Some of the more prominent examples of this trend were General Count N. V. von Adlerberg, former governor-general of Finland, who at his death in 1892 owned government bonds valued at 626,000 rubles but no real estate; Count I. D. Delianov, minister of education, who died in 1897 leaving an estate containing securities worth 217,000 rubles, but again no real property; and V. V. Apraksin, former *guberniia* marshal of nobility in Orel, who at his death in 1898 left real property worth

252,000 rubles and securities, mostly railroad bonds, worth over 3.3 million.[62]

Contemporary observers took note of the transfer of noble capital from agriculture to commerce and industry. Those who valued the first estate's traditional social role and style of life were loud in their dismay.[63] The trend continued, however, and was intensified by the revolution of 1905, which made land appear to some nobles to be an even more risky and less profitable form of investment than before. In 1894 Count A. D. Sheremetev owned twenty-nine estates totaling 226,100 *desiatiny* and worth perhaps 10 million rubles; he also owned securities with a value of 7.6 million. By 1913, of the count's total annual income of 1,550,000 rubles, 62 percent took the form of interest and dividends from his investments in commerce and industry, and only 32 percent was derived from agriculture and forestry; the remaining 6 percent came from his urban real estate holdings. His brother Sergei had total assets of 37.9 million rubles on March 1, 1917, of which 19 percent was in stocks and bonds, 28 percent in urban property, and 51 percent in rural land, buildings, and livestock. The Iusupovs owned only 41,000 rubles worth of securities in 1901, but after 1905 they sold and mortgaged many of their estates and increased their securities holdings to 5.1 million by 1915. A. A. Orlov-Davydov, a landowner in no fewer than eight *gubernii*, also had an income of 117,000 rubles in 1911 from his holdings of Russian and foreign stocks and bonds. It was not only the aristocracy who held such investments, for in 1910, of the 137,825 nobles residing in St. Petersburg, 49 percent lived on income from securities.[64]

The picture that emerges from the foregoing indicates that the nobles depicted in *The Cherry Orchard*, to take the most famous among many similar portrayals, reflect only one among many tendencies at work among the postemancipation nobility. Other nobles did in fact make a go of agriculture without serf labor, either farming on their own account or, more often, leasing their estates to land-hungry peasants. A significant number even purchased additional land. Mortgage debt was by no means a sign that an estate was on the road to liquidation. And noble landowners remained the dominant element among private owners of all but the smallest properties.

The fact remains, of course, that the majority of noble landowners did divest themselves of their estates, but this is not to say that they always, or even in the majority of cases, did so reluctantly and in order to satisfy their creditors. In many and perhaps even most cases the decision to sell was a voluntary one, facilitated by the nature of the nobility's historical relationship to the land and by the general unprofitability of Russian agriculture. The decision to sell was by and large an alternative to mortgaging the estate, not a product of indebtedness. And the capital realized from the sale of land, like that received from the mortgage banks, was often put to work more profitably in commerce and industry than it ever could have been in agriculture. The landed nobility was thus not so much undergoing a process of decline or impoverishment, the result of its alleged inability to adjust to farming without serf labor, as it was experiencing a radical transformation—one, in large part, of its own choosing. This transformation should be viewed as a process of separating out those who, because of personal inclination, a rational weighing of the economic potential of their properties as opposed to other forms of investment, personal inadequacy, bad luck, or a combination of two or more of these factors, opted to sell their remaining *desiatiny* and try their fortunes elsewhere. The minority that stayed on the land continued to diminish in numbers and in the aggregate acreage it owned, but increasingly it consisted of committed agrarian entrepreneurs.

When the state's traditional interest in the nobility as servitors waned, as it did in the 1860s, the nobility for the most part lost both its traditional social function and its privileged legal status. What remained was a dominant position among intermediate and large rural landowners and a clear sense of cultural superiority. Some nobles sought a new social identity in the first; the majority were influenced by the second to look elsewhere. Cultural castaways on their patrimonial estates, where they were isolated in a vast sea of traditional peasants, clergy, and merchants, many nobles took advantage of the greater mobility which the postreform period offered to escape to the mainland of the larger towns and cities, where they found a more congenial cultural environment and new social roles. This dramatic transformation could be deplored only by those who were more concerned with the preservation of the old order than with the creative adaptation of individual nobles to social change. Traditionalists did more than deplore "the decline of the nobility." With a fervor born of desperation they undertook to arrest, if not reverse, the nobility's divorce from the land and all it signified.

C H A P T E R 3

THE TRADITIONALIST COUNTERATTACK

THE DEFENSE OF PRIVILEGE

T HE belief in the first estate's helplessness to deal with the postemancipation world was cherished not only by those who felt little sympathy for the nobility but also by its warmest supporters and defenders. Neither group doubted for a moment that noble landowners were parting with their patrimonial estates under compulsion from insupportable debts, falling grain prices, and, most of all, their innate inability to survive in a free market for labor and land. Where the two groups differed was in the conclusions they drew from their analysis.

By definition, liberals approved of Russia's social evolution in general and the decline of the nobility in particular. Some did so from a position akin to that of the Westerners of the 1840s, viewing the traditional Russian estate society as comparable in all essential respects to the old regime in the West and fated to follow the same path as the West had taken since the French Revolution. V. O. Kliuchevskii, the country's leading historian, articulated this view in his 1886 lectures on the history of estates in Russia. He argued the existence of a historical law decreeing society's progress through three stages: a primitive undifferentiated stage; a stage in which the appearance of functional economic groups and the state gives rise to juridically unequal social categories (estates); and finally, the modern stage of social development, in which all individuals enjoy equal civil rights and personal obligations, such as military service, and in which political rights and material obligations, such as taxes, are distributed unequally, not among groups according to birth, but among individuals according to wealth. Like most discoverers of historical laws, Kliuchevskii regarded his findings in a positive light; he had no doubt that "the equalization of estates is a victory both for the general interest of the state and for personal freedom."[1]

A similar case was made by B. N. Chicherin, philosopher, legal theorist, historian, and a prominent liberal. Chicherin held that the existence of social estates was an important safeguard against tyranny in an absolute monarchy but that they had no place in a society in which the rights of individuals were constitutionally guaranteed and the power of the government limited. In his 1897 articles on the noble question for *Sankt-Peterburgskie vedomosti*, Chicherin argued that "the estate system, which is characteristic of a certain period of social development, yields to another civil order, based on general freedom and the equality of all before the law." In Russia this transformation had begun with the reforms of the 1860s: "With the introduction of civil liberty for all, the disintegration of the estate system is only a question of time."[2]

Others who approved of Russia's social evolution did so from a point of view which emphasized Russia's uniqueness. The Slavophiles Ivan Aksakov and A. I. Koshelev in the 1860s and the distinguished legal scholars N. M. Korkunov and Baron S. A. Korf a generation later insisted that social estates were an institution alien to Russia, borrowed from the West in the eighteenth century and never able to put down strong roots because of a basic incompatibility with Russia's egalitarian tradition. These commentators applauded the elimination of the legal distinctions separating the estates and the rapprochement of the nobility, divested of its old privileges, with the common people as marking Russia's return to her own true course of development.[3]

Minister of Finance Sergei Witte also insisted in 1897 on Russia's uniqueness, at least with respect to her political system. In contrast to the old regime monarchies in the West, according to Witte, the Russian monarchy had always stood above all the estates, allying itself with none, acting solely in its own interests, and imposing obligations upon the estates for the benefit of society as a whole. Rejecting demands that the state save the nobility from extinction by granting it special favors, Witte warned of disaster if the autocracy at this late date were to betray its own historical character for the alien model of "European monarchism, with its estate basis." With respect to economic and social development, however, Witte viewed Russia as anything but unique. Feudalism had given way to capitalism in the West, and Russia was destined to follow the same course: "Wealth is now to be found not in land but in finance, industry, manufacturing." And since the nobility was a relic of the feudal system, Witte foresaw the same fate for that group in Russia as it had already experienced in the West. The minister of finance had no regrets, for Russia's economic and social modernization was a "completely natural process," which neither could nor should be halted.[4] In short, there was no problem, and thus no need for corrective action.

The noble question owed its appearance in the early 1880s as one of the major public issues of the day not to those who shared the opinions just cited but to those who found Russia's evolution away from hereditary privilege and toward legal equality both distasteful and alarming. That the noble question should have been raised only in the 1880s, two decades after the reforms that had so diminished the legal distinctions among the estates, demands an explanation. The answer lies in two basic characteristics of old regime Russia: the autocracy's jealously guarded monopoly of political power and the nobility's origins as a service estate, endowed with rights and privileges by the state the better to serve the latter.

When, in the aftermath of Russia's humiliating defeat in the Crimean War, Alexander II resolved upon the necessity for serf emancipation, thereby threatening the nobility's most valued privilege, he did not seek the advice of the first estate and consulted them only afterward as to the details of the process of emancipation and the land settlement. Although "most nobles were opposed to the government's plan at each stage of its spasmodic evolution," and small groups of nobles repeatedly challenged provisional formulations of government policy, such challenges were invariably "rebuffed and rebuked" by the state and withdrawn by their authors.[5] The firmly established pattern of submission to the state in political matters, particularly those in which the state took the initiative, and of reliance on the tsar's favor for rewards and privileges held the overwhelming majority of nobles in its grip. Once serf emancipation and the subsequent reforms had been enacted, effective opposition was even less feasible than before for those who objected to the erosion of the nobility's rights and privileges. They were intent upon preserving the patterns and values of the past, but among these, political subservience to the state occupied a primary place. And as long as Alexander II lived, the thrust of the state's actions was to promote the principle of legal equality over that of legal privilege. It is this conundrum that explains the almost total absence of open dissent from the direction traveled by Russia in the 1860s and 1870s.[6]

There were, of course, a few exceptions, among them the anonymous author of *The Merging of the Estates, or the Nobility, the Other Estates, and the Zemstvo*.[7] Written in response to Aksakov and Koshelev, this tract argued that a strong landed nobility was essential to protect the monarchy and thereby save Russia from the threat of anarchy. Another exception was General R. A. Fadeev, a prominent member of the conservative, anti-Western circle for which the St. Petersburg daily, *Russkii mir*, served as a forum in the 1870s. Fadeev ardently defended the hereditary, privileged nobility, sole bearer in Russia of education, culture, and political consciousness, as "necessary for Russia's future."[8] A further dissenter, somewhat less outspoken, contented himself with writing a brief popular history of the nobility to the end of the eighteenth century, in which he noted with satisfaction that the great reforms had altered neither the basic estate structure of Russian society nor the preeminence of the nobility.[9]

He was, in fact, correct. The forms of privilege, such as the division of the population into estates and the corporate structure of the nobility, had survived the reforms intact. And the vestiges of the nobility's former legal privileges were present in its continued dominance of private land-owning, state service, and the learned professions (see table 9 and chapter 6). The retention of the forms of privilege encouraged reactionaries "to dream of some day forcing back into them the various classes of the nation, of reconstructing the social order on the old lines with some slight modifications."[10] It was necessary only for Alexander III to reverse the state's position and signal his sympathy with defenders of the traditional social order for discussion of the noble question suddenly to burst into the open. That is precisely what happened in the 1880s, when in both the serious monthly journals and the provincial assemblies of nobility wide-ranging discussions of the problem and its possible solutions were launched.

The liberal *Vestnik Evropy* was quick to dub the defenders of the old order "*soslovniki*," from *soslovie* (social estate).[11] Among the most articulate and influential of these was A. D. Pazukhin, an *uezd* marshal of nobility in Simbirsk *guberniia*. A lengthy article by Pazukhin entitled "The Contemporary Condition of Russia and the Estate Question" appeared in the January 1885 issue of Katkov's *Russkii vestnik* and in book form the following year. Katkov went on to arrange for Pazukhin's appointment as director of chancellery under Minister of Internal Affairs Tolstoi, in which post Pazukhin was able to implement parts of the program he had proposed.[12] A host of publicists followed Pazukhin over the next two decades, often borrowing from his arguments. Among the more prolific of this group were A. A. Planson, an *uezd* marshal in Ufa *guberniia* and a landowner in no fewer than five *gubernii*, author of two books and several shorter pieces; and A. I. Elishev, author of numerous articles in the conservative press, many of which were reprinted in his 1898 collection.[13] The state's new attitude also encouraged the provincial assemblies of nobility from the mid-1880s to draft, debate, vote, and forward to the government an endless stream of petitions concerned with various aspects of the noble question but mainly with soliciting state aid for noble landowners.[14]

In contrast to those who viewed with equanimity or approval the advance of legal equality, the *soslovniki* were unanimous in regarding Russia's social estates as indigenous formations qualitatively different from those of the West and therefore not necessarily destined for the same fate as had befallen the latter. Defenders of privilege like Pazukhin and

Elishev viewed estates as natural communities of interest which had developed spontaneously in Russia and which differed from one another not only in their social position and style of life but in their level of moral development and capacity to serve the state. These differences were recognized by the autocracy and by the estates themselves. Thus, differential rewards from the state were accepted as just by all, and the estates lived in harmony with each other and were content with their common subjection to the autocrat. This idealized portrayal of the Russian past was contrasted with the history of estates in the West, where, according to the *soslovniki*, the endless antagonisms and bitter rivalries among the estates and between them and the state had finally destroyed the traditional social order, estates and all.[15] Russia, then, was more fortunate than the West and might avoid the latter's fate.

The nobility was that estate possessed of a superior capacity for state service, developed over many generations through the cultivation of selfless devotion and loyalty to the sovereign and habits of command in dealing with their social inferiors and particularly with the peasants living on their lands. While at least one defender of privilege offered a genetic explanation of the nobility's superiority, citing Darwin in his support,[16] the majority emphasized the common ethnic origin of nobles and commoners as further proof of harmony among the estates, in contrast to the West, where the nobility's descent from alien conquerors created a barrier of distrust between it and the populace.[17] In Russia the nobility was equally indispensable to the state above it and the peasant masses below. The state valued the nobility as a more disinterested and trustworthy body of servants than could be found in any self-seeking professional bureaucracy.[18] The peasants trusted and respected the nobles as their natural protectors against the effects of crop failure and other acts of God, against their own vices of laziness, drunkenness, and quarrelsomeness, and against such human predators as moneylenders, tavernkeepers, and rapacious neighbors (*kulaks*). The peasantry's attitude toward the nobility, so the *soslovniki* argued, naturally extended to those members of the first estate who wielded authority in public office.[19] A further claim upon the gratitude of society was the nobility's role as the bearers of a higher culture and a higher morality in the rude Russian countryside.[20] Thus both the state and the people valued the nobility, the former for its service and support, the latter for its protection and guidance.

Or so matters stood until the great reforms, when liberal bureaucrats, journalists, and *intelligenty* had undermined a healthy social order in the mistaken conviction that Russia must ape the West.[21] With the virtual abolition of legal privilege and estate distinctions in the reign of Alexander II, Russia had started down the slippery slope that led, as the West's recent history proved, to political and social turmoil and moral decadence. The already largely successful attack on juridical inequality would be followed, logically and inevitably, by attacks on the unequal distribution of political power and of wealth. The replacement of landed nobles by bureaucrats in the administration of the state was only the first step in a progression via constitutionalism and democracy to political anarchy. And the peasantry, placed under the authority of bureaucrats who were strangers and whom they could not respect, were sinking into idleness, drunkenness, and crime and losing all regard for paternal or political authority, while in society at large honor, loyalty, and self-sacrifice were being drowned by egoism and materialism.[22]

The remedy for Russia's ills was unmistakably suggested by the very diagnosis of them: the state must repair the damage caused by its own actions while there was still time. The reforms (serf emancipation alone usually escaped denunciation), or at least their harmful impact upon the social order, must be undone and the government's unconscionable neglect of the nobility reversed for the sake not of the nobility alone, but of the state and society. All was not yet lost, for the estates still existed, and the body social continued to reject as foreign the reforms mistakenly introduced.[23] The salvation of the monarchy and of the peasant masses depended on the restoration of the first estate to its former position. But only through the possession of land in sufficient quantity to provide his family with material security could a noble perform his vital double function of servant to the state and leader of the rural community. A land-poor or landless noble was on his way to becoming, if he had not already become, a member of the bureaucracy, the *raznochintsy*, "the commercial-industrial class," the urban intelligentsia. A nobility without land was "an empty phrase," "an abnormal phenomenon," the principal enemy of privilege and of "the real nobility."[24] Pazukhin and a few others believed that the nobility's abandonment of the land could be halted merely by restoring the distinctions among the estates and the nobility's dominant position in the countryside, but the great majority of *soslovniki* argued that more direct forms of state assistance were needed to strengthen noble landownership.

The defenders of privilege were acutely conscious of serving in the front lines in a war to the death between two incompatible social orders, each with its distinguishing values. Like other traditional societies, the old order in Russia was agrarian, patriarchal, and static in the sense of being organized so as to maximize continuity and minimize change. It was a society in which the production of food and other necessities was both treated "as a definitely inferior function, fit only for persons of low if not servile status," and fused with other functions "in nexuses of relations with primarily noneconomic significance, or at best only very partial economic significance."[25] As even Nicholas II, not the most perceptive of men, noted, the landed estate was a microcosm of this society, providing a framework not only for the satisfying of the basic material needs of both the lord's household and the peasants but also for the protection and governance of the latter by the lord of the manor (see the next section, "The Regime's New Course"). Master and productive workers together constituted a family-type community.

Not being completely self-sufficient, however, the rural communities which contained the overwhelming majority of the inhabitants of any traditional society were always to some extent dependent upon merchants who traded in the products of the labor of others. Possibly because of a primitive belief that one's products are part of oneself and that to trade in goods produced by others is consequently a morally censurable activity, surely because the role of merchant necessarily embodied values alien to those of the rural community, traditional societies normally regarded merchants as outsiders who lacked "a natural and proper place in the society" and threatened its values and stability by their very existence. As recently put by a student of economic development:

> In the villages of almost all traditional societies great weight is placed on the duty of mutual self-help and on group solidarity. This sense of mutuality also runs vertically: between the simple folk and the successive layers of the elite there is a sense of reciprocal obligation, of mutual dependence. . . . The trader-financiers do not accept these obligations. They are lone wolves, or, if you choose, the first economic men, looking out for themselves first in a way that is not true of other members of the society and which other members of the society regard as antisocial and immoral.[26]

These outsiders were commonly kept in check by means of what Max Weber described as "the hindrance of the free development of the market" and of "the power of naked property *per se*" through withholding certain goods "from free exchange by monopolization. This monopolization may be effected either legally or conventionally."[27] In prereform Russia the most valuable good, land inhabited by serfs, had been legally monopolized by the hereditary nobility.

The breaking of that monopoly as a consequence of serf emancipation and the transformation of agricultural land into a commodity pure and simple, along with the destruction of the nexus of relationships between landed nobility and peasantry and the substitution of a purely economic relationship (landlord and tenant, employer and hired hand) represented, as the *soslovniki* were keenly aware, a crucial victory for "merchants' values" over those of the traditional community. Indeed, the great reforms were in part both the product of, and an important incentive to the further spread of, egalitarian and individualist values that were inimical to the hierarchical and corporate values of traditional society. By diminishing the significance of ascribed status, the reforms raised that of achieved status. By substituting a purely economic relationship for the former network of ties binding lord and peasant together and by transforming land into a simple commodity, the reforms facilitated the shift of emphasis to productive functions as a means of achieving status. To use Max Weber's terms again, Russia in the last third of the nineteenth century was a society in which the traditional "status order" was being undermined by "the pretensions of purely economic acquisition" and evolving into a society in which "functional interests" rather than status distinctions would be all important.[28]

In Russia, as compared with the West, the traditional value system and its powers of resistance to "merchants' values" were particularly strong.[29] Because of Russia's centralized and autocratic political structure, those groups that did not fit into the rural community were nevertheless subordinated and dominated by the traditional order to an extent unknown in the relatively decentralized and pluralistic societies of the West. Furthermore, the first estate, as guardian of traditional values, regarded the merchantry not only with the usual disdain and unease of an agrarian elite toward those who stood outside the rural community, but also with the contempt of the culturally "enlightened" (via Westernization) toward the bearded and caftaned merchants—living reminders, along with peasants and priests, of pre-Petrine barbarism.

If the traditional society and its values were idealized almost beyond recognition, the new order already making its appearance was excoriated with an energy born of disdain and contempt, fear and hatred. Pazukhin described a society without social estates as consisting of "chance groups of property owners," of individuals grouped according to purely mechanical property qualifications with no regard to the significant differences in "social position, style of life, upbringing, and level of moral understanding" which distinguish estates from one another. A society without estates, he argued, "stands on shifting, unsteady ground"; where social and political distinctions depend upon wealth alone, only money can promise security, and society dedicates itself to the worship of Mammon.[30] Other defenders of the traditional order contrasted its tranquility and patriarchal harmony, presided over by a selfless and loyal nobility, with the continuous strife, egoism, and materialism of a society dominated by merchants, moneylenders, *kulaks*, capitalists, Jews, and foreigners.[31]

The danger was real and present, and the stakes were high. And if the *soslovniki* believed not only in the rightness of their cause but also in its chances for success, this was due in large part to encouragement from the state.

THE REGIME'S NEW COURSE

A LEXANDER III moved quickly to distance himself from the reformist tendencies that had characterized the reign of his murdered father. In a manifesto of April 29, 1881, the new emperor swore to maintain intact the principle of autocracy and summoned all loyal Russians to the defense of traditional values. In 1883 he urged the representatives of the peasantry assembled in Moscow for his coronation: "Follow the advice and leadership of your marshals [of nobility]." And on the day of his coronation Alexander pointedly assured the first estate of his faith in them as "the bulwark of the throne" and of his great appreciation for "the useful and unselfish participation of nobles in local affairs."[32]

That this emphasis on traditional values, the nobility as the bulwark of autocracy, and nobles as the leaders of rural Russia was not a mere rhetorical flourish was demonstrated by Alexander's immediate dismissal of the officials identified with the reforms of the previous reign. In their place Alexander relied on men who shared his views in regard to traditional values and the role of the nobility—men like M. N. Katkov, Count D. A. Tolstoi, and Prince V. P. Meshcherskii. Katkov frequently used his daily paper, *Moskovskie vedomosti*, to advocate the maintenance in Russia of the system of social estates that had been weakened but not destroyed by the great reforms. Tolstoi, upon his appointment in 1882 as minister of internal affairs, assured the emperor that those reforms had been a drastic error. Not the least of their faults was that they threatened Russia's social tranquility by lowering the legal barriers among the several estates. Meshcherskii, one of Alexander III's few close friends, warned the emperor in a letter of June 11, 1884, that the diminution of distinctions among the estates in the previous reign was a step toward the abolition of the autocracy itself. Unlike his father, Alexander insisted on a uniform outlook among his advisers and ministers. His first minister of finance, N. Kh. Bunge, who was dismissed as too liberal in 1887, regarded the nobility as "a dying estate," according to Meshcherskii.[33] This was heresy in the eyes of Alexander and his closest advisers.

Alexander's son and successor was no less wholehearted a champion of traditional values and the estate model of society. On the day preceding his coronation in May 1896, Nicholas II admonished the representatives of the peasantry assembled in Moscow for the occasion to heed their marshals of nobility: "Remember the words spoken here by [my father] to the *volost* elders at the time of his accession to the throne. Among you are many who heard them in person. I want these words always to serve you as a firm guide."[34] Nicholas repeated the same advice in 1902 to a group of *volost* elders and village headmen in the Ukraine, only recently the scene of a serious peasant revolt, and then proceeded to confide to them the following vision: "I conceive of Russia as a landed estate of which the proprietor is the tsar, the administrator is the nobility, the steward is the *zemstvo*, and the workers are the peasantry."[35] Nicholas could have chosen no more vivid metaphor for Russia's traditional social order—nor a less relevant one for a society entering the twentieth century with a decade of rapid industrialization behind it.

The regime's new emphasis on the old order in the 1880s took concrete form in a series of actions reaffirming its intention of remedying the problems singled out by the *soslovniki*. Commissions were created to investigate ways of raising juridical barriers to the sale of noble lands and curtailing the ennoblement of commoners, although practical remedies in these two areas were not forthcoming until the following reign (see chapters 4 and 5). The State Noble Land Bank was founded in 1885, and restrictive admissions policies favoring the first estate in secondary and higher education were adopted (see chapters 4 and 6). In the same spirit the regime undertook to bolster the landed nobility's role in local administration by establishing the office of *zemskii nachalnik* (land captain) and reforming the *zemstvo* institutions (see chapter 7).

Alexander III's efforts to preserve and strengthen the role of privilege failed in any significant measure to affect the course of economic and social development upon which Russia had embarked with the great reforms. In fact, the state's policy of sponsoring industrialization did far more to promote Russia's transformation than the measures to bolster the position of the nobility did to impede change. Far from being solved, the noble question became the focus of renewed attention soon after Nicholas II succeeded his father in 1894.

One area in which this revival of interest was manifest was the press. The number of major editorials on the noble question in the reactionary *Moskovskie vedomosti* rose from one or two per year in the early part of the decade to sixteen in 1896 and forty-two the following year. That paper, of which Nicholas was a regular reader, and Meshcherskii's *Grazhdanin* conducted a running debate over the noble question with the liberal *Sankt-Peterburgskie vedomosti* during the late winter and early spring of 1897.[36]

Simultaneously a new campaign for government action in support of the traditional social order was launched in the noble assemblies. For the first time there was coordination and leadership at the national level by the *guberniia* marshals of nobility, who from 1896 on met together one or more times each year (see chapter 7, section entitled "Marshals of Nobility"). With some qualms about this initiative from below (although in this case "below" was no further down than Russia's first estate), and over the strenuous objections of Minister of Finance Witte, the government and the emperor yielded to the urgent request of many of the noble assemblies and their marshals for a commission to study the noble question and propose appropriate answers. On April 13, 1897, Nicholas published his rescript to I. N. Durnovo, chairman of the Committee of Ministers, appointing him to preside over a special conference to investigate possible means of assisting the nobility to continue playing its traditional role in society and the state, for, in the language of the rescript, "it is necessary for the good of Russia that the noble estate retain the place hitherto occupied by it."[37]

Apart from Durnovo, the conference consisted initially of eleven high-level bureaucrats, to whom three more were later added.[38] Three *guberniia* marshals of nobility joined the conference in March 1898, and the following February six more were named to one or both of the conference's newly created subcommittees.[39] At its first sessions the conference decided to concentrate its attention on that part of the hereditary nobility which remained in possession of land, for the members deemed landownership essential to the performance of the nobility's historical functions. Indeed, the body was at first styled the Special Conference on the Affairs of the Landed Nobility, although its name was soon changed to the Special Conference on the Affairs of the Noble Estate.[40]

Witte remained wholly opposed to the very concept of a conference on the noble question. He criticized the emperor's rescript for launching the government on "a false path," for repeating the mistakes of the 1880s by raising "once again promises and hopes which will remain unfulfilled because they are inexhaustible, and which consequently will be followed by disillusionment." Despite Meshcherskii's warning that any attempt to block the conference's efforts would only destroy his own career, Witte argued at the opening session on May 10, 1897, that the needs of noble landowners could not be treated in isolation from those of landowners in general and of peasants in particular. Even after the adoption of the agenda on May 25 he continued his efforts to have the conference treat the noble question together with the peasant question. Witte engaged in an acrimonious correspondence with Durnovo in early June in which he accused the chairman of misrepresenting the conference's views in the official journal prepared for the emperor and of other, similar high-handed actions. On June 20 the finance minister sent the emperor a memorandum arguing that the agenda adopted by the special conference ran counter to established government policies. And at the conference's first working session on November 29, Witte insisted that the group could only harm the nobility if it persisted in trying to achieve the impossible—a halt to Russia's evolution from an agrarian into an industrial society.[41]

Witte's efforts were to no avail, for the defenders of the traditional social order had Nicholas's support. Far from agreeing that their cause was a quixotic one, they had persuaded themselves that victory was within their grasp. In hailing the emperor's April 13 rescript, *Moskovskie vedomosti* triumphantly proclaimed: "The question whether Russia is to be a distinctive state, composed of estates, or is to surrender to the disastrous and dismal fate of western Europe, which lacks estates, has definitively been decided in the spirit of our precious historical legacy."[42] Such rejoicing was premature. The conference had before it a tall pile of petitions received by the Ministry of Internal Affairs from various *guberniia* assemblies of nobility over the preceding dozen years, the proposals of the 1896 conference of *guberniia* marshals, and the memoranda submitted by its own members. Many additional documents would be gathered and generated in the course of the conference's work.[43] It would be four and a half years before the group completed its assignment and six months more until the last of its proposals had been dealt with by the State Council. Only then would it be possible to decide which had been warranted: Witte's pessimism or the optimism of *Moskovskie vedomosti*.

EXERCISES IN FUTILITY: ATTEMPTS TO STABILIZE NOBLE LANDOWNERSHIP

ENTAIL

THE importance that the defenders of privilege attributed to landownership as an essential characteristic of noble status cannot be too strongly emphasized. Possession of, and residence on, a rural estate was identified with a traditional and morally superior way of life which was contrasted to the despised and feared manners and morals of the marketplace. As expressed in an 1898 encomium by the publicist N. P. Semenov, the life "of a landowner elevates the soul of man, develops in him noble [*blagorodnye*] feelings, strengthens his morals, binds him to his family and to his home district [*mesto*], while the life of a capitalist produces precisely the opposite effects.[1]

More concretely, land provided the financial security that enabled nobles to serve the state in a selfless fashion quite beyond the capability of *chinovniki* who were wholly dependent upon their salaries. In the view of some defenders of privilege, in fact, noble landowning and service were so closely identified that support for government measures favoring the former was predicated upon the reinstitution of some form of compulsory state service. A. I. Elishev, for one, was apprehensive lest, without "the restoration to the nobility of its former obligatory service role," a revived "wealthy and influential class of landed aristocracy, in no way bound to the state and enjoying rights without responsibilities" turn out to be "an artificial imitation of the west European aristocracy" and a center of political opposition which the state would find it difficult to destroy.[2]

Other *soslovniki*, however, regarded landowning as having replaced service as "the distinguishing characteristic of noble status."[3] The image of themselves as gentlemen landowners was in part the result of a marked tendency, both spontaneous and fostered by the state, among Russian nobles since the eighteenth century to imitate the style of life and juridical status—but not the political autonomy—of Western nobilities. For all their insistence upon the uniqueness of the relationships among social groups in Russia, the great majority of the defenders of privilege were captives of an imported concept of noble status. In the West, certainly, the "essential meaning" of nobility was derived from the fact that "for a thousand years the rationale for the privileged status of the nobility had rested upon the nobleman's leadership over, responsibility for, and protection of the peasants who lived in his seigniory."[4] In Russia, by contrast, the rationale for the privileged status of the nobility, including their monopoly of agricultural land and peasant labor until 1861, was their role as the first servants of the autocracy. By the late nineteenth century, however, the first estate had lost much of its service significance, and the coincidence between landowning nobles and serving nobles had been greatly reduced (see chapter 6). But the nobility retained enough of its land to hold onto its dominant position among rural landowners, as well as corporate institutions in which possession of land had always been a prerequisite for the full exercise of the rights of membership. By their own peculiar route, Russian landed nobles had arrived at a situation in some respects analogous to that of the nobility in the West.

If landowning had become the essential attribute of noble status in the minds of the *soslovniki*, then the central problem was to ensure that the not inconsiderable area of land still in the possession of the first estate remained there. Projections based on current rates of decrease in noble landownership indicated its total disappearance in Russia by 1920, 1950, or 1966, depending on whose calculations were used.[5] The most direct means of averting this calamity was to restore in some form the restricted market in land that had existed before 1861. The transformation of land into a commodity speculated in by merchants and *kulaks* was repeatedly denounced by the defenders of privilege in favor of the traditional view of "land as a means of securing the way of life" of both the nobility and the peasantry.[6]

In order to prevent the development of a landless rural proletariat, the state legislated in 1893 that peasant allotment land could not be mortgaged, nor could an allotment on which the redemption payments had been completed be sold except to another member of the same peasant commune or to someone willing to become a member.[7] The publicists Semenov and Elishev both cited the 1893 law as a precedent in arguing for a similar ban on the transfer of noble land to nonnobles. Such a ban had already been proposed, on Pazukhin's initiative, by the noble assembly of Simbirsk *guberniia* in 1889 and discussed in other assemblies in the same year.[8] A petition to the same effect from the Tula assembly was considered by the special commission chaired by N. S.

Abaza which during 1891–1895 studied various ways of strengthening noble landownership.

Although appealing by virtue of its simplicity and directness, the idea of a ban on the transfer of noble land to commoners raised several major difficulties, which caused it to be rejected both by the Abaza commission and in 1898 by the Special Conference on the Affairs of the Noble Estate. By restricting the circle of potential buyers of noble land to a limited number of wealthy members of the first estate, the measure would diminish the market value of such land and consequently the creditworthiness of its owners. Worse yet, it would promote the further concentration of noble land in the hands of a wealthy few and do nothing to halt the decline in the numbers of landed nobles.[9] If the landed nobility was to be preserved as a social force, the numbers of proprietors as well as of *desiatiny* had to be maintained, and if possible augmented.

In keeping with the assumption of most defenders of the old order that nobles who sold their estates were driven to do so by financial necessity, some traditionalists proposed to stem the decline of the landed nobility by blocking the sale of insolvent estates. In 1896 and 1897 several noble societies suggested that special agencies of either the central government or the societies themselves take over bankrupt noble properties, restore them to solvency, and return them to their owners. The most thoroughly thought-out proposal came from the Kherson assembly of marshals and deputies, which suggested a specially elected *guberniia* noble wardship council with power to assume control of any noble estate threatened with forced sale for debt. If successful in restoring a property to solvency within ten years, the council would return the estate to its owner as an entail, thereby protecting it against burdensome debt in future. If unsuccessful, the council would auction the property, giving preference to bidders of noble status and Orthodox faith.[10]

The January 1898 conference of *guberniia* marshals was less than enthusiastic over the Kherson proposal. Its members observed that it would be impossible to find enough able people to manage all the estates in question and that the wardship council's unconditional right to take over an estate in default would be too great an infringement upon the property rights of landowners who might prefer to see their estates sold in order to raise needed capital. Although the Kherson proposal was approved by the next marshals' conference in January 1899, it was rejected as unrealistic a few months later by the special conference on the nobility.[11]

Entail has been mentioned as part of the plan drafted by the Kherson noble society, and this was the juridical solution to the problem of the decline of noble landowning that found most favor among the defenders of privilege. Entail—the establishment of a predetermined, unalterable succession of heirs to a landed estate, thereby depriving them during the term of the entail of the power to alienate the property—had long been practiced in various forms by the nobilities of the West and nowhere more than in England, where it was still favored in the third quarter of the nineteenth century by both the nobility and the gentry. Approximately half of all the land in England was entailed in that period, and entail was the norm for estates of over 1,000 acres and not unusual for estates of 500–1,000 acres.[12] On the Continent entail was a declining institution in the late nineteenth century. In France it had been abolished after the 1848 revolution, and where it persisted (e.g., Denmark, Austria and Hungary, and most of the German states, including Prussia) it usually encompassed 10 percent or less of the land and was confined to very large properties.[13]

Entail was a long-established practice among the German and Polish nobles of Russia's western borderlands. In the Baltic *gubernii* in 1909 there were 266 entails (*Fideikommisse*) comprising 921,100 *desiatiny*—18 percent of all noble holdings in the region and 27 percent of all noble land.[14] Elsewhere in European Russia entail was unknown before the reign of Catherine II. In an effort to ensure that nobles engaged in socially useful activity and did not live idly off the income from their lands, Peter I had decreed in 1714 that a noble's real property must pass intact upon his death to one son of his choice; lacking a son, to a daughter; lacking children, to a collateral relative. What the law of 1714 introduced was single inheritance (*edinonasledie*), or the indivisibility of noble estates, rather than entail, for the owner remained free to dispose of his property as he pleased during his lifetime. Because the new law ran counter to the traditional Russian practice of sons' sharing equally in the inheritance of patrimonial property, it was more honored in the breach than in the observance and was repealed after only sixteen years.[15]

Between 1774 and 1830 the first *maioraty* (from the French *majorat*), entails whose inheritance was governed by primogeniture, were created by the sovereign in response to individual petitions from a few wealthy noblemen. The rising popularity of this institution (fourteen new *maioraty* were created between 1831 and 1845) led to the enactment in 1845 of general regulations concerning its operation.[16] *Maioraty* were inherited by right of seniority, with males taking precedence over females, and, like entails in Scotland, they were perpetual, being terminated only when there were no longer lineal descendants of the person who first inherited the property from the *maiorat's* founder. A *maiorat* could under no conditions be given away or sold, even to pay back taxes or the debts of a bankrupt life tenant. Nor could it be mortgaged except within narrow limits to repair damage to the property from war or an act of God or to provide cash settlements for the heir's siblings. The *maiorat* was designed to protect the wealthiest noble families against the possibility of ruin by profligate heirs. In order to qualify for the emperor's permission to create a *maiorat*, a noble had to (1) set aside property amounting to a minimum of 10,000 *desiatiny* of usable land or land yielding at least 12,000 rubles in annual income, without thereby infringing on the legal shares of his younger children in the patrimonial estate; (2) pay off or transfer to another property any mortgage on the land to be entailed; and (3) deposit in a state credit institution a contingency fund equal to three years' net income from the *maiorat*. In view of the declining number of properties of this size, the special conference on the nobility in 1898 recommended lowering the minimum size of *maioraty*. Despite the State Council's advice that the old minimum be retained on the grounds that the *maiorat* was designed to assist only large landowners, Nicholas II in 1899 decreed a reduction of the minimum to 5,000 *desiatiny* or an income of 6,000 rubles.[17] Only 784 noble landowners (0.7 percent of the total) owned over 10,000 *desiatiny* each in 1877; in 1905, after the halving of the minimum size, 1,319 noble landholdings (1.2 percent of the total) could qualify. The number of nobles who could meet the other requirements was even smaller. In fact, between 1845 and 1905 only sixty *maioraty* were established. By 1914 in the thirty-eight *gubernii* of European Russia without the Baltic and western regions, *maioraty* encompassed over 3.5 million *desiatiny*—25–30 percent of the area in holdings large enough to qualify, but only 10–15 percent of total noble acreage in those *gubernii*.[18]

Beginning in the 1870s entail was discussed as a solution to a much broader problem than the protection of a few dozen wealthy families against possible financial ruin. If applied to noble estates of intermediate size, entail promised to stabilize the numbers of landed nobles and the acreage in their possession, thereby halting the tendency of this social element to disappear from the Russian scene. In the 1870s and early 1880s there were several proposals to use the *maiorat* to protect estates much smaller than those covered by the law of 1845.[19] Entail became a major public issue, however, only in 1887. In May of that year N. E. Baratynskii, a retired landowner of Kazan *guberniia*, a former *zemstvo* member, and a member of a commission appointed by the Kazan noble assembly to study ways of stemming the decline of noble landowning, published a lengthy brochure favoring entail as the most promising solution to the problem. This was the first of five publications Baratynskii was to devote to the subject over as many years. Independently of the work of the Kazan commission, Prince A. V. Meshcherskii, *guberniia* marshal in Poltava, presented to his assembly of nobility in July 1887 a petition calling for the widespread use of entail for noble properties of intermediate size.[20]

More than a dozen other *guberniia* assemblies adopted similar petitions between 1887 and 1893, the majority of them modeled on that of the Poltava society.[21] More petitions from noble assemblies were devoted to entail than to any other aspect of the noble question apart from credit.

The subject was widely discussed in the press and the polemical literature, and entail for intermediate noble estates was recommended by the Abaza commission in 1895, the nationwide conference of *guberniia* marshals in 1896, the special conference on the nobility in 1898, and the State Council the following year.[22] Entail had all the appeal of a counterattack that would turn the tables on upstart capitalists by removing noble land from the marketplace, and all the glamour of an institution associated with the nobilities of the West, upon whom Russia's first estate had modeled itself for over a century. Lest it seem to be an anachronism, however, entail was frequently compared by the defenders of privilege to the quarter sections (160 acres) of public land sold to farmers and protected (so they wrongly believed) against alienation, subdivision, and forced sale for debt under the Homestead Act of 1862 in the United States, a country not known for its tolerance of anachronisms.[23]

Entail was promoted as an efficacious means of realizing the interest of state and society in ensuring that at least one member of every landed noble family in each generation retain an estate large enough to enable him to fill the traditional roles of local administrator and leader and guardian of the rural community. Owners of intermediate estates were the focus of concern because, as a group, they evidenced the lowest rate of absentee ownership, in contrast to both petty proprietors and landed magnates, and therefore played the most active role in local affairs.[24] If *raison d'état* and the nobility's own interests required the entailment of intermediate noble estates, then logic demanded that entail be made compulsory, as *Vestnik Evropy* pointed out in 1892. Indeed, Baratynskii called for compulsory entail on the grounds that voluntary entail would not achieve the desired results. The noble assembly of at least one *guberniia*, Simbirsk in 1890, took the same position. To sweeten the pill of compulsory entail, Baratynskii proposed that certain local administrative positions be reserved exclusively or preferentially for life tenants of entails and that the children of nobles who held estates no larger than the legal minimum for compulsory entailment and were still repaying debts incurred before the act of entail receive their education at state expense.[25]

The great majority of defenders of privilege and those noble societies that followed the lead of Poltava were unwilling to support so severe an abridgment of the nobility's property rights and favored instead voluntary entail, frequently suggesting such incentives as tax and educational advantages for tenants of entails, preferment in appointment to local and central government posts, and ex officio membership in the *uezd zemstvo* assemblies.[26] Bowing to the reality of the deeply rooted tradition of equal inheritance and fearing that compulsory entail, like Peter the Great's law on the indivisibility of noble estates, would be sabotaged by the nobility itself, the Abaza commission proposed that nobles be per mitted but not obligated to entail their estates, either during their lifetimes or in their wills; no incentives were offered. Compulsory entail was not seriously considered by either the special conference on the nobility or the State Council, but they did exempt entails from the inheritance tax by way of incentive.

A concrete definition of intermediate estates proved to be far from easy. Logic dictated a minimum size capable of supporting a noble family comfortably, but ideas on how large an annual income was required by a family of four, in addition to the housing and board provided by the estate, ranged from 1,500 to 3,500 rubles, which in turn presumed a property worth from 30,000 to 70,000 rubles. The lower figure, which was double the property qualification for a personal vote in the noble and *zemstvo* elections and implied a minimum size of 250–950 *desiatiny*, depending on the *uezd*, was in fact recommended by the Abaza commission.[27] Regarding such a minimum as unduly restricting eligibility for entail, the special conference halved it to 125–475 *desiatiny* and a value of 15,000 rubles, rationalizing that even 600 rubles a year would suffice for a modest existence in the country, especially if the head of the family received a supplementary income from a post in the local administration. The special conference also set a maximum size of twenty times the minimum, which the State Council raised to a flat 10,000 *desiatiny* while accepting the conference's recommended minimum. In 1905 some 27,000 noble estates (25 percent of the total) in the fifty *gubernii* of European Russia fell within these limits.[28] Unlike the *maioraty* formed under the 1845 law, entails of the new type were required to be economic entities, each containing an *usadba* (a residence complete with outbuildings, gardens, etc.).

Although a few proposals were for perpetual entails, like the *maioraty*, the great majority included an arrangement under which the entail could be terminated in the will of the second tenant, for example, the founder's grandson.[29] This was the form adopted by the Abaza commission; hence the designation temporary (*vremenno-*) or term (*srochno-*) entail for the new type, as opposed to the *maioraty*, which were called hereditary (*nasledstvennye*) entails or simply entailed estates (*zapovednye imeniia*). The special conference on the nobility gave each tenant after the first the option of terminating the entail in his will, but only if he was a direct descendant of the previous tenant and had direct descendants of his own to whom to leave the property. Automatic termination would occur if (1) the last tenant failed to name an heir and there were no more direct descendants either of the entail's first tenant or of the founder, unless the original act of entail covered such an eventuality, or (2) neither the legal heir nor any of his direct descendants belonged to the hereditary nobility. If valuable mineral deposits were discovered on the property, however, the entail could be terminated at any time with the permission of the *guberniia* assembly of marshals and deputies and the first department of the Senate. These provisions were all endorsed without change by the State Council.

The order of succession proposed by Meshcherskii in 1887 was essentially the one adopted by the special conference and the State Council.[30] The founder of the entail and all succeeding tenants were each to choose a single heir, giving priority to direct male descendants, then direct female descendants, and lastly, unless forbidden by the original act of entail, to collateral relatives descended from the founder. When no heir was available from any of these three groups, the entail could be left to a collateral relative not descended from the founder.

At the very heart of the concept of entail is the notion of legally constraining the life tenant from doing anything that might damage the interest of future generations of the family in the estate, such as encumbering it with debt. A thorny problem, therefore, was whether to permit the entailment of properties already burdened with mortgages—as 42 percent of all noble acreage was by 1896. The 1887 Poltava proposal assumed the ineligibility of mortgaged estates, but the assemblies of several other *gubernii* specifically extended eligibility to such properties in order to secure the support for entail of otherwise dubious members. Baratynskii recognized the necessity of including mortgaged estates, as did Planson, who proposed a ceiling of 50 percent of the property's value.[31] The Abaza commission recommended requiring the consent of all holders of mortgages or promissory notes for entail but no limit on previous indebtedness. In the special conference a ceiling of 60 percent of the estate's value was adopted in addition to requiring the creditors' consent. The State Council recommended much more restrictive conditions. To be eligible for entailment, an estate could be mortgaged only to the Noble Land Bank or its Special Department, the unpaid balance was not to exceed 60 percent of the estate's value, the owner had to have a minimum of 15,000 rubles in equity in the property, and the estate had to be free of any mortgage or tax arrears.

A less difficult problem was that of debts incurred after the entailment of an estate. The consensus among proponents of term entails was that such properties, like *maioraty*, should serve as security for loans only in narrowly delimited circumstances. Combining the suggestions of the Abaza commission and the special conference, the State Council confined the permissible reasons for incurring new debt to the provision of settlements for the tenant's siblings or children other than his heir and to unavoidable capital improvements and repairs necessitated by war or an act of God. Debts incurred to pay for improvements and repairs were not to exceed two years' net income from the estate or 8 percent of its value; in such cases total indebtedness, both old and new, was not to exceed 33 percent of the property's value. Entailed estates were to be mortgaged only to the State Noble Land Bank. According to the recommendations of the special conference and the State Council, term entails could be foreclosed and sold at public auction for default only on debts incurred before entailment, not on subsequent mortgages and not for tax arrears.

On May 25, 1899, the emperor approved the State Council's draft, and term entail became an option for hereditary nobles owning estates of intermediate size. The new law had aroused almost no opposition in its passage through the special conference and State Council. Its opponents, including Witte, regarded it as harmless, since they were convinced that no more than a few hundred landowners were likely to create term entails. Even many supporters of entail, such as Durnovo and V. K. von Pleve, secretary to the State Council, were no more optimistic about its appeal to the great majority of noble proprietors. At the beginning of 1896, when it first reviewed the Abaza commission's recommendations, the joint session of the departments of the State Council noted that the proposed legislation did nothing for petty proprietors and was dubious whether it would really be of much help to intermediate landowners. In fact all of these predictions were borne out: without legal compulsion few nobles chose to entail their estates. In 1899 and 1900 only thirteen landowners did so, and over the next eleven years only twenty-two more followed their example.[32]

FRAGMENTATION AND REDEMPTION OF PATRIMONIAL ESTATES

ENTAIL was promoted as a barrier to both the alienation and fragmentation of the nobility's landholdings. A less drastic remedy, focusing on fragmentation alone, was suggested repeatedly in the 1880s and 1890s as an alternative or supplement to entail: the setting of some minimum size, anywhere from 200 to 800 *desiatiny*, below which nobles would not be permitted to divide their properties.[33]

The proposed ban on the fragmentation of noble estates ran counter to the existing laws governing inheritance. Russian civil law distinguished between a patrimonial estate (*rodovoe imenie*), inherited by right of kinship, and acquired property (*blagopriobretennoe imushchestvo*), which included land purchased or received as a gift or grant as well as all personal property and liquid assets. Acquired land that was bequeathed to a kinsman with a legal claim to a share in the estate thereupon became patrimonial property, but patrimonial property purchased from a kinsman retained its classification. Kinsmen were defined as members of a single *rod*, which consisted of all the descendants of a common ancestor, regardless of their surnames. Acquired property could be disposed of by testament as the owner pleased, with only minor restrictions, and given away or sold by him during his lifetime. The inheritance of a patrimonial estate, however, was governed by laws which left nothing to the discretion of the owner but provided minor shares for his widow and daughters and divided the bulk of the property equally among his sons. During his lifetime the owner of a patrimonial estate could sell it, but not give it, to a stranger.[34]

Rather than ban the division of estates below a certain size, the Abaza commission chose a positive approach. It proposed that any owner, regardless of social estate, of a patrimonial property that was a working farm complete with *usadba* and did not exceed in size ten times the property qualification for a direct vote in *zemstvo* elections be permitted to bequeath it intact to one of his sons; lacking sons, to one of his daughters; and lacking children, to one of his collateral relatives. Persons other than the designated heir who were entitled by right of kinship to a share in a patrimonial estate bequeathed in this manner would be compensated with cash settlements, but their legal shares might be reduced by as much as 50 percent. The Abaza commission's plan met with little interest in the Special Conference on the Affairs of the Noble Estate; only Princes Obolenskii and Liven, who led the fight against entail, were enthusiastic.[35]

Over the next decade the staunchest advocate of a change in the inheritance laws governing patrimonial estates was Prince P. N. Trubetskoi, Moscow *guberniia* marshal of nobility and one of the few who had opposed entail at the 1896 marshals' conference. Arguing that not all families are alike and that a family's interests can better be judged by its head than by any legislators, Trubetskoi proposed that the owner, regardless of social estate, of a patrimonial property of any size be given the right to bequeath it among his direct descendants, or in the absence of such, among his collateral relations, either to a single heir or in shares which he himself would be free to determine and allocate. Endorsed by the conference of *guberniia* marshals in February 1901 and supported in principle by the special conference at its last session in November of that year, Trubetskoi's plan was referred to the Ministry of Justice and a commission which was revising the civil code. In 1912 Trubetskoi's proposal on patrimonial estates was finally enacted into law—too late to have any effect on the continuing fragmentation of noble properties.[36]

There was a further legal peculiarity of patrimonial estates. When such a property was sold outside the *rod* (unless to satisfy creditors), the kinsmen of the seller, but not his direct descendants during his lifetime, had the right to redeem the estate within three years from its new owner, repaying him the purchase price and reimbursing him for the transfer tax and any money spent on maintenance or capital improvements. The one case in which the right of redemption did not apply was the sale of uninhabited land by a member of one social estate to a member of an-

other. This exception dated from the period of serfdom and had originally been intended to facilitate the purchase of limited quantities of
noble land by commoners. As the emancipated serfs received their land
allotments (and all had done so by the end of the 1880s), all noble land
came to be classified as uninhabited and therefore not subject to redemption when purchased by a commoner.[37]

In the late 1880s and 1890s several noble societies petitioned for the
extension of the right of redemption to noble patrimonial estates sold to
commoners, while the Abaza commission favored a more general measure covering all sales of patrimonial properties across social estate
lines.[38] A large majority of the special conference on the nobility voted
to apply the right of redemption only to "patrimonial landed property
sold by hereditary nobles to members of other social estates." They rea-
soned that since the great majority of sales of patrimonial estates by
members of one social estate to members of another involved noble land,
the existing law was de facto discriminatory against nobles. The supporters of the measure admitted that they did not expect the right of
redemption ever to be widely used. Despite this disclaimer, a minority of
the conference saw the proposal on redemption as counterproductive, for
commoners would be wary of buying property they might be called
upon to return. A slackening of demand and lower prices for noble land
was one possible result. Ruses such as sales contracts with fictitious
prices were another. The State Council agreed with the minority and
killed the proposal.[39]

The right of kinsmen to redeem patrimonial estates sold to commoners
was never a very convincing means of halting the decline of the landed
nobility. And the inheritance laws were changed too late to halt or slow
down the continuing fragmentation of noble estates. The principal objective, and the only one to be achieved, in the campaign to preserve
noble landownership by juridical means was the institution of term
entail, but the practical results were ludicrously out of proportion to the
hopes pinned on this nostrum. Juridical remedies, however, were by no
means the only ones prescribed by the *soslovniki*. Various forms of material assistance to noble landowners held even greater appeal.

LONG-TERM CREDIT

ALONG with entail, credit was the means of stabilizing noble
landownership that attracted most attention in the *guberniia*
societies of nobility and from those who wielded the pen in defense of privilege. True, some of the latter distrusted credit as a snare
used by capitalists, worshipers of Mammon, to ruin honest upholders of
traditional values—landowners and peasants alike. As the anonymous
author of "The Indebtedness of Private Landowning" put it in 1880:

It would not be an exaggeration to say that our landowners . . . have sold themselves into bondage, which, although its form is more refined, has proved to be incomparably more cruel than was serfdom, in most cases, for the peasants. Credit is a dreadful instrument; its use, like that of opium, should be permitted only in exceptional cases.[40]

Similar sentiments were expressed over the next two decades by other *soslovniki*, some of whom wanted to prohibit mortgages altogether. Eleven of the thirteen members of the Abaza commission believed that a major virtue of entail was its denial to noble landowners of access to mortgage credit.[41]

Most defenders of privilege, however, demanded more and easier credit for noble landowners. What they had in mind was not credit of the sort employed by businessmen—money to be used in making more money and to be repaid out of profits—but rather loans made in furtherance of the state's interest in supporting the traditional social order. Because the state would not press too hard for repayment, such loans might better be described as grants-in-aid. Having become accustomed during the reign of Nicholas I to the state's use of mortgage loans in precisely this fashion, many nobles resented the withdrawal of such assistance in the late 1850s and desired its renewal. And the *soslovniki* frequently added the argument that the state owed such assistance to the landed nobility in partial compensation for the severe losses caused by serf emancipation and the subsequent reforms.[42]

It was these considerations, rather than any shortage of loan funds available through private banks, that explain the rising demand among the first estate in the late 1870s and early 1880s for government mortgage loans. In response to a steady stream of petitions from both noble and *zemstvo* assemblies, Alexander III in June 1885 established the State Noble Land Bank.[43] In the emperor's words, the bank was intended "to ensure that in future they [the nobles] have the means to execute with honor their very high calling." Alexander hoped that with the bank's help "more nobles may be persuaded to reside permanently on their estates, and there to exert their efforts mainly in the activities expected of them by virtue of their position," namely, by assuming "the leading roles in the command of the army, in local administrative and judicial affairs, in unselfishly caring for the people's needs, in disseminating by their example the principles of faith, loyalty, and wholesome dedication."[44]

The terms under which the bank operated left no doubt as to its purpose.[45] Loans were granted to hereditary nobles on the security of rural land already in their possession. The bank did not finance the purchase of land except, from 1894, for purchases by Great Russian from non-Russian (i.e., Polish) nobles in the nine western *gubernii*. Polish noble landowners in the western *gubernii* were not eligible for loans,[46] and the bank's sphere of activity was limited to the forty-seven *gubernii* of European Russia without the Baltic region, plus the North Caucasus and Transcaucasus. In contrast to the Peasant Land Bank founded two years earlier, whose loans carried the commercial interest rate of 7.5–8.5 percent until 1895, the Noble Land Bank at first charged only 5 percent on its mortgages and lowered its rate to 4.5 percent in 1889 and to 4 percent in 1894. The capitalization of the Noble Bank was also considerably larger than that of the Peasant Bank: by the mid-1890s the outstanding loan balance of the former was approximately six times as large as that of the latter.[47] In 1890, when the Noble Land Bank took over all the outstanding loans of the Society for Mutual Land Credit, contracted at rates of over 7 percent, the mortgagors were permitted to refinance them at the bank's much lower rate of interest. The bank would normally loan up to 60 percent of the value of an estate; in certain cases, if the loan was to repay debts incurred before the bank's establishment, the maximum might be raised to 75 percent. A higher special assessment of the property could also be requested, and more often than not was; as of November 1896, 65 percent of all properties mortgaged to the Noble Land Bank had been subject to special assessment.[48] Although the bank was empowered to loan money for terms of from eleven to sixty-seven years, in fact between 1902 and 1905, 97 percent of all mortgages by number, and 97–99 percent by value, were of sixty-one to sixty-seven years' duration.[49] After it had run for five years a mortgage could be refinanced—its term extended or the amount of the loan increased up to 60 percent of the current value of the property. If a mortgaged estate was acquired by a personal noble or by a commoner, the new owner was required to liquidate the debt to the bank within five years.

The treatment of delinquent borrowers was a delicate problem, for the Noble Land Bank's purpose was to keep the mortgaged land in the hands of its present owners. Mortgagors who fell into arrears on their semiannual payments were subject to a penalty of 0.5 percent per month for the first three months and 1 percent per month thereafter. After six months the bank could take possession of the property and, if the arrears were not paid up in another three months, sell it at public auction. Or a borrower in default might have his estate taken over by the elective noble wardship committee of his *uezd* for up to six years, or by the bank itself for up to two years, in order to pay off the arrears. While a property was in receivership, the arrears on its debt were subject to a penalty of 6 percent per annum. In case of natural disaster, fire, or the death of the owner of a mortgaged estate, two semiannual payments were permitted to be delayed for up to three years, subject to the same penalty, without making the property liable to foreclosure. In fact, as Witte pointed out to the Special Conference on the Affairs of the Noble Estate, foreclosure became a real threat to a delinquent borrower only when he fell behind by three or more payments. The majority of the Noble Land Bank's mortgagors took advantage of this leniency to fall moderately behind (see table 17). The likelihood of forced sale was even less than the figures might suggest; between 1891 and 1896 the bank sold at auction an average of forty-one estates each year—only three per thousand of all properties mortgaged to it.[50]

Despite the terms of its charter and the manner in which it operated, the Noble Land Bank from the beginning was criticized for not being sufficiently different from an ordinary commercial bank. Both Meshcherskii's daily memoranda for Alexander III and the heir apparent and Katkov's editorials in *Moskovskie vedomosti* attacked the bank's charter on precisely these grounds as soon as it was made public; more than a decade later the publicist Semenov condemned the bank for offering "stock-exchange bank credit" and taking a "commercial attitude toward land."[51] Even more outspoken was P. A. Krivskii, marshal of nobility of Saratov *guberniia*, who in 1896 claimed that Alexander III's original concept of the bank had been subverted by Witte's Ministry of Finance. As a result the bank put estates up for sale at the first appearance of arrears in payments and in general conducted its affairs no differently from "the private yid [*zhidovskie*] banks" that before 1885 had held noble landowners at their mercy.[52] Krivskii's diatribe was a not uncommon attempt to identify the commercial ethos as an alien threat to native Russian values—with the first estate cast as the defender of those values.

Concrete suggestions for changes in the Noble Bank's mode of operations flowed in a steady stream from the societies of nobility, publicists, and the conferences of *guberniia* marshals. The suggestions covered a broad range of questions: the greater use of wardship to prevent or at least postpone foreclosure of properties in arrears, a ban on forced sales of noble properties or the restriction of such sales to members of the first estate, lower interest rates, financing by the bank of nobles' purchases of land or even purchases of land by the bank for resale on easy terms to nobles, the transfer of the bank to another ministry (agriculture or internal affairs) perceived as more sympathetic to the nobility than the Ministry of Finance, and the election of representatives by the nobility to participate in the bank's administration.[53]

The most intense feeling was excited by the question of arrears in debt payments, which affected four out of five of the bank's borrowers. In March 1896 the conference of *guberniia* marshals called for a three-year moratorium on mortgage payments, the cancelation of a portion of the arrears, and the addition of the balance of the arrears to the debt principal—with no penalties in the form of higher interest rates on arrears. Precedents existed for the latter two recommendations, for in 1889 the Noble Bank had forgiven six million rubles in delinquent payments

TABLE 17.   ARREARS OF NOBLE LAND BANK'S MORTGAGORS ON
NOVEMBER 1, 1896 (PERCENT)

STATUS OF LOANS	NUMBER OF LOANS	VALUE OF LOANS
Current	21	20
One payment in arrears	38	35
Two payments in arrears	26	26
Three or more payments in arrears	16	19

Source: TsGIAL, f. 593, op. 1, d. 101, l. 248.

and added the remaining five million to the principal of the loans. The proposal of the 1896 conference was supported in memoranda from Krivskii and other marshals and by publicists like Planson.[54] In March 1897 Witte countered with a plan to lower the bank's interest rate but at the same time to clamp down on borrowers in default, but this provoked vehement opposition from many marshals of nobility and from Durnovo.[55]

The emperor attempted a compromise between Witte's proposal and that of the 1896 marshals' conference in his May 29, 1897, *ukaz* to Witte. Nicholas rejected the idea of a moratorium on mortgage payments after being persuaded by some of the most prominent marshals (P. N. Trubetskoi of Moscow, A. D. Zinoviev of St. Petersburg, and M. A. Stakhovich of Orel) that such a blatant act of government favoritism would seriously damage the public image of the first estate. On all loans contracted before May 1, 1897, the interest rate was lowered to 3.5 percent per annum; it remained at 4 percent for loans made after that date and in fact was raised to 5 percent in July 1900.[56] All payments in arrears at the end of April 1897, together with accumulated penalties, constituted a special debt up to a maximum of 12 percent of the amount of the original loan. This debt carried an interest rate of 3.5 percent and was to be repaid in semiannual installments set at one-fourth of the regular mortgage payments. In future the penalty on delinquent payments was to remain at 0.5 percent per month for the duration of the delinquency instead of doubling after the third month, as previously. A further amendment to the Noble Bank's charter in February 1900 permitted that institution to rescue from default the most heavily indebted delinquent estates—those on which the mortgage debt plus the payments in arrears exceeded 60 percent of the property's value. With the mortgagor's consent, the bank might buy part of the estate on its own account, using the purchase money to lighten the debt burden on the remaining portion. Acreage acquired by the bank in this way was to be sold within two years if possible, and preferably to hereditary nobles; after two years such lands were to be turned over to the Peasant Bank for sale.

These changes did little to lower the rate of delinquency among the Noble Bank's borrowers. In the period 1898–1905 notice of impending sale for arrears in payments was given on 42,839 estates, an annual average of 5,355—almost one-fourth of all estates mortgaged to the bank. The number of properties actually sold at auction during the same period, however, did decline from its earlier (very low) level and averaged only 29 per year, or 1.3 per thousand estates mortgaged to the bank.[57] The rate of sale at auction rose again for the period 1906–1913 to an annual average of 50, or 1.8 per thousand—still very low.[58]

Most nobles who borrowed from the bank, then, not only enjoyed the use of generous sums of money at low rates of interest and with very long repayment periods but also continued to take advantage of the bank's lenient treatment of delinquents to fall behind, many of them seriously, in their payments, knowing that they ran little risk of losing their land. Even though it remained under the jurisdiction of the Ministry of Finance, the Noble Land Bank's activities did not diverge too widely from the *soslovniki*'s concept of credit.

Nicholas II's *ukaz* of May 1897 extended from five years to ten the deadline for liquidating a mortgage held by the Noble Bank on an estate sold to a personal noble or commoner. The ability of commoners to assume the very attractive mortgages held by the bank and retain them for a decade would certainly tend to raise the market value of noble estates and benefit particularly nobles who sold land, but the bank's raison d'être was not to facilitate and encourage such sales but to render them unnecessary. The *ukaz* also prohibited discussion by any government agency of further revisions in the Noble Bank's charter. Trying to ride out the wave of sentiment in favor of privilege and the nobility that had crested with the creation of the Special Conference on the Affairs of the Noble Estate, Witte had been successful in keeping the bank off the conference's agenda. When the latter body nevertheless took up the problem of credit at the beginning of 1899, Witte and the bank's director, Prince Liven, made a strong case that the frequent changes over the past decade (periodic decreases in the bank's interest rate and the addition of arrears in payments to the loan principal) were unsettling and led mortgagors to delay their payments in anticipation of further favors; the bank needed a moratorium on such changes if it was to function in a responsible manner. The emperor agreed and reminded the special conference to avoid any discussion of the bank's charter.[59]

SHORT-TERM CREDIT AND MUTUAL AID FUNDS

THE related subject of noble mutual aid funds was not barred from the special conference's deliberations, but Witte managed to preempt this area with a plan of his own. Interest in mutual aid funds first arose in the 1880s as a means of providing noble landowners with short-term loans of working capital. Short-term credit on the personal note of the borrower was available from the State Bank from 1884. While commercial borrowers paid from 4.5 to 7.5 percent, depending on the term of the loan (three to twelve months), landowners paid a flat 6 percent. This difference led to charges that landowners were being forced to pay higher interest than businessmen, which was true on three- and six-month loans, but as Witte pointed out in 1897, most landowners' loans were for twelve months. The State Bank's loans to landowners were intended to provide up to two-thirds of the total annual working capital of an estate, provided that the sum of the new loan and previous debts did not exceed 60 percent of the property's value. Such loans tended to be abused by landowners, who renewed them continuously, treating them like long-term loans. The total of landowners' loans outstanding from the State Bank reached 9.2 million rubles at the beginning of 1893 and 26.8 million in 1896.[60]

Nobles treated the commodity credit available from the State Bank beginning in 1893 in the same manner. Loans were made for nine months, renewable up to a total of eighteen months, on the security of a landowner's grain so that he could avoid having to sell immediately after the harvest when prices were lowest. Interest rates fluctuated between 5 and 6 percent. Landowners tended to renew their loans repeatedly rather than sell their grain at what they regarded as unattractive prices. At the beginning of 1896, 41.8 million rubles in commodity credit was outstanding. The total of promissory note and commodity loans to landowners by the State Bank in that year equaled approximately 8 percent of the nobility's mortgage debt.[61]

Periodic calls for the state to provide even easier short-term credit to landowners culminated in the program endorsed by the 1896 and 1899 marshals' conferences: short-term loans at rates below those prevailing in the money market and commodity loans renewable indefinitely as long as the grain remained unsold.[62] Witte made several small concessions to this pressure in 1897 by raising the limit and lowering the interest rates on the State Bank's promissory note loans to landowners and entrusting the review of applications for such loans to a committee consisting exclusively of landowners instead of one on which merchants were in the majority, as hitherto. Witte also insisted, however, that short-term credits that had in effect been converted into long-term loans through repeated renewal or that had raised total indebtedness beyond the legal limit (75 percent of the property's value) be repaid. The result was a precipitous decline in the State Bank's outstanding promissory note loans from 27 million rubles in 1896 to less than 8 million in 1901. Although private banks were permitted to make such loans to landowners from 1898, only 2 million rubles of such credits was outstanding at the beginning of 1902.[63]

Dissatisfaction with the available types of short-term credit gave rise to the idea of noble mutual aid funds, which had a continuing appeal to defenders of privilege in the 1880s and 1890s. While the various proposals differed in details, they all shared certain basic features: the funds would be capitalized on the basis of deposits, contributions, or levies from their members and contributions or loans from the government; members would be entitled to borrow from the fund or from the State Bank; and loans from the government to either the funds or to individual members would be secured by the collective landholdings of the members.[64]

Mutual aid funds were in fact established in the early 1890s by the noble societies of Chernigov, Poltava, Kursk, and Tula *gubernii* without state assistance and with a very narrowly defined purpose—to make loans to local nobles to enable them to pay the arrears on their mortgages.[65] Funds of this type were the model for Witte's 1897 proposal for noble mutual aid funds (*kassy*) to be capitalized by the societies of nobility and, on a matching basis, by the state to provide short-term loans on properties threatened with sale for default on mortgages held by the Noble Land Bank.[66] The rejection of Witte's plan by many *guberniia* societies and by the January 1898 marshals' conference was based on objections to both the purpose and the financing of the proposed funds. It was argued that they should provide loans for working capital and commodity loans, as well as help for those behind in their mortgage payments to either private banks or the Noble Bank, and that the capitalization of the funds should be borne by the state alone, since the *guberniia* societies could not raise the requisite sums.[67]

In response to the widespread criticism of Witte's plan, the special conference's subcommittee on measures to support noble landowning, chaired by Minister of Agriculture A. S. Ermolov, in February 1900 endorsed a counterproposal for mutual aid funds to provide the first estate with abundant and cheap short-term credit. The funds would be financed entirely with state loans totaling 200 million rubles, and their members would be collectively responsible for prompt repayment. In a lengthy and scathing critique of the subcommittee's plan, Witte objected that 200 million rubles was quite beyond the state's means (he estimated the total cost to the state of his own plan at only 7.5 million) and that collective responsibility for repayment would be a worthless guarantee unless it were extended to all noble landowners instead of being restricted to the funds' member-borrowers. Witte's adamant opposition succeeded in blocking consideration of the subcommittee's proposal by the full special conference.[68] In November 1901 the conference approved Witte's plan, amending it only to make owners of estates mortgaged to private land banks eligible as well for loans from the mutual aid funds. Discussion of the measure in the State Council the following spring raised all of the objections and doubts that had been voiced previously, but Witte successfully resisted all suggestions that the funds should serve any purpose other than assisting mortgagors in arrears on their payments. He insisted that the transfer of noble land into the hands of commoners was taking place in response to profound economic and social forces. The government's responsibility was not to halt this transfer, for it could not even if it would, but to see that it proceeded in a gradual and orderly manner so as not to disrupt Russian agriculture; that was the only proper function of the proposed mutual aid funds.[69]

The legislation passed by the State Council and approved by the emperor on June 3, 1902, authorized any *guberniia* assembly of nobility to establish a mutual aid fund "to provide assistance to local hereditary noble landowners in paying their mortgage debts, in order to avert the sale of their estates at public auction."[70] The funds were to make loans for up to five years, at no more than 6 percent interest, and for up to 20 percent of the total outstanding debt secured by the property, provided that the loan did not raise the indebtedness of the property beyond 90 percent of its value. The funds could also make one- or two-year loans "in the event of various kinds of misfortunes which might befall said nobles," for example, the death or serious illness of the head of the family, crop failure, cattle disease, or fire. A fund might assume the management of properties in default on their debt to it or subject to forced sale by the Noble Land Bank—in the latter case only with the owner's consent and for a maximum of six years. If a property indebted to a mutual aid fund passed into the possession of a nonnoble, the loan had to be liquidated within six months. The funds were to be financed by onetime grants from the state; by special annual taxes voted by the *guberniia* assemblies on the lands of nobles; and by matching grants for the first decade of a fund's existence, equal each year to the amount raised the previous year by the special tax. Any losses incurred by a fund were to be covered by its profits from earlier years or, if these were insufficient, by borrowing from its capital. Should repeated losses consume half of its capital, a fund was to be terminated.

It is uncertain how many mutual aid funds were established under the 1902 law, or whether indeed any were established. In any case there was no decline in the already very low rate of forced sale of noble properties in the years after 1902.[71] In view of the opposition to the Ministry of Finance's plan from the *guberniia* marshals and assemblies, Witte could have entertained few illusions as to the funds' success. They were clearly designed as a harmless diversion from the much more attractive and expensive proposal for all-purpose short-term credit financed primarily by the state.

WORKBOOKS AND LAND GRANTS

JURIDICAL measures to stem the alienation and fragmentation of noble estates and the provision of easier credit to noble landowners by no means exhausted the ways in which state aid was suggested to solve the problem of the landed nobility's declining numbers and acreage. Some proposals drew only insignificant support, such as a recommendation that the state provide interest-free loans to noble societies to enable them to take the entire grain trade into their own hands and thereby eliminate grasping middlemen, or appeals for special privileges for nobles who operated distilleries on their estates and were suffering from the loss of their former monopoly in this area.[72] Other ideas were enacted into law but proved no more efficacious in stabilizing noble landownership than did entail or mutual aid funds. Among these were the notion of giving noble landowners greater legal authority over the peasants they hired as agricultural laborers and the resort to grants of state land to strengthen the landed nobility.

In 1884 on the initiative of their *guberniia* marshal, P. A. Krivskii, the Saratov noble assembly petitioned the government to institute a compulsory workbook in which each agricultural laborer would have recorded, for the use of future employers, all his jobs and any breaches of contract for which he had been fined or dismissed. A laborer who left his job before the expiration of his contract could be returned forcibly to his employer without even the necessity of a court order. When the proposal was discussed in the State Council, K. P. Pobedonostsev objected (as he had a decade earlier when he had helped block a similar scheme) that the imposition of such strict labor discipline smacked of serfdom. The climate of opinion at court was now different, however, as reflected in Katkov's and Meshcherskii's advocacy of the plan, and it passed the council and was approved by the emperor on June 12, 1886.[73] Its provisions proved impossible to apply in all their severity, however, and at the turn of the century Krivskii and others were still complaining that noble landowners were being driven to ruin for want of adequate legal protection against lazy, drunken, and negligent hired hands.[74]

If compulsory workbooks smacked of serfdom, land grants to nobles had an even more anachronistic ring to them. V. K. von Pleve, secretary of the State Council, was not in the least self-conscious in 1900 about citing the experience of sixteenth-century Muscovy in support of his proposal to the special conference that state lands in Siberia be given to nobles as latter-day *pomestia*, entailed for three generations to preclude their purchase by commoners.[75]

State lands had not generally been granted to nobles since the reign of the emperor Paul, but in the nineteenth century both grants and subsidized sales of state lands to nobles had been used on occasion either to provide for impoverished families from *gubernii* where available land was scarce or to strengthen the Russian presence in the borderlands. An example of the former was the resettlement in the 1840s of almost eight hundred noble families from Smolensk and Riazan on land grants ranging from sixty to eighty *desiatiny* each in Tambov, Simbirsk, and Samara. Attempts to grant or sell state lands in Tobolsk, the westernmost *guberniia* of Siberia, to Russian nobles between the 1840s and 1860s met with no success, but in the 1870s almost half a million *desiatiny* taken from the Bashkirs in Ufa and Orenburg were sold by the government to Russian nobles at prices from 70 to 80 percent below market value; most of the purchasers never settled on their new estates, reselling them instead at a very substantial profit. And after 1865 the state sold to Russian nobles at attractive prices over half a million *desiatiny* confiscated in the western *gubernii* from Polish nobles who had participated in the recent revolt.[76]

There was thus adequate precedent behind the numerous proposals of the *soslovniki* between the 1880s and the early 1900s to use grants of state land to halt the decline of the landed nobility. Such projects more often than not focused on landless members of the hereditary nobility who were in state service. Grants of up to eight hundred *desiatiny* were proposed in lieu of ranks and orders or of pensions, or even in partial payment of salaries. Frequently conditions were suggested which would limit the alienability, divisibility, or mortgageability of such land grants. And several projects charged the Noble Land Bank or some other state institution with acquiring estates placed on the market by nobles or foreclosed for debt and reselling them to nobles.[77]

In fact the only measures along these lines seriously considered by the government under Alexander III and Nicholas II involved lands in the least promising of all the borderlands and arose as a by-product of the construction of the Trans-Siberian Railroad. As early as 1893 the Siberian Railroad Committee decided to reserve lands for settlement by educated and cultured landowners as well as by peasants in the areas through which the railroad would run. The committee hoped the estates of the former would serve as models for the peasants. The question that provoked lively debate within the government in the years 1898–1901 was whether to give nobles preference, or even exclusive rights, in the sale and leasing of such lands. On one side of the question were ranged the Siberian Railroad Committee's preparatory commission and the majority of the State Council, who, concerned primarily with Siberia's economic development, favored the sale and leasing of state lands to individuals, regardless of social estate (but excluding Jews, *inorodtsy*, and foreigners), who would cultivate the land properly. On the other side were the Special Conference on the Affairs of the Noble Estate and the minority of the State Council, who viewed the establishment of a landed nobility in Siberia as at least as important a goal as economic development.[78] Landed nobles were needed in Siberia both as a "local service estate" and as a source of leadership and guidance for the peasantry, but nobles could not be expected to compete successfully with bourgeois types for the purchase or lease of state lands. In its own interest, therefore, the state should sell and lease such lands to nobles only. The law which Nicholas II enacted on June 8, 1901, was a compromise: leases of state lands in Siberia for ninety-nine years, with the option to buy on favorable terms at the expiration of the lease, would be restricted to nobles alone, while sales of such lands, in order to maximize the return to the state, would be at public auction to the highest bidder regardless of social estate.[79]

In the meantime a companion proposal of the Siberian Railroad Committee, approved by the emperor on June 22, 1900, provided for nobles who lacked the means to buy or lease the larger parcels (up to three thousand *desiatiny* each) dealt with in the 1901 law. The 1900 act offered grants of sixty to one hundred *desiatiny* of state land in Tobolsk and Tomsk *gubernii* and in the Irkutsk, Amur, and Steppe governments-general to "hereditary nobles who worked the land with their own personal labor and that of the members of their families." Requests for these grants were to be made to the governor of the applicant's home *guberniia* and required the support of his *uezd* and *guberniia* marshals of nobility. A grant would be forfeited if not occupied within two years, if abandoned thereafter for five years or more, or if taxes remained unpaid for five years, and it could neither be alienated nor mortgaged.[80] How many such grants were made is not known; given the nobility's lack of interest in the regions in question, the program's success may safely be presumed to have been minimal.

In the case of the 1901 law covering the lease and sale of larger allotments, the State Council's view of it as innocuous but unlikely to realize the hopes of its sponsors was more than borne out by events. Fifty-nine parcels of arable land, averaging slightly more than two thousand *desiatiny*, were set aside along the route of the railroad as far east as Irkutsk *guberniia*. No sales or leases were concluded before the 1905 revolution, however, as a result of opposition from local authorities, who were protective of the peasantry's interests, and of mass protests in Eniseisk *guberniia* in 1902 against the earmarking for sale or lease to large proprietors of lands previously leased to peasants for pasture and haymeadows. After 1905 the lands in question were redesignated for peasant settlement.[81]

The common denominator of all the proposals discussed in this chapter was the desire to preserve the landed nobility by insulating it from the free play of market forces. It was an article of faith, and even a point of pride, among the *soslovniki* that nobles could not compete successfully with aggressive and materialistic merchants and *kulaks* under the conditions of legal equality that had prevailed since the great reforms. Almost all of the measures that were enacted, however, like entail, met with a striking lack of response from noble landowners, who overwhelmingly failed to take advantage of such protection as was offered. This reaction suggests that the defenders of privilege were quite out of touch with the sentiments and desires of the overwhelming majority of intermediate noble landowners. The latter group, praised by the *soslovniki* as the true core of the first estate, almost to a man placed freedom to sell, divide, or borrow on the security of their property above any attachment to the idea of a lasting family seat or concern for the future of their social order. Voluntary entail and other measures like Siberian land grants could not but fail because the champions of such measures had their sights trained determinedly on an idealized past, while the great majority of the landed nobility was not to be dissuaded from making the best terms possible with the present.

The only measures to which large numbers of landed nobles responded positively were those designed to provide them with easy credit. The exception is illuminating. Easy credit was demanded by traditionalists for their particular reasons. Such credit was equally attractive to noble landowners for their own quite different purposes—to cover routine and extraordinary living expenses, certainly, but also to invest in commerce, industry, and even agriculture. Agriculture as a field for investment appealed only to a few, but those few agrarian entrepreneurs were coming to dominate the landowning rump of the first estate.

SHARING NOBLE STATUS:
PROBLEMS OF MEMBERSHIP

ENNOBLEMENT VIA STATE SERVICE

I N the minds of the *soslovniki* it was a crucial matter to provide juridical and material means by which to stem the flow of scions of old
landed families into the urban, modernizing world dominated by
types viewed as alien to the values of the nobility. That was the rationale
behind the measures aimed at stabilizing noble landownership. No less
essential a part of the traditionalist program, however, was the raising of
barriers against the influx—partly real but mostly chimerical, as we shall
see—of those same alien types into the nobility. No other aspect of the
noble question drew more attention in the 1880s and 1890s, and the first
problem to which the 1897 special conference turned was that of re-
defining the qualifications for membership in the first estate.

Privilege and exclusiveness are inseparable concepts, and the entry of
commoners, especially civil servants, into the ranks of the nobility had
caused consternation to the defenders of privilege ever since the reign of
Catherine the Great. There were three means by which commoners
could acquire hereditary noble status: by special patent from the sovereign, by reaching the prescribed level of the Table of Ranks, or through
the award of membership in one of four honorific orders open to commoners. The first was of little significance; only twenty-three individuals
were ennobled by special patents between 1872 and 1896, leading one
contemporary authority to describe this mechanism as "virtually a dead
letter."[1]

Promotions in rank for civil servants and officers had been responsible
for the majority of cases of ennoblement in the eighteenth and first half
of the nineteenth centuries. Pressure from the nobility to abolish automatic ennoblement through the Table of Ranks arose as early as

Catherine II's Legislative Commission. This pressure was the product of a number of factors: a growing status consciousness and exclusiveness among the first estate, the inflation of class ranks as promotions were given increasingly to bureaucrats for time served rather than for merit, and the rising absolute number of ennobled commoners as the bureaucracy grew in size.[2] Nicholas I and Alexander II rejected the idea of abolishing ennoblement through the Table of Ranks but did raise the requisite ranks for ennoblement—in 1845 from class fourteen for officers and eight for bureaucrats to class eight for officers and five for civil servants, and in 1856 to class six for officers and four for civil servants. Officers in class six held the rank of army colonel or naval captain first class. Civil servants in class four held the rank of actual state councillor (equivalent to major general or rear admiral) and included the directors of departments and heads of chancelleries of the central ministries, the over-procurators of departments of the Senate, the presidents of provincial courts, and *guberniia* governors. Unlike lower ranks, class four rank was not conferred for length of service alone but only upon nomination by the appropriate minister or department head and confirmation by the emperor.[3]

As a result of the raising of the class ranks required for ennoblement, membership in honorific orders supplanted the Table of Ranks as the principal means of commoners' acquiring noble status in the second half of the nineteenth century. Between 1875 and 1884, 60 percent of all cases of ennoblement were via receipt of orders rather than ranks; in the period 1882–1896, the figure rose to 72 percent.[4] Officers as well as civil servants now found entrance into the nobility much easier through decorations than promotions. As of January 1, 1897, there were 852 staff and junior officers in the army and 87 in the navy who were ennobled commoners; 63 percent of the former and 74 percent of the latter had acquired hereditary nobility through receipt of an order of St. George or St. Vladimir, the rest by promotion in rank.[5] The order of St. George was awarded to commissioned officers for distinguished service, the order of St. Vladimir for twenty-five years' service with an unblemished record.[6] The fourth (lowest) degree of either order carried hereditary noble status. For civil servants and for individuals not in service, the possibilities for ennoblement through receipt of decorations had been progressively restricted between 1826 and 1856 to the order of St. Vladimir, all degrees, and to the first degrees of the orders of St. Anna and St. Stanislav. All three orders, but especially the latter two, were awarded not only to outstanding high-ranking government servants but to leading figures in business, the professions, scholarship, and the arts. Only personal nobles and distinguished citizens, however, thereby acquired hereditary nobility, and the first degree of the order of St. Anna was rarely awarded even to members of these substates. By far the most commonly bestowed decoration that carried noble status was the fourth degree of the order of St. Vladimir, commonly awarded to civil servants in class seven or above either for outstanding performance or for long service with an unblemished record.[7] An authority on the laws of status observed in 1886 that "now even a collegiate councillor [class six] rarely lacks an order of Vladimir in his buttonhole," and complained, "It is as difficult for a soldier to win a George, fourth degree, as it is easy for a bureaucrat to win an order of Vladimir, fourth degree."[8] And as an ever-growing number of nonnobles entered the bureaucracy and the officer corps, the proportion of commoners among the recipients of the Vladimir fourth degree rose from 12 percent in the years 1875–1881 to 22 percent in 1892–1896.[9]

Annual additions to the first estate by all means other than natural increase averaged 1,000, including both the ennobled person and his dependents, for the period 1825–1845; 1,270 for 1875–1884; 1,393 for 1882–1896; and 1,569 for 1892–1896—a rise of over 50 percent. In all, the nobility gained approximately 50,000 members through the process of ennoblement between 1858 and 1897—20,000 in the period 1858–1874, and 30,000 in 1875–1896.[10] Despite the growing influx of commoners, mostly via state service, the relative weight of newcomers in the first estate as a whole remained remarkably steady. In 1858 approximately 6.5 to 7 percent of the nobility consisted of persons ennobled in the thirty-three years since 1825 and the dependents and descendants of such persons (41,000–42,000 out of 610,000–626,000). In 1897 roughly 7.5 percent consisted of persons ennobled in the thirty-nine years since 1858, plus their dependents and descendants (66,000–67,000 out of 886,000).[11] All of the figures on ennoblement are for cases confirmed by the Senate's Department of Heraldry upon petition by the ennobled person. Even if a growing proportion of unreported cases is assumed for the period after 1858 (and noble status, although rapidly losing its material significance, nonetheless retained its appeal for most middle-ranking officials and officers), the relative weight of the newcomers in 1897 would hardly have exceeded 8 percent; had it not been for the purge of Polish nobles in the 1860s, the figure would have been below 7 percent—exactly where it stood four decades earlier. It was not, therefore, any increase in the rate at which commoners were joining the first estate that caused this phenomenon to be viewed by the defenders of privilege in the late nineteenth century as a more serious threat than ever before. The reason for their concern is to be sought rather in the nobility's rapid loss of its character as a landowning estate, a transformation which the ennoblement of landless bureaucrats and officers could only hasten.

Closing off, or at least narrowing, access to noble status via state service was a favorite theme of the *soslovniki*.[12] As *Russkii vestnik* summed up their case in 1890, the landed noble who entered government service out of a sense of responsibility and honor was a totally different specimen from the bureaucrat of common birth who pursued his career purely out of self-interest. Conferring noble status upon the latter served only to confuse the two in the public mind. Nor was that the worst of it. Any upstart functionary, once ennobled for his timeserving and bootlicking, could purchase a scrap of land somewhere and claim membership in a noble society and a role in local administration on an equal basis with scions of old landed families. Ennoblement had perhaps once been useful in attracting calculating *raznochintsy* into service, but this was no longer the case, argued *Russkii vestnik*, now that noble status was devoid of any substantial advantages.[13]

On the other side of the issue the liberal *Vestnik Evropy* argued that noble status was not yet an empty honor but still conferred some rights and privileges, which were likely, moreover, to increase if even a few of the *soslovniki*'s demands were to be satisfied. Postulating that "the harm inflicted by privilege increases in inverse proportion to the number of persons possessing it," *Vestnik Evropy* concluded that if the nobility could not be eliminated, then at least it should be as open as possible to talent. *Russkaia mysl* supplied ammunition to the liberals by correctly pointing out that the number of commoners ennobled by all means taken together was dwarfed by the number added to the first estate through natural increase.[14]

Even a few of the defenders of privilege sided with the liberals on this question. General Fadeev in the early 1870s and Katkov in 1885 both argued that the Russian nobility had never been "an exclusive caste" like the feudal aristocracy of France or Germany but simply "the upper stratum of the people, created historically and constantly replenished by recruitment from below." Raising the requisite service rank for ennoblement, as was repeatedly proposed, would betray this tradition, would endow the nobility with an uncharacteristic exclusiveness, and would create a group of high government officials who, denied noble status, would be enemies of the first estate. Similar objections were raised in 1897 by Witte, who pointed out the danger to the nobility of a future in which "Russia would be administered by nonnobles" who had been deprived of the possibility of ennoblement, and in 1885 by Minister of War P. S. Vannovskii with reference to the officer corps. Vannovskii noted that refusing entry into the first estate to officers of nonnoble birth would result in high-ranking commoners' exercising authority over the large number of hereditary nobles serving in staff and junior officer ranks. This would aggravate a problem that had existed on a limited scale since 1856, when the ranks of lieutenant colonel and major had ceased to confer hereditary nobility.[15]

In March 1883 Alexander III responded to the concern over the ennoblement of commoners by appointing a commission under S. A. Taneev, director of His Majesty's Own Chancellery, to examine the question. Although the emperor was inclined to abolish the Table of Ranks altogether, the Taneev commission in January 1885 recommended only the raising of the requisite rank for ennoblement to class three in both the civil service and the officer corps. Bureaucrats in class three held the rank of privy councillor and posts such as deputy minister; officers in class three held the rank of lieutenant general or vice admiral. The Taneev commission also proposed the elimination of ennoblement through receipt of the third and fourth degrees of the order of St. Vladimir, the fourth degree of St. George, and the first degrees of St. Anna and St. Stanislav. Had the proposed changes been in effect during the decade 1875–1884, the commission estimated, only 70 persons, including dependents, would have been ennobled through receipt of ranks or orders instead of the 12,701 persons who were actually raised to the first estate in this manner. As a result of the opposition of Vannovskii and of other ministers, the Taneev commission's recommendations were ultimately buried in the State Council.[16] Under Alexander III the only step taken to reduce the number of commoners ennobled through state service was to restrict the award of the fourth degree of the order of St. Vladimir to those who had served a specified number of years in class ranks with an unblemished record; this term was set at twenty years in 1887 and raised to thirty-five years in 1892. And the fourth degree of the order of St. Vladimir no longer conferred noble status when it was awarded to philanthropists or others not actively in state service.[17]

Although temporarily checked, efforts to restrict the ennoblement of commoners became even more frequent after the mid-1880s. Over the next decade the government received petitions from the noble assemblies of many *gubernii* asking either for the curtailment or the outright abolition of ennoblement via ranks and orders. And the first national conference of marshals of nobility in 1896 voted almost unanimously to raise the requisite rank for ennoblement to class three in the civil service and class four in the military, and approved by a large majority the abolition of ennoblement through receipt of any order but that of St. George.[18]

The majority of the Special Conference on the Affairs of the Noble Estate sympathized with the desire of one of its members "to deliver the landed nobility from the bureaucratic element, which is alien to it."[19] The conference recognized, however, that raising the rank for ennoblement would make little difference, since the greater number of civil servants who reached the fourth class already held the order of St. Vladimir. By an overwhelming majority, therefore, the conference voted instead in late January 1898 to eliminate the fourth degree of St. Vladimir as a means of ennoblement and to restrict the award of the third degree to bureaucrats in class four or above and officers in class six or above, that is, to individuals who, if of common birth, would already have been ennobled by promotion in rank.[20]

Despite some sentiment in the State Council in favor of more drastic measures, that body ended by endorsing the recommendations of the special conference early in 1900, and they were promulgated by the emperor's decree to the Senate of May 28, 1900. Although the requisite civil service rank for ennoblement remained unchanged, new regulations in 1898 and 1900 made that rank harder to attain. A bureaucrat could henceforth be promoted to class four only after serving a minimum of five years in class five and in an office appropriate to that rank, provided also that he had been in class ranks for a minimum of twenty years.[21] The combined effect of these regulations and the abolition of ennoblement through receipt of the fourth degree of the order of St. Vladimir was a drastic reduction in a commoner's chances for acquiring noble status through the civil service.

The May 28 *ukaz* also eliminated another path into the first estate. By unanimous consent and with little discussion both the special conference and the State Council had recommended the abolition of the procedure whereby a man whose father and grandfather had each served a minimum of twenty years in civil or military ranks conferring personal nobility, upon entering service himself, could claim membership in the hereditary nobility. Nicholas II agreed that such persons should be required to prove themselves worthy of ennoblement on the same basis as other commoners.[22]

PERSONAL NOBILITY

IN the decades-long discussion over means of restricting ennoblement via state service, the cause of most anxiety was the commoners—or to be more exact, nonnobles (*nedvoriane*), for Russian contains no precise equivalent of the English "commoner" or French "*roturier*"—who held intermediate-level civil service ranks. The "nonnobles" in question in fact belonged to the personal nobility, a component, albeit inferior, of the first estate since the reign of Peter the Great. For a century and a quarter personal nobility was conferred on commoners who attained junior civil service ranks (classes nine through fourteen).[23] Then, as the requisite ranks for attaining hereditary nobility were raised in 1845 and again in 1856, so too were the ranks that conferred personal nobility on civil servants. At the same time personal nobility was substituted for hereditary nobility as a reward for commoners who reached junior officer or the lower staff officer ranks in the army and navy. From 1856 civil service ranks in classes five through nine and military ranks in classes seven through fourteen conferred personal nobility upon men of common birth. Civil servants could also attain personal nobility through the receipt of various honorific orders which formerly had carried hereditary noble status: the second through fourth degrees of the order of St. Anna from 1845, the second and third degrees of St. Stanislav from 1855, and the fourth degree of St. Vladimir from 1900. Personal nobility was conferred as well upon merchants who received a rank of the ninth class or higher for their civic or charitable work, and also, at the emperor's discretion, upon any deserving individual for whatever reason.[24]

As a result of these changes the personal nobility grew rapidly in size from the middle of the nineteenth century—much more rapidly than the hereditary nobility. Precise figures are unavailable, since in every population estimate from 1858, and in the 1897 census, personal nobles were grouped together with *chinovniki* (in the narrow sense of commoners holding civil service ranks in classes ten through fourteen). The total number of personal nobles and *chinovniki*, including wives and minor children, was estimated at 276,809 in 1858, and the 1897 census counted 486,963—an increase of 76 percent as compared with only 45 percent for the hereditary nobility.[25]

The relationship of the personal to the hereditary nobility had been an ambiguous one from the beginning. Under the 1785 charter personal nobles were excluded from the exercise of the first estate's corporate rights: they were barred from enrolling in the genealogical registers of the noble societies, from participating in the triennial assemblies, and from holding such elective estate offices as marshal, deputy, or secretary.[26] And they were deprived of the first estate's most valuable privilege—the right to own land inhabited by serfs. On the other hand personal nobles shared the useful personal rights of the hereditary nobility. Serf emancipation diminished the legal distance between the hereditary and the personal nobility, but the extension of the common personal rights of all nobles to the members of the other estates at the same time eliminated the most important bond between the two noble subestates.

Other ties were of considerably less significance. Before the great reforms personal nobles were eligible to hold certain local administrative posts normally filled by hereditary nobles elected or nominated by the *guberniia* assemblies. After the great majority of these posts were abolished in the 1860s, the only office to which personal nobles could, in an emergency, be elected was that of assessor of the *uezd* police bureau. When these bureaus were eliminated in 1889, personal nobles who were landowners and met certain other qualifications became eligible for nomination and appointment to the new post of *zemskii nachalnik* in the absence of qualified hereditary nobles. Very few personal nobles owned land, but as of 1890 those who did were grouped together as equals with hereditary noble landowners in the first curia of *zemstvo* electors. Whether landowners or not, personal nobles had some claim in case of need to financial support from the *guberniia* societies of nobility, although the societies understandably gave preference to their own members in the distribution of their charitable and scholarship funds. Undoubtedly because of this claim, from 1851 the lands of personal nobles were taxable by the *guberniia* societies on the same basis as the lands of hereditary nobles. The estates of personal as well as hereditary nobles could be placed in wardship by the *uezd* and *guberniia* marshals and the deputy assemblies for reasons of extreme mismanagement or apostasy from Orthodoxy. And marshals of nobility were on occasion responsible for testifying concerning the conduct and character, and for certifying the insanity, of individual personal as well as hereditary nobles under their jurisdiction.[27]

From the very beginning personal nobles were shunned by the hereditary nobility, and both state and society regarded personal nobles as de facto members of the urban estate. From the reign of Nicholas I the children of personal nobles upon coming of age were registered as hereditary distinguished citizens, and personal nobles themselves, if they so requested, were given the legal rights of hereditary distinguished citizens.[28] V. O. Kliuchevskii articulated a commonly held view in his 1886 university lecture course, "The History of Estates in Russia," when he argued that the personal nobility could not in any real sense be considered

a special division of the nobility, because it does not share the distinctive rights of the nobility . . . ; it is no more than an honorary rank for life, to which the title of nobility is applied not because personal nobility confers the same rights, but because it is acquired by the same means, as hereditary nobility: by imperial grant, by ranks in service, and by receipt of an order. The actual rights of personal nobles are identical to those of the so-called *hereditary distinguished citizens*.[29]

A renowned figure from a nineteenth-century literary classic may be of some use in illustrating society's attitude toward the personal nobility. In *The Overcoat* Gogol introduces the self-effacing clerk, Akakii Akakievich, as a "permanent titular councillor." What Gogol did not need to add for the benefit of his contemporaries is that the rank of titular councillor (class nine in the civil service) carried with it personal noble status, as did civil service ranks in all lower classes as well. Promotion to the next rank (class eight) conferred hereditary nobility. The usage "permanent titular councillor" had gained currency to describe the Akakii Akakieviches, who were not about to become hereditary nobles through promotion in rank. Even after the mid-century raising of standards, the rank of titular councillor continued to confer personal nobility. So the identification of Akakii Akakievich as a personal noble in the minds of literate Russians remained valid until the end of the old regime.

The future of the relationship between the personal and the hereditary nobility was repeatedly raised in the debate over the noble question.

Fadeev in the early 1870s suggested granting personal nobles "full equality during their lifetime with respect to all the political and other rights of the nobility," and in January 1898 the Kazan assembly of marshals and deputies proposed to admit to their society personal nobles of the *guberniia* who, by their interest in agriculture and their educational background, demonstrated a community of interest with the hereditary nobility.[30] The prevailing sentiment among the defenders of privilege, however, was for a total divorce of the personal from the hereditary nobility. At times even the abolition of the personal nobility was proposed, as by an anonymous publicist in 1881 and by the marshals and deputies of St. Petersburg *guberniia* in December 1898.[31]

The majority of the Special Conference on the Affairs of the Noble Estate recommended a less extreme but nonetheless radical solution. Having characterized the personal nobility at its first session as "an independent estate having nothing in common with the real, that is, hereditary, nobility," the conference later proposed that all laws dealing with the personal nobility be removed from the section of volume nine of the Code of Laws that dealt with the hereditary nobility and relegated to a separate place in the same volume; that marshals of nobility and the deputy assemblies be freed of all responsibility for personal nobles; and that personal nobles be transferred from the first to the second curia of *zemstvo* electors, the latter comprising nonnoble individual proprietors and corporate property owners other than peasant communes. A personal noble was, of course, merely a lower form of the *chinovnik* who attained hereditary noble status; both were regarded by the conference as possessing values and attitudes, shaped by their upbringing and their work, which were incompatible with those of the traditional, that is to say landed, hereditary nobility. A large minority of the special conference, however, objected to any change in the existing relationship between the two strata of the first estate on the grounds that service, not landowning, was the primary vocation of, and traditional qualification for membership in, the nobility. Most personal nobles had acquired their status through government service, and through further service many would eventually attain hereditary nobility.[32]

Although a handful of members of the State Council agreed with the majority of the special conference that the nature of the hereditary nobility should be protected by putting as much distance as possible between it and the personal nobility, the council overwhelmingly supported the maintenance of the status quo, pointing out that no apparent harm had come to the hereditary nobility from its 180-year association with the personal nobility. A firm believer in the Petrine system linking noble status to government service, Nicholas II accepted the State Council's recommendation in 1902, leaving unresolved the ambiguity of the personal nobility's position.[33]

At the same time the emperor sided with the council's minority and decreed a change that reaffirmed the bond between the two noble subestates and, more important, that was of material advantage to the societies of nobility. Since 1851, rural real estate owned by personal nobles had been taxed by the *guberniia* societies on the same basis as land belonging to hereditary nobles. Unlike the latter category, however, which together with personal property escheated to the appropriate noble society after 1883, the personal and rural real property of personal nobles continued to escheat to the state.[34] Although the overwhelming majority of personal nobles owned no land and were by no means wealthy, in individual cases an escheated estate might have considerable value, and in St. Petersburg and Moscow, which contained sizable numbers of personal nobles, potentially large aggregate sums were at stake. Similarly, in some *gubernii* the tax revenue from the property of personal nobles was a welcome addition to the society's treasury. Giving material considerations precedence over the desire to divorce the personal from the hereditary nobility, both the January 1898 marshals' conference and the Special Conference on the Affairs of the Noble Estate recommended that the noble societies be given unlimited rights to the escheated property, personal and real, urban and rural, of the personal as well as hereditary nobility.[35] The State Council, however, agreeing with Sipiagin's subcommittee of the special conference, voted to sacrifice material interest to principle by not only denying the *guberniia* societies any claim to the escheated property of personal nobles but also depriving the societies of their right to tax the lands of personal nobles. Under Russia's autocratic system the State Council merely proposed, while the emperor disposed. Nicholas II awarded the property in question to the noble societies, while reaffirming their right to tax personal nobles' rural real estate.[36]

Since 1894, urban real estate belonging to either personal or hereditary nobles had been subject to taxation by the noble societies instead of by the municipalities in which such property was located. A similar transfer of escheatage rights was decreed by Nicholas II with respect to urban real property of hereditary nobles in 1898 and of personal nobles in 1902.[37]

ENNOBLEMENT VIA LANDOWNERSHIP

DISTANCING the hereditary nobility from the personal nobility and making it harder for career bureaucrats to exchange personal for hereditary noble status were negative means of strengthening the first estate's traditional identification with landownership. A positive approach was the ennoblement of commoners who were substantial landowners. Various schemes to achieve this end were proposed from the 1860s on, frequently by the noble societies themselves in the reign of

Alexander III. Both the Taneev commission in 1885 and the first conference of *guberniia* marshals in 1896 recommended that the noble societies
be allowed to petition the government for the ennoblement of landowners who met certain standards of usefulness to their rural communities,
moral character, size of landholdings, and length of ownership.[38]

The case for the ennoblement of wealthy landowners was based on the
urgent need, in the eyes of the defenders of privilege, to halt and even
reverse the sharp decline in the numbers of landowning nobles.
Pazukhin, for one, was concerned lest, even with a change in the government's policy toward privilege, the landed nobility of some districts
might already have been so weakened in numbers that they would not be
able effectively to act as the state's most valued servants and the peasantry's trusted protectors without an infusion of "strong new elements." By
that he meant landowners of substance living in a manner befitting a
nobleman. An anonymous defender of privilege writing a few months
after Pazukhin, also in *Russkii vestnik*, repeated the same argument and
added that the possibility of ennoblement would encourage landowners
to live like gentlemen and to engage in socially useful activity. Another
soslovnik, V. Liaskovskii, defended the proposal by insisting that "when
the distinguishing characteristic of noble status was service, that was also
the natural path by which a *raznochinets* attained nobility," but state service, with the possible exception of the officer corps, was no longer
either the monopoly of the nobility or the career choice of most nobles.
It would therefore be logical to switch from service to landownership as
the primary attribute of noble status and to offer ennoblement to landowners as well as to state servants. In any case, a resident proprietor of
an estate that had been in the family for several generations would have
much more in common with the landed nobility of his district than a
chinovnik born and bred in the city.[39]

A different tack was taken by a substantial majority of the 1897 special
conference, which argued that *zemstvo* activity and similar contributions
to the life of the rural community were actually but another form of
service to the state and as such should be considered grounds for
ennoblement. Local service, furthermore, could best be evaluated by
bodies such as the noble assemblies which were more intimately ac-
quainted with the quality of the work performed than any St. Petersburg
bureaucrats ever could be. Minister of War A. N. Kuropatkin, who was
invited to participate in the special conference's deliberations on this
question, offered yet another argument in favor of the ennoblement of
landowners. The best background for an officer, Kuropatkin was convinced, was the wholesome physical and moral upbringing which could
be provided only in the bosom of a rural noble family. Given the declining number of such families since serf emancipation and the rising demand for officers, it was imperative that measures such as the one under

consideration be taken to preserve the traditional breeding ground for officers.[40]

The major obstacle facing the ennoblement of landowners nominated by noble societies was that the proposal broke with long-established practice in two ways. It would have established an alternative to state service as a regular means of entry into the first estate, and it would have granted to the nobility itself control over the admission of new members. Both points provoked strong opposition not only among liberals but also among conservatives like the minister of internal affairs, Count D. A. Tolstoi. In advising Alexander III against a petition on this subject from the Riazan *guberniia* noble assembly in 1885, Tolstoi urged "that the Russian nobility is not of feudal origin and that the right of self-definition cannot be granted to it without altering its historic significance as a service estate."[41] The liberal *Vestnik Evropy* objected that giving the noble societies the right of co-optation would not only be incompatible with the nobility's historic relationship to the state but would invite serious abuse. Unlike the objective and impersonal mechanism of ennoblement through ranks and orders, the ennobling of landowners would involve necessarily vague qualifications and subjective judgments of character. A *guberniia* assembly of nobility, moreover, was too large a body, too changeable in composition from one triennial meeting to another, and too narrow in its interests to be entrusted with such judgments. Standards for admitting new members would likely be lowered as the numbers and strength of the older landed nobility declined and its need for new blood rose, and, in any case, the assembly was a poor judge of the value of a man's services to state and society—the only justification for awarding him privileged status.[42]

Another liberal journal, *Russkaia mysl*, applauded the fact that since the 1860s intermediate and large landowners, nobles and nonnobles together, had constituted a group analogous to the English gentry, defined not by legal privilege but by their leadership of the rural community. This leadership was evident in the domination of the *zemstvos* by the electors of the first curia. (The journal could not, of course, foresee that the *zemstvo* act of 1890 would exclude nonnobles from the first curia.) To attach hereditary privileged status to the ownership of a landed estate was both unnecessary and somewhat absurd, given the rapid turnover in such properties in recent years.[43] The latter point was pursued by two of the participants in the 1896 marshals' conference. V. A. Kapnist of Kharkov and A. D. Durnovo of Kursk argued that the ennoblement of landowners, in addition to undermining the historical significance of ennoblement in Russia, would only accelerate the purchase of noble properties by commoners.[44]

In the Special Conference on the Affairs of the Noble Estate a small group consisting of Witte, Minister of Justice N. V. Muraviev, D. S. Sipiagin, and S. D. Sheremetev insisted that the ownership of land and success in agriculture could not be construed as service to the state and should not be made grounds for ennoblement. State service, moreover, could be properly evaluated only by the government, not by local organs of the nobility. In Witte's view the nobility would profit less from the ennoblement of bourgeois landowners than from its own further *embourgeoisement*. Deeper involvement in industry and finance would save the first estate from becoming completely a social anachronism, identified exclusively with state service and agriculture. If property owners were to be ennobled, let it be for their services to the state, and let the group of eligibles include all property owners, not just gentlemen landowners. Developing this line of thought, Witte proposed that the definition of state service be broadened to keep pace with the changing times. Ministers and directors of government departments should be urged to bring to the attention of the Committee of Ministers individuals in the professions, the business world, the arts, and the sciences who were deserving of ennoblement, especially if the fourth degree of the order of St. Vladimir, sometimes awarded to such persons, was no longer to confer noble status. Witte's proposal was adopted by the special conference virtually without argument, doubtless because, given the very sparing use in the past of ennoblement by exercise of the emperor's prerogative, no one anticipated a flood of new nobles from this direction. Only Sipiagin and Sheremetev were opposed, adhering to their position that state service could be performed not in a landowner's riding habit or in a frock coat but only in a civil servant's or officer's uniform.[45]

The conference's recommendation concerning the ennoblement of outstanding industrialists, financiers, professional men, scholars, and the like was rejected by the State Council on the grounds that such persons were already amply rewarded in material terms and had no need of further motivation or recognition.[46] Nicholas II concurred. The special conference's proposal concerning the *guberniia* societies' nomination of landowners for ennoblement was, on the other hand, adopted without change by a small majority of the State Council. A candidate was to have at least a secondary education, to own landed property in the *guberniia* which had been in his family's possession for a minimum of twenty years and two generations and was assessed for tax purposes at 30,000 rubles or more, to be a permanent resident in his district, and to have been active in community affairs. If a nomination received the support of two-thirds of the assembly of marshals and deputies it would be forwarded via the *guberniia* marshal, the governor, the minister of internal affairs, and the Committee of Ministers to the emperor.[47]

In his May 28, 1900, decree to the Senate, Nicholas II sided with the sizable minority of the State Council led by the four who had earlier opposed the ennoblement of landowners in the special conference.[48] Service to the state in a formal capacity remained, as it always had been, the basic criterion for membership in Russia's first estate. Although it was important to stem the decline in numbers of the landed nobility, it was even more important from the autocracy's point of view to maintain both the intimate connection between government service and noble status and the state's exclusive power to determine the membership of the nobility. Attempts just before and after the 1905 revolution to revive the idea of noble societies' co-opting nonnoble landowners proved fruitless.[49] There remained the possibility of informally and quietly bringing to the government's attention individual landowners worthy of ennoblement. This was the course urged upon the *guberniia* societies by Senator F. G. Terner, who as a member of the State Council had voted for giving the societies the right to nominate landowners for membership.[50]

ENROLLMENT IN GUBERNIIA NOBLE SOCIETIES

A NEWLY ennobled family was entitled to enroll in a *guberniia* society of nobility. If the family owned land, it would enroll in the society of the *guberniia* in which its property was located. Typically, however, such a family was headed by a landless *chinovnik*, who was permitted to enroll in the society of his choice.[51] Although a landless member of a noble society had no vote in the triennial elections, he was eligible for election to any office, and if he held a class rank or had completed secondary school, he had a vote on all matters other than elections. To preserve the societies from the inimical influence of ennobled *chinovniki* and their progeny, the defenders of privilege sought to erect barriers against their enrollment. In response to pressure from the *guberniia* societies over the previous decade, the government in 1895 raised the maximum fee charged for enrolling a new family in the *guberniia* genealogical register from 60 rubles, where it had stood since 1840, to 200 rubles. Pressure continued, however, for an even higher limit, in fact an exclusionary initiation fee, the Kaluga nobility calling for a fee of 10,000 rubles.[52] In January 1898 the special conference on the nobility proposed a differential enrollment fee: a maximum of 200 rubles for nobles owning real property in sufficient quantity to qualify for a direct vote in noble and *zemstvo* elections (125–475 *desiatiny* of land, depending on the *uezd*, or other real estate worth 15,000 rubles) and a maximum of 1,000 rubles for all others. In 1900 the special conference's recommendation was rejected by the State Council, which preferred to attack the problem directly by simply denying enrollment altogether to applicants whom the *guberniia* societies deemed undesirable.[53]

A truly radical solution to the problem of preserving the traditional character of the noble societies had been advocated in the 1890s by the publicist A. A. Planson: free and compulsory enrollment of all landowning nobles and the exclusion of all others. Individuals rather than families would be enrolled in the societies, and if an individual disposed of his land, he would automatically be stricken from the list of members. Noble landowners who failed to enroll in the society of the *guberniia* in which they owned property would be fined. The landed nobility and the *guberniia* societies would thus be one.[54] Planson's proposal would not have prevented newly ennobled *chinovniki* who had acquired even a morsel of land from joining the noble societies. It therefore proved much less attractive than the idea of giving the societies some control over the admission of new members.

The Code of Laws charged the *guberniia* deputy assemblies simply with verifying an applicant's proof of nobility and gave them no authority to pass on the applicant's desirability as a member. When the Vladimir deputy assembly rejected an applicant as undesirable in 1888, the Senate ruled in the applicant's favor and directed the assembly to enroll him. From 1885 on, a number of noble societies petitioned in favor of changing the law to permit them to refuse enrollment to undesirable applicants and to expel such persons who might have been enrolled in the past. The 1896 conference of marshals of nobility unanimously supported this idea.[55] Although the special conference on the nobility rejected the proposal to permit noble societies to expel members (the State Council subsequently supported the conference on this point), a majority did favor granting the societies the right to refuse enrollment to nobles who owned no real property in the *guberniia*. The rationale for this recommendation was that a noble who paid no real estate taxes to the *guberniia* society should not have access to the charitable funds supported by those taxes.[56]

In accepting the special conference's proposal in his *ukaz* of May 28, 1900, Nicholas II rejected the State Council's plan to give the noble societies the right to reject any applicant, whether or not he owned real property. The council had made the telling point that unsuitability for membership in a noble society was a matter of morals and character, and that there was no necessary connection between these qualities and the ownership of property. Furthermore, a propertied member enjoyed rights and a potential influence in the society's affairs, for good or ill, going far beyond those of a member who owned no real property.[57] The problem was that two contradictory concerns were at issue—the desire to bar from the *guberniia* societies newly ennobled *chinovniki*, who in a very small number of cases were landowners, and the desire to strengthen the identity of the societies as associations of noble landowners. Since the risk of including undesirable landed *chinovniki* was small, the emperor gave precedence to the latter goal while minimizing the extent of the discretionary authority given to the noble societies.

In June 1904 Nicholas II implemented the State Council's recommendation that a national genealogical register be established for nobles who were not enrolled in any *guberniia* society. Maintained by the Senate's master of heraldry, the national register served three distinct constituencies: landless nobles who had been refused membership in a *guberniia* society, nobles owning property in *gubernii* which lacked corporations of nobility, and Jewish nobles. Except for Jews, nobles enrolled in the national register (for the nominal fee of three rubles per family member) were still eligible for membership in a *guberniia* society, especially if they acquired land in a *guberniia* containing such a society.[58]

The problem of the eligibility of Jews for membership in the societies of nobility affords a glimpse into one of the more interesting contradictions in Russian society revealed by the discussion of the noble question. A Jewish noble in imperial Russia was a paradox. The status of noble was synonymous with the highest degree of legal privilege, while the status of Jew signified extreme deprivation of rights; only a convicted criminal possessed fewer legal rights than a Jew. And yet the 1897 census listed 108 Jewish hereditary nobles of both sexes and all ages in the fifty *gubernii* of European Russia, and another 88 elsewhere in the empire. The number was small—in fact only an infinitesimal fraction of the total Jewish population of 3.7 million in the fifty *gubernii*—but nonetheless demands explanation.

Jews in late nineteenth-century Russia occupied a singular legal position.[59] Together with such nomadic peoples as the Samoeds of the far north and the Kalmyks and Kazakhs of the steppes, Jews were classified as *inorodtsy*, that is, alien subjects of the emperor, as distinct both from the native population (a legal category including both Russians and non-Russian ethnic groups like the Poles and Georgians) and from resident foreign nationals. Despite this classification the law treated Jews as an inferior part of the native population, defining their status not in the Statute on *Inorodtsy* but in a separate section of the laws concerning social estates. Other *inorodtsy* were free to exchange their status for that of natives by abandoning their nomadic way of life and joining one of the estates into which the native population was divided; religion was irrelevant to this change of legal status. Jews, however, were already a sedentary people and were included in the estate system by being assigned to the *meshchanstvo*. In the fifty *gubernii* of European Russia in 1897, 95.0 percent of all Jews were *meshchane*; 1.7 percent had risen into the merchantry and 0.15 percent into the distinguished citizenry; 2.75 percent were peasants.[60] Jews were distinguished from other members of these estates by legal disabilities from which there was no escape except through conversion to Orthodoxy or some other officially recognized variety of Christianity.

Before the great reforms conversion was also the only means by which a Jew might enter the first estate, and such cases were extremely rare. Alexander II was the first emperor to confer noble status on Jews who had not converted.[61] Much more important was the partial opening of state service to Jews. Although Jews continued to be barred from the officer corps until 1917, Jews who held a medical or other advanced degree had been eligible since the 1860s for civil service appointments.[62] Jews who entered the bureaucracy in this way began their service in ranks in classes eight through ten. Class nine rank conferred personal nobility, and the receipt of the fourth degree of the order of St. Vladimir (until 1900) or a promotion to actual state councillor conferred hereditary nobility. It was by this route that the great majority of the 108 hereditary and 2,905 personal nobles listed as Jews in the 1897 census acquired their privileged status. The ratio of hereditary to personal nobles (1:27 for Jews as compared with 2:1 for the total population of European Russia) reflects both the fact that the first estate had been open to Jews for only a generation and the difficulty Jews faced in being promoted into the higher ranks.[63]

Like their coreligionists in other estates, Jewish nobles were distinguished by legal disabilities from gentile nobles. Senate rulings in 1898 and 1901 affirmed that Jewish hereditary nobles did not enjoy the general right of members of the first estate to enter the civil service and could do so only if they could meet the high educational qualifications imposed on Jews belonging to lower estates. In another case, however, the Senate decided in December 1898 that one Grinkrug, who had appealed the rejection of his membership application by the St. Petersburg deputy assembly, could not be denied enrollment since his noble status was unquestionable. A few Jews may have enrolled in noble societies before this; others had been refused membership but had not pursued the matter further. One previous rejection that had been appealed to the government had brought a ruling from Alexander III's minister of justice, N. A. Manasein, that the Moscow society of nobility was under no obligation to accept Jews as members.[64]

The Senate's finding in favor of Grinkrug provoked indignation among the defenders of privilege. On the basis of a technical irregularity, the St. Petersburg society refused a second time to enroll him. In November 1899 a nationwide conference of *guberniia* marshals called for legislation enabling noble societies to exclude Jews, and the following month N. V. Muraviev, Manasein's successor, made the same recommendation.[65]

Early in 1900 the Special Conference on the Affairs of the Noble Estate resolved the fundamental incompatibility between Judaism and nobility in Russia by proposing that in future "Jews may not acquire hereditary nobility by ranks in service and by the grant of orders." If the conference regarded bureaucrats of common birth in general as alien in upbringing and character to the treasured traditions of the first estate, it viewed Jewish bureaucrats as nothing short of a mortal threat to the nobility. As members of a religious community which had preserved its identity in the midst of Christian society for a millennium and a half, Jews would remain for all time a totally unassimilable element in the nobility. While the numbers of Jews ennobled through state service might never be large, their descendants would be very numerous, and they too would be nobles. Worse yet, if permitted to enroll in *guberniia* societies, Jews would "have a baneful, corrupting influence" on the corporate life and moral character of the first estate. Why the nobility should be so susceptible to the Jews' "anational, cosmopolitan views and strivings," their single-minded pursuit of material self-interest, and their spirit of intrigue—all so alien to the nobility's own values—was a question never raised in the conference.[66]

In contrast to the special conference, the majority of the State Council felt that the ennoblement of a small number of Jewish bureaucrats posed no threat to the first estate—as long as Jews were prevented from infiltrating the societies of nobility. The *guberniia* societies deserved the same degree of protection as was already accorded to the *zemstvos* and municipal *dumas*, from whose activities Jews had been excluded since 1890. Nicholas's *ukaz* of May 28, 1900, implemented the State Council's recommendation and prohibited the enrollment of Jewish nobles in the *guberniia* genealogical registers.

The settlement of the various aspects of the problem of membership in the first estate and in the societies of nobility at the turn of the century reflected the state's interest in reaffirming the nobility's identity as a service estate (maintenance of service as the principal path into the nobility—even for Jews—and of the links between the hereditary and personal nobilities) and in retaining sole control of the process of ennoblement (refusal to grant *guberniia* societies the right of co-optation). The settlement also reflected the concern of the defenders of the old social order to preserve the traditional character of the first estate, which they regarded as indissolubly linked to landowning (more restrictive qualifications for the ennoblement of bureaucrats and bourgeois, right of *guberniia* societies to reject landless nobles as members). In fact, the leitmotiv running through the long discussions of ennoblement, membership in the societies, and the relationship of the hereditary to the personal nobility was the same as that characterizing the debate over the measures treated in the preceding chapter: anxiety over the nobility's rapidly fading identity as a landowning estate. "Noble" and "landowner" had traditionally been virtually synonymous terms. This was less and less the case with every passing decade after serf emancipation.

CHANGING CAREER AND EDUCATIONAL PATTERNS

THE NOBILITY AND STATE SERVICE

I F nobles had traditionally been identified with landowning, they had been even more strongly identified with state service, especially during the seventeenth and eighteenth centuries, when Russia's estate system was receiving its final form. For a century after it ceased to be a legal obligation in 1762, state service, preferably the army, remained the only proper career for nobles driven by financial need or by personal ambition. Even those not so driven usually served long enough to secure the rank which brought with it status in the eyes of society and recognition from the state that they had done their duty. The typical noble of the first half of the nineteenth century was not only the owner of a modest estate but also a retired civil servant or army officer of modest rank.

After the great reforms, this picture changed, but not so radically as has been argued by Soviet and Western scholars who have focused on two phenomena only: the declining percentage of hereditary nobles among civil servants and officers and the declining percentage of landowners among the members of both groups. As in the case of noble landownership, the commonly cited statistics tell an important part of the story but by no means the whole story.

Between 1755 and the 1850s, despite an enormous increase of approximately 4,000 percent in the number of *chinovniki* and the growing professionalization of the bureaucracy in the first half of the nineteenth century, the percentage of nobles by birth in class ranks declined surprisingly little, from 50 percent to 44 percent. In the following four decades, however, while the total number of *chinovniki* rose by a much more modest 295 percent, the relative weight of the nobility dropped to 31 percent,

TABLE 18. NOBLES IN THE CIVIL SERVICE, 1755–1897

	NOBLES AS % OF ALL CHINOVNIKI			% OF ALL NOBLE CHINOVNIKI, 1897
RANKS	1755	1850s	1897	
Higher	87.6	77.6	71.6	3.3
Middle	76.9	52.5	37.9	60.9
Lower	34.4	33.2	22.3	35.8
All	49.8	43.7	30.7	100.0

Source: The percentages for 1755 are from S. M. Troitskii, *Russkii absoliutizm i dvorianstvo v XVIII v.* (Moscow, 1974), p. 215; for the 1850s, calculated from data in Walter M. Pintner, "The Evolution of Civil Officialdom, 1755–1855," in Walter M. Pintner and Don K. Rowney, eds., *Russian Officialdom* (Chapel Hill, 1980), pp. 192, 199–200; for 1897, from A. P. Korelin, "Dvorianstvo v poreformennoi Rossii (1861–1904 gg.)," *Istoricheskie zapiski 87* (1971): 160.

Note: For 1755 and the 1850s the higher ranks include classes one through five; the middle ranks, classes six through eight. For 1897 the higher ranks include classes one through four; the middle ranks, classes five through eight. Had class five been included in the higher ranks for 1897, nobles would have constituted a smaller percentage of all *chinovniki* in both the higher and middle ranks.

the largest decline occurring in the middle and lower ranks (see table 18).[1] By the end of the nineteenth century the great majority of *chinovniki*, except in the topmost ranks, were recruited from the sons of personal nobles (most of whom had themselves been bureaucrats or officers), clergy, distinguished citizens, and merchants. At the highest levels, however, nobles by birth retained a near monopoly of bureaucratic posts. In 1903 they constituted 98 percent of the State Council, 100 percent of the Committee of Ministers, 88 percent of the Senate, 84 percent of all deputy ministers and department heads, 100 percent of provincial governors, and 94 percent of vice governors. These figures were virtually identical with those for 1853.[2] An increasing number of these nobles, in all likelihood, were the sons or grandsons of ennobled *chinovniki*, but it is impossible to determine how many.[3]

The officer corps presents a somewhat different picture from the civil service. Starting from a higher level (86–88 percent) in the third through sixth decades of the eighteenth century,[4] the percentage of officers of noble birth declined over the next hundred years, particularly as a result of promotions of commoners from the ranks in wartime, to only 56 percent in 1864. In the next third of a century, however, the relative weight of the first estate suffered only a slight further loss (see table 19). Among generals and admirals (classes one through four) and staff officers (classes six through eight), the percentage of nobles actually *increased*. The explanation for the nobility's success in holding their own in the officer corps is twofold: the slight growth in the size of the corps (only 16 percent in thirty-three years)[5] and the first estate's privileged access to commis-

TABLE 19. NOBLES IN THE ARMY AND NAVY OFFICER CORPS,
1864 AND 1897

	NOBLES AS % OF ALL OFFICERS		% OF ALL NOBLE OFFICERS	
CLASSES	1864	1897	1864	1897
1–4	87.7	91.9	2.8	5.1
6–8	68.8	71.0	16.6	20.4
9–13	53.0	46.3	80.5	74.6
All	55.8	51.2	99.9	100.1

Source: Korelin, "Dvorianstvo," p. 157.

Note: In the late nineteenth century there were no military ranks in classes five or fourteen. Totals of 99.9 and 100.1 are due to rounding off.

sioned officer ranks through the cadet corps (a subject treated later in this chapter in the section on education). Far from being turned away from military careers by the growing professionalization of the officer corps, as reflected in the increase in the average length of service for all officers from ten years in the reign of Nicholas I to eighteen years in the first decade of the twentieth century,[6] nobles were part of this development. They may even be said to have turned it to their advantage by dominating the military schools that were so important a part of this growing professionalization.

The figures in table 19 would appear to contradict the bitter complaints of the defenders of privilege about the takeover of the officer corps by men of inferior breeding and character. Those complaints did, however, have some basis. Although the corps continued to be dominated by men of noble birth, at the end of the century three-fourths of all noble officers served in junior ranks, where they were in the minority, and over half of all noble army officers served in the infantry, where they were outnumbered by commoners three to two (see table 20). In the navy the sense of being inundated by commoners was much less acute. Engineers and technical officers, the great majority of whom were of nonnoble origin, were segregated in separate corps with distinctive ranks (for example, colonel instead of captain), while the line officers remained overwhelmingly of noble birth.[7]

Of the commoners who held almost half the positions in the officer corps at the end of the century, 46 percent were sons of personal nobles, that is, of staff and junior officers and middle-ranking bureaucrats.[8] Since three-fourths of all officers were the sons of either hereditary nobles or career state servants, it is misleading to characterize the corps on the eve of World War I as "a middle-class occupation." In fact, the hereditary nobility strengthened its position in the first decade of the

TABLE 20.   DISTRIBUTION OF NOBLE ARMY OFFICERS (ALL RANKS)
BY BRANCH OF SERVICE, 1895

BRANCH	NOBLES AS % OF ALL OFFICERS	% OF ALL NOBLE OFFICERS
Guards cavalry	96.3	3.7
Guards infantry	90.9	6.2
Guards artillery	89.4	1.2
Regular artillery	74.4	19.4
Regular cavalry	66.7	11.7
Engineers	66.1	4.8
Regular infantry	39.6	53.0
All	50.8	100.0

Source: Derived from data in P. A. Zaionchkovskii, "Soslovnyi sostav ofitserskogo korpusa na rubezhe XIX-XX vekov," Istoriia SSSR, no. 1(1973), p. 149.

new century; by 1912, nobles constituted 55.0 percent of all commissioned officers and 50.8 percent of those in junior ranks.[9]

During the second half of the nineteenth century, while the percentage of nobles among chinovniki was declining sharply and among officers was slipping only moderately, the historical connection between state service and landowning was subject to even greater pressure. In 1755 approximately 60–65 percent of all civil servants in class ranks had been landowners. A century later, after more than a generation of growing professionalization, only 25–28 percent owned land. Even in the higher ranks, where the proportion of nobles by birth declined only slightly, the percentage of landowners fell from 88–90 percent in 1755 to 57 percent in 1853 and only 29 percent in 1902.[10] The percentage of landowners in the State Council dropped from 93 percent to 57 percent between 1853 and 1903, in the Committee of Ministers from 94 percent to 59 percent, in the Senate from 73 percent to 48 percent, and among deputy ministers and department heads from 64 percent to 31 percent.[11] The divorce between the bureaucratic elite and the landowning elite, already in progress by mid-century, was carried much further during the next five decades.[12] Two forces were at work to produce this result, and it is impossible to weigh their relative importance. On the one hand, more of the top-ranking bureaucrats were probably coming from families that had made a career of state service for several generations past and had never been landowners. On the other hand, many of the bureaucratic elite were scions of landowning families that had recently exchanged their estates for stocks and bonds, as described in chapter 2.

Although data are lacking on landownership among the middle and lower ranks of the bureaucracy at the turn of the century, an estimate that 13–14 percent of all chinovniki were landowners in 1902 would not be unreasonable, if we assume that the ratio between the relative weight of landowners in the higher ranks and that of landowners in all ranks was the same in 1902 as it had been in 1853. Among the army elite, composed almost exclusively of nobles by birth, the proportion of landowners was even lower than in the comparable ranks in the civil service—only 17 percent among the first four classes in 1903–1904.[13]

While many members of the service elite held substantial property in forms other than land, at the lower levels of both the civil service and the officer corps most nobles undoubtedly "lived on their relatively modest salaries, having essentially no other sources of income of any kind." In fact, so dependent were these nobles on their government salaries that in the period 1892–1896 more than six hundred officers, most of them nobles, annually transferred to better-paying posts in the civil service despite the lesser prestige attached to the bureaucracy as opposed to the officer corps.[14]

It is time to turn from these demonstrations of the declining relative weight of both nobles and landowners in state service and to ask some different questions of the data. How many nobles and landowners were in state service in the middle and at the end of the nineteenth century, and what percentages do these numbers represent of the pool of eligible nobles and landowners? There were some 37,600 *chinovniki* in 1857 and 19,400 officers in 1864 born of noble fathers; by 1897 the number of noble *chinovniki* had risen to an estimated 104,400, that of noble officers only to 20,700.[15] Thus, despite the sharp decline in their relative weight in the bureaucracy, noble *chinovniki* increased in numbers by 178 percent in the second half of the century. Students of the nobility have made much of the decline but have failed to notice the increase. A 6 percent increase in the number of noble officers, meanwhile, was sufficient to keep to a minimum the nobility's loss in relative weight in a much more slowly expanding branch of state service. Both the bureaucracy and the officer corps, then, continued to attract large and growing numbers of nobles.

In order to complete our picture of the nobility's relationship to state service, it is necessary to compare the number of nobles who actually opted for a service career with the total number who might have done so. The number of nobles from European Russia serving in class ranks as a percentage of all adult males in the same region who had been born into the nobility was an estimated 17–19 percent for the civil service in 1857/1858 and 34–36 percent in 1897; for the military the ratio was 8–9 percent in 1863/1864 and 7 percent in 1897. The apparent doubling of the percentage of adult male nobles serving in the bureaucracy in the four decades following 1857/1858 is illusory. On the eve of serf emancipation the normal pattern for nobles involved retirement after no more than a decade in state service. The percentage of adult male nobles who at one time or another had been in service was probably two to three times the percentage that was serving in any given year. Thus, at the beginning of the great reforms, some 34–57 percent of all adult male nobles in European Russia served in bureaucratic class ranks at some point in their lives, and 16–27 percent in commissioned officer ranks. By 1897 the professionalization of both the bureaucracy and the officer corps had largely destroyed the traditional pattern of early retirement.[16]

Thus in the second half of the century the percentage of adult male nobles serving in the bureaucracy probably did experience a moderate decline, while in the officer corps the decline was much more dramatic. The opportunity to obtain a commission became increasingly restricted, as a result both of the very limited expansion of the corps and the less rapid turnover produced by longer terms of service. These factors are undoubtedly of greater significance in explaining the nobility's declining role than those cited by Manning: the shift in emphasis from the cavalry (favored by nobles) to the artillery (allegedly disdained by nobles) and the rising cost of serving in the guards and cavalry regiments.[17] In fact, the data in table 20 reveal that 77 percent of all noble officers in 1895 served in units other than the cavalry or the guards, and the number in the regular artillery alone almost equaled the total in the cavalry and the guards.

A similar picture, at least for the bureaucracy, is presented by the number of landowners in state service—although here we are working with fewer firm data and more educated guesses. Between 1853 and 1902 the number of landowners among the *chinovniki* grew from 21,000–24,000 to 44,000–48,000—an approximate doubling. In the officer corps there were an estimated 4,500–5,200 landowners in 1864 and 3,400 in 1903–1904—a decrease of roughly 30 percent. If we assume that all landowners in state service were nobles (an assumption that is almost totally warranted for the eve of serf emancipation and departs only slightly from reality for the end of the century), the percentage of male noble landowners in European Russia who were serving in the bureaucracy was 18–24 percent in 1864 and 40–51 percent in 1902; in the officer corps the figures are 4–5 percent for 1864 and 3–4 percent for 1902/1903. Correcting for the pattern of early retirement, we arrive at estimates for 1864 of 36–72 percent for the civil service and 8–15 percent for the military. Just as in the case of adult male nobles, the percentage of male noble landowners serving as *chinovniki* suffered a moderate decline, the percentage serving as commissioned officers, a precipitous one.

From the preceding calculations, we may reasonably conclude that in the early 1860s a majority, and perhaps even three-quarters, of all adult male nobles in European Russia and a similar proportion of male noble landowners were in state service at some point in their lives. By the turn of the century the percentage of adult male nobles who were in service had fallen to about 40, of male noble landowners to about 50. In the intervening years, of course, the pool of nobles eligible for service had greatly expanded, while the number of noble landowners had significantly contracted. It is clear that despite their declining relative weight among state servants, and especially among *chinovniki*, neither nobles nor noble landowners had by any means abandoned their historical role of servants of the state.

Despite the persistence among the first estate of the tradition of state service, the days when almost every nobleman also held both land and class rank were but a nostalgic memory in the minds of the *soslovniki*. In 1897, 36–38 percent of all adult male nobles by birth in European Russia were in service, and of these, two-thirds owned no land at all; of the remaining third, all but a small minority were absentee petty proprietors. Another 14–22 percent of adult male nobles were full-time landowners.[18] Thus, an aggregate of 50–60 percent of all adult male nobles were still to be found in the traditional roles of landowner and state servant. However, these roles, which in the eighteenth and early nineteenth centuries had been for the most part joined in the same individuals, were now being played almost entirely by nobles who were *either* landowners *or* career bureaucrats or officers, but not both. Almost all of those who were making careers in state service were as cut off from the nobility's traditional way of life, rooted in landownership, as were the significantly larger number (approaching half of all nobles) who were now playing roles other than the two historically identified with the nobility.

These new roles were in areas opened up by Russia's economic and social development since mid-century—the free professions, the arts, commerce, and industry—while one of them, that of revolutionary, was the product of Russia's political rigidity. Nobles were especially well represented among the new professional class whose numbers grew so rapidly from the 1860s—scientists, engineers, lawyers, doctors, teachers, professors, journalists, writers, and so on. In an 1880 sample of 826 university professors, 18 percent were sons of hereditary nobles.[19] The Moscow municipal census of 1882 listed close to 3,000 nobles (14–15 percent of all self-supporting hereditary nobles) as working in the free professions.[20] One of the minor characters in Tolstoi's *Anna Karenina*, set in the 1870s, comments on this trend. He is an unnamed retired army officer and resident landowner whom Levin encounters at the meeting of his *guberniia* noble assembly. This model of the traditional nobleman sees little future for his kind; his own son is not at all interested in managing the family estate but is bent upon a career as "a scholar or a scientist."[21]

The business world, too, attracted the persons, as well as the capital, of many nobles. The wealthier ones and those with the more distinguished pedigrees often joined the boards of directors of banks, railroads, and every other type of corporate enterprise. Such positions were sometimes the financial salvation of hard-pressed nobles like those in Terpigorev's *Oskudenie* and like Ranevskaia's brother, Gaev, in *The Cherry Orchard*, or of spendthrift aristocrats like Anna's brother, Prince Oblonskii, in Tolstoi's novel. Oblonskii anxiously pursues a sinecure on a corporate board which would pay 7,000–10,000 rubles a year while permitting him to continue in his government post, which carries a salary of only 6,000.[22]

His financial need is strong enough to overrule his qualms about being the first in his family to follow a career other than state service—worse yet, one that would necessitate his associating with Jewish railroad magnates. Oblonskii was in good company, for the list of aristocratic family names that graced the boards of directors of banks alone at the beginning of the twentieth century included Bobrinskii, Volkonskii, Vorontsov, Golitsyn, Meshcherskii, Obolenskii, Shakhovskoi, and Shcherbatov. Some, like the fictitious Oblonskii, were paid simply for the use of their names to lend respectability to the enterprises of upstart commoners; others took an active part in the affairs of their firms, in which they often were shareholders.[23] A small but important minority founded their own firms and played a leading role as captains of industry and commerce— like those who were in the front ranks of the Moscow, the St. Petersburg, and the southern entrepreneurial groups.[24]

In 1882 there were in Moscow 730 noble proprietors of commercial and industrial enterprises, frequently of a very modest size. Nor did the participation of nobles in the world of business halt there, for the municipal census of that year counted 2,413 nobles working in white- and blue-collar jobs in commerce, industry, and transport; including entrepreneurs, 15.5 percent of all self-supporting nobles worked in this sector. When these are added to the 14–15 percent in the free professions and the 4.9 percent at the bottom of the social ladder (domestic servants, prostitutes, and those with no declared occupation), it becomes apparent that more than a third of all self-supporting nobles in Moscow in 1882 were working in nontraditional occupations. Furthermore, a large part of the 24.7 percent who were *rentiers* drew some or all of their income from investments in the nonagricultural sector.[25] While Moscow undoubtedly had a higher percentage of nobles in nontraditional roles than did European Russia as a whole, over the next decade and a half the fifty *gubernii* caught up to and perhaps surpassed the level that the old capital had reached in this respect by 1882. Moscow itself, meanwhile, moved even further ahead.

While the role of revolutionary appealed to relatively few members of the first estate, without them the revolutionary movement would have been deprived of a good part of its leadership; Herzen, Bakunin, Pisarev,

Lavrov, Mikhailovskii, and Plekhanov were but the most prominent examples of the phenomenon of the noble revolutionary. A sample of 384 St. Petersburg radicals in the late 1870s indicates that 38 percent were children of noble landowners, and another 24 percent had noble bureaucrats for fathers.[26]

PREFERENTIAL TREATMENT OF NOBLES IN SERVICE

SO close was the historical association between nobility and state service in Russia that it could not be ignored even by those *soslovniki* most captivated by the image of nobility borrowed from the eighteenth-century West. Most had no desire to ignore the connection. For the great majority of traditionalists, a landed estate was the only proper setting for the life of a true noble, but state service was still the primary reason for the nobility's existence and for its privileged status. Along with ways to halt the growing separation of the first estate from its lands, accordingly, the *soslovniki* searched for means to restore the identification of noble status with state service. They approached the problem along two routes: direct restrictions and preferential treatment with respect to service careers, on the one hand, and the educational preparation of nobles for state service, on the other.

Neither the civil service nor the officer corps had ever been the exclusive preserve of the nobility. The state had nevertheless consistently demonstrated a preference for nobles in positions of responsibility. Peter the Great had given definitive form to this preference by making service a lifelong obligation for all noblemen, thereby seeking to satisfy the state's personnel needs without significant recourse to commoners. Even Peter's provision that all commoners who reached a certain level in the Table of Ranks should receive hereditary noble status and be "considered equal to the best older nobility in all dignities and privileges"[27] was not intended to encourage any influx of nonnobles into state service. It was rather an attempt to preserve the identification of service with noble status by co-opting into the first estate any commoners who managed to attain responsible posts in the army, navy, or civil bureaucracy. In fact in 1724 Peter forbade the appointment of commoners, except in unusual circumstances, to the lowest positions carrying class rank.[28]

No sooner had the state abolished compulsory service for nobles than it resorted to a number of measures designed both to restrict the entry of commoners into service and to give nobles a formal advantage over those commoners who did enter into competition with them. In the military, where nonnoble officers were relatively rare in the eighteenth century, beginning in 1764 noncommissioned officers of noble birth were given formal preference over commoners for promotion to the lowest commissioned officer rank, and the minimum term of service required before such a promotion was significantly shorter for nobles than for commoners. At the beginning of the nineteenth century, promotion of nonnobles to the officer corps was forbidden altogether; under Nicholas I commoners were again made eligible for commissioned officer rank, but normally only after twelve years of service, as compared with two years for nobles.

With the exception of the diplomatic corps, the civil service traditionally held less attraction than the military for the first estate; even before the abolition of compulsory service for nobles, commoners accounted for half of all *chinovniki*. Until the reign of Catherine the Great, the civil service had been open to all except proprietary serfs, but in the last quarter of the eighteenth century and the first quarter of the nineteenth the social base from which civil servants were recruited was progressively narrowed. From 1827 the civil service was normally open only to hereditary nobles and to the sons of the following: personal nobles, officers and *chinovniki*, Christian clergy, commercial councillors and merchants of the first guild, degree-holding scholars and artists, and chancellery clerks. The state's need for trained personnel, however, overrode its predilection for servitors from the privileged estates; the 1827 law permitted education to compensate for low social status. Except for Jews, anyone barred from entering the civil service on the basis of social origin was nevertheless eligible if he was a graduate of an institution of higher, and in some cases secondary, education.[29]

Holders of university or medical degrees and honors graduates of gymnasia received immediate appointments as *chinovniki*; all others entering the civil service began their careers as chancellery clerks. From early in the reign of Nicholas I, chancellery clerks were divided according to social origin. Hereditary nobles were eligible for promotion to the lowest class in the Table of Ranks after a much shorter apprenticeship than nonnobles—two years if they had only an elementary education and one year if they had a secondary education. *Chinovniki* of noble birth also enjoyed more rapid promotions than commoners. From 1834 the latter were required to spend roughly twice as long in class nine as nobles before being eligible for promotion to class eight. This was the step which until 1845 conferred hereditary noble status. The predominance of nobles at the upper and middle levels of the civil service in mid-century was due not so much to these formal advantages, however, as to the fact that "except at the lowest provincial levels, more nobles entered service and they entered at a higher level than nonnobles."[30]

The era of the great reforms eliminated virtually all the legal advantages nobles had enjoyed in entering and rising through class ranks in the military and civil service. Promotion to the lowest commissioned officer rank henceforth was based solely on examination. The civil service remained closed to the *meshchanstvo* and peasantry but was opened in 1861 to Jews holding a university or medical degree. And from 1856 all *chinovniki*, regardless of social estate, were subject to the same rules for promotion through the ranks. The only privileges hereditary nobles retained were (1) more rapid promotion from chancellery clerk to the lowest class rank for nobles who lacked a university or medical degree or an honors diploma from a gymnasium; (2) automatic promotion upon transfer from the military to the civil service and upon retirement, if at least one year had been served in the last rank held before retirement; and (3) the right to transfer from the civil to the military service without forfeiting class rank.[31]

Both in the civil and the military service nobles continued to enjoy informal advantages of education and social connections that facilitated their access to responsible positions, particularly from the early 1880s when the autocracy committed itself to a pro-noble policy. The relationship between education and service will be treated in the following section. A curious example of government policy was Minister of War P. S. Vannovskii's attempt to promote dueling among officers as a means of bolstering the image of the corps as a noble preserve. Borrowing from an 1874 law of the German Empire, the only Western power that still permitted officers' duels, Vannovskii directed in 1894 that a duel be mandatory if a military court found that an insult to an officer's honor could be satisfied in no other way. An officer refusing a duel under these circumstances had to resign his commission within two weeks or face dismissal. In the wake of this directive, the number of reported duels jumped from an annual average of one in the period 1876–1890 to between eighteen and nineteen in 1894–1904. Although jurists questioned the legality of duels among officers, Nicholas II strongly favored the practice, and as of 1897, duels were permitted as well between officers and civilians.[32] Measures such as this may well have helped to discourage commoners from contemplating a military career.

The defenders of the traditional order proposed a number of direct measures to restore the identification of the first estate with its historical calling. At one extreme stood Fadeev and Elishev, who in the 1870s and 1890s, respectively, urged the reinstitution of compulsory service for the nobility. This drastic step was necessary, they argued, if control of the civil service was to be wrested from the *raznochintsy*, men without any social estate identity. Although such people might possess the formal education (*obrazovanie*) required to perform their official duties, they could never acquire the moral character, the self-discipline, the selfless devotion to the state, that allegedly were the products of inheritance and of an upbringing (*vospitanie*) in the bosom of a noble family. Fadeev's and Elishev's proposal represented only a minority viewpoint among the *soslovniki* and received no serious support. Instead of coercing the nobility, a more popular approach was to protect its members from competition once they entered state service. In the 1890s Planson argued for the restoration of significant preferential treatment for nobles in service. *Moskovskie vedomosti* and *Grazhdanin* went further and called for the establishment of the nobility's monopoly over state service—a monopoly the first estate had never enjoyed even during their halcyon years in the eighteenth century.[33]

This was one aspect of the noble question on which the autocracy and the *soslovniki* did not see eye to eye. The state's urgent need for qualified civil servants could no longer be satisfied by relying primarily on the first estate. By the late nineteenth century a majority of adult male nobles were choosing careers other than service, and this trend was unlikely to be altered by any measure short of the reinstitution of compulsory service, an idea which had no significant backing inside or outside of government. The debate within the regime under Alexander III was rather over whether to retain or to diminish even further the existing minimal privileges accorded nobles in service.[34] No decision was reached, and in the early years of the next reign the whole question of revising the statute on the civil service was entrusted to a commission chaired until his death in 1899 by E. A. Perets, a former secretary of the State Council. So as not to duplicate the work of the Perets commission, the subject was excluded from the deliberations of the Special Conference on the Affairs of the Noble Estate. This did not prevent several of the members, including Sipiagin and Stishinskii, from voicing their concern lest the nobility's existing privileges in the civil service be eliminated. The draft statute submitted by the Perets commission in 1901 to the State Council compromised by opening the lower ranks of the service to all, regardless of social estate, who had a secondary education while reserving the middle and upper ranks primarily for "people who are not only seriously educated but properly brought up," that is, nobles.[35] Discussion of the draft continued for five years, and only the shock of revolution persuaded the government in October 1906 to extend "to all Russian subjects irrespective of social origin, except *inorodtsy*, the same rights in regard to state service as are enjoyed by members of the noble estate, all special privileges based on estate membership being hereby eliminated in the holding of government posts."[36]

The final triumph of legal equality over privilege in the civil service completed a process that was already very far along in the late nineteenth century. It was a process the state was clearly not willing to halt. The officer corps, on the other hand, offered more hope for the preservation of the nobility's dominance. The nobility's position there was much stronger than in the civil service, and the state was somewhat more disposed to assist. For this purpose the most promising approach was through the schools that prepared young men for a military career.

EDUCATION

IN the first half of the nineteenth century the bulk of new officers were graduates of the cadet corps, schools reserved exclusively for nobles which provided military training along with a general secondary education. The first cadet corps was established in 1731; by 1825 there were five—four in and around St. Petersburg and one in Moscow. They were attractive to the nobility because their graduates received officers' commissions immediately upon entry into service and because in the corps sons of nobles avoided the necessity of rubbing shoulders with commoners that they faced if they attended civilian secondary schools. In response (1) to the first estate's demand for more such facilities and their location closer to the nobility's homes and (2) to the state's desire to avoid commissioning any more officers from the rank-and-file soldiery than was absolutely necessary, fourteen additional noble cadet corps were established in the provinces under Nicholas I.[37]

In the mid-1860s all the cadet corps except for the Page Corps[38] and the Finland Cadet Corps were reorganized by Minister of War D. A. Miliutin into military gymnasia with a broadened curriculum, civilian teachers, and a student body drawn from all social estates. By the end of Alexander II's reign there were eighteen of the reformed military schools. Their graduates, along with those of the civilian secondary schools, underwent a further two or three years of preparation in the new higher military schools, also open to members of all social estates, before being commissioned as second lieutenants (class twelve in the Table of Ranks).[39]

Miliutin's successor, General Vannovskii, in 1882 restored their former designation of cadet corps to the military schools, discharged the civilian faculty, and assured the exclusive nature of the schools by establishing the following order of priority for accepting boarding students, who constituted the majority of the student body: (1) sons of officers, whether hereditary or personal nobles; (2) sons of hereditary nobles who held class rank in the civil service; and (3) sons of hereditary nobles who had been in neither the officer corps nor the bureaucracy, and of army chaplains and army doctors. Only the Siberian, Don, Second Orenburg, and Nikolaevsk cadet corps accepted members of other social groups. From the mid-1880s several of the higher military schools limited their student bodies to graduates of the cadet corps and thus, in effect, almost exclusively to nobles. The naval cadet corps established in 1894 in St. Petersburg admitted first, sons of naval officers, and second, sons of hereditary nobles not in the naval officer corps.[40]

Miliutin's efforts to democratize the military gymnasia caused a growth of 80 percent in total enrollment between 1870/1871 and 1880/1881, but the relative weight of sons of nobles and *chinovniki* in both the gymnasia and the progymnasia fell only slightly—from 89 percent to 83 percent. With the reversal in policy under Alexander III, total enrollment in the cadet corps was stabilized at the 1881 level until the end of the century. Hereditary nobles alone constituted 62–71 percent of the students in the cadet corps in the years 1881–1897 and 54–55 percent of those in the higher military schools.[41] These figures explain the continued dominance of nobles in the higher and middle ranks of the officer corps, for in the last two decades of the century, six years of study in a cadet corps followed by two years in a specialized higher military school was the standard preparation for those who rose to staff or general officer rank. Those destined to end their careers as junior officers, by contrast, were in large part the product of the two-year *junker* schools created by Miliutin to prepare for the officers' examination noncommissioned officers and others lacking a complete secondary education. Only 27 percent of the students in the *junker* schools in 1897 were hereditary nobles.[42]

The restrictive admissions policy introduced in 1882 and the continued dominance of students of noble birth in the cadet corps left the defenders of privilege unsatisfied. They complained that in the competition for the limited number of places in the corps sons of nobles were increasingly at a disadvantage because the sons of merchants could better afford the not inconsiderable expense involved. The merchantry, lacking the nobility's inherited traits of character, were alleged to be poor officer material. If not checked, warned an anonymous publicist in 1897, alluding to the Dreyfus affair, this trend would produce the same results in Russia as it already had in the French and Austrian armies. There even Jews, the quintessential merchants, had risen into positions of command, and the outcome had been "colossal scandal."[43] Expanding opportunities for nobles to receive an education in the cadet corps would be the best protection for Russia against a like fate. Defenders of the traditional order saw the cadet corps not only as the training ground of future officers but as the ideal type of school, emphasizing the traditional virtues of honor, loyalty, and service; stressing physical and moral development as well as booklearning; and providing a properly supervised environment where young noblemen could live and learn in the company of their peers. Sharing this broader view of the corps' mission, several noble assemblies and the 1896 conference of *guberniia* marshals called for the inclusion of agricultural science in the corps' curriculum.[44]

In fact only 25 percent of all noble boys in secondary school in 1897 were in the cadet corps, but whether this was primarily by choice, for want of an adequate number of places, or because of cost is impossible to say.[45] Total annual charges for a boarding student, whether in a cadet corps or a civilian gymnasium, in the 1890s ran between 400 and 500 rubles.[46] At the turn of the century in the thirty-seven *gubernii* with noble elections three-quarters of all noble landholdings were too small to qualify their owners for a direct vote; that is, they were worth less than 15,000 rubles and could therefore be assumed to yield an annual income of under 750 rubles. The strain that the education of even a single son imposed on the budget of most landed noble families is readily apparent.

The remedy was obvious: the expansion of the corps to accommodate more students and the provision of financial aid for the sons of nobles who could not afford the cost of a military education. Proposals along these lines were submitted by numerous assemblies of nobility and by the 1896 conference of *guberniia* marshals and endorsed by the Special Conference on the Affairs of the Noble Estate in 1898.[47] Witte professed to sympathize with the special conference's rationale that sons of nobles, and landed nobles in particular, because of their superior moral and physical development and their families' tradition of service, provided the best officer material. He questioned, however, whether the state's existing investment in the cadet corps was yielding the anticipated return. In recent years 10 percent of each graduating class of the cadet corps and the higher military schools had been choosing careers other than the military, and over six hundred officers annually had been transferring from active service to the reserves; the civil service, where salaries were higher and life easier than in the military, was attracting graduates of both the cadet corps and the higher military schools. Simply providing additional places in the cadet corps for sons of nobles would not, according to Witte, necessarily increase the number of nobles entering the officer corps. The minister of finance proposed either a ten-year period of compulsory service in the army for graduates of military schools or a ban on their transfer into the reserves before reaching a certain rank, together with the curtailment of the privileges they currently enjoyed if they transferred to the civil service.

Minister of War A. N. Kuropatkin, who had been invited to participate in the conference's discussion of education, responded to Witte with the arguments that current plans to raise the pay of officers would slow down the exodus into the bureaucracy and that in any case officers made excellent civil servants. The conference endorsed Kuropatkin's proposal to establish two new cadet corps, thereby bringing the total to twenty-three in addition to the Page Corps and the Finland Cadet Corps,[48] and 415 full scholarships for sons of hereditary nobles who had not been officers. Witte agreed to fund these scholarships at the rate of 450 rubles for a total of 186,750 rubles annually. Added to the existing 585 full scholarships in the cadet corps, funded by endowments given by various societies of nobility and private philanthropists, the new scholarships meant that one of every six nobles in the cadet corps would have his way completely paid. The conference's draft was approved in all details by the State Council and on May 25, 1899, by the emperor. The awarding of the scholarships was to be shared by the cadet corps and the noble societies, and the state would provide matching funds for any new scholarships established by societies of nobility for use in civilian secondary and higher schools. In awarding both types of scholarship, the societies were to give preference first to sons of nobles who had held elective noble or *zemstvo* office or served as *zemskie nachalniki*, and second to sons of "needy members of the society who lived on their estates and occupied themselves with agriculture."[49]

Two new corps were established in 1899 in Warsaw and Odessa, two more the following year at Sumy in Kharkov *guberniia* and at Khabarovsk in the Far East, and another in 1902 at Vladikavkaz in the North Caucasus. But the expansion of enrollment in the cadet corps by 20 percent between 1897 and 1903 benefited commoners more than nobles, for the percentage of hereditary nobles among the students fell steadily from 67 percent in 1897 to 62 percent in 1903.[50]

A. A. Arseniev, Tula marshal of nobility, turned the special conference's attention to the plight of impoverished noble landowners who could not afford to give their children an elementary, let alone a secondary, education. Before the army reform of 1874 the sons of such families could always make their way in the world by joining the army; as nobles serving in the ranks they would receive preferential consideration for officers' commissions. After the reform, however, all officer candidates, regardless of social estate, had to take an examination which presumed at least an elementary education. In March 1899 Arseniev proposed the establishment at government expense of three-year elementary schools for sons of needy nobles; their graduates would be admitted automatically to the eleven existing two-year *junker* schools to prepare for the officers' examination. Kuropatkin was not enthusiastic over either the likely quality of education in the projected schools or its actual quality in the *junker* schools. The conference approved his proposal to substitute for both Arseniev's elementary schools and the *junker* schools new five-year rural boarding schools with a curriculum equivalent to that of the five lower grades of the seven-year cadet corps. The government would provide up to 150,000 rubles to build each school and 50–75 percent of its annual operating expenses, the rest to be borne by the society of nobility which had petitioned for the school's establishment and selected its pupils. Although passed by the State Council and approved by Nicholas II on April 2, 1903, the plan for the so-called cadet schools was never implemented because of lack of interest on the part of the *guberniia* societies.[51]

In the minds of traditionalists the cadet corps may have been the ideal type of school for the first estate, but in fact only 25 percent (5,900) of all hereditary noblemen's sons attending secondary schools on January 1, 1897, were enrolled in military schools; 56 percent (13,200) were enrolled in boys' gymnasia and progymnasia and 19 percent (4,600) in technical/ vocational schools.[52] The Russian gymnasium (*gimnaziia*), an academic secondary school with a curriculum including Greek and Latin, dated from the middle of the eighteenth century but occupied a central position in the educational system only from the first quarter of the nineteenth. At that time a gymnasium was established in almost every *guberniia* capital to prepare students for the newly expanded university system. Under Nicholas I both gymnasia and universities were reserved primarily for the sons of hereditary and personal nobles and *chinovniki*. In the 1860s two new types of secondary school were created. The progymnasium, offering a course of study identical to that of the first four years of the seven-year gymnasium and located for the most part in *uezd*, rather than *guberniia*, seats, produced graduates qualified for direct entry into the civil service. The technical/vocational (*realnoe*) school was a seven-year institution like the gymnasium but one in which modern languages were substituted for Greek and Latin and the emphasis was on the physical sciences, mathematics, engineering, bookkeeping, and in general, subjects of a practical orientation. Graduates of the technical/vocational schools were expected to go directly into business or industry or, in a few cases, on to higher education in a technical institute.

Admission to all three types of schools, and to the universities, was divorced from considerations of social origin in the early 1860s, with a resultant decline in the percentage of students from noble and *chinovnik* families (see table 21). In the reign of Alexander III the government restricted access to secondary and higher education for members of the lower social orders, thereby stemming the decline in the percentage of sons of nobles and *chinovniki* in the student body of the universities and, to a lesser extent, of the technical/vocational schools and reversing the trend in the gymnasia and progymnasia. Under Nicholas II, admissions policies once again gave little weight to estate membership. At the beginning of 1897 hereditary nobles alone accounted for 20 percent of the pupils in the boys' gymnasia and progymnasia and 15 percent of those in the technical/vocational secondary schools.[53] If the balance between hereditary nobles, on the one hand, and sons of personal nobles and *chinovniki*, on the other, remained stable over time, then one out of three gymnasium students was a hereditary noble in 1853, but only one out of six in 1904. In the universities the hereditary nobility constituted 23 percent of the student body in 1880 and the same percentage in 1897.[54]

What is striking about the figures on the relative weight of nobles in nonmilitary secondary and higher education is not that they reveal a decline after the democratizing reforms of the 1860s but that the decline was not much more precipitous. This is particularly true in view of the very substantial expansion of total student enrollments under both Alexander II and Nicholas II—an increase of 405 percent between 1855 and

TABLE 21. HEREDITARY AND PERSONAL NOBLES AND NONNOBLE
CHINOVNIKI AS A PERCENTAGE OF ALL STUDENTS, 1853–1904

YEAR	BOYS' GYMNASIA AND PROGYMNASIA	TECHNICAL/ VOCATIONAL SECONDARY SCHOOLS	UNIVERSITIES
1853	80		65 (1855)
1865	70		67 (1864)
1870–1871	60–65	55–60	—
1875	52	50	46
1880–1881	48	41	47
1890–1891	56	40	—
1894	56	37	46 (1895)
1897–1898	52	36	52 (1900)
1904	44	31	—

Source: Data for the gymnasia and technical/vocational schools are from Nicholas Hans, *History of Russian Educational Policy (1701–1917)* (London, 1931), p. 236 (for 1853, 1865, 1875, 1894, 1904), and from L. G. Beskrovnyi, *Russkaia armiia i flot v XIX veke* (Moscow, 1973), pp. 180–81 (for 1870–1871, 1880–1881, 1890–1891, 1897–1898); for the universities, from Allen Sinel, *The Classroom and the Chancellery: State Educational Reform in Russia under Count Dmitry Tolstoi* (Cambridge, Mass., 1973), p. 101 (for 1864 and 1881), from L. V. Kamosko, "Izmeneniia soslovnogo sostava uchashchikhsia srednei i vysshei shkoly Rossii (30–80-e gody XIX v.)," *Voprosy istorii*, no. 10 (1970), p. 204 (for 1855 and 1875), and from V. R. Leikina-Svirskaia, *Intelligentsiia v Rossii vo vtoroi polovine XIX veka* (Moscow, 1971), pp. 60, 62–64 (for 1880, 1895, 1900).

Note: Dashes indicate that data were unavailable to me.

1904 in the boys' gymnasia and progymnasia, and 488 percent in the universities.[55] The relatively moderate decline in the nobility's share of total enrollments reflects not only the first estate's continuing easy access, as compared with other social orders, to secondary and higher education, but also their rising appetite for schooling. Between 1880 and 1897 the absolute number of hereditary nobles enrolled in universities increased by 90 percent, which is considerably more than twice the growth in the size of the first estate during the same period.[56] The nobility's growing interest in higher education is also revealed by the fact that in the 1897 census 19.4 percent of all male nobles and *chinovniki* aged twenty to fifty-nine (that is, those who were born after 1837 and therefore graduated from secondary school after the accession of Alexander II) were reported as having had some nonmilitary education beyond the secondary level, compared with only 11.7 percent of those sixty and older.[57] This increasing demand for extended formal education was a function of the changing nature of Russian society in general and of the first estate in particular. As one contemporary observed, in postreform Russia "membership in a particular estate had much less significance, even in the eyes of the law, than the attainment of a given educational level."[58] Even in state service, educational qualifications had come to have roughly the same value as membership in the first estate, and one way nobles retained their dominant position in the higher bureaucratic ranks was by acquiring much more formal education than previously.[59] And the professional and business careers to which the nobility turned increasingly after the great reforms required more extensive schooling than did either state service or estate management as traditionally approached by Russian nobles. Thus the fact that for every noble son attending a cadet corps in 1897 there were three attending nonmilitary secondary schools should be seen not only as evidence of a shortage of available places in the schools beloved of traditionalists[60] but also as the result of a preference among many noble youngsters or their parents for a broader education, perhaps leading to university and a career in the free professions.

Most defenders of privilege regarded the gymnasia with intense suspicion. Open to the sons of ambitious merchants, bureaucrats, and worse, the gymnasia were a powerful instrument of social leveling. Staffed with commoners and filled with the children of commoners, the schools had an enormous potential for corrupting the tender minds and characters of noble youths. In addition to demanding the expansion of opportunities for the education of nobles in the cadet corps, the *soslovniki* argued for changes in the gymnasia themselves.

In an attempt to overcome the nobility's prejudice against sending their sons to school together with the sons of nonnoble *chinovniki*, merchants, and clergy, the government had from the beginning of the nineteenth century permitted the noble societies to maintain dormitories (*pansion-priiuty* or *internaty*) exclusively for the use of noble students whose parents were unable to take up residence during the school year in the *guberniia* capitals, where the gymnasia were located. By mid-century such dormitories served forty-seven of the seventy gymnasia; boarding students wore a distinctive uniform and sat apart from the other pupils in class.[61] The dormitories were abolished in the more liberal atmosphere of the 1860s. Although two traditionalist ministers of education, D. A. Tolstoi and I. D. Delianov, encouraged their revival in the 1870s and 1880s, dormitories had been reestablished by noble societies in only seven *gubernii* by the beginning of Nicholas II's reign.[62] Dormitories for nobles appealed very strongly to publicists for the cause of privilege. Elishev argued that government-funded, supervised dormitories in all *gubernii* with noble societies would serve two essential functions. They would provide moral supervision for noble youths forced to live away from home—youths who currently were compelled to share lodgings with the sons of their fathers' former cooks and footmen and who, lacking proper adult supervision, were liable to develop such vices as reading the works of Chernyshevskii, Pisarev, and Tkachev. Dormitories would also be very useful in countering the baneful influence of the schools themselves, which by admitting the sons of rootless and ambitious *raznochintsy* were exerting "a corrupting influence on noble children."[63]

At least seven noble societies in 1897 favored the expansion of the system of dormitories for nobles, and the special conference saw them as a means of giving noble youth enrolled in gymnasia the same desirable home-type environment provided in the cadet corps. The conference recommended the establishment of dormitories in all *gubernii* in which noble elections were held and justified government financing by arguing that the students who would benefit were future state servants. Witte was sympathetic and offered government aid up to 100,000 rubles to each *guberniia* society to establish a dormitory and up to one-half the annual operating expenses, the balance to be raised by the society itself. The State Council proved even more generous, and under the provisions of the law of May 25, 1899, the government paid the full cost of construction and one-half the operating expenses — a total of 2 million rubles in 1900 and 1 million each in 1901 and 1902.[64] Administered jointly by the Ministry of Education and the noble society of its *guberniia*, each dormitory served noble boys enrolled in any civilian secondary school in its town. Priority in admission together with full room-and-board scholarships went to sons of local nobles who had held elective noble or *zemstvo* office or served as *zemskie nachalniki*.

As important as dormitories for nobles were in isolating them from the bourgeois types who were predominant in the student body of the gymnasia, other measures were called for to deal with the *soslovniki*'s criticism of the schools' teaching and administrative personnel and course content. Planson in particular among the publicists charged gymnasium and technical/vocational school teachers, inspectors, and directors, men for the most part of lowly birth, with discriminating against their noble charges and in favor of children of nonnoble parents in return for bribes and gifts from the latter. Planson suggested that the noble societies and the *guberniia* marshals be given a role in supervising secondary education in order to secure fair treatment of students from the first estate.[65] Although the 1896 marshals' conference and at least five *guberniia* societies in 1897 took the same position and made similar recommendations, the special conference never took up the allegations of discrimination or the question of extending the nobility's supervisory role to civilian secondary education. It did, however, echo the frequent criticism of the classical curriculum of the gymnasia, which one *soslovnik* publicist denounced as being imbued with "the formal and soulless Roman logic" which underlay the economic and political system of the West rather than with "sensible and honest Russian thinking."[66] The conference's views on this point and its call for more technical/vocational schools were seconded by the State Council but produced no results.

If the segregation of nobles from commoners in secondary schools was a desirable goal, exclusive schools for nobles were an even more efficacious instrument than dormitories. Although the establishment of gymnasia solely for the nobility had been suggested in the past and was requested by five *guberniia* assemblies in 1897, the idea was not taken up in the special conference. A. N. Kulomzin, executive secretary of the Committee of Ministers, and A. A. Arseniev did argue for more institutions on the model of the Alexander Lycée and the School of Jurisprudence—nine-year schools combining secondary and a limited higher education and open only to hereditary nobles—but the rest of the conference members felt that this type of school could not provide an education equal to that offered in the universities.[67]

By the end of the nineteenth century, education in Russia had long since lost its former primary function of training noblemen for state service. Even the autocracy now recognized the usefulness of an educated populace for military effectiveness and economic growth. And if the lower orders were discovering education's uses in a society in which achieved roles were displacing ascribed roles as determinants of social status, the nobility was also embracing education in preparation for new careers apart from state service—careers in which estate distinctions were irrelevant. The proposals of the *soslovniki* stemmed from their refusal to accept the situation that had developed in education, but they received little support from either the state or the rank and file of the nobility. Both the government's position and the visionary nature of the traditionalists' approach to education are clearly revealed in the following excerpt from a memorandum of March 6, 1899, written in response to requests received by the special conference for the establishment with government funding of exclusive boarding schools for noble girls. The author was Count N. A. Protasov-Bakhmetev, curator of the Imperial Alexander Lycée and director of the Fourth Department of His Imperial Majesty's Own Chancellery for the Institutions of the Empress Maria, an agency which administered a number of educational institutions for women:

From a pedagogical point of view it would hardly be useful to charge the schools with the task of reinforcing the separation of the estates from one another when that separation is so weakly maintained in real life. On the one hand the ranks of the hereditary nobility are constantly being filled with new people from the service estate; on the other, the hereditary nobility is constantly mixing with the merchantry and the bureaucracy through marriage. Furthermore, since serf emancipation the country seat and landed estate have been transformed into a form of capital, easily transferable from one owner to another. It therefore seems to us that one can scarcely prepare noble girls for life mainly in a country seat, when for the majority of nobles the country seat no longer exists.[68]

The world the defenders of privilege were trying to preserve was slipping away, with the willing assistance of much of the nobility, faster than the traditionalists were ready to admit.

FURTHER EXERCISES IN FUTILITY: ATTEMPTS TO RESTORE NOBLE LEADERSHIP IN THE COUNTRYSIDE

THE COUNTERREFORMS OF ALEXANDER III

A CRUCIAL element of the old order in Russia was the paternalistic role the nobility had played until the 1860s vis-à-vis the peasantry in particular and rural affairs in general. The members of the first estate had played this role both individually as serfowners and corporately through their *guberniia* societies and the officials elected by the latter. The virtual elimination of this role as a consequence of the great reforms was a central concern of traditionalists, and much of their energy was devoted to finding means of restoring the nobility's role in the countryside in one or another form.

As early as the beginning of the 1870s, General Fadeev urged that the administration of rural areas "should be entirely in the hands of persons elected by the nobility," or at the very least persons appointed by the government from among the local nobility.[1] The realization of this proposal had to await the more favorable climate of opinion fostered by Alexander III's new course. In 1884 P. A. Krivskii, Saratov *guberniia* marshal of nobility, raised in earnest the idea of a new type of official, to be recruited from the local nobility, who would exercise tutelage over the peasantry. His suggestion found favor among some of the traditionalist provincial governors, *zemstvo* leaders, and marshals of nobility added to the Kakhanov commission on the reform of local government in November 1884.[2]

Among this group was A. D. Pazukhin, who after the disbanding of the Kakhanov commission in May 1885 was recruited by Minister of Internal Affairs Tolstoi to work on strengthening estate distinctions in local government, as Pazukhin had proposed in his celebrated January

1885 article.[3] Pazukhin's 1886 plan for the establishment of the office of *zemskii nachalnik* was very close in spirit to Krivskii's suggestion, and the latter, in fact, participated in the discussion of Pazukhin's draft within the Ministry of Internal Affairs. A majority of the State Council accepted the idea of restricting the new post to nobles but rejected two basic features of Pazukhin's plan: the merging of administrative and judicial authority in a single official and the limitation of his jurisdiction to the peasantry alone, in isolation from the other inhabitants of the *uezd*. The council's majority feared that the new office would be taken (as, indeed, it was meant) as "a measure aimed at the restoration, albeit in altered form, of those rights of the nobility over the peasantry that were lost with the emancipation of the serfs and in any case as a law inimical to the peasantry's equality of rights and their self-government."[4] The council adopted instead by a three-to-one majority a proposal by Minister of the Imperial Court Vorontsov-Dashkov to create an *uezdnyi nachalnik* as a kind of mini-governor, with authority over the entire population in his district, regardless of social estate. Subordinate to the *uezdnyi nachalnik* would be *uchastkovye nachalniki*, with similar authority at the sub-*uezd* level. Neither of the new posts would include judicial authority.[5] Guided by Tolstoi and Meshcherskii, Alexander III sided with the minority of the State Council and enacted Pazukhin's project on July 12, 1889.

The *zemskie nachalniki* replaced not only the *uezd* and *guberniia* bureaus for peasant affairs as overseers of the peasantry's estate institutions but also the justices of the peace elected by the *uezd zemstvo* assemblies. Each *zemskii nachalnik* was responsible for a district (*uchastok*) of which there might be as many as five in an *uezd*. He was nominated jointly by the governor and the *guberniia* marshal of nobility (after the latter had consulted with the *uezd* marshal and the members of the *guberniia* noble assembly from the district in question) and appointed by the Ministry of Internal Affairs. Eligibility for nomination was ideally restricted to former marshals of nobility who had served at least three years and to hereditary nobles aged twenty-five and older who owned at least one-half the quantity of land necessary for a personal vote in noble and *zemstvo* elections and either had a higher degree or had served three years as an arbiter of the peace, a member of a local bureau for peasant affairs, or a justice of the peace. In the absence of qualified hereditary nobles, personal nobles could be appointed if they met certain property and educational or service requirements. If candidates were lacking from both the local hereditary and personal nobility, the Ministry of Internal Affairs could appoint nobles from other *uezdy* or *gubernii* and even commoners. The operation of the 1889 law was restricted to European Russia minus both the Baltic region and the nine western *gubernii* where noble elections had been suspended.[6]

From its establishment the new institution did not satisfy the more outspoken *soslovniki*. Meshcherskii's *Grazhdanin* insisted that the *zemskie nachalniki* should be nominated by the assemblies of nobility rather than by the governors and *guberniia* marshals, many of whom were accused of being too liberal to be trusted with this charge. *Moskovskie vedomosti* questioned whether the *zemskii nachalnik* had been given sufficient authority to keep order among the peasants.[7]

The opponents of privilege offered a different type of criticism. *Vestnik Evropy* rebutted the arguments in Pazukhin's 1885 article by reminding its readers that the nobility had scarcely distinguished itself by its participation in local government in the century preceding serf emancipation. A landowner writing anonymously in the same journal in 1887 pointed out the illogic in restricting local offices to nobles when the upper levels of the civil service were open to commoners. Nor did it make any greater sense to attempt to restore the nobility's monopoly of local government when they had long since lost their monopoly of landowning. To restructure local government in this way in order to stem the nobility's exodus from the land, as Pazukhin proposed, would be worse than futile.[8]

A similar criticism of the new office was voiced shortly after its establishment by one much more sympathetic to the cause of privilege than those who contributed to and read *Vestnik Evropy*. In the words of F. D. Samarin, marshal of nobility in Bogorodsk *uezd* of Moscow *guberniia* and a nephew of the famous Slavophile:

> It would be a great delusion to think that by this means the state can to any extent prop up the noble estate. There is no doubt but that in *uezdy* where the nobility is still fairly numerous and not totally ruined, all elective local offices remain in its hands. In other areas, even under the operation of the new law, many vacancies in the office of *zemskii nachalnik* can scarcely be filled without resorting to persons of nonnoble origin.

Even a noble from another *uezd* or *guberniia*, appointed for want of a qualified local noble, "will, in the absence of any connection with the locality, be as much a *chinovnik* as any other," Samarin pointed out.[9]

Some years later Count Witte delivered a much more cynical verdict on the whole concept of the *zemskii nachalnik*. He condemned as an "illusion" the notion that there had ever been in Russia, much less that there still existed, a sufficient number of "honorable" noble landowners enjoying local "general esteem" so that even one such could be found "to watch over, judge, and govern the peasants" in each of the new *uchastki*.[10]

Numbers did indeed pose a problem. In January 1889 the emperor had argued that rural justices of the peace had to be abolished "in order to assure that the necessary number of reliable land captains will be available."[11] Despite the elimination of the justices of the peace, it still proved impossible to recruit the 2,200 to 2,300 men required from the pool of local noble landowners who could meet the service or educational qualifications. The result was the appointment of noble landowners in reduced circumstances to whom the salary of 1,600 rubles plus 600 rubles for expenses was the most appealing part of the job; of retired army officers, strangers to the community, "who have appeared from God knows where"; and of bureaucrats, some of them not even nobles. By 1893 *Grazhdanin* was contemptuously characterizing *zemskie nachalniki* as "*chinovniki*, automatons, living from day to day, reading official *guberniia* circulars, scribbling away, filing their busy work in the proper places."[12] A 1903 government survey of ten *gubernii* containing 584 *zemskie nachalniki* confirmed the dearth of qualified nobles: 21 percent of the holders of the post lacked a secondary education, and 5 percent were neither hereditary nor personal nobles.[13] A recent estimate has it that the proportion of local noble landowners among the *zemskie nachalniki* declined from two-thirds or more in the early 1890s to "well under half" by 1905 and fell even further in the following years.[14]

The establishment of the office of *zemskii nachalnik* by no means laid to rest the traditionalists' desire to restore to the first estate control over local administration. Only the paucity of landed nobles in many *uezdy* prevented the St. Petersburg nobility in 1898 from calling for a noble monopoly of local offices; they proposed instead that legal priority be given to local nobles in making appointments to these posts. Such considerations did not stop the publicist N. P. Semenov in the same year from urging the restoration of local government exclusively to hereditary nobles, lest the nobility lose its historical identity as a service estate.[15]

As late as 1904, nothing daunted by the proven difficulty of recruiting qualified *zemskie nachalniki*, the publicist Vladimir Paltov proposed a detailed plan for 30,000 unsalaried officials called *prikhodskie nachalniki* (parish captains) to be elected by the *uezd* assemblies of nobility from among the nobles of the parish who owned at least two hundred *desiatiny* of land. Where a sufficient number of such nobles did not exist, the government would grant state land or foreclosed noble properties in parcels of two hundred *desiatiny* to noble *chinovniki* so that they might qualify for the office. The *prikhodskii nachalnik* would assume primary responsibility for administrative, tax-collecting, judicial, and police functions in the parish, assisted by officials elected by the noble landowners, clergy, and heads of peasant households. The existing peasant *volost* and *uezd* police officials would be abolished, and the *uezd zemstvo* assembly would be replaced by an assembly of the *prikhodskie* and *zemskie nachalniki* of the *uezd* chaired by the marshal of nobility.[16] Paltov's plan was as clear a statement as could be wished of the traditionalists' vision of an ideal rural society freed of the influence of merchants, *kulaks*, and nonnoble *chinovniki* and confided to the care of noble landowners exercising public authority in a paternalistic manner.

After the 1905 revolution, the office of *zemskii nachalnik* underwent two important changes. The October 1906 *ukaz* that "all special privileges based on estate membership [are] hereby eliminated in the holding of government posts" was recognized by the Ministry of Internal Affairs in May 1913 as applicable to the position of *zemskii nachalnik*. The office thereby lost its special character and became just another bureaucratic appointment. The same 1906 *ukaz* also curtailed the *zemskii nachalnik*'s authority (along with that of the head of the household, the commune, and the *volost*) over the individual peasant. And in June 1912 the reestablishment of rural justices of the peace with jurisdiction over peasants and nonpeasants alike deprived the *zemskii nachalnik* of the judicial functions he had exercised since 1889. Implementation of this last change was slow, however, especially after the war began, and had affected no more than twenty *gubernii* by 1917.[17]

While the tutelage of noble landowners over the peasantry was the ideal of the traditionalists, the *zemstvo* was anathema to them. Fadeev spoke for many *soslovniki* when he condemned the *zemstvo* as the embodiment of the principle of *vsesoslovnost* (the mixing of social estates), a principle which society was bound to reject "as a scandalous, fictitious, and dangerous falsehood against Russian reality."[18]

The idea of restructuring the *zemstvo* along estate lines was warmly endorsed by the traditionalists whom Tolstoi added in 1884 to the Kakhanov commission on the reform of local government, dominated till then by liberals. The resulting division among the members gave Tolstoi a pretext to persuade the emperor to disband the commission after it had issued a report proposing the abolition of the peasantry's estate institutions at the *volost* and *selskoe obshchestvo* levels and their replacement with an all-estate (*vsesoslovnaia*) *volost* administered by an official elected by the *uezd zemstvo* assembly. This report was hardly a "backward-looking document full of nostalgia for prereform Russia" and of "gentry bias," as it has recently been characterized.[19] It is true that the *uezd zemstvos* were controlled by noble landowners, but the latter were in most cases liberals, not nostalgic traditionalists. The *soslovniki*, moreover, abhorred the *zemstvo* for representing property owners grouped according to the nature of their property rather than by social estate. A proposal to ignore estate distinctions at the *volost* level as well could hardly be termed reactionary or biased in favor of the nobility in any sense that would have pleased traditionalists.

By 1886 Pazukhin had prepared a draft for a revised *zemstvo* statute that unambiguously affirmed social differentiation and inequality along traditional lines.[20] The essential points of his plan were (1) the redefinition of the three curiae which elected the *uezd zemstvo* assemblies on the basis of estate membership rather than according to the type of property owned, as under the 1864 statute;[21] (2) the allocation of seats in the *uezd* assemblies so as to favor the first curia (hereditary and personal nobles and nonnoble *chinovniki*) over the second (merchants and *meshchane*) and diminish the representation of the third (peasants);[22] (3) the lowering of the property qualification for a direct vote in the first curia to adjust for the shrinkage in noble acreage since 1864;[23] (4) the raising of the acreage required for an indirect vote via the assembly of small landowners, who were represented by electors in the first curia;[24] (5) the award of ex officio membership in the *guberniia zemstvo* assemblies (previously composed entirely of persons elected by the *uezd* assemblies) to the *uezd* marshals of nobility, who already presided over the *uezd zemstvo* assemblies; (6) the granting of automatic membership in the *zemstvo* assemblies at both levels to owners for at least ten years of properties above a certain substantial size, almost 80 percent of whom would have been nobles;[25] and (7) the replacement of the executive boards elected at both levels by the assemblies by three-man bureaus consisting at the *uezd* level of one representative each of the nobility, the urban estate, and the peasantry appointed by the governor and at the *guberniia* level of three nobles nominated jointly by the governor and the *guberniia* marshal of nobility.

Pazukhin's plan received broad support during 1887 from the societies of nobility, some of which wanted to go even further and liquidate the *zemstvo* altogether. In January of the following year Tolstoi introduced the draft statute into the State Council with the explanation that by calling once again upon the nobility to assist it in local government, the state would be acknowledging publicly that in Russia the political and social system continued to rest on a basis of social estates. Since 1864, Tolstoi claimed, the selection of *zemstvo* representatives had wrongly been assigned to "a mass of taxpayers undifferentiated as to estate," within which the influence of bourgeois property owners whose "interests and aspirations are totally opposed to noble landowning" was increasing with every passing year.[26]

As passed by the council and approved by the emperor on June 12, 1890, the new *zemstvo* statute differed from Pazukhin's draft only in three significant points. The statute shifted individual peasant proprietors from the third to the second curia of voters, made no provision for automatic seats in the assemblies for large landowners, and retained unchanged the elected *uezd* and *guberniia* executive boards. Thus the estate principle was embodied in the *zemstvo* institutions, albeit not as thoroughly as Pazukhin had wished, and the *zemstvos* retained somewhat more autonomy than Pazukhin had envisioned, although their work was subjected in each *guberniia* to review by a new bureau for *zemstvo* affairs, which included the *guberniia* marshal of nobility and was advisory to the governor.[27]

Under the 1890 statute, 55 percent of all seats in the *uezd zemstvo* assemblies were allocated to the first curia; during the years 1883–1886 only 42 percent had been held by hereditary and personal nobles and nonnoble *chinovniki*. In the *guberniia* assemblies the same social groups' share rose from 82 percent in the period 1883–1886 to 90 percent in 1897; in the *uezd* and *guberniia* executive boards from 56 percent and 89 percent, respectively, in 1883–1886 to 72 percent and 94 percent in 1903.[28] The increase in the already high proportion of nobles had no effect at all, however, on the work of the *zemstvo* institutions; in fact, the latter demonstrated an increased antipathy to estate distinctions in the 1890s.[29] Clearly the nobility was not using its numerical predominance in the *zemstvos* in the manner anticipated by Pazukhin and other *soslovniki*. Rather, the *zemstvos* continued to attract the energies of the more public-spirited noble landowners, while the majority, including the more traditional minded, continued to ignore them.

The counterreforms of 1889–1890 failed to satisfy the traditionalists' aim of restoring the first estate's influence over the peasantry and over rural life in general for several reasons. The number of landowning nobles eligible and willing to serve was rapidly decreasing; the *zemskii nachalnik*, when all was said and done, was more of a bureaucrat than a landowner enjoying the deference of his social inferiors; and even the reformed *zemstvos* did not attract the interest of traditionalist nobles. But the problem went further, for the nobility's own corporate institutions, formerly a vital element in the first estate's leading role in the countryside, were also a cause of deep concern to the *soslovniki*.

NOBLE SOCIETIES

IN the four decades following the great reforms, both the constituency to which the *guberniia* noble societies catered and the societies' sphere of competence were drastically constricted—the former gradually, as noble landowning contracted, and the latter suddenly, as a result of the reforms themselves. The combined effect was to aggravate the apathy that the first estate had always demonstrated toward its corporate institutions.

Serf emancipation and the diminution of the nobility's acreage through the ensuing land settlement necessitated a revision in the property qualifications for participating in the triennial elections of the *guberniia* societies. As of 1870, for a personal vote a noble had to own from two hundred to eight hundred *desiatiny*, depending on the *uezd*, of agricultural land (worth roughly ten thousand rubles at 1870 prices)—the same property qualification established six years earlier for a personal vote in the first or landowners' curia in balloting for members of the *uezd zemstvo* assemblies—or nonagricultural real property worth at least fifteen thousand rubles. To be represented in the elections by an elector chosen in concert with the other small landowners of his *uezd*, a noble henceforth had to own a minimum of ten to forty *desiatiny*.[30] In 1877, of the approximately 88,000 noble landowners in the thirty-seven *gubernii* of European Russia with noble elections, an estimated 20 percent met the property qualification for a personal vote in elections, and another 50 percent owned sufficient land to exercise an indirect vote. The remaining 30 percent of noble landowners were entitled, as previously, to a personal vote on all other matters before the assembly, but were disfranchised in elections.[31] The practice instituted in the late 1830s was continued, under which a personal vote in elections was given to nobles whose landholdings qualified them merely for an indirect vote but who had attained a rank of class six in the military (colonel) or four in the civil service (actual state councillor) and also to nobles, whether or not they were landowners, who had served three years in the office of marshal.[32]

Until 1875 the possession of class rank or membership in an honorific order was a prerequisite, along with the ownership of land, for the exercise of voting rights in the noble assemblies. In that year, however, the completion of a secondary education was recognized as a valid substitute for class rank, as was three years' service in one of several newly created local offices such as justice of the peace or member of the executive board of a *zemstvo* or municipality.[33] No doubt the change was necessitated by the growing divorce between those nobles who owned land in significant quantities and those nobles who served the state.

Between 1875 and 1889 eligibility for election to the offices at the disposal of the noble assemblies was limited to nobles who had class rank or a secondary education or had served three years in a *zemstvo*, municipal, or similar local office; landownership had not been required of officeholders since 1831. In 1889, however, coincident with the creation of the post of *zemskii nachalnik*, all adult hereditary noblemen were again made eligible for election, as they had been before 1875.[34] Even with this enlargement of the candidate pool, finding suitable nobles for elective office often proved difficult, and sometimes impossible.

In 1890 the revised *zemstvo* statute lowered the property qualification for a personal vote in the first (now the *noble* landowners') curia; in 1896 the Senate applied the change to the noble assemblies as well. Henceforth the ownership of between 125 (in certain *uezdy* of the Black Soil center) and 475 *desiatiny* (in certain northern and eastern *uezdy*), that is, of agricultural land worth roughly fifteen thousand rubles at 1890 prices, or of other real property valued at the same figure, was sufficient for a personal vote in the triennial noble elections. Acreage equal to one-twentieth of the amount required for a personal vote entitled its owner to indirect representation, as had been the rule since 1831. The lowering of the property qualification succeeded in maintaining the numbers of those whose land entitled them to a personal vote, but the ranks of those with the right to an indirect vote were nonetheless greatly thinned by the decline in noble landowning. Of the approximately 73,000 noble properties in 1905 in the thirty-seven *gubernii* with noble elections, roughly 25 percent were large enough to qualify their owners for a personal vote, and another 45 percent for an indirect vote, in elections. An estimated 18,000 belonged to the first group in both 1877 and 1905, while the number in the second group declined from 44,000 to 33,000.[35]

The 18,000 fully enfranchised members of noble societies in 1905 were part of a group of 31,000 nobles in all fifty *gubernii* of European Russia whose estates met the same property qualification when it was incorporated in the Duma electoral law of that year.[36] These 31,000 noble landowners, whose families contained only 12 percent of the hereditary nobility of European Russia, had weathered the transition from farming with a servile labor force in a restricted market for land to farming in a situation where supply and demand governed the wages of agricultural labor, the price of land, land rents, and commodity prices. Although a diminutive fraction of the first estate, these 31,000 constituted the dominant element among the class of individual proprietors of landholdings of over two hundred *desiatiny*, owning 59 percent of all such properties and 69 percent of the acreage contained in them in 1905.[37] Estranged from the overwhelming majority of their fellow nobles by their occupation and style of life and by no means uniformly sympathetic to the backward-looking program of the *soslovniki*, this small group of landed nobles controlled the corporate machinery designed for the entire first estate in the reign of Catherine the Great, when noble status was virtually synonymous with landholding.

Representing and serving a dwindling proportion of the first estate in the decades after serf emancipation, the *guberniia* noble societies had also suffered a drastic curtailment of their sphere of activity in the 1860s when, deprived of their role of providing local administrative, judicial, and police personnel, they were confined almost exclusively to estate concerns. Decades of quiescence followed an abortive attempt on the part of some societies to play an active political role between 1859 and 1865.

Invited by the government to elect committees to discuss the implementation of serf emancipation and to send representatives to St. Petersburg to consult with the bureaucrats drafting the legislation, the societies of nobility soon discovered that the regime would brook no questioning of the basic principles involved. Alexander II's angry ban in November 1859 on any further discussion of the peasant question in the noble assemblies only stimulated broad-ranging debates in many assemblies over the following two years on the political, social, and administrative structure of postemancipation Russia, culminating in a series of proposals for some sort of representative national legislature.[38] St. Petersburg responded by forbidding the noble assemblies to petition the emperor on "general legislative questions," which were reserved exclusively to the central government. When in January 1865 the Moscow *guberniia* assembly voted an address to the emperor calling for two representative bodies composed of delegates elected, respectively, by the *zemstvos* and by the nobility, Alexander reacted with a rescript insisting that the initiative in questions of reform belonged solely to the autocrat. Affirming that "no estate has the right to speak in the name of other estates" and that no one may petition the emperor regarding "the general welfare and needs of the state," Alexander ordered that in future the nobility not be permitted to pose "such hindrances" to the exercise of the ruler's prerogative. The effect of the emperor's instructions was the abrogation of the noble assemblies' right, granted in 1831, to petition the government regarding local administrative abuses and shortcomings, even if such abuses affected groups other than the nobility.[39]

Except in the Baltic region, where until the 1880s the noble assemblies (*Landtage*) played a local political role more extensive than that of the prereform assemblies elsewhere,[40] and in the nine western *gubernii*, where noble assemblies and elections were suspended indefinitely as a consequence of the Polish national revolt of 1861–1863,[41] the noble societies led a tranquil existence after 1865, concerning themselves almost exclusively with matters little calculated to arouse the interest of most of their members. Perhaps the most important of the estate functions they performed was the exercise of wardship over the property of orphaned, mentally ill, senile, and otherwise legally incompetent nobles. The number of noble properties in wardship reached 15,670 in 1885 and 16,429 in 1895; in the latter year such estates had an aggregate value of over 243 million rubles and yielded a gross annual income of 16 million and a net annual income of 3.6 million. Wardship matters were handled by a committee in each *uezd* or group of *uezdy* consisting of two to four members elected by the *guberniia* assembly of nobility and chaired by the *uezd* marshal. Throughout the last third of the nineteenth century the nobility successfully resisted recurrent proposals from the bureaucracy to entrust all wardship matters, regardless of the social estate of the ward, to a common set of administrative institutions.[42]

Administrative expenses related to wardship were the largest single item in the triennial budget adopted in 1890 by the Moscow *guberniia* noble assembly, claiming 53,100 rubles, or 29 percent of the total budget. Second in size was the appropriation for expenses of the deputy assembly, which maintained the society's genealogical register and enrolled new families after scrutinizing their credentials—42,720 rubles, or

24 percent of the budget. The next largest item (34,500 rubles, or 19 percent) was the cost of maintaining a dormitory exclusively for nobles' sons enrolled in Moscow's secondary schools. Noble societies also engaged in a number of charitable activities for the benefit of those of their members who were financially needy—pensions and grants for widows and the aged, scholarships, orphanages, old-age homes, and hospital beds. In the 1890s the St. Petersburg noble assembly was appropriating up to 12,000 rubles per triennium for these purposes, the Moscow assembly even more.[43]

The charitable activities of the noble societies were in part supported by the income from various endowment funds established by members over the years. In St. Petersburg there were six such funds in 1898, with a total endowment of 360,890 rubles. Roughly 90 percent of the societies' budgets, nevertheless, was financed by a tax of 1 percent per annum levied on the income from rural and urban real estate in the *guberniia* owned by both hereditary nobles, whether registered members of the society or not, and personal nobles. Moscow and St. Petersburg *gubernii* were atypical in that they contained an unusually large quantity of urban real estate owned by nobles of those and other provinces and were subject to unusually great demands on their charitable resources. In the 1880s a number of noble proprietors of houses in the city of Moscow who still identified with their native *gubernii* unsuccessfully challenged the legality of their being taxed for the benefit of members of the Moscow noble society.[44]

The nobility's lack of interest in the triennial assemblies had been a cause of much concern to the government in the first half of the nineteenth century; the situation went from bad to worse after the great reforms. Even at the height of the *guberniia* societies' political activity early in the 1860s, the number of nobles voting on major motions in the assemblies was often only a small percentage of the fully enfranchised members of the society, for example, 20 percent in 1859 in Riazan, 29 percent in 1860 in Vladimir, 34 percent in 1859 and only 15 percent in 1862 in Tver. Only the assemblies in the two capitals registered substantially higher turnouts—50 percent in 1862 and 43 percent in 1865 in Moscow, and 88 percent in 1860 and 64 percent in 1862 in St. Petersburg.[45]

After losing both their role as providers of local officials to the state and their right to petition the government on questions of general concern to the rural community, the assemblies were even less successful than before in commanding the serious interest of their members. Writing in 1869, the liberal Slavophile A. I. Koshelev placed on these recent developments responsibility for the fact that "the assemblies of the nobility are as few in number as they are deserted." Koshelev cited several cases in which the nobles of a particular *uezd* lacked a quorum to elect their marshal or wardship committee, forcing the officials in question to be chosen by the combined nobles of two *uezdy* or by the *guberniia* assembly as a whole. According to Koshelev, only the St. Petersburg and Moscow assemblies, because of their locations and the large number of resident nobles in each capital, continued to draw a good attendance. In twenty-six *gubernii* for which data were collected in the late 1890s by the Special Conference on the Affairs of the Noble Estate, only 21 percent of all nobles who had the right to participate in the triennial assemblies actually did so, and of these, 91 percent met the property qualification for a personal vote in elections.[46]

This level of participation is borne out by figures for several individual *gubernii*. In Moscow there were 1,842 noble estates of all sizes in 1905, of which approximately 550 met the property qualification for a personal vote in noble elections. The total vote for *guberniia* marshal was 283 in 1890, 312 in 1899, and 256 in 1902. When allowance is made for multiple ownership and for the fact that some landowners lacked the necessary service or educational qualifications for a vote, a level of participation of about 50 percent of the fully enfranchised members is indicated. Saratov *guberniia* in 1905 contained 1,275 noble landholdings of all sizes, of which approximately 600 were large enough to secure for their owners a personal vote in elections. The 225 votes cast for *guberniia* marshal in 1902 suggest a rate of participation of roughly 40 percent for the fully enfranchised members of the society. Matters other than elections drew even less interest. Only half the number who voted in Saratov in 1902 were present at the 1896 assembly for a discussion of the decline of noble landownership in the *guberniia*. And fewer than 15 percent of the noble landowners of Penza and 5 percent of those of Kherson voted on proposals to petition the government to broaden the use of entail when that question was discussed in extraordinary assemblies in both *gubernii* in the early 1890s.[47]

A. A. Planson, a leading defender of estate privilege who owned land in five *gubernii* and had been marshal of nobility in Ufa *uezd*, complained that the policies pursued by the regime since the early 1860s had demoralized the nobility to such a degree over three decades that "the majority takes no part in the affairs of its estate and is gradually becoming totally alienated from the interests of the nobility." (Note the conviction that "the interests of the nobility" were not necessarily identical to the attitudes of the majority of nobles.) Planson cited an example from his own *uezd*, where in February 1892 an extraordinary session of the noble assembly was convoked; of 167 fully enfranchised nobles, only 3 turned up for the meeting. Planson further complained that of four actual state councillors in his *uezd* who took part in *zemstvo* elections, were nobles by birth, and were long-time residents on their estates, he alone was an active member of the noble society, while the other three "take a constant and active part in *zemstvo* affairs because their monetary and personal interests are involved with those affairs."[48]

Indeed, not only were most nobles deserting the countryside for urban careers, but among the shrinking percentage who remained on the land, those of a liberal inclination tended to prefer the *zemstvos* as a forum of public activity down to 1905, leaving the noble assemblies to traditionalists of Planson's stripe. The latter frequently used the assemblies as vehicles for expressing their own aspirations on such matters as entail, credit, and ennoblement—aspirations not often shared by the majority who ignored the assemblies. This lack of correspondence between the views of the *soslovnik* minority who were responsible for the many petitions on the noble question in the 1880s and 1890s, on the one hand, and the attitudes of the great majority of landowning, not to mention non-landowning, nobles, on the other, was the Achilles heel of the traditionalist cause. It was a much more important factor than the nobility's alleged lack of "a sense of direction," or even than its "social diversity,"[49] in thwarting the aims of the *soslovniki*.

The nobility's apathy toward their assemblies was not in the least mitigated by a symbolic act of confidence in those bodies on the part of Alexander III. In response to petitions from several noble societies from 1881 on, the emperor in his rescript of April 14, 1888, restored to the *guberniia* assemblies the right they had enjoyed between 1831 and 1865 of petitioning the governor and the central administration concerning "local abuses or inconveniences noted in local administration, even if these stemmed from some general enactment," that is, affected estates other than the nobility.[50] In fact this gesture proved worrisome to some traditionalists. *Moskovskie vedomosti* took the position that the nobility "needs now to think much more about its obligations than about its rights," and it warned against construing the restoration of the right of petition as permitting addresses on "matters of general significance" as opposed to estate and local questions.[51] Others urged the need for amplification, asking that the noble societies explicitly be assured the right to address the emperor directly on local matters touching other social estates. Both the special conference on the nobility and the State Council favored such an assurance, and it was included in the law approved by the emperor on June 10, 1902.[52]

The same law contained a feeble effort to deal with the continuing high level of absenteeism from the triennial assemblies: a fine of up to seventy-five rubles for a first offense and a reprimand from the *guberniia* marshal for a second offense—the reverse of the practice until then. The penalty for a third offense remained unchanged—exclusion from the assembly for a period of up to one entire session.[53] The efficacy of the last penalty in raising attendance strikes a latter-day observer as more than a little doubtful. Fines for first offenders in particular, and punitive measures in general, were opposed by Sipiagin's subcommittee of the special conference. The subcommittee was of the opinion that "the reluctance to attend the assemblies of nobility which is currently observed is a sign of the decline suffered by the nobility's interests," and it optimistically predicted that

> as soon as the rural nobility revives—a revival which may be anticipated as a result of the measures now being undertaken by the government to improve the economic and political situation of the noble estate—those elements of the nobility that at present do not find in the *guberniia* capitals an important enough sphere of activity for their intellect and energy will undoubtedly flock to them once again.[54]

In fact the revival the subcommittee anticipated never took place, and not until the extraordinary events of 1904–1906 did the nobility show much interest in the *guberniia* assemblies.[55]

Two other sections of the 1902 law were the result of several years of discussion among the *soslovniki* of ways and means to strengthen the noble societies. For one, the societies were for the first time given the legal status of corporate persons, with the right to acquire and alienate property, enter into contracts, and sue and be sued in the courts.[56] For another, in an effort to provide more continuity in the work of the societies in the intervals between the triennial meetings of the *guberniia* assemblies, the assembly of marshals and deputies (established in 1831 primarily to verify the right of individual nobles to vote in elections) was elevated to the role of an executive committee, which role it had played informally upon occasion. Other proposed solutions to the problem of continuity, including annual meetings of the *guberniia* assemblies and utilizing as an executive committee either the *guberniia* and *uezd* marshals or the deputy assembly (composed of one member from each *uezd* and constituting a kind of secretariat to the society), had been rejected by the special conference. The law of 1902 expanded the responsibilities of the assembly of marshals and deputies specifically to embrace the discussion and resolution of business referred to it by the government or by the *guberniia* marshal (its chairman) and the preparation of the agenda for the *guberniia* assembly, including any petitions to the emperor.[57]

As long as the noble societies evoked little interest among the great majority of the first estate, even among its landowning minority, the 1902 structural reforms were of little consequence. The reforms did, however, help at least in a small measure to prepare the societies for their new role after 1905—as lobbies for the interests not of the first *estate* but of the *class* of substantial landowners, among whom nobles were the dominant element. In fact, some of the petitions sent to St. Petersburg by the noble societies in the late 1880s and 1890s, especially those concerned with easy credit, grain storage facilities, railroad tariffs for agricultural commodities, and the like, may easily be seen as the first indications of this new role.

MARSHALS OF NOBILITY

ALTHOUGH the noble assemblies were largely divested of their role in the political life of the *uezd* and *guberniia* in the 1860s, the office of marshal, particularly *uezd* marshal, underwent a very different evolution. In the prereform period the marshal was primarily a representative, spokesman, and leader of his fellow nobles, although from time to time the government charged him with other duties for want of enough local administrative personnel of its own. His governmental responsibilities were not so burdensome as to require his continuous attention and in his absence were easily handled by the judge of the *uezd* court. The latter, like the marshal, was elected by his fellow nobles but, unlike the marshal, was salaried and resided permanently in the *uezd* seat.

In order to coordinate and supervise the *zemstvos*, peasant self-government institutions, and other local bodies that resulted from the great reforms, the government turned increasingly to the *uezd* marshal. Lacking any substantial direct representation at the *uezd* level, St. Petersburg transformed the marshal into the de facto administrative head of the *uezd*. He served as chairman of the *uezd zemstvo* assembly and played an important role in *zemstvo* elections by presiding over both the first curia, consisting of individual landowners whose estates met the legal minimum size and of representatives of those whose estates fell below the minimum, and the preliminary congress of petty landowners, which chose those representatives. The *uezd* marshal was also chairman of the *uezd* conference of arbiters of the peace, the officials nominated by the nobility to carry out the land settlement attendant upon serf emancipation, and, from 1874, of that body's successor, the *uezd* bureau for peasant affairs. When universal conscription was introduced in the same year, the marshal became chairman of the *uezd* draft board; he also presided over the *uezd* bureau for the supervision of taverns, created in 1885, and over the *uezd* temperance committee, which succeeded the bureau in 1894. And from 1887 he was chairman of the *uezd* commission that determined the compensation to be paid to owners of property taken by right of eminent domain.[58]

An illuminating example of the government's attitude toward the marshals of nobility during the period of the reforms belongs to the years 1873–1874. Concerned about the tide of populist activism, Alexander II endorsed the suggestion of several of his more conservative advisers to entrust to the *guberniia* and *uezd* marshals supervision over the public elementary schools in their jurisdictions with the aim of halting the propagation of ideas injurious to the health of the state, society, and the family. The emperor's rescript to the minister of education, Count D. A. Tolstoi, summoned Alexander's "faithful nobility to defend the elementary school . . . against pernicious and dangerous influences" and to uphold "religion and morality" as the basis of education, explaining that members of the first estate "have always set an example of honor and devotion to civic duty."[59] The 1874 statute on elementary schools accordingly made the *uezd* marshal chairman of the *uezd* school council, giving him responsibility for the establishment of new schools and the maintenance of order in the schools, and the right to discharge undesirable teachers. At the same time the *guberniia* marshal was charged with supervising all elementary education within his jurisdiction.[60]

In recognition of his expanded duties, which now made permanent residence in the *uezd* seat necessary, the *uezd* marshal's office was raised from class six to class five in 1878, but the occupant did not receive the corresponding rank until he had served three terms and had been elected to a fourth. Marshals were paid no salaries by the noble societies, but the *zemstvos* frequently granted them stipends by way of compensation for the time and energy they expended on their ex officio duties, which were now more burdensome than their purely estate functions. Some noble assemblies also reimbursed marshals for travel and office expenses. In a very real sense the *uezd* marshals were no longer "so much the representatives of the nobility as agents of the government, executors of its will and of its multifarious administrative directives."[61]

Since the state was much more strongly represented at the *guberniia* than the *uezd* level, the *guberniia* marshal functioned primarily as the leader and spokesman for the first estate, rather than as a government agent. He was nevertheless a member of many *guberniia* administrative bodies and the chairman of two—the *zemstvo* assembly and the school council—and was justifiably described in the Code of Laws as occupying the "first place after the governor" in the *guberniia*.[62]

Before serf emancipation, according to A. Romanovich-Slavatinskii, author of the standard work on the history of the nobility, few nobles wanted to serve as marshals, and the office attracted only "rich, idle landowners" who could afford the expenses of the position, including the expected lavish entertaining of their fellow nobles, especially during the triennial assemblies. The small number of nobles wealthy enough and willing to serve were, according to this view, repeatedly reelected— three terms being common, five not at all rare, and even seven or nine not unheard of. Marshals also, according to Romanovich-Slavatinskii, usually belonged to ordinary provincial families possessing neither a title nor ancient lineage.[63] This characterization of the prereform marshal of nobility accords closely with the following portrayal in a sketch by Terpigorev, which pertains to the first decade after serf emancipation:

Our *uezd* marshal, who had served four consecutive three-year terms, had died about two months before, and now we were faced with the difficult task of electing a man who would satisfy at one and the same time both all the 'parties' and all the demands of the position of marshal, that is, he had to be either a strong and intelligent person, standing a head taller than all the rest, or else a colorless personality; but in either case he had to be a person of at least ample means, if not rich.[64]

The legal scholar Baron S. A. Korf, writing at the beginning of the twentieth century, also insists upon the marshals' long tenure of office but claims, in contrast to Romanovich-Slavatinskii, that a small group of prominent nobles resident in each *guberniia* eagerly sought and virtually monopolized the office of marshal, attracted by its prestige and power. And a recent Soviet study continues this tradition, claiming that in the postreform period one-third of all *guberniia* marshals served more than three terms each.[65]

The conventional view outlined above stands in need of correction, at least insofar as the *guberniia* marshals are concerned, and probably in the case of the *uezd* marshals as well. Between 1777 and 1910 in the forty-seven *gubernii* of European Russia in which the office existed for some part of this period, 983 different noblemen served as *guberniia* marshals.[66] Of this number, 888 were elected and the remainder appointed—49 in the western *gubernii* after elections were suspended from the 1860s in the wake of the Polish revolt, 4 in Olonets between 1812 and 1858, and 42 who were named by the governors of their *gubernii* to fill out unexpired terms but were never elected in their own right. Well over half of all elected marshals were elected to only one term, and more than three-quarters to no more than two terms (see table 22).[67] The distribution does not differ significantly for those marshals first elected before 1861 as opposed to those who took office after that date. Approximately one of every five *guberniia* marshals belonged to a family that numbered among its members another holder of the same office, and sometimes more than one.[68] Only in Mogilev, however, did the office become for a while the virtual monopoly of a single family: I. O. Golynskii, his brother, and his three sons held the office for forty-eight of the sixty-three years between 1781 and 1844. In a very few cases a family supplied marshals to two or more *gubernii*.[69] These were the exceptions, however. In the great majority of cases the post of *guberniia* marshal was not monopolized by any single family or group of families, and frequent turnover in office rather than long tenure was the norm.

TABLE 22. DISTRIBUTION OF ELECTED *GUBERNIIA* MARSHALS IN EUROPEAN RUSSIA BY NUMBER OF TERMS, 1777–1910

NO. OF TERMS	NO. OF MARSHALS	% OF ALL ELECTED MARSHALS
1	521	58.7
2	163	18.4
3	90	10.1
4	54	6.1
5–7	53	6.0
8–10	7	0.8

Source: S. Liubimov, *Predvoditeli dvorianstva vsekh namestnichestv, gubernii i oblastei Rossiiskoi imperii, 1777–1910 g.* (St. Petersburg, 1911), passim.

No comparable study has been made of the duration in office of *uezd* marshals, but if Moscow *guberniia* was at all typical in this regard, the results would be similar to those for *guberniia* marshals (see table 23). Instances of a father and son each serving as *uezd* marshal were slightly more common in Moscow than was true of the office of *guberniia* marshal nationwide. And in two of the thirteen *uezdy* the marshalship was monopolized by a single family for a lengthy period.[70] In Moscow at least, while frequency of turnover in the office of *uezd* marshal was almost exactly the same as that for *guberniia* marshal nationwide, there was a somewhat greater tendency for certain families successfully to assert a continuing claim to the position.

TABLE 23. DISTRIBUTION OF *UEZD* MARSHALS IN MOSCOW *GUBERNIIA* BY NUMBER OF TERMS, 1782–1910

NO. OF TERMS	NO. OF MARSHALS	% OF ALL MARSHALS
1	189	61.2
2	55	17.8
3	28	9.1
4	20	6.5
5–7	10	3.2
8–11	7	2.3

Source: Moskovskoe dvorianstvo. Spiski sluzhivshikh po vyboram, 1782–1910 (Moscow, 1910), passim.

In order to construct a picture of the type of nobleman who was elected as *guberniia* marshal at the end of the nineteenth century, I examined the government service records of twenty-nine marshals who served in twenty-six *gubernii* of European Russia from January 1899 to December 1904.[71] This sample includes 57 percent of the fifty-one individuals who held the office during these years in the thirty-seven *gubernii* in which the marshal was elected by his peers. A majority of the sample were forty-five years of age or younger when first elected (see table 24).

TABLE 24. DISTRIBUTION OF *GUBERNIIA* MARSHALS BY AGE
AT FIRST ELECTION, 1899–1904

AGE	NO.	% OF SAMPLE
31–35	5	17.2
36–40	4	13.8
41–45	8	27.6
46–50	7	24.1
51–55	3	10.3
56–60	1	3.4
61–65	0	0.0
66–70	1	3.4

Source: Government service records, TsGIAL, f. 1283, op. 1, various *delo* numbers.

Eighteen of the marshals (62.1 percent) had some higher education; of these, thirteen had attended a university.[72] Of the eleven who had only a secondary education, seven were the products of the Page Corps or the cadet corps. Twenty-two marshals (75.9 percent) had been in state service—thirteen in the bureaucracy, one in the army, and eight in both. The twenty-one who had been in the bureaucracy had averaged eleven years in service, while the nine who had been in the army had served, on average, only five years on active duty. All but five of the marshals had served the local community as an honorary justice of the peace or school superintendent or, in a few cases, as a member of a *zemstvo* assembly, *zemstvo* board, or municipal *duma*. Twenty had previously served as *uezd* marshals, averaging seven years in that post.

All twenty-nine individuals in the sample were landowners. The size of their holdings was not given in two cases (see table 25). A majority of the entire sample owned between 1,000 and 10,000 *desiatiny*.[73] Twenty-

TABLE 25. DISTRIBUTION OF *GUBERNIIA* MARSHALS BY SIZE OF
LANDHOLDINGS, 1899–1904

NO. OF DESIATINY	NO. OF MARSHALS OR WIVES	% OF SAMPLE
500–1,000	3	11.1
1,001–5,000	10	37.0
5,001–10,000	6	22.2
10,001–20,000	3	11.1
20,001–50,000	3	11.1
50,001–80,000	2	7.4

Source: Government service records, TsGIAL, f. 1283, op. 1, various *delo* numbers.

Note: The acreage figures are totals for land owned by the marshals and/or their wives in all *gubernii*.

five had inherited land, fourteen had purchased land, seven had wives who owned land in their own names, and ten owned additional estates in *gubernii* other than those in which they served as marshals.

The sample indicates that four decades after serf emancipation the typical *guberniia* marshal had been born into a moderately wealthy family of provincial landowners and had received a university education. After spending his twenties in the civil service, he had retired early in his thirties to his patrimonial estate, consisting of 5,000–6,000 *desiatiny* located in a single *guberniia*. For the next decade he had served the local rural community in a variety of posts, and after two terms as *uezd* marshal of nobility, he had been elected in his mid-forties to the office of *guberniia* marshal, from which he would retire by the age of fifty. This outline of a typical marshal's career is at variance with Manning's claim that nobles often used the position of marshal as "a stepping stone to high government office."[74] Current and former marshals were often called upon to serve on government commissions such as the Kakhanov commission and the Special Conference on the Affairs of the Noble Estate, but this is quite another matter.

The *guberniia* marshal at the turn of the century, like the corporate structure that he headed, was strikingly unrepresentative of the social estate whose official spokesman he was. He was a landowner in a period when landless families had come to constitute the greater part of the nobility, and he had combined state service with the responsibilities of a resident rural landed gentleman at a time when the overwhelming majority of his peers had abandoned one or the other of these traditional pursuits, and almost half had abandoned both. Further, he belonged to that small minority (fewer than 9 percent of landed nobles and approximately 4 percent of all nobles) who owned more than 1,000 *desiatiny*. Both the office of marshal and the corporate structure of the first estate in general had, in fact, come to represent not the entire nobility nor even a large part of it but only the small minority of nobles who constituted the dominant element in the new class of substantial rural landowners.

This change was acknowledged by neither the autocracy nor the defenders of privilege. Both Alexander III and Nicholas II began their reigns by extolling the marshals as the natural leaders not of the nobility alone but of the entire rural community. The marshals of nobility, especially the *uezd* marshals, were key components of every traditionalist plan for the reform of local government in the quarter century preceding 1905. Pazukhin, who expressed thanks that the institution of marshal was "spared by some miracle and not blown away by the hurricane of reform" in the 1860s, regarded it as a splendid example of selfless and conscientious service to state and society. He viewed the *uezd* marshal as "the most popular person among the peasants" and successfully proposed him for chairman of the *uezd* congress of *zemskie nachalniki*. The *uezd* marshal would also have presided over the appointed bureau with which Pazukhin had unsuccessfully sought to replace the *uezd zemstvo* board.[75]

On the whole, traditionalists shared Pazukhin's idealization of the marshals and focused their attention on the problem of attracting able candidates, especially for *uezd* marshal, despite the continuing exodus of nobles from the countryside. The three remedies that received the most serious consideration were the payment of a salary, the provision of an assistant, and the granting of civil service ranks and pensions.

The idea of a salary for the *uezd* marshal was ruled out by Sipiagin's subcommittee of the Special Conference on the Affairs of the Noble Estate. In May 1899 the subcommittee acknowledged the increasing number of otherwise well qualified nobles who were finding it impossible to bear the expenses related to the office. Sipiagin's group nevertheless insisted that "the unpaid nature of his service is the basis of that authority which the marshal enjoys in local government" and ought therefore to be preserved as long as possible.[76] There the matter rested.

An alternative means of reducing the personal and financial sacrifice demanded of the *uezd* marshal was to supply him with an assistant who would assume many of the routine responsibilities of the office. In the spring of 1900 the special conference endorsed the idea of an assistant *uezd* marshal to be elected in the same manner as the marshal himself. The proposal differed from one presented seven years earlier by the publicist A. A. Planson mainly in that the conference recommended that the position carry no salary.[77] The State Council in 1902 was wary of the conference's plan, arguing that dividing the responsibilities of the office would undermine its authority. The council stipulated therefore that the marshal's assistant act merely as a replacement for a marshal who was unable to perform his duties, rather than as a genuine aide. Nicholas II, however, sided with the council's minority and the special conference's plan; the law of June 10, 1902, provided for assistant marshals in *uezdy* where noble societies deemed them necessary, each marshal to employ his assistant as he saw fit. In fact few societies availed themselves of this opportunity to ease the *uezd* marshal's burden of work; both the assemblies and the marshals tended to be suspicious of any division of the *uezd* marshal's authority.[78]

Although the special conference had ruled out salaries for marshals, it favored rewarding them with civil service ranks and pensions. *Uezd* and *guberniia* marshals who had not already attained these ranks in the civil service were named state councillors (class five) and actual state councillors (class four), respectively, upon election to a fourth term. The conference recommended that an *uezd* marshal receive the rank of collegiate councillor (class six) upon the completion of two full three-year terms, and state councillor after three full terms; a *guberniia* marshal would become a state councillor after two terms, an actual state councillor after three. All marshals would be eligible for government pensions based on the period they had spent in office. The State Council demurred on the ground that noblemen had an obligation to their peers to hold estate office and that such service was its own reward and should not be viewed as a means for advancement in a bureaucratic career. Again the emperor overruled the council's majority, and the 1902 law granted civil service ranks to all two- and three-term marshals as recommended by the special conference.[79]

A few *soslovniki* were surprisingly unenthusiastic about the marshals. A case in point is A. I. Elishev, who deplored the fact that "the marshal of nobility as a radical, preaching the abolition of estate distinctions [*soslovnost*] in general and of his own estate in particular, is by no means a rarity in our time."[80] It is not necessary to accept Elishev's use of the term "radical" in order to agree that it was not uncommon for noble marshals to take a position not at all consonant with the traditionalists' defense of estate distinctions. A by no means unique example was Prince B. A. Vasilchikov, Novgorod *guberniia* marshal, whose 1897 response to a questionnaire from the special conference declared: "the interests of each individual nobleman are much more completely expressed by the interests of the profession to which he belongs than by the interests of his estate. . . . To anticipate an awakening of estate consciousness and solidarity in this diversified mass at the end of the nineteenth century does not seem possible."[81]

A very important forum for the expression of such liberal views, as well as traditionalist ones, on the part of noble marshals was the national conferences of *guberniia* marshals which met from 1896 on. As early as 1884 the Poltava noble society, supported by those of several other *gubernii*, had petitioned for the convocation of a nationwide conference of *guberniia* marshals to represent the interests and articulate the needs of the first estate on the occasion of the centenary of Catherine's charter. Sensitive as always to the remotest threat of political rivalry, the government had refused to cap the network of provincial estate institutions with a body at the national level. Minister of Internal Affairs Tolstoi rejected the petition of the Poltava society on the grounds that (1) since it affected the interests of the entire first estate, it was beyond the competence of the Poltava assembly, and (2) the Code of Laws included no provision for a conference of *guberniia* marshals. The autocracy had never yet allowed its own interests to take second place to those of any social group, the nobility included, if it sensed the slightest conflict between the two, and it remained faithful to that tradition right to the end. In January 1896, however, when the nobility of St. Petersburg *guberniia* again called for collective consultation among the marshals, the government consented. Nicholas II was anxious to translate into action his fine phrases about the nobility's leading role, and he had just been warned by

M. A. Stakhovich, marshal of Orel *guberniia* and a prominent moderate spokesman for the landed nobility, that unless the government moved quickly to relieve the plight of that group, its members would soon lose entirely their ability to serve the state.[82]

Minister of Internal Affairs I. L. Goremykin accordingly summoned twenty-seven of the *guberniia* marshals to a month-long conference in St. Petersburg in February and March of 1896 at which various means of support for noble landowners were discussed, along with such questions as the ennoblement of commoners and the corporate role of the nobility in local administration. Goremykin kept a close watch on the conference and for eight months after its adjournment forbade public discussion of the memorandum which the marshals had addressed to the emperor. This document contained an indictment of the government for the material harm it had caused the first estate by its policies since the 1860s and most recently by its favoritism toward industry, banking, and the railroads at the expense of agriculture.[83]

Subsequent conferences of *guberniia* marshals met in Moscow over the next thirteen years, usually once each year but sometimes twice, for four to five days at a time. Attended by anywhere from fifteen to twenty-five marshals, these meetings were "private, unofficial discussions" not convoked by the government, as the 1896 conference had been. They did, however, at least until 1905, obtain preliminary permission from the minister of internal affairs and usually reported to him on the results of their deliberations.[84] Permission did not signify unqualified approval, for the government remained uneasy about the potential threat posed to its political monopoly by these gatherings. Minister of Internal Affairs V. K. von Pleve expressed this unease as follows in 1902:

> I suppose that congresses of marshals of nobility for the exchange of views on questions of an estate nature might be useful not only for establishing a community of views and unity of action, but also for ensuring that these actions duly conform to the views of the government. . . . The talks held hitherto in Moscow among certain *guberniia* marshals of nobility have not provided sufficient evidence to determine whether, in drawing up an agenda for such meetings, it is possible to distinguish between estate matters and general affairs of state.[85]

Pleve's doubts proved well founded three years later when the conferences of *guberniia* marshals, dominated by men who shared Prince Vasilchikov's views on the primacy of professional and class over estate identity, became an influential lobby for constitutional reform.

THE CLOSING OF THE SPECIAL CONFERENCE

THE June 10, 1902, law dealing with the first estate's corporate institutions was the last major piece of legislation to come out of the work of the special conference on the nobility.[86] The conference itself had met for the last time the previous November 24. Anticipating the problem of keeping attention focused on the nobility's needs after the end of the special conference, *Moskovskie vedomosti* had in the spring of 1897 suggested that a permanent government agency be established to serve as a channel for communication with the *guberniia* societies. The idea was taken up in 1900 by D. S. Sipiagin, the new minister of internal affairs, who proposed the creation of a special department for the affairs of the nobility within his ministry. The imperial rescript that dissolved the conference on January 1, 1902, pointed in the same direction by promising that "the further strengthening of the Empire's first estate would occupy an appropriate place in the ongoing work of the government."[87]

Sipiagin's proposal, however, soon ran into indifference and even opposition in the State Council. A majority of the council felt that the proposed agency would serve no positive purpose and worried lest the other estates react negatively to such an overt expression of official favoritism toward the nobility. The majority was also concerned about the nobility's lack of enthusiasm for the new agency; the January 1902 conference of *guberniia* marshals had objected that such an agency would only interpose a bureaucratic barrier between the nobility and the autocracy. V. K. von Pleve, who had succeeded Sipiagin upon the latter's assassination in April 1902, overrode the doubts of the majority by insisting that (1) the opposition of the *guberniia* marshals was not to be equated with the opposition of the first estate as a whole, and that (2) even if a majority of the nobility did oppose the proposed agency, the government had every right to take steps in the pursuit of its own higher interests. The latter argument speaks volumes about the relationship between the autocracy and the nobility. On June 12, 1902, the emperor authorized the establishment of the Ministry of Internal Affairs' chancellery on matters relating to the noble estate.[88] The new agency fulfilled the State Council's prophecy by producing little but paperwork during its six-year existence.

The relatively intense period of public discussion and legislative activity that had lasted since the middle of the 1890s left the traditionalists divided. At one extreme were those like A. A. Chemodurov, the Samara *guberniia* marshal, who in September 1902 criticized the special conference for not having "worked out any radical measures for the salvation of the nobility." Chemodurov called for the creation of committees of noble landowners in each *guberniia* to debate such measures, taking as his model the committees established in the late 1850s to assist in the drafting of the emancipation legislation.[89] Among most defenders of privilege, however, interest in further legislative assistance ebbed abruptly once the special conference had demonstrated the relatively narrow limits of feasibility in this area. In both the societies of nobility and the press, discussion of the noble question fell off sharply from its peak in the late 1890s. At the other extreme from Chemodurov, Senator F. G. Terner, a former tutor of Alexander III, observed with satisfaction in 1903: "A critical period of gains for the nobility has thus ended; all that the government has considered it possible to do to satisfy the desires of the nobility has been done, and the noble question can be considered as having been resolved, at least for the time being."[90]

Pace Senator Terner, the legislative remedies produced by the special conference on the nobility were at best palliatives, not cures, for the supposed illness the *soslovniki* diagnosed in Russian society. Not even under the most favorable circumstances could these measures have halted or even appreciably slowed Russia's transition from a society based on estate privilege to one based on the legal equality of individuals. The failure of the traditionalists' program was due in no small degree to the fact that Russian nobles, rather than waiting for the state to protect them from the winds of change, were themselves taking an active role in their economic and social transformation. By the end of the century, the first estate was no longer a meaningful social entity. In the place it had formerly occupied in the countryside was emerging a self-conscious class of substantial landowners. And the 1905 revolution hastened the process.

THE BIRTH OF A CLASS: NOBLE LANDOWNERS
IN REVOLUTION AND AFTER

1905 AND THE ADVANCE OF LEGAL EQUALITY

THE period 1905–1914 has been the focus of much recent attention on the part of both Soviet and Western scholars. I shall, therefore, not explore in any detail the history of these years but simply follow the story of the nobility and the question of privilege into this final phase of the old regime, using the findings put forth in the preceding chapters to obtain some insights into this critical period.

The revolution of 1905 marked the long-delayed beginning of Russia's political modernization, even though the hopes of the revolutionary year were subsequently, and rapidly, disappointed. Both autocracy and legal privilege were dealt serious blows, although not serious enough fundamentally to alter the nature of the old regime. The first estate was materially affected by the revolution and the changes it wrought. Members of the nobility, moreover, were major participants in these dramatic events. To the limited extent that the various revolutionary elements possessed a common program in 1905, it was provided by the liberation movement, which was composed largely of *intelligenty* from that part of the first estate that had been absorbed into the modern urbanized sector of Russian society. Allied with them were provincial nobles, liberals active in the *zemstvos*, who were spiritually members of the same subculture.[1]

In the opening years of the twentieth century, the emigré journal *Liberation* and the illegal Union of Liberation launched a campaign for an elected national legislature, while a series of annual national *zemstvo* congresses called for the strengthening of the *zemstvos* and the reform of the administrative structure governing the lives of the peasants. Both groups firmly believed in the necessity of substituting legal equality for distinctions based upon social estate wherever the latter still existed. Emboldened by Japan's victories in Manchuria, which revealed the old regime's vulnerability, the liberation movement capped three years of activity with the *zemstvo* congress of November 1904. An eleven-point resolution adopted by the congress summed up the program of the liberal intelligentsia and the *zemstvo* liberals by calling for—among other things—parliamentary government and civil liberties guaranteed by law, with equal political and civil rights for all citizens regardless of social estate, and for the elimination from *zemstvo* elections of the principle of representation by estates.[2]

In the several months following the congress the continuing campaign of the liberals, now based on the congress's program, gained the support of a significant part of the provincial nobility. This support came not only from the noble-dominated *zemstvos* but also, surprisingly, from the *guberniia* noble assemblies, which had traditionally attracted a more conservative constituency than had the *zemstvos*. Eleven of the seventeen noble assemblies meeting during December 1904 and January 1905 endorsed the *zemstvo* congress's call for a national representative assembly.[3] The behavior of the nobility's corporate organs can be explained as the product of several factors: the long-standing antipathy to the bureaucracy on the part of the landed nobility, especially of its more traditionalist elements; the related conviction among some nobles, conservatives as well as liberals, that the first estate should have a voice in the governance of Russia; and the ability of the liberals temporarily to seize the initiative in the noble assemblies.

The bureaucracy, whose divorce from the landed nobility had proceeded quite far by the end of the century, was widely regarded by noble landowners as an alien and hostile body composed of socially rootless timeservers and of misguided worshipers of the West. For more than a decade these bureaucrats had been sacrificing the interests of agriculture to those of commerce and industry. Traditionalist nobles also resented the usurpation by the bureaucracy of the place of the first estate, the historical nursery of the monarch's advisers and of the implementers of his will. In 1905 these feelings were expressed in a willingness to back the liberation movement's demands for public participation in the legislative process; nobles assumed that they would naturally be the leaders in any representative assembly.

Of equal importance are the facts that only a minority of those eligible to participate attended the noble assemblies in the winter of 1904/1905, although the turnout was larger than usual, and that at the meetings the liberals alone were organized and in possession of a concrete program.[4] The great majority of noble landowners either ignored the meetings as usual or else attended in a state of resentment over the past, concern for the future, and bewilderment in the face of mounting attacks on the autocracy. Like the autocracy, conservative noble landowners were on the defensive. They looked to St. Petersburg for leadership but found there only weakness and vacillation. In these circumstances it is understandable that many noble assemblies found themselves temporarily following the lead of their more liberal, activist, and better organized members.

Hard on the heels of the liberals' agitation for constitutional reform came the popular outcry over the surrender of Port Arthur to the Japanese and the Bloody Sunday massacre in St. Petersburg. Shaken by these events and persuaded that the call for change could be ignored no longer, Nicholas II in his rescript of February 18 to Minister of Internal Affairs A. G. Bulygin announced his intention of establishing a consultative national representative assembly. In the accompanying manifesto, in pointedly traditionalist language, the emperor summoned "all true Russians . . . men of good intentions from all estates and ranks, everyone in his place and his estate," to defend the fatherland and the throne.[5] As the revolutionary tide continued to flow during the summer and fall of 1905, however, Nicholas was forced first to accept the principle of representation by property ownership rather than social estate and then to concede real legislative authority to the projected national assembly.

The *guberniia* marshals, the de jure leaders of the first estate but the de facto representatives of an emerging class of substantial landowners, rejected the principle of representation by estates at their March-April 1905 conference. By a vote of twenty to six they proposed that the Bulygin Duma, as the proposed consultative assembly came to be called, be chosen by voters divided into interest groups or classes along the lines of the 1864 *zemstvo* franchise. Although the few noble assemblies that met in extraordinary sessions during the summer manifested sharp divisions over the nature of the suffrage, the June conference of twenty-five *guberniia* marshals, overriding a traditionalist minority who favored representation in the Duma by estates, refused to reverse their April vote. More broadly based pressure for elections conducted on the principle of legal equality came from the three national *zemstvo* congresses held during the spring and early summer, which unanimously opposed representation by estates and endorsed the Union of Liberation's call for universal, equal, secret, and direct suffrage. The May *zemstvo* congress even sent to the emperor a delegation headed by Prince S. N. Trubetskoi, professor of philosophy at Moscow University and half brother of the Moscow *guberniia* marshal of nobility. Warning Nicholas against any attempt to base the franchise upon estate membership, Trubetskoi maintained that "the Russian Tsar is not a nobles' Tsar, not a peasants' Tsar, or a merchants' Tsar, not a Tsar of estates but the Tsar of all Rus."[6]

A last stand in defense of representation in the Duma by social estate was made by four of the five members of the general public included in the predominantly bureaucratic Peterhof Conference in late July. These four included former *guberniia* marshals Count A. A. Bobrinskii and A. P. Strukov and were supported by A. S. Stishinskii, former deputy minister of internal affairs and member of the special conference on the nobility and currently a member of the State Council. Stishinskii made a personal plea to the emperor, warning that an electoral system based on property rather than social estates would be a blow from which the nobility would not recover. The fifth representative of the public was the historian V. O. Kliuchevskii, whose lectures two decades earlier had characterized social estates as anachronisms. Kliuchevskii joined the majority of the conference in recommending an electorate divided according to property ownership rather than estate membership.[7]

Under the electoral law of August 1905, members of the Duma, except for those from the twenty-six largest cities, were to be chosen under a system similar to that in effect for elections to *uezd zemstvo* assemblies between 1864 and 1890. In each *guberniia* an assembly of electors named by three curiae of voters composed respectively of individual landowners, urban property owners, and representatives of the communal peasantry was to select the Duma deputies. When four months later the Duma was given real, if limited, legislative power and the electoral law was revised in fulfillment of the promises made by the regime in the October Manifesto, a fourth curia was added for industrial workers, and the minimum property requirement for voting in the petty landowners' curia was abolished. The petty landowners' curia chose representatives who sat in the first curia together with landowners whose holdings qualified them for a personal vote. As a result of the abolition of the minimum property requirement, individual peasant proprietors of nonallotment land came to be heavily represented in the first curia and even to dominate it in *gubernii* where larger landholdings were less common. Nationwide, in the 1906 elections close to 30 percent of the *guberniia* electors chosen by the first curia were peasants, and 54–55 percent were large landowners, mostly nobles.[8]

The advance of the spirit of legal equality did not stop with the Duma electoral law but was also manifested in the October 1906 decree that ended many of the restrictions on the personal rights of peasants and eliminated "all special privileges based on estate membership" from the civil service.[9]

Despite these important gains for the principle of legal equality at the expense of estate privilege, gains which made even more hollow the formal structure of legal distinctions among the estates, the structure itself remained intact. And it was reflected, however uncertainly, in the State Council after its reconstitution in February 1906 as the upper house of Russia's new parliament. Thenceforth only half the council's members were appointed by the emperor. The other half were elected in a manner that gave an ambiguous role to the corporate estate institutions of the nobility and the merchantry—ambiguous, because it is not clear whether these institutions were given a voice as the representatives of traditional social orders or of modern interest groups. The latter supposition is the more likely: the state turned to the corporate estate institutions for the sake of convenience.[10] Of the council's ninety-eight elected members, seventy-four were representatives of the rural landowning class: eighteen members selected from among themselves by a national congress of electors chosen by the noble societies of all *gubernii* with noble elections; thirty-four members chosen by the *guberniia zemstvo* assemblies; sixteen members elected by the landowners (without regard to estate membership) of the *gubernii* of European Russia that lacked *zemstvos*; and six members chosen by the landowners of the ten Polish *gubernii*. Of these seventy-four only eighteen were by statute members of the nobility, but in fact the great majority were members of the estate that still dominated private landowning in Russia. The landed nobles in the State Council were politically divided among themselves on most issues but tended to unite in defense of their own class interests.[11]

A distant second place in the council was occupied by twelve representatives of trade and industry, selected from among its own membership by a national congress of electors chosen by a variety of organizations: committees of trade and manufacturing, stock exchange committees, and *upravy* of the merchant estate. Six elected members of the reformed council represented the Orthodox church, and a like number the Academy of Sciences and the universities. Thus the elected half of the State Council was designed to represent several major interest groups but was chosen in a manner that gave a voice to the corporate estate organs of both the nobility and the merchantry.

The 1905 revolution marked another important step in Russia's evolution from an estate society based on legal privilege toward a mass society based on legal equality without, however, definitively breaking with the principle of distinctions among the estates. The perpetuation of that principle was to confuse more aspects of post-1905 politics than just the composition of the State Council.

LAND EXPROPRIATION AND ELECTORAL REFORM

WHAT had started as a campaign for constitutional reform broadened after Bloody Sunday into a mass movement. The peasant revolt that began in the spring of 1905 and persisted through the summer of 1907 was the most serious in Russia in 130 years. Its economic impact on the landed nobility has already been discussed (see chapter 2, especially sections on "Sales and Purchases of Noble Land" and "Mortgage Debt"). Its political consequences were no less

significant. The peasant revolt, together with the threatened expropriation of large and intermediate landowners and the unsympathetic character of the first Duma, cut short the landed nobility's flirtation with
liberalism. The depth of peasant feeling revealed in 1905 persuaded both
liberal *intelligenty* and enlightened bureaucrats that a compulsory redistribution of land in favor of the peasantry was a political necessity. The
centrist Octobrists and all parties to the left of them endorsed the notion
of expropriation, and at the end of 1905 a proposal for limited expropriation was drafted within the government with Witte's blessing. The elections of March 1906, moreover, produced a lower house overwhelmingly
in favor of compulsory land reform. The landed nobility reacted by simultaneously rejecting the leadership of the liberals, formulating an alternative plan for pacifying the peasantry, and organizing as a pressure
group to defend its interests under the new political dispensation that
had resulted from the 1905 revolution.

The repudiation of the liberals, who had dominated the *guberniia* noble
and *zemstvo* assemblies during the struggle for constitutional reform and
who were now held responsible for the attack on property rights, began
in the winter of 1905/1906 and culminated a year later in a decisive shift
to the right in the *zemstvo* and noble elections. Even such moderates
among the *guberniia* marshals of nobility as Prince P. N. Trubetskoi of
Moscow and M. A. Stakhovich of Orel were denied reelection because of
their prominent roles in the liberation movement. Trubetskoi's trium-
phant opponent in the Moscow noble elections, A. D. Samarin, marshal
of Bogorodsk *uezd* since 1899, rebuked his predecessor for having been
too obliging to, and too much under the influence of, "extreme leftist
elements."[12]

The landed nobility's alternative to the expropriation of private proprietors was the transformation of the communal peasantry into a class of
individual landowners. This alternative was first proposed publicly by
the All-Russian Union of Landowners, a gathering of 203 individuals,
almost exclusively nobles, from thirty-three *gubernii* which met in Moscow in November 1905. Among the leading spirits in establishing the
union were N. A. Pavlov, a close associate of Meshcherskii on
Grazhdanin, and A. A. Chemodurov, who headed the executive council.[13] The group's second congress in February 1906 openly criticized the
plan for the expropriation of private land rented to peasants that had
been drafted by N. N. Kutler, director of the Department of Land Use
and Agriculture (formerly the Ministry of Agriculture), and called for
the dismissal of Prime Minister Witte, whom they held responsible for
the expropriation project. In January 1906 expropriation was rejected
and the elimination of the peasant commune in favor of a class of individual peasant proprietors was endorsed also by a national conference of
both *guberniia* and *uezd* marshals of nobility convened specifically for this

purpose. Several *guberniia* noble societies and *zemstvo* assemblies quickly followed suit. Encouraged by this support for his own inclinations,[14] Nicholas II dismissed Kutler in February and Witte in April, and the principle of the inviolability of private property was written into the final draft of the new Fundamental Laws.[15]

These steps did not, however, end the threat of expropriation, for it was taken up by the majority of the parties and factions in the first Duma, which began its deliberations at the end of April. The following month the first Congress of Representatives of Noble Societies, a group established principally to lobby for the defeat of expropriation, added its voice to the campaign for the transformation of the communal peasantry into a class of individual proprietors. In May also, the government definitively rejected the expropriation of land from private owners in favor of the abolition of the commune and the consolidation of peasant holdings. When the Duma insisted on pressing for the expropriation of land not worked by its owner, the government dissolved the lower house in July 1906. P. A. Stolypin, the new prime minister, took advantage of the period before the meeting of the second Duma to enact by decree in November 1906 an agrarian program which in general outline resembled the proposals of the landed nobility: the gradual abolition of communal landowning and the consolidation of peasant allotments, leading, it was hoped, to the development of an industrious peasantry imbued with the conservative mentality of small landed proprietors. When the second Duma also insisted on the expropriation of private land, it too was dissolved at the beginning of June 1907.[16]

In the course of their campaign to defeat expropriation and promote their alternative plan, the landed nobility began for the first time to organize as an interest group. As already indicated, an All-Russian Union of Landowners was formed in November 1905 upon the initiative of provincial landowners from *gubernii* like Samara and Saratov, where the physical menace from the peasantry was most acutely felt. During the winter of 1905/1906 there was growing sentiment for a permanent national organization, composed of specially elected delegates from the *guberniia* noble societies, to defend the interests of the landed nobility against the threats posed by both rebellious peasants and misguided liberal bureaucrats. Support for such an organization came from two different constituencies: conservative provincial landowning nobles active in local affairs, such as those who had formed the All-Russian Union of Landowners, and like-minded landed magnates living in the capital, such as those who had formed the Patriotic Union the previous spring to defend the principle of representation by estates in a purely consultative national assembly. Working through the noble societies, which were by now ending their brief flirtation with liberalism, the sponsors of the idea of a permanent national organization of the nobility had to overcome opposition from the *guberniia* marshals. Many of these, like P. N. Trubetskoi, V. V. Gudovich, and M. A. Stakhovich, were moderates of the Octobrist type, and most of them correctly saw this initiative as an attempt to bypass the marshals, and perhaps also to undercut the Duma before it could hold its first session. Under pressure from twenty-six of the noble societies, the April 1906 conference of *guberniia* marshals reluctantly endorsed the call for a meeting to create a permanent national organization.[17]

The gathering that took place in May was the first of twelve week-long Congresses of Representatives of Noble Societies over the next decade. Continuity between congresses was provided by a Permanent Council of fifteen, one-third of whom were elected by each annual congress. Membership in the organization, which was commonly referred to as the United Nobility, was open to all *guberniia* societies of nobility on a voluntary basis, and each society's delegation exercised a single vote in the congress. Despite some initial boycotts and later defections, the membership grew from twenty-nine in May 1906 to thirty-nine in March 1913, out of a potential forty-one societies with elections, including the four in the Caucasus.[18] The organization's initial resentment of the liberal stance taken by so many of the marshals in 1905 was expressed in the overwhelming choice of the conservative A. A. Bobrinskii over Trubetskoi and Gudovich as chairman by the first congress. This resentment was dissipated only by the defeat of such moderates as Trubetskoi and Stakhovich in the noble elections in the winter of 1906/1907. Many of the remaining moderates among the marshals moved closer to the position of the United Nobility as a result of both the radical attitude of the first two Dumas on the land question and the continuing peasant disturbances. From 1907, accordingly, the *guberniia* marshals of the constituent societies became ex officio voting members of the annual congresses and of the Permanent Council.[19]

The United Nobility was a bundle of contradictions, reflecting both the transitional state, between absolutism and constitutionalism, of Russian political life after 1905 and the ambiguous position of the first estate in the final years of the old regime. Although composed of member societies which were themselves the official corporate institutions of the nobility, the congress was formed by individuals acting in a private capacity, exercising the right of assembly newly guaranteed to all citizens. The United Nobility was not part of the first estate's corporate structure, membership in it was voluntary, and its decisions were not binding even on the noble societies that belonged to it. And although based on the first estate's corporate institutions, the organization in fact represented and defended the interests only of the 12 percent of the nobility whose families owned substantial quantities of land. The perennial chairman of the United Nobility's Permanent Council was a perfect example of the organization's Janus-like nature: a titled aristocrat and former *guberniia* marshal, an advocate in 1905 of a Duma representing the several estates, Count Bobrinskii was also an entrepreneur of the new type, a "sugar magnate" who was active among the leaders of trade and industry in Moscow.[20]

The United Nobility enjoyed an especially close relationship with the state. Its founders and leaders were men who, by virtue of their social position and/or public office, had direct access to the government and the court. The first congress, for example, assembled in the reception hall of the Department of Land Use and Agriculture at the invitation of its director, A. S. Stishinskii, one of the United Nobility's founders. Chairman Bobrinskii was received in audience by the emperor at least once a year.[21] In pursuing its aims the organization at first favored these high-level connections, and they continued to be utilized throughout its existence. Increasingly, however, the United Nobility relied on the presence within the State Council of many of its staunchest supporters. One-third of the delegates to the first congress and nine of the fifteen members of the original Permanent Council were elected members of the upper house, and virtually all of the eighteen State Council members elected by the noble societies and roughly half of the thirty-four elected by the *zemstvos* were participants in the United Nobility.[22]

The Congress of Representatives of Noble Societies can most accurately be described as a lobby for a special interest group, formed in order to take advantage of the more open nature of politics under the post-1905 quasi-parliamentary system. The establishment of the United Nobility was a sign of growing misgivings among the landed nobility about the course of state policy. The organization defended the interests of those intermediate and large landowners who stood to the right of the Octobrists and who controlled the noble societies from 1906. While the first congress was preoccupied with the question of land reform, the next several (November 1906, March 1907, and March 1908) focused on other issues: the reform of the process whereby the Duma was elected and the defense of the landed nobility's traditional role in the administration of the *uezd*.

The results of the elections to the first Duma were a great disappointment to many and perhaps most of the landed nobility. Their leadership was rejected by the peasantry, and the dominant group in the lower house was the left-of-center Constitutional Democrats, who adamantly favored the expropriation of large landowners. In the eyes of many landed nobles the electoral system was largely to blame. Slightly fewer than one-third of the *guberniia* electors in European Russia were assigned to the first curia, which, moreover, included not only peasant proprietors but also many representatives of peasant smallholders. Almost 30 percent of the *guberniia* electors chosen by the first curia in 1906 had been peasants. Noble landowners could not be elected to the Duma, in most cases, without substantial peasant support. In each of the first two Dumas only one-fifth of the deputies were noble landowners, and almost all of them either belonged to or were allied with parties which favored the expropriation of large private landholdings.[23]

Moderately conservative landed nobles, like those who dominated the 1907 national *zemstvo* congress, saw the solution to this problem in a suffrage weighted heavily in favor of wealth, as measured by either the amount of *zemstvo* tax paid or the quantity of land owned. But the more extremist traditionalists favored a more drastic approach. As early as January 1906, two months before the first Duma elections, the Tambov *guberniia* noble assembly, from whom the initiative came for the formation of the United Nobility, called once more for a Duma elected by the several estates and endowed with merely consultative authority. In September and October, after the dissolution of the first Duma and before the elections to the second, at least three other noble societies endorsed Tambov's call for representation by estates. Four more favored representation based both on estates and on groups sharing a common style of life. The ambivalence of the latter group of noble societies, based on a recognition of the already considerable gap between Russia's formal estate divisions and social and economic reality, also characterized the discussion of electoral reform in October and November in the Permanent Council and in the second congress of the United Nobility. Even those participants in the second congress who argued for elections by estates defined the nobility in terms of landowning rather than according to the Code of Laws. Other delegates preferred to speak of *bytovye* groups, that is, groups defined by a common style of life, arguing that the traditional estates had in fact been replaced by groups of individuals sharing a "similar life style, based on property, occupation, education, etc." In the end the second congress hedged and adopted a resolution calling for the Duma to be elected in future "both by estates where such are organized and by natural customary (*bytovye*) groups or classes of the population."[24]

Despite its unwillingness to abandon in principle the concept of social estate, the second congress in its concrete proposals for electoral reform in fact demonstrated a clear preference for class representation over estate representation in the Duma. In the March 1906 elections in many *gubernii*, when the first curia assembled to choose its delegates to the *guberniia* electoral college, the representatives of the petty proprietors had outnumbered the more substantial landowners. Nationwide, approximately two-thirds of the former were peasants, and almost two-thirds of the latter were nobles. To rectify this situation the second congress proposed that the first curia be divided into separate curiae for large and for petty proprietors. While the new curia of petty proprietors would have been dominated by peasants, and that of large landowners by nobles, it is also a fact that approximately two-thirds of all noble landowners would have been assigned, on the basis of the size of their holdings, to the smallholders' curia.[25] Thus the United Nobility in November 1906 revealed itself as a lobby not for the interests of the first estate, or even of its landed minority, but of the 31,000 nobles who met the property qualification for a direct vote in the first curia and constituted the great majority of the class of large and intermediate landowners.

After the elections of January 1907 produced a second Duma more radical in its political complexion than the first, the government was won over to the cause of electoral reform but not to the traditionalists' view that the Duma should represent the several estates. Prime Minister Stolypin in fact regarded the estate principle as an anachronism. He opted instead for one significant change in the assignment of voters to electoral curiae and radically altered the relative weight accorded to each curia in the *guberniia* electoral colleges. The revised electoral law of June 1907, promulgated by decree the day after the dissolution of the second Duma, confirmed a previous Senate ruling which barred from voting in the landowners' curia any peasant proprietor who, through membership in a commune, was already represented in the third curia. By this means the overwhelming majority of individual peasant landowners were excluded from the first curia.[26] The redistribution of *guberniia* electors under the 1907 law reduced the percentage of all electors assigned to the peasants' curia in European Russia from 42 percent to 22 percent and raised the percentage assigned to the landowners' curia, newly purged of most of its peasant members, from 33 percent to 50 percent. Henceforth the first curia's electors held "an absolute majority in twenty-seven of European Russia's fifty-one provinces, half the vote in four others, and a plurality closely approaching half almost everywhere else." Under the 1905 electoral law, the first curia had received a majority of electors in only two *gubernii*, from 31 percent to 50 percent in thirty-one, and from 9 percent to 30 percent in the remaining eighteen.[27] The 1907 revision raised the proportion of nobles among all deputies from approximately one-third in the first two Dumas to just under one-half in the third and fourth Dumas, and the proportion of noble landowners from one-fifth to two-fifths.[28] The doubling of the percentage of noble landowners doubtless contributed to the markedly more conservative complexion after 1907 of the noble deputies in particular.

The electoral law of June 1907 completed the process of conferring a grossly disproportionate share of political power under the quasi-parliamentary system upon large and intermediate landowners, most of whom belonged to the first estate. They were now the largest single force in the Duma, just as in the previous year they had been made the predominant constituency among the elected half of the reformed State Council. They wielded this power not as nobles but as landowners. Except for the eighteen representatives of the noble societies in the upper house, the electoral law gave no privileges to the first estate as such. The government's insistence on adhering to property rather than social estate as the basis for suffrage in Duma elections provoked no opposition from the United Nobility, because the interests of its constituents—large and intermediate noble landowners—were in any case being promoted. When, however, St. Petersburg turned its attention to the reform of local government, thereby threatening the prerogatives of its constituents, the United Nobility took a strong and successful stand in defense of estate privilege.

LOCAL GOVERNMENT REFORM

REFORM of rural administration at the *uezd* and *volost* levels had been discussed intermittently within the government ever since the early 1880s. In the early years of the twentieth century attention had focused on inadequacies in the offices of *uezd* marshal of nobility and *zemskii nachalnik* and on the absence of representative institutions below the *uezd* level for any but the communal peasantry. The distinguished jurist, Baron Korf, for one, argued that it was an anomaly for an estate official like the *uezd* marshal to occupy such a central position in *zemstvo* and peasant affairs.[29]

Drawing on the ideas that had come out of these discussions, the project that Stolypin introduced in the Council of Ministers in December 1906 proposed that (1) virtually all the political functions of the *uezd* marshal of nobility be assumed by an appointed vice-governor or *uezdnyi nachalnik*; (2) the administrative duties of the *zemskii nachalnik* likewise be transferred to an official appointed without local input; (3) a *volost zemstvo* representing all inhabitants take the place of the peasant *volost* institutions; and (4) representation in the *uezd* and *volost zemstvo* assemblies be based on the amount of *zemstvo* taxes paid. Had it been enacted, Stolypin's reform would have drastically reduced the landed nobility's local political role. The long reign of the *uezd* marshal as administrative chief of the *uezd* would have come to an end, as would the segregation of the communal peasantry under the administrative and judicial control of an amateur official selected from among the local landed nobility. And the first estate's influence in the *zemstvo*, to whose tax revenues they contributed very little, would have been greatly diminished.[30]

Stolypin's project reflected not only the long-standing recognition, in both the bureaucracy and educated society, of the shortcomings of rural administration but also the prime minister's own personal conviction that social estates were anachronisms in the twentieth century. He held this view despite, or perhaps as a result of, his service as a state-appointed *uezd* marshal of nobility in Kovno in the 1890s and as Kovno *guberniia* marshal during 1900–1903. In introducing his project for local government reform in the Council of Ministers, Stolypin argued that "the grouping of Russia's population by estates represents something concrete only to the extent that this division corresponds to real differences among distinct class elements; when it exceeds these limits, it is a purely fictitious construct."[31] In short, only class distinctions were now of significance; estate distinctions pure and simple no longer corresponded to Russian social reality. Two months later, in February 1907, Stolypin left no room for doubt about his attitude when he insisted to A. A. Naryshkin, a leader of the United Nobility, that the estate principle was an anachronism that had to be removed from local government.[32] The same thinking lay behind Stolypin's abolition in June 1908 of the interior ministry's chancellery on noble affairs.

Stolypin's attack on the estate principle in local government, on the power and influence wielded by the *uezd* marshal and the *zemskii nachalnik*, and on the landed nobility's control of the *zemstvo* was seen as a challenge by the United Nobility. Once their flirtation with liberalism in 1905 had ended, the corporate institutions of the first estate—the *guberniia* and *uezd* marshals and the assemblies that chose them—were perceived by the conservatives who now dominated them as useful instruments for the defense of the landed interest. The *guberniia* societies of nobility were in fact the foundation upon which the United Nobility had been erected, and that influential lobby accordingly focused its attention during much of 1907 and 1908 on Stolypin's proposed reforms, playing a vital role in their defeat.

With Stolypin's project already under attack from the January 1907 conference of *guberniia* marshals, in the Council of Ministers, and in the State Council, the Permanent Council of the Congress of Representatives of Noble Societies in February urged the prime minister to permit the noble and *zemstvo* assemblies to discuss his proposal before he submitted it to the Duma. Not yet reformed through revision of the electoral law, the Duma was still regarded as a threat by the United Nobility, and the Permanent Council hoped through widespread criticism to kill the project before it reached the lower house. Although enjoying the support of the Octobrists as well as the Constitutional Democrats on this issue, Stolypin bowed to this pressure, and the introduction of the legislation in the Duma was delayed until December 1908, by which time many *guberniia* noble societies had expressed their opposition. In so doing they were following the lead of the third congress of the United Nobility, which in March 1907 had condemned the prime minister's project on the grounds that it "would completely destroy the significance of the nobility in the localities."[33]

The case for maintaining that significance was argued eloquently before the fourth congress the following March by F. D. Samarin, one of the elected representatives of the noble societies in the State Council. Samarin had chaired the Moscow noble assembly's commission to study the Stolypin project and was the congress's official reporter on the subject. Using rhetoric familiar to any reader of the literature of the 1880s and 1890s on the noble question, Samarin defended the traditionalist conception of Russian society as an organic union of "mutually related social groups," namely, the clergy, nobility, and peasantry. The implementation of Stolypin's proposals, which followed the pernicious example of the French Revolution in recklessly disregarding the legacy of the past, would shatter this union, leaving society fragmented into antagonistic groups and the monarchy in a precarious situation. Samarin was particularly ardent in defending the *uezd* marshal as an independent and impartial authority, impervious alike to bureaucratic and popular pressure—in short, the ideal state servant and the embodiment of the nobility's raison d'être.[34]

The fourth congress adopted a resolution which echoed Samarin's sentiments and sent a delegation to the emperor to present their case against the reforms. Nicholas II gave them a sympathetic hearing and subsequently added eight *guberniia* marshals, United Nobility activists all, to the Ministry of Internal Affairs' Council on the Affairs of the Local Economy. The council had been charged with reviewing all proposals on local government before their submission to the Duma. In December 1908 these noble representatives dissented from the council majority's endorsement of the proposal to reform the *uezd* administration, protesting that if a bureaucrat were appointed to govern the *uezd*, "the population will naturally conclude that the marshals, and consequently the entire landed nobility which elects them, have lost the tsar's confidence."[35] This sharp condemnation, combined with the adamant opposition of the national conference of *guberniia* marshals in January 1909 and of the fifth congress of the United Nobility the following month, brought Stolypin's initiative to a halt while the prime minister watered down his proposals (for example, by eliminating the *uezdnyi nachalnik*) in the hope of getting something through the two legislative chambers. Although parts of his program passed the Duma in 1911/1912, even these were blocked in the State Council, thanks largely to the efforts of United Nobility activists like Stishinskii.[36]

The thwarting of Stolypin's efforts to reform local government left the landed nobility, or more precisely its fully enfranchised members, secure in their hold over the life of the countryside. The marshal of nobility continued to play the role of de facto administrative chief of the *uezd*, the *zemskii nachalnik*'s (somewhat watered-down) paternalistic authority over the peasants continued to serve as a surrogate for the lost power of noble landowners over their serfs, and intermediate and large noble landowners continued to control the *zemstvos*. In addition, the same group dominated the elected half of the State Council and also the Duma and could count on the sympathetic attention of the imperial court. The political power of this small minority rested not on legal privilege, which by now was all but eliminated, but on their disproportionate ownership of land in what was still an overwhelmingly agrarian society.

This wealthy and politically influential group was by no means clear in its own mind whether it constituted an estate or a class, and the discussions in the congresses of the United Nobility reflected this confusion. At the first congress one participant, Iu. A. Arseniev of Tula, insisted that "we speak not as a service estate but as an agricultural estate," while another, Prince P. L. Ukhtomskii of Kazan, wondered whether the new organization represented "a government estate" or "an agricultural class."[37] The debate over electoral reform in the noble societies and in the second congress revealed widespread support for the notion of society divided into groups defined by education, occupation, wealth, and style of life rather than by legalistic estate distinctions which no longer reflected social reality. Once the battle over local government reform had been won by the conservatives and traditionalists in 1909, the United Nobility concentrated on lobbying for the class interests of agrarians in general and intermediate and large proprietors in particular. The organization pressed, for example, for state aid for *zemstvo*-provided agricultural services (agronomists, veterinarians, advisers on livestock breeding, model farms and cooperatives, discount purchases of improved seed and agricultural equipment, and so on) and for more roads and grain elevators in the countryside.[38] In March 1913 the ninth congress resuscitated the idea of ennobling and enrolling in *guberniia* noble societies commoners who owned agricultural properties of substantial size.

And yet, Stolypin's proposals to reform local government evoked a great deal of rhetoric devoted to extolling the idealized virtues of estate society. The nobility was praised as the provider of selfless service to the state and moral leadership to the peasantry; Russian society was romantically depicted as an organic union of distinct estates, each making its particular contribution and all linked through mutual respect.

Why this relapse into the language and thinking of a bygone era on the part of men who on other occasions acted and thought increasingly like a modern interest group? Is it because, as Arno Mayer argues, the old elite may have acted in many ways like a modern class but in its heart and mind remained a "feudal" nobility? The truth is probably more complex. It must be remembered that the institutions whose influence over rural administration Stolypin's projected reforms would have ended had a dual character: formally they were the corporate institutions of the first estate, but in practice they had become one of the major instruments whereby the small minority of the nobility composed of large and intermediate landowners protected its class interests. What had been designed in the eighteenth century as a corporate structure for the entire nobility had been gradually transformed into the instrument of a small class of noble landowners who were increasingly aware both of the interests that bound them together (and to nonnoble landowners) and of the social distance between them and the majority of the first estate, who had been lost to the professional, commercial, and industrial world of the cities.

In part, then, the renewed concern for the defense of the estate principle was a reaction to an attack on institutions which, while serving the class interests of large and intermediate noble landowners, were at the same time estate organs in the eyes of the law. In part, also, this concern reflected the fact that noble landowners continued to dominate the life of the *uezd* not simply as landowners but also as nobles. Large and intermediate landowners who were not nobles were excluded from the political leadership of the *uezd*. They had no voice in the choosing of the marshal of nobility, the most important official in the *uezd*; until 1913 they did not form part of the manpower pool from which the *zemskii nachalnik* was selected; and they were not included after 1890 in the first curia of *zemstvo* electors, which was disproportionately represented in the *uezd* assembly. Attempts to make the *guberniia* noble societies more fully representative of the class of substantial landowners had failed more than once in the last two decades of the nineteenth century, and the United Nobility's effort in 1913 met the same fate. The obstacle remained as before: the state refused to permit the *guberniia* societies to co-opt nonnoble members of the landowning class by ennobling them for service to agriculture and the local community. To the very end the old regime remained faithful to the principle that service to the state alone warranted ennoblement.[39]

The persistence of estate rhetoric was in some degree a manifestation of cultural lag—the use of familiar terms like "estate" to describe unfamiliar phenomena like "class"—but principally it was a reflection of the transitional nature of Russian society and its institutions in the closing decade of the old regime, and of the autocracy's stubborn adherence to archaic forms. The labor of the first estate to give birth to a class of self-conscious landowners able and willing to defend their common interests began before 1905 and was not yet complete by 1914. The process was already far advanced and quite irreversible, but it was shielded from view by the screen of Russia's antiquated estate structure—a structure that, despite Stolypin's critical attitude, retained the unquestioning support of the monarchy.

C O N C L U S I O N

NOBILITY, AUTOCRACY, AND REVOLUTION

BEFORE the great reforms the Russian nobility had constituted a
legally privileged estate possessed of great landed wealth, a dominant role in state service, and social preeminence. By the eve of
the 1917 revolution Russia's first estate had been reduced to little more
than a legal fiction confined to the Code of Laws and the minds of traditionalists. Deprived of its privileged legal status and no longer identified
with distinctive social roles or a distinctive style of life, the nobility was
no longer a social reality. There were, of course, noblemen who still
followed traditional careers in agriculture or state service, but rarely both
any longer. For every such nobleman, moreover, there was now another
who was neither a full-time landowner nor a servant of the state.

Having divested themselves of their land, moved to the cities, and
become career bureaucrats or taken up occupations unknown to or
shunned by their forebears, the overwhelming majority of the first estate
were in fact no longer recognizable as nobles. Accordingly, I have made
no attempt in the preceding pages to provide a complete picture of the
nobility at work and play during the half century before the revolution,
no attempt to describe an average day in the life of a typical Russian
nobleman or noblewoman. For the period before serf emancipation typical nobles from the several strata of the noble estate can be described
with respect to style of life, occupation, upbringing, formative
influences, marriage patterns, budgets, and so forth. But for the early
twentieth century an attempt at such a description would be fruitless.
Nobles had become almost as diverse in their styles of life as Russian
society itself; they were officers, bureaucrats, agrarian entrepreneurs,
schoolteachers, doctors, philosophers, revolutionaries, journalists,
lawyers, artists, businessmen, scientists, engineers, white- and even
blue-collar workers.

The transformation the nobility underwent during the half century following serf emancipation has conventionally been referred to as "the decline of the nobility," for it involved a sharp decrease in the absolute number and percentage of noble families who owned land and in the aggregate acreage owned by the first estate. This "decline," moreover, has usually been seen as a pathological development, the result of the hopelessly anachronistic attitudes and spendthrift behavior that made the nobility helpless victims of economic and social change.

The analysis in chapter 2 of land sales and purchases, land prices and rents, and mortgage debt provides the basis for a contrasting conclusion: the divestiture of their land on the part of so many nobles after serf emancipation was a sign of a healthy ability to adjust to a radically changed social and economic environment. The abolition of the right to own serfs, the most valuable form of noble privilege, eliminated the strongest bond between the first estate and its landholdings. For the most part lacking the emotional attachment to their properties that was characteristic of Western nobilities, and accustomed to regarding their estates as assets to be exploited in order to support a life focused on town and court rather than the countryside, Russian nobles showed little hesitation about treating land as simply a form of capital, once emancipation had created a free market in agricultural land.

While some nobles turned to farming their estates for profit, many more cashed in on their land's appreciating value by leasing it to neighboring peasants, by using it as security for loans, or, in areas where farming was least likely to be lucrative, by selling it to land-hungry peasants who were willing to pay inflated prices which bore little relationship to the land's profitability. Money borrowed against land or realized from its sale was not infrequently invested to better advantage in the commercial and industrial sector of Russia's developing economy. The nobility's divorce from the land was further facilitated by the opening up or expansion in the cities of opportunities in the free professions, the arts, commerce, and industry—a development that exerted a strong pull upon nobles who felt the tedious boredom of existence in the cultural wasteland of rural Russia. Further evidence that the first estate was by no means simply being victimized by social change but was adapting rapidly to it is the nobility's increased appetite after serf emancipation for both secondary and higher education for their sons.

Nor was the minority of the first estate that still retained its ties to the land composed of helpless proprietors gradually succumbing to mounting debts, their estates doomed to eventual forced liquidation. In fact the landowning remnant of the nobility, particularly the owners of large and intermediate properties, in the last decade of the old regime formed an economically sound and powerful group. The capital value of their land had reached an unprecedented level, the ratio of mortgage debt to that value was very modest, and nobles still retained a hugely disproportionate share of the private individually owned agricultural land in Russia.

A very large part of the nobility had thus successfully merged with the modern "social-class reference groups" that were struggling to supplant the traditional estates.[1] Their forests and cherry orchards were no doubt the subject of nostalgic memories, but for the majority of nobles the behavior patterns and symbols of the past had no such paralyzing effect as has usually been assumed. Long before the 1917 revolution abolished their anachronistic status as Russia's first estate, most nobles had learned to live, and many even to thrive, in a world where legal equality had replaced hereditary privilege.

The majority of the nobility, who made the transition to a new way of life more or less successfully, received little attention except to be upbraided as renegades or bemoaned as victims by traditionalist defenders of estate distinctions and legal privilege. The landowning remnant, on the other hand, was the object of much solicitous concern in the quarter century before 1905 from those same traditionalists as well as from the autocratic state. This concern was manifested in a great variety of proposals to halt the "decline" of the nobility, most of which were studied by the Special Conference on the Affairs of the Noble Estate, and in a number of legislative acts. By their lack of enthusiasm for schemes designed to protect them against social change, however, the overwhelming majority of the remaining noble landowners demonstrated that they were not interested in becoming a fossilized social element, insulated by juridical means and material subsidies from the free play of market forces and protected against the further diminution of their acreage at the price of surrendering their freedom to divide, mortgage, or sell that acreage as they saw fit.

In fact estate consciousness was rapidly disappearing among the remaining noble landowners, and class consciousness was developing in its place. Landed proprietors of substance and education, regardless of social origin, were widely regarded among the landed nobility as constituting a single social class, which was the natural constituency of the *guberniia* noble societies. This growing class consciousness was increasingly apparent after 1905 as large and intermediate noble landowners closed ranks to defend their material interests against threats from the peasantry, the intelligentsia, and the bureaucracy. Interest-group politics based on class drew more response from substantial landowners than the schemes of the *soslovniki*, based on the estate concept of society, ever had. Both nobles who divested themselves of their estates and those who retained them adapted more successfully to social and economic change than even their friends and champions gave them credit for.

This adaptation took place without the assistance or encouragement of the state, although it was the state's actions that had made it impossible for the nobility to continue in its old ways. The relationship between state and nobility during the last half century of the old regime is infinitely more complex than its depiction in current Soviet historiography, which in its most doctrinaire form insists that "the autocracy as a whole right up to its overthrow remained the instrument of the dictatorship of a single class, namely the class of reactionary noble landowners."[2] In fact, Russia under the last three tsars is a classic illustration of the truth of Alexander Gerschenkron's observation, in response to views such as that just quoted, that "the interests of the state are something *sui generis* and in some periods not just as important, but infinitely more important than class interests."[3] In pushing through the great reforms in the 1860s and promoting rapid industrialization a generation later, the autocracy was serving primarily its own interests and secondarily those of Russia by enhancing its political and military strength. Its humiliating defeat in the Crimean War had dramatized the rapidly growing power disparity between Russia and the modernizing societies of the West. In pursuing its own goals the state sacrificed the privileges and special interests of the nobility, most notably in the emancipation of the serfs and their endowment with land. The changes that were set in motion by the reforms transformed the first estate virtually beyond recognition. Such had not been the autocracy's intent, but such was the result of the course it followed from the reign of Alexander II on.

In an analogous fashion the autocracy reacted to the revolutionary situation of 1905 by conceding a quasi-parliamentary system that, like the reforms of the 1860s, attempted to protect the interests of the landowning nobility insofar as possible while at the same time giving priority to those of the state. Defenders of privilege responded to the 1906 Fundamental Laws much as they had to the reforms of the 1860s.

Although the state never swerved from its course of promoting economic development and hence, indirectly, further social change, it nevertheless responded positively in the 1880s and 1890s when traditionalists argued for the preservation of privilege and estate distinctions in general, and in particular those pertaining to the nobility. This seeming paradox and the confusion it created as to the direction of Russia's development was heightened by the autocracy's official rhetoric under the last two tsars. That rhetoric fostered the illusion that the nobility's role in Russian life had not changed, while the everyday evidence of Russian social reality belied this. How are these contradictions to be explained?

During its last half century the autocracy was caught in a dilemma. It recognized that it could not hold its own in a world of modernizing states without promoting economic and social modernization in Russia. But economic and social modernization posed a threat to social stability and, worse yet, implied political modernization as well. Constitutionalism was the political mode identified with the new social order in the West, but constitutional monarchy was unacceptable to Russia's rulers, who were as jealous of the form as of the substance of their power. The old regime tried to limit the risks involved in the necessary economic and social modernization that it launched in the 1860s by maintaining the formal structures of the social estates and the sense of place and deference that such a system instills in its members. Modernization in the political sphere was successfully resisted until 1905. It is these two features that distinguish Russia's experience from the West's in the period following peasant emancipation in the two societies: in Russia the hierarchical estate system was preserved not just through the inertia of custom but with the full force of the law, and in Russia the onset of political modernization was delayed a full four decades after economic and social modernization began.

Absolute monarchy, to which the last tsars desperately clung, is the purest expression of the principle that also underlies social estates— hereditary privilege sanctioned by law. Traditionalists repeatedly warned that an attack on the estate principle was implicitly an attack on the monarchical principle as well. Public pronouncements in support of legal privilege and of the nobility, and legislation designed to strengthen both, in fact served the interests of the autocracy more than they did those of the nobility. Despite the Cassandra cries of the *soslovniki*, the first estate was making its peace with the new order in one way or another. That government pronouncements and legislation did nothing to stem the process of social change was less important to the regime than the ideological value of these acts, for they indirectly affirmed the legitimacy of absolute monarchy.

In this respect the 1905 revolution changed nothing. The gap between social and now political *reality* on the one side, and official *ideology* on the other, widened, but the autocracy acknowledged none of this. Nicholas II was compelled to reject the estate principle in establishing the Duma, just as he was compelled to grant the Duma real legislative power. Similarly, the estate principle was embodied in only the most limited and ambiguous way in the restructured State Council, eliminated from the civil service, and attacked by Prime Minister Stolypin. And yet the sovereign's loyalty to the past survived unshaken. Even after he had reluctantly consented to the October Manifesto and the Fundamental Laws, Nicholas persisted in the view that Russia fortunately remained an absolute monarchy. As late as October 1913 he suggested to his minister of internal affairs a return to "the previous tranquil course of legislation," with majority and minority reports to be presented to the emperor for his decision when the two legislative chambers could not agree on a bill.[4]

Seen in this light, the retention until 1917 of the legally sanctioned hierarchy of estates was completely logical. Absolute monarchy and hereditary legal privilege remained linked to the end, although the monarchy was no longer truly absolute, and the first estate and its privileges were forms largely without substance.

What, then, can we conclude about the respective responsibility of the nobility and the autocracy for the potentially explosive situation Russia found herself in on the eve of World War I? Any response to this question is colored by one's view of the nobility in the preceding half century. A leading Soviet student of the nobility, Iu. B. Soloviev, sees the autocracy and the first estate as equally responsible for Russia's plight: the failure of Stolypin's efforts to introduce needed reforms comes down finally to "the inability of the autocracy and the nobility, which preserved their old natures, to execute that abrupt break with the past that was required to adapt to new conditions." The autocracy and the nobility marched hand in hand to their rendezvous with revolution, both of them "firmly wedded to outmoded forms of life," refusing to be reconciled with the post-1905 political system, and trying, "wherever possible, to return to the past."[5]

Manning, whose version of "the decline of the nobility" includes the gentry's "turn to the land" and its consequent political resurgence in the twentieth century, also is convinced of the nobility's basic inflexibility. She sees this trait as the major factor in "the crisis that eventually consumed the Old Regime."[6] The events of 1905–1907 "redressed the precarious balance of power within the state" by taking political authority from the bureaucracy and returning it to the provincial gentry and their aristocratic allies. The gentry then proceeded to use their power for the next decade to block all attempts at needed reforms; they were willfully blind to the nation's urgent needs and problems and could think only of defending their own interests and privileged position.[7] Unable "to deal with the newly emerging industrial society around them" and unwilling to share power with or to consider the needs of other groups, the landed gentry frustrated the government's attempts to do so.[8]

In this study I have tried to offer an alternative view to the conventional image of a nobility declining because of its inability to adapt to change; developments in the old regime's last years both support and are illuminated by this alternative view. The history of the years 1905–1914 contains much evidence that noble landowners learned quickly to take advantage of Russia's new quasi-parliamentary system with its opportunities for political organization and lobbying in defense of their special interests. A recent study of gentry politics in the last decade of the old regime finds that landed nobles adjusted rapidly to the new political order they had "neither sought nor created."[9] The creative response of noble landowners in the western *gubernii* was the Nationalist party, which saw itself as representing the *class* interests of agrarian entrepreneurs rather than the *estate* interests of nobles.[10] A somewhat different example of the same phenomenon was the United Nobility.

The landed nobility's political power after 1905 was in no sense a restoration. It was a phenomenon as novel as Russia's (limited) participatory
politics under the quasi-parliamentary system. Similarly, the uses to
which nobles put their new power reveal no particular inflexibility or
incorrigibility on their part. On the contrary, they behaved much as one
would expect of a conservative group of wealthy men who still enjoyed
high social status and a sense of their historical right to assist the tsar in
governing Russia. They defended their own interests and, to the extent
that they concerned themselves at all with the interests of others and the
needs of the nation as a whole, persuaded themselves that in pursuing
their own interests they were satisfying these broader concerns as well.
In short, noble landowners acted as special interest groups typically act
in even the most democratic states.

If the landed nobility enjoyed preponderant influence in the post-1905
political order, it was because of their facility at taking advantage of the
opportunities presented by the new system and because of the structure
of the system itself. While yielding to pressure from below, the regime
had rigged Russia's first experiment with political modernization so as to
sacrifice as little as possible of the principles of absolutism and social
hierarchy. Conservative landowners were able to thwart the government's attempts at moderate reform, first because of the absence under
the new political dispensation of other special interest groups with coun-
tervailing power to offset that of the landed proprietors, and second
because the court, which retained a very important political role, was
unsympathetic to and unsupportive of Stolypin's efforts.

The monarchy had designed the new political order, with minimal
input from anyone outside the bureaucracy. The 1907 modifications
augmenting the relative weight in the Duma of landowners at the expense of peasants were necessary to correct the miscalculation of the
previous year about the peasantry's willingness to follow the political
lead of their social betters in the countryside; the 1907 changes did not
fundamentally alter the already extremely unbalanced nature of the system. Thus, in the final analysis, we come back to the autocracy, to the
preponderant role of the state—by no means an unfamiliar phenomenon
in Russian history.

The transition from estate society to class society has been a difficult
one under even the most favorable circumstances. In Russia the difficulty
was increased by the fact that traditional status distinctions received
formal support from the state to the very end of the old regime. By
defending the traditional model of society as a hierarchy of hereditary
privileged groups, the autocracy hoped to immunize Russia against social
upheaval and prolong indefinitely its own political monopoly. Instead the
policy pursued by the state after 1881 exacerbated the inevitable strains

involved in adjusting old values and institutions to a new model of society and ultimately produced a result opposite to the one intended and desired. A new social order based on legal equality was developing in Russia after the great reforms, and nobles were participating in this new order at every level. In large part because of the autocracy's stubbornly traditionalist stance in defense of institutions and patterns of behavior based on privilege, however, the tension between the new influences and the old forms was particularly acute. Even the long-delayed advent of a limited participatory political system in 1906 was structured so as to give a dominant role to the owners of substantial rural properties—an emerging class that nevertheless still bore the unmistakable traces of its historical origin in Russia's legally privileged first estate.

The autocracy's unwillingness to facilitate the necessary reconciliation of old and new contributed in no small measure to the old regime's failure to navigate safely the treacherous shoals that imperil the course of modernization. From the shipwreck of 1917 no vestige of either monarchy or nobility survived. This stands in sharp contrast to the West, where constitutional monarchs—still privileged if retaining only vestigial powers—and hereditary nobilities—no longer legally privileged but still socially, economically, and consequently politically powerful—became familiar features of modern society. The responsibility for the shipwreck of 1917, the victims of which included the monarchy and the nobility, but more important, most of the people of the former Russian Empire, belongs primarily not to the nobility, or even to its landowning remnant, but to the autocracy. It was the autocracy, not the nobility, that could not rid itself of its fixation on the past and adapt successfully to the modern world.

STATUS GROUPS WITHIN THE NOBILITY

T HE 1785 charter issued by Catherine the Great divided the hereditary nobility into six categories (*razriady*) for purposes of enrollment in the provincial genealogical registers. The categories, which had no legal significance and did not at all reflect more important differences in wealth, service rank, and education, were as follows: (1) families of persons ennobled by special patent from the sovereign since 1685; (2) families of persons ennobled since 1721 by virtue of having achieved commissioned officer rank; (3) families of persons ennobled since 1722 by virtue of having achieved the requisite rank in the civil service; (4) families of naturalized Russian subjects who had been nobles in their native countries; (5) families of titled nobles; and (6) untitled families which had enjoyed noble status since before 1685. By the end of the nineteenth century a majority of noble families belonged to categories two and three (see table A-1), but the pre-1685 nobility, constituting little more than a quarter of the entire first estate, considered itself the true, blueblooded nobility and viewed the first three categories especially with condescension.[1]

At the end of the nineteenth century there were in the empire as a whole some eight hundred titled families, divided more or less evenly into princes, counts, and barons.[2] By far the greater number of princely families were to be found in Georgia and in Poland. Among the nobility of European Russia there were some forty princely families descended from the ruling house of Kievan Russia (including such names as Bariatinskii, Dashkov, Dolgorukii, Dolgorukov, Gagarin, Gorchakov, Kropotkin, Lvov, Lobanov-Rostovskii, Obolenskii, Odoevskii, Repnin, Shakhovskoi, Shcherbatov, Ukhtomskii, Volkonskii, and Viazemskii), from Gedymin, the fourteenth-century founder of Lithuania (including Golitsyn, Khovanskii, Kurakin, and Trubetskoi), or from Georgian or

TABLE A-1. DISTRIBUTION OF NOBLE FAMILIES BY GENEALOGICAL
CATEGORY IN FIFTEEN *GUBERNII*, 1893–1910

CATEGORY	% OF FAMILIES
1	9.9
2	33.7
3	28.2
4	0.5
5	1.7
6	26.0

Source: A. P. Korelin, *Dvorianstvo v poreformennoi Rossii 1861–1904 gg.* (Moscow, 1979), pp. 32–33. Korelin's percentages have been corrected.

Turkic princes (including Bagration, Imeretinskii, Iusupov, Meshcherskii, and Urusov). Another twenty or so families enjoyed the title of prince by virtue of a forebear's having received it from the emperor, a practice begun by Peter I in 1707. The title of count was unknown in Russia before 1706, when Peter first conferred it. In the period 1855–1908 alone, eighty-eight new counts were created. In some cases the title was of foreign origin, having been confirmed after the family was naturalized.

Baronial families fell into three different groups. A small minority had received the title from the emperor, normally at the time of ennoblement for outstanding service to the state in finance, trade, or industry; there were thirty-one such families by 1900, of whom seven had received the title since 1856. The remaining baronial families were divided fairly evenly between Baltic Germans who had borne the title from the period before Russia's annexation of their homeland and those (both foreigners subsequently naturalized and native Russians) who had received the title from a foreign government.

SIZE, DISTRIBUTION, AND ETHNIC
COMPOSITION OF THE NOBILITY

ACCORDING to the 1897 census a total of 885,754 hereditary nobles of both sexes and all ages resided in the fifty *gubernii* of European Russia; an additional 334,415, for the most part members of non-Russian ethnic groups, lived elsewhere in the empire, primarily in the Caucasus and in Poland.[1] Official estimates of the number of nobles in the fifty *gubernii* exist for the period of the great reforms—610,000 in 1858, 677,000 in 1863, and 544,000 in 1870[2]—but must be used with caution. Large discrepancies appear when forward and backward projections are made from the official estimates and the census total and are then compared with the figures for the later and earlier dates. Such projections are based on known rates of natural increase for the total population of the fifty *gubernii* by five-year periods from 1861; on data on the number of persons, both heads of families and their dependents, who entered the nobility either via the Table of Ranks or through the receipt of an honorific order; and on a standard formula for projecting natural increase: $P_1 \times 2.72^{(rt/2)} = P_2$, where P_1 and P_2 are the population totals at the beginning and end of a given period, r is the average annual rate of increase during the period, and t is the duration of the period in years.[3]

Including the addition of 5,000–6,000 new members via ennoblement, a population of 610,000 nobles in 1858 would have grown to only 660,000 by 1863; it would have taken a population of 626,000 in 1858 to reach the official estimate of 677,000. Some, but probably only the lesser part, of the discrepancy of 17,000 can be attributed to the enrollment of previously unregistered nobles by the deputy assemblies of the six Lithuanian and Belorussian *gubernii*, which were notoriously lax in the scrutiny they gave to the required proof of noble status.[4]

The 1870 official estimate presents an even greater problem. A population of 677,000 nobles in 1863 would have grown by natural increase to 740,000–741,000, and including cases of ennoblement, to about 749,000, or 205,000 more than the official figure for 1870. After the suppression of the Polish revolt of 1863, noble elections in the western *gubernii* were suspended, and government-appointed marshals and deputies of nobility conducted a purge of the first estate, invalidating previously accepted claims to noble status. The numerical losses that resulted from this process were much greater than those attributable to death in battle during the revolt or to execution or deprivation of rights after judicial proceedings.[5] The total magnitude of the losses is not known, but was probably less than 205,000.

A population of 544,000 nobles in 1870 would have grown by natural increase alone to 800,000 by 1897, and including ennoblement and the natural increase of the newly ennobled, to 840,000–845,000 —considerably short of the census total which is the one relatively reliable figure in this whole series. In order to reach the census total of 886,000, the noble population in 1870 would have had to number between 570,000 and 575,000, without making allowance for any purged Polish nobles who may have been restored to the ranks of the first estate after that date. If the number of nobles in 1870 was indeed closer to 575,000, then the loss caused by the purge of Polish nobles after 1863 was only 175,000 (using the official estimate of noble population for 1863) or even 160,000 (using the projection of 660,000 nobles for 1863).

The preceding calculations produce the following probable ranges for the size of the hereditary nobility of European Russia in the third quarter of the nineteenth century: 1858: 610,000–626,000; 1863: 660,000–677,000; 1870: 544,000–575,000.

As a result of both geography and history, the hereditary nobility of European Russia was very unevenly distributed, thinning out dramatically in both absolute numbers and as a percentage of the total population as one moved from the west and southwest toward the east and north.[6] In 1858, before the purge of the Polish nobility, 62.8 percent of the first estate of European Russia lived in the nine western *gubernii* (Vilno, Kovno, Grodno, Minsk, Mogilev, Vitebsk, Volynia, Podolia, and Kiev) annexed from Poland in the period 1772–1795; in 1897 these same provinces still contained an impressive 46.1 percent. The *gubernii* containing the new and old capitals, St. Petersburg and Moscow, held 5.5 percent of the nobility in 1858 and 14.6 percent four decades later. Thus, in 1897 three out of five nobles lived in the eleven *gubernii* mentioned.

In each of these eleven *gubernii* in 1897 the nobility formed 1 percent or more of the total population. In several the relative weight of the first estate was much higher: 3.3 percent in Minsk, 4.3 percent in St.

Petersburg, 4.4 percent in Vilno, and 6.4 percent in Kovno. In 1858 their relative weight had been even greater (for example, 5.5 percent in Minsk, 5.8 percent in Vilno, and 9.1 percent in Kovno) in all of the western provinces but Kiev, where, as in the two capital *gubernii*, the rapid urban growth during the second half of the century drew many nobles from other *gubernii*. In absolute numbers of nobles in 1897, these eleven ranged from Kovno with 99,000, St. Petersburg with 90,000, and Minsk and Vilno with 71,000 each to Vitebsk and Mogilev with 22,000 each and Grodno with 19,000.

If to these eleven are added Kherson and Poltava, two *gubernii* adjacent to Kiev, in each of which there were 27,000 nobles who constituted 1 percent of the total population, the enlarged group of thirteen *gubernii* contained two out of three hereditary nobles in European Russia in 1897.

At the other extreme was a group of nineteen *gubernii* lying almost entirely to the north of the latitude of St. Petersburg and/or to the east of Moscow, which together held only 10.1 percent of the first estate in 1897, up from 8.9 percent in 1858. In eighteen of these *gubernii* the nobility's relative weight in the total population was no higher than 0.4 percent in 1897; the exception was Olonets with 0.6 percent. The absolute number of nobles ranged from 1,200 in Archangel to 8,100 in Tambov.[7] In the remaining eighteen *gubernii*, containing 23 percent of the first estate in 1897, the number of nobles ranged from 20,000 in the Don Army Oblast to 3,700 in Estonia (in only four were there fewer than 8,000 nobles), and the relative weight of the nobility from 1.2 percent in Courland to 0.4 percent in Orel.

The level of urbanization among the nobility in 1897 varied greatly from one *guberniia* to another and bore little or no relationship to that of the total population, except in the four provinces containing the country's largest cities—St. Petersburg, Moscow, Kherson (Odessa), and Livonia (Riga)—where both the nobility and the total population registered their highest urban percentages.[8] Urban nobles accounted for between 72 percent and 97 percent of the first estate in these four *gubernii*; in Kharkov, which contained the sixth largest city in European Russia; and in seven northern and eastern *gubernii* in which noble landowners were numerically very weak—Archangel, Nizhnii Novgorod, Kazan, Astrakhan—or in which many of those landowners were absentees— Vologda, Iaroslavl, and Vladimir. At the opposite extreme, the eleven *gubernii* with the lowest percentages of urban nobles (12–36 percent) included all of the western provinces but Kiev, plus adjacent Poltava and Smolensk and distant Ufa. In Kiev *guberniia* the presence of the country's fifth largest city balanced an unusually strong concentration of resident noble landowners and resulted in a first estate that was 55 percent urban; elsewhere in the west the second factor predominated.

In the western *gubernii* the nobility showed both its greatest numerical strength and its strongest resistance to urbanization; the west was also the region in which the ethnic Russian element in the first estate was weakest. Great Russians constituted 47.0 percent of all hereditary nobles in European Russia in 1897, followed by Poles (26.2 percent), Belorussians (9.9 percent), Ukrainians (7.2 percent), Lithuanians (4.5 percent), and Germans (2.5 percent).[9] In the twenty-nine central, northern, and eastern *gubernii* in which 66 percent of the Great Russian nobility lived, they formed 75 percent or more of the first estate. Bessarabia, Kherson, Tauride, Ekaterinoslav, and Kharkov in the south, and Orenburg in the east contained an additional 14 percent of the Great Russian nobles, who formed local majorities of 56–71 percent. The remaining 20 percent lived in fifteen borderland *gubernii* where they formed pluralities in Chernigov (48 percent) and Kiev (41 percent); large minorities (22–35 percent) in Ufa, Estonia, Livonia, Grodno, Volynia, Podolia, and Poltava; and small minorities (4–18 percent) in Courland, Vitebsk, Mogilev, Vilno, Minsk, and Kovno.

The other major ethnic groups among the first estate in European Russia were all deeply rooted in the borderlands, particularly in the west, and only the Germans and Poles had spread into the Great Russian *gubernii* in significant numbers. Spurred by the existence of primogeniture in the Baltic provinces and by a strong tradition of state service, almost half of the Baltic German nobility lived outside their historic homeland—18 percent in St. Petersburg *guberniia* and 30 percent scattered throughout the rest of European Russia, where they constituted from 1 to 3.5 percent of the nobility in no fewer than twenty-six *gubernii*. In the Baltic provinces, where 52 percent of the German nobles lived, they formed 62 percent of the first estate in Estonia, 50 percent in Livonia, and 38 percent in Courland.

Two-thirds of all Polish nobles in the empire in 1897 lived in European Russia rather than in the former kingdom of Poland. Like the Baltic Germans, but for different reasons, the Polish nobility in European Russia was also widely scattered outside its home provinces—the nine western *gubernii* plus Courland (see chapter 5, note 54). This region nevertheless still held 83 percent of the Polish nobles of European Russia. They formed majorities of 52–58 percent among the nobles of Kovno, Vilno, Grodno, and Vitebsk; pluralities of 40–50 percent in Volynia, Podolia, and Courland; and minorities of 28–40 percent in Kiev, Mogilev, and Minsk.

Each of the remaining ethnic groups among the nobility of European Russia was of purely regional importance. Five *gubernii* contained 97 percent of all Belorussian nobles, who formed majorities of 52–58 percent among the first estate of Minsk and Mogilev and minorities of 17–33 percent in Vilno, Vitebsk, and Grodno. Kovno and Vilno were the home of 98 percent of the Lithuanian nobility, who constituted 37 percent of the nobles in the former *guberniia* and 4 percent in the latter. Ninety-two percent of the Ukrainian nobility lived in eight *gubernii* — Volynia, Podolia, Kiev, Chernigov, Poltava, Kharkov, Ekaterinoslav, and Kherson. They formed a majority of 68 percent among the nobles of Poltava and minorities of 13–41 percent in the other seven *gubernii*. Numerically minor ethnic groups constituted locally significant minorities (and in one case a majority) among the nobles of several provinces: Estonians in Estonia (4 percent); Romanians in Bessarabia (22 percent); Crimean Tatars in Tauride (13 percent) and Minsk (5 percent); Volga Tatars in Ufa (55 percent) and in Penza, Orenburg, Saratov, and Samara (4–18 percent); and Bashkirs in Orenburg (9 percent) and Ufa (5 percent).

Levels of urbanization among the nobility varied greatly by ethnic group. Most urbanized in 1897 were Germans living outside the Baltic region (79.0 percent), Poles residing outside the nine western *gubernii* and Courland (76.4 percent), Great Russians (71.8 percent), and Germans in the Baltic *gubernii* (66.0 percent). Together these groups constituted 54 percent of the first estate in European Russia. The other ethnic groups were all far below the average for all nobles: Crimean Tatars (35.1 percent), Poles in the western *gubernii* and Courland (23.6 percent), Ukrainians (18.4 percent), Estonians (18.2 percent), Romanians (9.6 percent), Volga Tatars (7.5 percent), Belorussians (4.8 percent), Lithuanians (3.3 percent), and Bashkirs (1.6 percent).

Personal nobles and *chinovniki* were much more urban than the hereditary nobility and also much more ethnically homogeneous. For levels of urbanization see chapter 2, note 1; for ethnic composition see table B-1.

TABLE B-1. ETHNIC COMPOSITION OF HEREDITARY AND PERSONAL
NOBILITY AND OF TOTAL POPULATION OF EUROPEAN
RUSSIA, 1897 (PERCENT)

ETHNIC GROUP	HEREDITARY NOBLES	PERSONAL NOBLES & *CHINOVNIKI*	TOTAL POPULATION
Great Russians, Belorussians, & Ukrainians	64.1	88.0	80.0
Poles	26.2	6.1	1.2
Lithuanians	4.5	0.6	1.4
Germans	2.5	3.1	1.4
Others	2.7	2.2	16.0

Source: Obshchii svod rezultatov perepisi, 2:378.

A P P E N D I X C

NUMBER AND PERCENTAGE OF NOBLE
LANDOWNERS

I N 1861 the number of noble landowners in forty-four *gubernii* of
European Russia was reported as 123,622; the addition of estimates
for Bessarabia, the Don Army Oblast, and the three Baltic provinces would bring the total to approximately 129,000.[1] Since a landowner was counted once in each *guberniia* in which he owned land, this
figure should be reduced by perhaps 2,000–3,000 to adjust for multiple
listings. In 1877 the first thorough land census conducted in European
Russia, excluding only the Don Army Oblast and one *uezd* of Bessarabia,
counted 114,716 landowners belonging to both the hereditary and the
personal nobility, listing a landowner once in each *uezd* in which he
owned property.[2] With the omitted areas the total would have been close
to 118,000, including perhaps 4,000–5,000 multiple listings and an equal
number of personal nobles. A government survey in 1895 covering
forty-four *gubernii* reported 114,781 separate estates in the possession of
the hereditary nobility alone;[3] with Bessarabia, the Don Army Oblast,
the three Baltic *gubernii*, and Archangel the total number of estates
would have been approximately 120,000–121,000—of landowners,
perhaps 113,000–115,000. The land census of 1905, the most complete
of any conducted under the old regime, counted 107,247 properties in
the hands of both hereditary and personal nobles in the fifty *gubernii*,[4] a
figure which included perhaps 6,000–7,000 estates owned by nobles who
held more than one each, and 4,000–5,000 owned by personal nobles.
By 1912 the number of properties owned by hereditary and personal
nobles in forty-seven *gubernii* (excluding Archangel, Viatka, and Estonia)
increased to 115,035, probably because once the 1906–1907 panic was
over, a larger share of noble land sales than formerly was of parts of

properties rather than of entire estates, while properties continued to be divided through inheritance.[5] With the three missing *gubernii* included, the total would be approximately 116,000, including 6,000–7,000 multiple listings and 4,000–5,000 personal nobles.

A significant minority of noble families contained more than one landowner, cases in which both husband and wife owned property being the most common. Making the adjustments indicated above, and assuming two landowners per family in 10 percent of all landowning families, one arrives at the approximations of the number of noble landed families found in table C-1. Using the data from appendix B on the size of the nobility and employing known rates of natural increase for the total population and annual averages of commoners ennobled through service, one can approximate the number of hereditary nobles for the required years (see table C-2). On the basis of tables C-1 and C-2 and on the assumption that the average noble family contained 4.5 persons,[6] the approximate percentage of nobles belonging to landed families can be calculated (see table C-3).

TABLE C–1.   ESTIMATED NUMBER OF NOBLE LANDOWNING
FAMILIES, 1861–1912

YEAR	NO. OF FAMILIES
1861	114,500–115,500
1877	98,000–100,000
1895	103,000–104,500
1905	86,500–88,000
1912	94,500–96,500

TABLE C–2.   ESTIMATED NUMBER OF HEREDITARY NOBLES, 1861–1912

YEAR	NO. OF HEREDITARY NOBLES
1861	640,000–657,000
1877	609,000–643,000
1895	855,000–860,000
1905	1,025,000–1,030,000
1912	1,169,000–1,174,000

Note: The figures for 1905 and 1912 are based on the assumption that the same rate of growth through natural increase and the ennoblement of commoners prevailed after 1897 as in the 1890s. In fact, after 1900 the entry of commoners into the first estate via the civil service undoubtedly slowed down. Even if the rate of ennoblement of commoners were cut by one-half, however, the estimated number of nobles in 1912 would be reduced by only 14,000.

TABLE C-3. ESTIMATED PERCENTAGE OF NOBLES BELONGING TO
LANDED FAMILIES, 1861–1912

YEAR	%
1861	78–81
1877	69–74
1895	54–55
1905	38–39
1912	36–37

Note: Korelin, "Dvorianstvo," p. 140, arrives at an estimate for 1861 of 80–85 percent by dividing the estimated number of noble landowners in that year (128,500) by the estimated number of nobles (675,000) and multiplying by 4.5 to get "around 88% (in fact, 86 percent), and then reducing this figure to allow for a probable overestimation of the number of landowners because of multiple counting of owners of estates in different *gubernii* and a probable underestimation of the number of nobles. Actually, Korelin's figure of 150,000 families or 675,000 nobles is rather too high than too low. On p. 151, Korelin gives a figure of 55 percent for the early 1890s with no explanation as to how it was derived.

A P P E N D I X D

DECREASE IN NOBLE ACREAGE

Manning (*Crisis*, p. 146) gives the same figures as in table 3 for noble acreage at the end of 1905 and for the aggregate loss in 1906–1909, but she elsewhere (p. 373) presents a totally different (and incompatible) set of figures drawn from a variety of less reliable sources. Table D-1 compares Manning's figures and mine for comparable periods.

TABLE D–1. COMPARISON OF DATA ON AVERAGE ANNUAL DECREASE
IN NOBLE ACREAGE, 1877–1914 (000's OF *DESIATINY*)

MANNING, *CRISIS*, P. 373		MY CALCULATIONS	
1877–1895	824	1878–1897	926
1895–1905	604	1898–1905	894
1905–1914	673	1906–1914	1,135
1877–1914	728	1878–1914	970

Sources: Manning's figures are taken from the 1877 and 1905 land censuses, various data for 1895, and *Russkii kalendar* for 1905–1914. My calculations are based on data in *MSDZ* 21 (1912): xxiii; ibid. 24 (1915):63, 66–67; and Anfimov and Makarov, pp. 86–87.

Note: Manning's figure of 832,898 for the period 1877–1895 is a typographical error; it should read 823,898. On page 363, Manning gives a different set of data for 1905–1914, which yield an average annual decrease of 731,000 *desiatiny* instead of 673,000.

A P P E N D I X E

MORTGAGE DEBT OF THE NOBILITY

HE estimates of mortgage debt in table 14 represent, for each year other than 1863 and 1914, the sum of the outstanding loan balances of the Noble Land Bank and of its Special Department plus prorated shares of the loan balances of the Kherson Land Bank and the joint-stock land banks, according to the percentage of all privately owned acreage in estates of over one hundred *desiatiny* that belonged to the nobility; only estates of this size qualified for mortgages from the private banks. This procedure was suggested by *O zadolzhennosti zemlevladeniia v sviazi s statisticheskimi dannymi o pritoke kapitalov k pomestnomu zemlevladeniiu so vremeni osvobozhdeniia krestian (Vremennik tsentralnago statisticheskago komiteta*, no. 2 [1888]), p. xii, and the figure for 1863 is from ibid., p. v.

Figures for the Noble Bank's Special Department have been adjusted by interpolation from July 1 to January 1, and for the Kherson Land Bank from September 1 to January 1. The percentage of privately owned acreage in estates of more than one hundred *desiatiny* that was held by the nobility is known for 1877, 1887, and 1905 and has been extrapolated or interpolated for other years as follows: 1873, 86 percent; 1883, 80 percent; 1893, 75 percent; 1906, 68 percent. For 1873 and 1883 the estimates for the total mortgage debt on noble land include a declining unpaid balance on the pre-1861 debt, calculated from data in *O zadolzhennosti zemlevladeniia*, pp. vi, x.

The procedure used to estimate the nobility's mortgage debt for 1873, 1883, 1893, and 1906 rests on the assumption that noble and nonnoble proprietors were equally likely to borrow from the private banks, but in fact, after the opening of the Noble Land Bank, nobles were less likely than commoners to do so. In all probability, then, the estimates for 1893 and 1906 are somewhat inflated, and the actual ratio of mortgage debt to land values in those two years is at least several percentage points lower than stated in the table. The estimate for the nobility's mortgage debt in 1914 is based on the assumption that in that year, as in 1905, the Noble Bank held 56.5 percent of the first estate's mortgage debt to all banks.

NUMBER AND PERCENTAGE OF NOBLES
AND LANDOWNERS IN STATE SERVICE

THE number of nobles in the civil service was estimated by multiplying the percentage of all *chinovniki* who were sons of hereditary nobles (table 18 above) by the total number of *chinovniki* in 1857 and 1897.[1] The number of nobles in the officer corps was similarly arrived at, using percentages from table 19 above and totals of officers for 1864 and 1897.[2]

In 1897 there were approximately 250,000 adult male nobles in the fifty *gubernii* of European Russia. This estimate was arrived at in the following manner: (1) of the 887,477 male hereditary and personal nobles and nonnoble *chinovniki* in the empire in 1897, 59.5 percent were twenty or older; (2) if the same age distribution is assumed for the 583,824 male hereditary nobles, 347,000 would have been twenty or older;[3] (3) of this 347,000, approximately 3,000 were men who had been ennobled through receipt of the appropriate ranks or orders;[4] (4) of the remaining 344,000, 72.6 percent, or 250,000, are assumed to have resided in European Russia—the same percentage of the entire hereditary nobility that lived in the fifty *gubernii* in 1897 (see appendix B).

Of all hereditary nobles of both sexes and all ages in European Russia in 1897, 250,000, or 28 percent, were adult males. Assuming that the percentage was the same a generation earlier and using population estimates from appendix B, we arrive at the following approximations of adult male nobles in European Russia: 171,000–175,000 in 1858 and 185,000–190,000 in 1863.

Although 72.6 percent of the empire's hereditary nobles resided in European Russia, it is reasonable to assume that a somewhat higher proportion, say 80–85 percent, of all nobles in state service were from the fifty *gubernii*, since the overwhelming majority of *chinovniki* and officers serving in the Caucasus, Central Asia, Siberia, and the Far East were from European Russia, as well as of those who served in the fifty *gubernii*. Multiplying the total number of nobles in civil and military service for the several years by 80–85 percent and then dividing by 171,000–175,000 for 1857/1858, 185,000–190,000 for 1863/1864, and 250,000 for 1897, we arrive at the following estimates for the number of nobles from European Russia serving in class ranks as a percentage of all adult males in the same region who had been born into the first estate: 17–19 percent in 1857/1858 and 34–36 percent in 1897 for the civil service and 8–9 percent in 1863/1864 and 7 percent in 1897 for the military.

The percentage of landowners among *chinovniki* is known for 1853 and can be estimated for 1902; the percentage of landowners in the top four classes of the officer corps is known for 1903 (see section entitled "The Nobility and State Service" in chapter 6). If the ratio of the percentage of landowners in the first four classes to the percentage in all fourteen classes was the same in the military as it was in the civil service, then approximately 8 percent of all army and navy officers in 1903 were landowners; the total number of officers in that year has been extrapolated from data for 1897 and 1900.[5] The estimate of 13–15 percent for the military in 1864 rests on the assumption that the ratio of the percentage of landowners among officers to the percentage of landowners among *chinovniki* was the same in 1864 as in 1902/1903. Although all of the above assumptions may not be valid, they are similar to those made by Zaionchkovskii in estimating the total number of *chinovniki* for 1903, and they at least provide some rough approximations with which to work.

The figures given in the section entitled "The Nobility and State Service" in chapter 6 were obtained by applying the above percentages to the total number of *chinovniki* and officers for the various years and interpolating where necessary. In order to estimate the size of the pool of male noble landowners, the figures in appendix C for all hereditary noble landowners have been diminished by 15–20 percent to eliminate women proprietors.

NOTES

ABBREVIATIONS

d.	*delo* (item)
ed.	*edinitsa* (item)
f.	*fond* (archival subdivision)
GBL	Gosudarstvennaia Biblioteka SSSR imeni Lenina
Gos.	Gosudarstvennyi
l.	*list* (folio)
ll.	*listy* (folios)
MSDZ	*Materialy po statistike dvizheniia zemlevladeniia v Rossii*
op.	*opis* (inventory, shelf list)
PSZ	*Polnoe sobranie zakonov Rossiiskoi imperii*
SZ	*Svod zakonov Rossiiskoi imperii*
t.	*tom* (volume)
TsGADA	Tsentralnyi gosudarstvennyi arkhiv drevnikh aktov, Moscow
TsGAM	Tsentralnyi gosudarstvennyi arkhiv goroda Moskvy, Moscow
TsGIAL	Tsentralnyi gosudarstvennyi istoricheskii arkhiv, Leningrad

CHAPTER 1

1. Jerome Blum, *The End of the Old Order in Rural Europe* (Princeton, 1978), p. 3.

2. Ibid., p. 440. See also T. H. Marshall, *Class, Citizenship, and Social Development* (Garden City, N.Y., 1964), p. 193, and Roland Mousnier, *Les hiérarchies sociales de 1450 à nos jours* (Paris, 1969), pp. 19–20.

3. Blum, *End of the Old Order*, pp. 440, 5.

4. Ibid., p. 441. Modern society is commonly characterized as "class society" in deference to what are usually considered its most important social formations. The term "class society" is too well established to be abandoned at this late date, but two precautions should be borne in mind. Class is only one and often not the most important basis of social differentiation in modern society; ethnic and religious divisions, for example, are sometimes more significant. Second, modern society ideally accords no juridical recognition to classes or to any other social groups; it recognizes only individuals who are equal to one another in both rights and obligations.

5. Blum, *End of the Old Order*, p. 419.

6. Ibid., p. 420.

7. Ibid., pp. 420–21, 424.

8. Arno J. Mayer, *The Persistence of the Old Regime: Europe to the Great War* (New York, 1981), pp. 5–6, 12–13.

9. Ibid., pp. 127, 133, 135, 186–87.

10. Ibid., pp. 277–78, 282, 301. This alleged counteroffensive coincides more or less with the onset of political reaction in Russia under Alexander III, but Mayer's concept of a "remobilization of the old order" is difficult to reconcile with the state's sponsorship of industrialization during the same reign.

11. Mayer, pp. 301–2.

12. Ibid., p. 304.

13. Terence Emmons, *The Formation of Political Parties and the First National Elections in Russia* (Cambridge, Mass., 1983), p. 2.

14. Alfred J. Rieber, *Merchants and Entrepreneurs in Imperial Russia* (Chapel Hill, 1982), p. xxv.

15. Ibid., p. 416.

16. Ibid., pp. xxv, 416.

17. S. N. Terpigorev, *Oskudenie* (Moscow, 1958), 1:22–24, 37–41, 68, 99–149.

18. A. M. Anfimov and I. F. Makarov, "Novye dannye o zemlevladenii Evropeiskoi Rossii," *Istoriia SSSR*, no. 1 (1974), pp. 87–88.

19. Roberta T. Manning, *The Crisis of the Old Order in Russia* (Princeton, 1982), pp. 3, 25.

20. Manning, *Crisis*, pp. 11, 43. Daniel R. Brower, *Training the Nihilists* (Ithaca, 1975), similarly refers to "the financial crisis of the landowners, to whom the city offered a place of refuge and work" (p. 51).

21. Manning, *Crisis*, p. 8.

22. Ibid., pp. 4, 8. Manning's estimate of 4 billion is about right. Not counting mortgage loans already repaid, through the end of 1905 nobles received slightly more than 3¼ billion rubles from government compensation payments, peasants' supplementary payments, net sales of land, and mortgage loans. See chap. 2 below.

23. Manning, *Crisis*, p. 8.

24. Ibid., pp. 8, 10.

25. Ibid., p. 9.

26. Ibid.

27. Ibid. See also Gary M. Hamburg, *Politics of the Russian Nobility: 1881–1905* (New Brunswick, 1984).
28. Manning, *Crisis*, pp. 10–11.
29. Ibid., p. 20 and passim.
30. Leopold H. Haimson, "Conclusion: Observations on the Politics of the Russian Countryside (1905–14)," in Leopold H. Haimson, ed., *The Politics of Rural Russia 1905–1914* (Bloomington, 1979), pp. 262–63, and Robert Edelman, *Gentry Politics on the Eve of the Russian Revolution* (New Brunswick, 1980), pp. 16–17.
31. Manning, *Crisis*, pp. 36–38.
32. Ibid., p. 11.
33. Ibid., pp. 30–32, 36–38, 40, 43, 48.
34. Ibid., pp. 41–42.
35. Ibid., pp. 3, 38, 42–46, 48.
36. Ibid., p. 49 and passim. See chap. 8 below.
37. Manning, *Crisis*, p.20.
38. V. O. Kliuchevskii, *Sochineniia* (Moscow, 1956–59), 3:55. For the treatment of estates in the 1649 code, see ibid., 3:157–61; 6:437, 444, 451–52.
39. For the former view, see Günther Stökl, "Gab es im Moskauer Staat 'Stände'?" *Jahrbücher für Geschichte Osteuropas*, n.s., 11 (1963):323, and Hans J. Torke, "Continuity and Change in the Relations between Bureaucracy and Society in Russia, 1613–1861," *Canadian Slavic Studies* 5 (1971):458–59. For the latter view, see Richard Pipes, *Russia under the Old Regime* (New York, 1974), pp. 107, 113. Rieber recognizes the existence of estates in Russia after 1785 but emphasizes the point that Russia never had "an estate system identical to that of Western Europe"; a Russian estate, according to him, was "an intermediate social form [between caste and class] possessing a legal identity and collective privileges but no inviolate corporate rights" (p. xxii). Rieber believes that seventeenth-century Muscovy was a "castelike" society (p. xxi), and that caste and class "represent the two most extreme forms of social organization: one closed, rigid, hereditary; the other open, mobile, and socioeconomic in character, with estates constituting an "intermediate form" (p. xx). Rieber thus follows in the footsteps of Marshall (p. 194) and Mousnier (pp. 19–20) in distinguishing estate society not only from class society but also from caste society. Max Weber, on the other hand, considers caste systems to be an extreme variant of estate society, status distinctions in a caste system being "guaranteed not merely by conventions and laws, but also by *rituals*" (H. H. Gerth and C. Wright Mills, eds., *From Max Weber* [New York, 1946], p. 188). In contrast to a caste society like traditional India, Muscovite Russia never used religious sanctions to regulate contacts among the estates.
40. Manning and Edelman are but the latest in a long line of modern historians who translate *dvorianstvo* as "gentry." Among the few exceptions are Robert Jones, *The Emancipation of the Russian Nobility 1762–1785* (Princeton, 1973), and Daniel Field, *The End of Serfdom: Nobility and Bureaucracy in Russia, 1855–1861* (Cambridge, Mass., 1976). Despite her initial differentiation between the noble estate as a whole and the gentry (provincial noble landowners) (p. xiii), Manning proceeds throughout her book to equate Russia's "leading estate" with "the landowning gentry" (e.g., pp. 3–4).
41. Marshall, p. 201.
42. C. B. A. Behrens, *The Ancien Régime* (London, 1967), p. 56.
43. The following discussion is based on "Svod zakonov o sostoianiiakh" in volume 9 of *SZ*. Revised editions of volume 9 were published in 1842, 1857, 1876, and 1899. Specific terms for social estate—*soslovie*, signifying shared es-

teem, and *sostoianie*, signifying shared status—came into general use only at the beginning of the nineteenth century. Until the 1740s the concept of estate was expressed by *chin* (rank), from then until the end of the century by *stan* (position or standing), which emphasized the aspect of status, and by *rod* (kinship group), which emphasized the hereditary and endogamous nature of the estates. See Dietrich Geyer, "'Gesellschaft' als staatliche Veranstaltung; Bemerkungen zur Sozialgeschichte der russischen Staatsverwaltung im 18. Jahrhundert," *Jahrbücher für Geschichte Osteuropas*, n.s., 14 (1966):35n.

44. While the celibate Western clergy recruited its members from the other estates, and its hierarchs frequently from the nobility, the Russian clergy was self producing, like the other estates, and recruited its hierarchs primarily from within itself. One consequence was the relatively low social honor enjoyed by even the higher clergy in Russia, compared with the very high status of noble-born prelates in the West.

45. Hereafter the terms "nobility," "noble," and "first estate," when unqualified, refer to the hereditary nobility alone. For the six categories (*razriady*) into which the hereditary nobility was divided in 1785, see app. A.

46. A. D. Gradovskii, *Sobranie sochinenii* (St. Petersburg, 1899–1908), 7:353.

47. V. M. Kabuzan, *Narodonaselenie Rossii v XVIII-pervoi polovine XIX v.* (Moscow, 1963), pp. 154–55. See app. B for a demographic profile of the nobility.

48. Franklin L. Ford, *Europe 1780–1830* (New York, 1970), pp. 31–34, 39, 41.

49. Except as otherwise noted, this discussion is based on the 1785 charter, in *PSZ*, 1st ser., vol. 22, no. 16187, and on *SZ*, vol. 9.

50. *O sostave, pravakh i preimushchestvakh rossiiskago dvorianstva* (St. Petersburg, 1897), pp. 113–15.

51. Gradovskii, 7:348.

52. Prokopii Ustimovich, *Mysli i vospominaniia pri chtenii zakonov o dvorianstve* (Moscow, 1886), pp. 152–53.

53. A. Romanovich-Slavatinskii, *Dvorianstvo v Rossii ot nachala XVIII veka do otmeny krepostnago prava* (St. Petersburg, 1870), pp. 201–3, 214.

54. Geyer, pp. 23–29; Karl-Heinz Ruffmann, "Russischer Adel als Sondertypus der europäischen Adelswelt," *Jahrbücher für Geschichte Osteuropas*, n.s., 9 (1961):167, 177. For the state's attempts to make servicemen collectively responsible on the *uezd* level for certain administrative functions between the sixteenth century and the reign of Peter I, see Kliuchevskii, 2:235–37; 4:152, 157–58, 184–85; 5:127; 6:459–60; Romanovich-Slavatinskii, pp. 403–5.

55. 1775 statute in *PSZ*, 1st ser., vol. 20, no. 14392; Paul Dukes, *Catherine the Great and the Russian Nobility* (Cambridge, Eng., 1967), pp. 61–63, 225; Romanovich-Slavatinskii, pp. 270–71, 411, 420–21, 430, 446–47, 453–54, 465–74. For the background of the 1775 reform, see Jones, especially pp. 37, 46, 50–88, 180–88, 192, 204, and Dukes, especially pp. 169–75, 222.

56. Jones, p. 283; Geyer, p. 36. Peter the Great's Table of Ranks was a system of parallel military, civil, and court ranks arranged in fourteen classes, with class one at the top and class fourteen at the bottom.

57. See S. Liubimov, *Predvoditeli dvorianstva vsekh namestnichestv, gubernii i oblastei Rossiiskoi imperii, 1777–1910 g.* (St. Petersburg, 1911).

58. B. N. Chicherin, *Neskolko sovremennykh voprosov* (Moscow, 1862), pp. 113–14; Romanovich-Slavatinskii, pp. 461, 473.

59. Kliuchevskii, 5:190.

60. *Russkii arkhiv*, 7 (1869): col. 1977.

61. Romanovich-Slavatinskii, pp. 420, 470, 491–98.

62. *PSZ*, 2d ser., vol. 6, no. 4989.

63. Large landowners were defined as those who owned a minimum of 3,000

desiatiny of land or 100 male serfs; intermediate landowners, between 150 and 3,000 *desiatiny* or between 5 and 100 serfs; and petty proprietors, fewer than 150 *desiatiny* or 5 souls. Intermediate landowners were represented by one elector for each 3,000 *desiatiny* and 100 souls owned by the members of the group who had turned out for the most recent *uezd* assembly. One *desiatina* equals 2.7 acres.

64. Romanovich-Slavatinskii, pp. 435–39, 452; *O sostave*, pp. 78–79, 81, 84.

65. Romanovich-Slavatinskii, pp. 498–99; Baron August, Freiherr von Haxthausen-Abbenburg, *The Russian Empire* (London, 1856), 2:197–98, 211–13; Chicherin, pp. 114–15.

66. The governor's permission was henceforth necessary for the convocation of the *guberniia* assembly, he opened its sessions in person and closed them by written order, and he received from the *guberniia* marshal a list of all those in attendance and a report on all resolutions adopted. Without the governor's permission an assembly session could not be prolonged beyond fifteen days, and in case of disorder in the assembly, the governor was personally to reprimand those responsible and warn them against a recurrence. Romanovich-Slavatinskii, pp. 445–46; *O sostave*, pp. 97–98.

67. 1785 charter, art. 90; *PSZ*, 2d ser., vol. 6, no. 4989, and 2d ser., vol. 11, no. 9322.

68. Romanovich-Slavatinskii, p. 423; *Russkii kostium 1750–1917* (Moscow, 1060–65), 2:102–3.

69. Rieber errs in stating that "in the Collection of Laws of 1892 . . . the government restored the division of the population into four sosloviia: nobility, clergy, townspeople, and rural inhabitants" (p. xxiii). That division needed no restoration, for it had never been abolished. What was restored in the 1892 edition of the statute on *zemstvo* institutions in volume 2 of the *Code* (not the *Complete Collection*) *of Laws* was the division of owners of rural and small-town real property into estates for purposes of electing *uezd zemstvo* assemblies (see chap. 7 below).

70. Romanovich-Slavatinskii, p. 266.

71. G. A. Dzhanshiev, *Epokha velikikh reform*, 8th ed. (Moscow, 1900), pp. 208–11.

72. A. A. Kornilov, *Kurs istorii Rossii XIX veka*, 2d ed. (Moscow, 1918), 2:261.

73. F. M. Dostoevskii, *The Brothers Karamazov*, bk. 12, chap. 1.

74. Ustimovich, pp. 149–50, 155–56, 161–62.

75. "Ustav o sluzhbe po opredeleniiu ot pravitelstva," 1896 ed., art. 6, *SZ*, vol. 3. See chap. 6 below for the abolition of estate distinctions in state service in 1906.

76. N. M. Korkunov, *Russkoe gosudarstvennoe pravo*, 7th ed. (St. Petersburg, 1909), 1:276–78.

77. *O sostave*, pp. 71–72.

78. Romanovich-Slavatinskii, p. 470. Of the other three members of the bureau, one was chosen by the townsmen and two by the peasants.

79. *O sostave*, pp. 52–56; A. P. Korelin, "Rossiiskoe dvorianstvo i ego soslovnaia organizatsiia (1861–1904 gg.)," *Istoriia SSSR*, no. 5 (1971), pp. 72–73. Several arbiters of the peace were named for each *uezd* to settle disputes between noble landowners and their former serfs while the latter remained in a state of "temporary obligation," i.e., until they had concluded agreements with their old masters for the redemption of their land allotments. The arbiters had to approve each of those agreements, which delimited the peasants' allotments and established the amount the landowner would receive as compensation. They also supervised the peasantry's estate institutions at the *selskoe obshchestvo* and *volost* levels. The *uezd* conferences of arbiters were responsible to a *guberniia* bureau for

peasant affairs, a body which combined local bureaucrats with four representatives of the first estate. When the arbiters of the peace were abolished in 1874, some of their functions were transferred to a new *uezd* bureau for peasant affairs constituted in a similar fashion.

80. Until a landowner concluded a redemption agreement with his former serfs (see note 79 above), his estate could not be transferred to anyone but another noble. Lands allotted to former serfs were owned collectively by peasant communes and were subject to redemption payments owed to the state, which advanced to the former serfowners the compensation for the peasant allotments taken from them.

CHAPTER 2

1. *Obshchii svod po imperii rezultatov razrabotki dannykh pervoi vseobshchei perepisi naseleniia, proizvedennoi 28 ianvaria 1897 goda* (St. Petersburg, 1905), 1:92, 172; *Statisticheskiia tablitsy Rossiiskoi imperii. Vyp. 2. Nalichnoe naselenie imperii za 1858 god* (St. Petersburg, 1863), pp. 276–77. In the urban-rural breakdown of the 1858 official population estimate, hereditary nobles were grouped together with personal nobles and nonnoble bureaucrats; of this larger group 32.9 percent was urban in 1858, 57.6 percent in 1897. Personal nobles and officials alone were 78.4 percent urban in 1897 and must have been at least 60–70 percent urban in 1858, at a time when they were barred from owning land inhabited by serfs. Since the ratio of hereditary nobles to personal nobles and nonnoble bureaucrats remained constant throughout the period at 2:1, the hereditary nobility alone in 1858 could not have been more than 15–20 percent urban. The population as a whole was 9.4 percent urban in 1858, 12.9 percent in 1897.

2. *Obshchii svod rezultatov perepisi*, 1:90, 92, 102, 105. The figures for the entire urban population are much lower: only 47.8 percent were living in *uezdy* other than those in which they had been born, and 30.9 percent had left their native *gubernii*.

3. The urban percentage of the total population of European Russia continued to increase in 1897–1914 at the same rate as in 1858–1897, reaching 15 percent in 1914. If the urban percentage of the nobility also continued to increase at the same rate as in the past, it would have reached approximately 80 percent in 1914; if it increased at only half the rate of 1858–1897, it would have reached approximately 60 percent by 1914.

4. The former serfs received 33,756,000 *desiatiny* in land allotments (G. T. Robinson, *Rural Russia under the Old Régime* [New York, 1932], p. 87), while the nobility retained 87,181,000 *desiatiny* in the forty-seven *gubernii* of European Russia minus the Baltic region, where serfs had been emancipated without land in the second decade of the nineteenth century (*MSDZ* 24 [1915]:66–67).

5. Haxthausen-Abbenburg, *Russian Empire*, 2:3, 174, 209–10.

6. Francis H. E. Palmer, *Russian Life in Town and Country* (New York, 1901), pp. 10–13.

7. Anatole Leroy-Beaulieu, *The Empire of the Tsars and the Russians* (New York, 1893–1896), 1:368.

8. Romanovich-Slavatinskii, pp. 165–67.

9. "Zadolzhennost chastnago zemlevladeniia," *Otechestvennye zapiski*, Feb. 1880, pt. 2, pp. 153–54; Sh., "Dvorianstvo v Rossii," *Vestnik Evropy*, Mar. 1887, p. 275; Z., "Sovremennye sofizmy. Novyia soslovnyia tendentsii v nashei pechati," *Vestnik Evropy*, July 1898, p. 336; Vladimir Paltov, *"Vzgliad i nechto" o dvorianstve* (Moscow, 1904), pp. 138–39.

10. Richard Pipes, *Russia*, p. 10. See also Baron August, Freiherr von Haxthausen-Abbenburg, *Studies on the Interior of Russia* (Chicago, 1972), pp. 37–39.

11. Manning, *Crisis*, may be correct in claiming that less land passed "out of gentry hands annually (both proportionately and in absolute terms) in the 1909–1917 period than in any comparable period since the onset of the Long Depression in grain prices of 1877–1896" (p. 364), but four out of nine years in the period in question were the atypical war years 1914–1917. On the other hand, since Manning is presumably using the same unreliable source from which she drew the figures for 1905–1914 on p. 363 (see table D-1), her claim is probably incorrect.

12. *MSDZ* 21 (1912):xiii; ibid. 24 (1915):xi.

13. *MSDZ* 21 (1912):xiv; ibid. 24 (1915):xi: Anfimov and Makarov, p. 86.

14. F. G. Terner, "Dvorianstvo," *Vestnik Evropy*, Mar. 1903, p. 47. Other contemporary observers who noted the nobility's ability to compete successfully for the purchase of land were V. Ionov, "Fakty i illiuzii v voprose dvizheniia chastnoi zemelnoi sobstvennosti," *Zhizn*, Apr. 1900, pp. 195–96, 209; V. V. Sviatlovskii, *Mobilizatsiia zemelnoi sobstvennosti v Rossii (1861–1908 g.)*, 2d ed. (St. Petersburg, 1911), p. 141; M. Iasnopolskii, "Razvitie dvorianskago zemle-vladeniia v sovremennoi Rossii," *Mir bozhii*, Dec. 1903, pt. 1, pp. 215, 222–27; I. G. Drozdov, *Sudby dvorianskago zemlevladeniia v Rossii i tendentsii k ego mobilizatsii* (Petrograd, 1917), p. 16.

15. Anfimov and Makarov, p. 88.

16. Derived from data for 1863–1902 in *MSDZ* 11 (1904):37; 12 (1905):12–13; 14 (1907):12–13; 15 (1908):12–13; 16 (1908):12–13; 17 (1909):14–15; for 1905–1908 in ibid., 20 (1911):22–23, 28–29; 21 (1912):22–23, 28–29; 22 (1913):22–23, 28–29; 23 (1914):22–23, 28–29; and for 1905–1914 in Anfimov and Makarov, p. 85. On this point, see also George L. Yaney, *The Urge to Mobilize* (Urbana, 1982), p. 139.

17. Alternative limits of 250, 500, and even 1,000 *desiatiny*, depending on the region, were at times suggested as the minimum for an intermediate holding, i.e., one large enough to enable a cultured nobleman to support his family without recourse to a supplementary income. See Sh., "Dvorianstvo v Rossii," Mar. 1887, pp. 249, 258; K. Golovin, "Krupnoe zemlevladenie v Zapadnoi Evrope i v Rossii," *Russkii vestnik*, May 1887, pp. 135–36.

18. S. N. Terpigorev, *Potrevozhennye teni* (Moscow, 1959), pp. 283–84.

19. N. P. Zalomanov, *Dvorianskoe zemlevladenie i mery k ego sokhraneniiu i raz-vitiiu* (St. Petersburg, 1899), p. 16.

20. Quoted in Korelin, "Dvorianstvo," p. 148.

21. L. P. Minarik, "'Statistika zemlevladeniia 1905 goda' kak istochnik po izucheniiu krupnogo pomeshchichego zemlevladeniia Rossii v nachale XX veka," in *Maloissledovannye istochniki po istorii SSSR XIX–XX vv.* (Moscow, 1964), pp. 64–66; A. M. Anfimov, *Krupnoe pomeshchiche khoziaistvo Evropeiskoi Rossii* (Moscow, 1969), pp. 31, 382–86. See also L. P. Minarik, "Kharakteristika krup-neishikh zemlevladeltsev Rossii kontsa XIX-nachala XX v.," in *Ezhegodnik po ag-rarnoi istorii Vostochnoi Evropy 1963 g.* (Vilnius, 1964), pp. 693–708, and idem, "Proiskhozhdenie i sostav zemelnykh vladenii krupneishikh pomeshchikov Rossii kontsa XIX-nachala XX v.," *Materialy po istorii selskogo khoziaistva i krestianstva SSSR* 6 (1965):356–95.

22. G. Ershov, ed., *Raspredelenie pozemelnoi sobstvennosti v 49-ti guberniiakh Ev-ropeiskoi Rossii v 1877–78 gg. (Statisticheskii vremennik Rossiiskoi imperii*, 3d ser., vol. 10) (St. Petersburg, 1886), pp. 86–89; *Statistika zemlevladeniia 1905 g. Svod dan-nykh po 50-ti guberniiam Evropeiskoi Rossii* (St. Petersburg, 1907), p. xvi. Chernigov

and Poltava alone contained 24 percent of all noble estates of one hundred *desiatiny* and under in 1905.

23. N. A. Egiazarova, *Agrarnyi krizis kontsa XIX veka v Rossii* (Moscow, 1959), pp. 48, 71; P. A. Khromov, *Ekonomika Rossii perioda promyshlennogo kapitalizma* (Moscow, 1963), pp. 205–7; George Pavlovsky, *Agricultural Russia on the Eve of the Revolution* (London, 1930), p. 192; Anfimov, *Krupnoe pomeshchiche khoziaistvo*, p. 373. Gary M. Hamburg, "Land, Economy, and Society in Tsarist Russia: Interest Politics of the Landed Gentry during the Agrarian Crisis of the Late Nineteenth Century" (Ph.D. diss., Stanford University, 1978), asserts that the agricultural depression was directly responsible for the heavy mortgaging and selling of noble land. The areas Hamburg claims were hardest hit by the depression (the Black Soil center and the Volga), however, were regions of relatively moderate decline in noble acreage (pp. 74–76).

24. For landowners' methods of exploiting their estates in the Baltic and western *gubernii* and on the southern steppes and lower Volga, see N. M. Druzhinin, "Pomeshchiche khoziaistvo posle reformy 1861 g. (Po dannym Valuevskoi komissii 1872–1873 gg.)," *Istoricheskie zapiski*, 89 (1972):208–14; Anfimov, *Krupnoe pomeshchiche khoziaistvo*, p. 180; Egiazarova, pp. 69–70; P. P. Maslov, "Razvitie zemledeliia i polozhenie krestian do nachala XX veka," in L. Martov, P. Maslov, and A. Potresov, eds., *Obshchestvennoe dvizhenie v Rossii v nachale XX-go veka* (St. Petersburg, 1909–1914), 1:3–4, 9–11; N. P. Pershin, *Agrarnaia revoliutsiia v Rossii* (Moscow, 1966), 1:67–78.

25. Robinson, p. 94.

26. Alexander Gerschenkron, "Problems and Patterns of Russian Economic Development," in Cyril E. Black, ed., *The Transformation of Russian Society* (Cambridge, Mass., 1960), p. 44.

27. Iasnopolskii, p. 214; Anfimov, *Krupnoe pomeshchiche khoziaistvo*, pp. 81–82, 365; idem, *Zemelnaia arenda v Rossii v nachale XX veka* (Moscow, 1961), p. 21; Peter I. Lyashchenko, *History of the National Economy of Russia to the 1917 Revolution* (New York, 1949), p. 466.

28. Minarik, "Kharakteristika krupneishikh zemlevladeltsev," pp. 624–25.

29. Anfimov, *Krupnoe pomeshchiche khoziaistvo*, p. 375.

30. Quoted in Lyashchenko, p. 466.

31. Anfimov, *Zemelnaia arenda*, pp. 195–96.

32. V. Ia. Laverychev, *Krupnaia burzhuaziia v poreformennoi Rossii 1861–1900* (Moscow, 1974), p. 68; Anfimov, *Krupnoe pomeshchiche khoziaistvo*, pp. 274–78.

33. All ruble amounts are in silver rubles, worth approximately fifty cents from the late 1890s to 1914. Data on land prices for the periods 1854–1858 and 1863–1902 are from *MSDZ* 13 (1907): table 4; for 1903–1905, from ibid. 21 (1912):xxxii.

34. These aggregate values have been calculated by multiplying the acreage figures for 1862 and 1905 (from *MSDZ* 24 [1915]:66–67) by land prices in each *guberniia* for those years. To minimize year to year fluctuations, the average prices for 1854–1858 and for 1863–1867 have been averaged to obtain 1862 prices, and the averages for 1903–1905 have been used for 1905. Using a variety of sources not necessarily compatible with each other, Anfimov places the aggregate value of noble land in 1861 at 1.345 billion rubles, and in 1905 at 4.945 billion, resulting in an increase in value of 268 percent (*Krupnoe pomeshchiche khoziaistvo*, p. 358).

35. Based on data in S. G. Strumilin, *Ocherki ekonomicheskoi istorii Rossii i SSSR* (Moscow, 1966), pp. 89–90.

36. Average land prices for 1905–1906 are in *MSDZ* 21 (1912):xxxii; for 1907–1908, ibid. 23 (1914):xxi–xxii; for 1909, ibid. 24 (1915):xxi; for 1912,

Anfimov, *Krupnoe pomeshchiche khoziaistvo*, p. 358. Estimates of inflation in the period 1905–1913 range from 2.3 percent to 3.7 percent per annum—the average is 2.8 percent (Strumilin, pp. 89–90).

37. Khromov, *Ekonomika Rossii*, pp. 31–32; Anfimov, *Zemelnaia arenda*, pp. 191–92.

38. I. D. Kovalchenko and L. V. Milov, *Vserossiiskii agrarnyi rynok XVIII-nachalo XX veka. Opyt kolichestvennogo analiza* (Moscow, 1974), p. 267.

39. Terner, pp. 17, 46, 48–53.

40. Quoted in A. N. Volkov-Muromtsev, *Memoirs of Alexander Wolkoff-Mouromtzoff* (London, 1928), p. 363.

41. P. A. Zaionchkovskii, *Provedenie v zhizn krestianskoi reformy 1861 g.* (Moscow, 1958), pp. 309–10.

42. These sources of long-term credit were the Noble Bank, founded in 1754 and reorganized in 1786 as the State Loan Bank; the Petersburg and Moscow foundling homes' reserve capital; and the reserve capital of the *guberniia* charity boards established in 1775. See S. Ia. Borovoi, *Kredit i banki Rossii (seredina XVII v.-1861 g.)* (Moscow, 1958), pp. 46–49, 63, 68–71, 118–23, 183, 192, 194–95, 197, 200.

43. Walter M. Pintner, *Russian Economic Policy under Nicholas I* (Ithaca, 1967), p. 39.

44. *O zadolzhennosti zemlevladeniia v sviazi s statisticheskimi dannymi o pritoke kapitalov k pomestnomu zemlevladeniiu so vremeni osvobozhdeniia krestian* (*Vremennik tsentralnago statisticheskago komiteta*, no. 2 [1888]), p. v; Borovoi, *Kredit*, p. 197.

45. Pavlovsky, p. 101; Anfimov, *Krupnoe pomeshchiche khoziaistvo*, p. 318.

46. Excluding the Baltic *gubernii*, which had their own noble land banks, and also Archangel, Olonets, Bessarabia, and the Don Army Oblast. See *Tsifrovyia dannyia o pozemelnoi sobstvennosti v Evropeiskoi Rossii* (St. Petersburg, 1897), pp. 38–39.

47. Ibid.

48. TsGIAL, f. 593, op. 1, d. 101, ll. 251–53.

49. *Guberniia* ratios were calculated in the manner described in table 14 and appendix E, using data on the mortgage debt of landed serfowners in 1859 from *O zadolzhennosti zemlevladeniia*, table following p. xx; a prorated share of the mortgage debt on all private individually owned land at the beginning of 1906, from *Ezhegodnik Rossii 1908 g.*, pp. xciv–xcv; and estimated aggregate values for noble land at the end of 1862 and 1905.

50. Anfimov, *Krupnoe pomeshchiche khoziaistvo*, p. 320.

51. In Samara, where noble land losses were exceptionally high, many landowners had received their estates as grants from the state in the decade or two immediately preceding serf emancipation, had never settled on or personally undertaken to farm them, and thus readily converted them into other forms of capital starting in the 1870s.

52. B. B. Veselovskii, "Dvizhenie zemlevladeltsev," in L. Martov, P. Maslov, and A. Potresov, *Obshchestvennoe dvizhenie v Rossii v nachale XX-go veka* (St. Petersburg, 1909), 1:297. Hamburg attributes the interest in a Noble Land Bank among the landowners of the Black Soil *gubernii* to the fact that "these were the areas most burdened by mortgage debts to private land banks" ("Land," p. 93); elsewhere he claims that the "agrarian crisis would seem to be the primary reason for [the] high rate of indebtedness" among the nobility (ibid., p. 27).

53. I. F. Gindin, *Gosudarstvennyi bank i ekonomicheskaia politika tsarskogo pravitelstva (1861–1892 gody)* (Moscow, 1960), p. 106.

54. *Ezhegodnik Rossii 1908 g.*, pp. xcii–xciii.

55. See chap. 4 below for the requirement that commoners liquidate mortgages

held by the Noble Land Bank within ten years. Had the previous trend (a 25 percent increase in repayments in each quinquennium) continued, 175 million rubles would have been repaid in the period 1906–1913; the amount actually repaid was 41 percent above this figure.

56. See, for example, P. N. Miliukov, *Ocherki po istorii russkoi kultury*, pt. 1, 6th ed. (St. Petersburg, 1909), pp. 234–35; A. A. Planson, *O dvorianstve v Rossii. Sovremennoe polozhenie voprosa* (St. Petersburg, 1893), pp. 60–61; V. [P.] V[o-rontsov], "Dvorianskoe zemlevladenie posle reformy," *Russkaia mysl*, Oct. 1898, pt. 2, pp. 91–92, 97.

57. See, for example, L. Z. Slonimskii, "Pozemelnyia zadachi," *Vestnik Evropy*, Aug. 1894, p. 812, and Sept. 1894, p. 342.

58. This point was made for the pre-emancipation period by Michael Confino, "Histoire et psychologie: A propos de la noblesse russe au XVIIIᵉ siècle," *Annales: Economies-Sociétés-Civilisations* 22 (1967):1195, and by Roderick E. McGrew, "The Politics of Absolutism: Paul I and the Bank of Assistance for the Nobility," *Canadian-American Slavic Studies* 7 (1973):26.

59. Anfimov, *Krupnoe pomeshchiche khoziaistvo*, pp. 320–24; Gindin, p. 106; B. G. Litvak, *Russkaia derevnia v reforme 1861 goda. Chernozemnyi tsentr 1861–1895 gg.* (Moscow, 1972), p. 379.

60. Manning, *Crisis*, p. 8.

61. A. S. Nifontov, "Formirovanie klassov burzhuaznogo obshchestva v russkom gorode vtoroi poloviny XIX v. (Po materialam perepisei naseleniia g. Moskvy v 70–90-kh godakh XIX v.)," *Istoricheskie zapiski* 54 (1955):243.

62. Laverychev, p. 69.

63. See, for example, "Zadolzhennost chastnago zemlevladeniia," pp. 153–54.

64. Laverychev, pp. 69–70; Anfimov, *Krupnoe pomeshchiche khoziaistvo*, pp. 286–87, 304–5.

CHAPTER 3

1. Kliuchevskii, 6:285, 288–89, 298.

2. Chicherin as quoted in *Vestnik Evropy*, July 1897, p. 370, and in Iu. B. Soloviev, "Pechat o politicheskoi roli dvorianstva v kontse XIX v.," in *Problemy krestianskogo zemlevladeniia i vnutrennei politiki Rossii. Dooktiabrskii period* (Leningrad, 1972), p. 215. See also Leonard Schapiro, *Rationalism and Nationalism in Russian Nineteenth-Century Political Thought* (New Haven, 1967), pp. 95–96.

3. I. S. Aksakov, "Dvorianskoe delo," in A. I. Koshelev, ed., *Golos iz zemstva* (Moscow, 1869), 1:33–49; A. I. Koshelev, "Chto takoe russkoe dvorianstvo, i chem ono byt dolzhno?" and "O dvorianstve i zemlevladeltsakh," in Koshelev, *Golos iz zemstva*, 1:28–41, 52–69; Korkunov, 1:274–75; Baron S. A. Korf, "Predvoditel dvorianstva, kak organ soslovnago i zemskago samoupravleniia," *Zhurnal ministerstva iustitsii*, Mar. 1902, pt. 2, pp. 109–10. See also Koshelev's *O sosloviiakh i sostoianiiakh v Rossii* (Moscow, 1881). Similar views were expressed by the historian K. D. Kavelin in 1862 (*Sobranie sochinenii* [St. Petersburg, 1897–1900], vol. 2, cols. 126–27, 147) and in Sh., "Dvorianstvo v Rossii," June 1887, pp. 442–47, and Z., pp. 324–25, 327.

4. Quoted in Soloviev, "Samoderzhavie i dvorianskii vopros v kontse XIX v.," *Istoricheskie zapiski* 88 (1971):159–61, 164–65; I. F. Gindin and M. Ia. Gefter, eds., "Trebovaniia dvorianstva i finansovo-ekonomicheskaia politika tsarskogo pravitelstva v 1880–1890-kh godakh," *Istoricheskii arkhiv*, no. 4 (1957), p. 137.

5. Field, pp. 361–62.

6. L. Z. Slonimskii, "Ekonomicheskie zametki. Selskokhoziaistvennyi krizis i

dvorianskoe zemlevladenie," *Vestnik Evropy*, July 1897, pp. 318–19; A. I. Elishev in *Russkoe obozrenie*, Apr. 1897, p. 930.

7. *Sliianie soslovii, ili dvorianstvo, drugiia sostoianiia i zemstvo* (St. Petersburg, 1870).

8. R. A. Fadeev, *Russkoe obshchestvo v nastoiashchem i budushchem (Chem nam byt?)*, in *Sobranie sochinenii* (St. Petersburg, 1889), vol. 3, pt. 1, pp. 64, 66 [a series of articles which first appeared in *Russkii mir*, then as a book in 1874].

9. I. A. Porai-Koshits, *Ocherk istorii russkago dvorianstva ot poloviny IX do kontsa XVIII veka, 862–1796* (St. Petersburg, 1874), pp. vii–x.

10. Leroy-Beaulieu, 1:309.

11. *Vestnik Evropy*, Apr. 1885, p. 816.

12. A. D. Pazukhin, *Sovremennoe sostoianie Rossii i soslovnyi vopros* (Moscow, 1886). According to Rieber, Pazukhin's article in *Russkii vestnik* was a revision of a memorandum he had submitted to the government a few years earlier, perhaps while he was serving on the Kakhanov commission (p. 95n.). The creation in 1889 of the office of *zemskii nachalnik* and the reform of the *zemstvo* institutions the following year were largely Pazukhin's work. See chap. 7 below.

13. Planson, *O dvorianstve v Rossii*; idem, *Sosloviia v drevnei i sovremennoi Rossii, ikh polozhenie i nuzhdy* (St. Petersburg, 1899); A. I. Elishev, *Dvorianskoe delo* (Moscow, 1898).

14. For a summary of the points raised in these petitions, prepared in July 1897 for the Special Conference on the Affairs of the Noble Estate, see TsGIAL, f. 1283, op. 1, d. 4, ll. 1–3.

15. Pazukhin, pp. 44–52; Elishev, *Dvorianskoe delo*, pp. 78, 125; idem, "Sliianie soslovii," *Russkoe obozrenie*, Sept. 1897, pp. 282–83; F. E. Romer, "Padenie dvorianstva," *Russkii vestnik*, Feb. 1900, p. 739; Paltov, pp. 9–10.

16. Paltov, p. 135. The concept of noble blood always lurked just below the surface of public discussions of the noble question. In May 1899 a subcommittee of the special conference on the nobility considered a proposal to deprive of their noble status "those nobles who have fallen into total poverty and have lost any connection to their social estate," who were illiterate and lived as "simple plowmen," often worse off than their peasant neighbors. The majority of the members rejected the idea, proposing instead to offer impoverished nobles educational opportunities, loans, and even grants of land in Siberia, with a view to reviving in their descendants "those traits of character which are inherent in the hereditary nobility and have been temporarily suppressed only because of an unsuitable manner of life." (TsGIAL, f. 1283, op. 1, d. 13, ll. 16–17.) The confidence that inherent traits could not be obliterated by an ignoble style of life belied the usual assertion of defenders of privilege that it was precisely the nobility's manner of life and upbringing that endowed it with its superior capability for state service and therefore justified its privileges.

17. Pazukhin, p. 30; Paltov, p. 7; Romer, pp. 738–39; Elishev, *Dvorianskoe delo*, pp. 81–82, 125, 148; Elishev in *Russkoe obozrenie*, Apr. 1897, pp. 934–35; idem, "Ocherki dvorianskago dela," *Russkoe obozrenie*, Nov. 1897, pp. 285–88.

18. Elishev, *Dvorianskoe delo*, pp. 8, 82–85; M. K. Polivanov, *Mysli o pomestnom nachale v Rossii* (Vladimir, 1897), pp. 4–5; N. P. Semenov, *Nashe dvorianstvo* (St. Petersburg, 1898), pp. 13–14; Paltov, pp. 158–59.

19. Valerii Liaskovskii, "Pomestnaia sluzhba," *Russkoe obozrenie*, June 1893, pp. 550–53; Paltov, pp. 48, 144–48, 154.

20. Semenov, pp. 18–25; Elishev, "Sliianie soslovii," p. 291.

21. Pazukhin, pp. 10–11; Elishev, *Dvorianskoe delo*, pp. 126, 188; Elishev in *Russkoe obozrenie*, May 1897, p. 486, Sept. 1897, pp. 280–82, and May 1898, pp. 303, 310; Planson, *Sosloviia*, pp. 9–10; Paltov, p. 90.

22. Planson, *Sosloviia*, pp. 15–25; Romer, pp. 747–48; Semenov, pp. 14–16, 44–45; V. V. Iarmonkin, *Zadacha dvorianstva* (St. Petersburg, 1895), pp. 1–3; Elishev, *Dvorianskoe delo*, pp. 87–93; Elishev in *Russkoe obozrenie*, May 1897, pp. 484–85.

23. Elishev, *Dvorianskoe delo*, pp. 61–62; Elishev in *Russkoe obozrenie*, May 1898, p. 304; Semenov, pp. 14–15.

24. Pazukhin, p. 29; editorial in *Moskovskie vedomosti*, no. 8 (1865), reprinted in M. N. Katkov, *O dvorianstve* (Moscow, 1905), p. 43; I. N. Durnovo's memorandum to Nicholas II, Apr. 2, 1897, TsGIAL, f. 1283, op. 1, d. 236, ll. 1–9; Liaskovskii, p. 552; Elishev, *Dvorianskoe delo*, pp. 108–9, 118, 187, 193. A *raznochinets* in the technical sense was a person, for example a professional man, who had left the estate of his parents but had not enrolled in another.

25. Talcott Parsons, "Some Principal Characteristics of Industrial Societies," in Cyril E. Black, ed., *The Transformation of Russian Society* (Cambridge, Mass., 1960), p. 20.

26. Everett E. Hagen, *On the Theory of Social Change* (Homewood, Ill., 1962), pp. 60–61.

27. Gerth and Mills, pp. 192–93.

28. Ibid., p. 192.

29. See, for example, Alexander Gerschenkron, *Economic Backwardness in Historical Perspective* (Cambridge, Mass., 1962), pp. 59–62. David S. Landes, *The Unbound Prometheus* (Cambridge, Eng., 1969), has noted that "the farther east one goes in Europe, the more the bourgeoisie takes on the appearance of a foreign excrescence on manorial society, a group apart scorned by the nobility" (p. 129).

30. Pazukhin, pp. 13, 42–43.

31. Elishev, *Dvorianskoe delo*, pp. 87–93; Planson, *Sosloviia*, pp. 15–25; Romer, pp. 747–48; Semenov, pp. 14–16, 44–45; Iarmonkin, *Zadacha*, pp. 1–3.

32. Quoted in Gosudarstvennyi sovet, *Otchet po deloproizvodstvu za sessiiu 1899–1900 gg.* (hereafter, Gos. sovet, *Otchet za [dates]*), 2:586–87. For the 1881 manifesto, see P. A. Zaionchkovskii, *Krizis samoderzhaviia na rubezhe 1870–1880-kh godov* (Moscow, 1964), pp. 369–75.

33. Iu. B. Soloviev, *Samoderzhavie i dvorianstvo v kontse XIX veka* (Leningrad, 1973), pp. 169, 171, 179; P. A. Zaionchkovskii, *Rossiiskoe samoderzhavie v kontse XIX stoletiia* (Moscow, 1970), pp. 48, 61–64, 70–72, 74–77, 89–90, 141; Heide W. Whelan, *Alexander III and the State Council: Bureaucracy and Counter-Reform in Late Imperial Russia* (New Brunswick, 1982), pp. 76–78.

34. Quoted in Gos. sovet, *Otchet za 1899–1900*, 2:587.

35. Quoted in *Khrestomatiia po istorii SSSR, 1861–1917* (Moscow, 1970), pp. 302–3.

36. Soloviev, *Samoderzhavie i dvorianstvo v kontse XIX veka*, pp. 252–70.

37. Ibid., pp. 234–35, 246–49. Durnovo's Apr. 2 memorandum, with the emperor's note of approval in the margin, is in TsGIAL, f. 1283, op. 1, d. 236, ll. 1–9. For Witte's position, see Witte to Pobedonostsev, [Apr.] 12, 1897, "Perepiska Vitte i Pobedonostseva (1895–1905 gg.)," *Krasnyi arkhiv* 30 (1928):98–99. The text of the Apr. 13 rescript is in G. E. Blosfeldt, ed., *Sbornik zakonov o rossiiskom dvorianstve* (St. Petersburg, 1901), p. 213.

38. The original eleven were: A. S. Ermolov, minister of agriculture and state domains; I. L. Goremykin, minister of internal affairs; N. V. Muraviev, minister of justice; Witte; Count I. I. Vorontsov-Dashkov, minister of the imperial court; A. N. Kulomzin, executive secretary of the Committee of Ministers; N. S. Abaza, a member of the State Council; Count S. D. Sheremetev, also a member of the State Council and a former *guberniia* marshal of nobility in Moscow; Pleve; D. S. Sipiagin, a former deputy minister both of state domains and of internal

affairs, since 1895 the official in charge of receiving petitions to the emperor, and from 1899 to 1902 minister of internal affairs; and A. S. Stishinskii, who had worked in the Ministry of Internal Affairs in the late 1880s on the counter-reforms and was subsequently to serve as deputy minister in that department under Sipiagin and Pleve from 1899 to 1904. In May 1897, A. A. Golenishchev-Kutuzov, the secretary and director of chancellery for the dowager empress Maria Fedorovna, was added to the conference, as were Prince A. D. Obolenskii, deputy minister of internal affairs, and Prince A. A. Liven, director of the State Noble Land Bank, in October.

39. The three marshals who were added in March 1898 were L. M. Muromtsov of Riazan, P. A. Krivskii of Saratov, and A. A. Arseniev of Tula. The six marshals who were named to the subcommittees were V. A. Kapnist of Kharkov, M. N. Leontiev of Vladimir, P. N. Trubetskoi of Moscow, A. D. Zinoviev of St. Petersburg, B. A. Vasilchikov of Novgorod, and A. P. Strukov of Ekaterinoslav. TsGIAL, f. 1283, op. 1, d. 236, ll. 11, 16, 23, 44, 50, 64–66.

40. TsGIAL, f. 1283, op. 1, d. 4, ll. 185–93. The memoranda produced by the conference's members are in ibid., ll. 12–53 and 103–66. The conference's first title appears as the printed letterhead on a note from Durnovo to Goremykin of April 17 (TsGIAL, f. 1283, op. 1, d. 22, l. 1); the second, as a handwritten correction to the printed letterhead on a June 4 note from Durnovo to Witte (TsGIAL, f. 1283, op. 1, d. 4, l. 174).

41. The quotation is from Witte to Pobedonostsev, [Apr.] 12, 1897, "Perepiska Vitte i Pobedonostseva," pp. 98–99. See also Soloviev, "Samoderzhavie i dvorianskii vopros," pp. 152–53, 159–61, 164–65. Witte's memorandum for the May 10 session is in TsGIAL, f. 1283, op. 1, d. 4, ll. 98–101; his correspondence with Durnovo is in ibid., ll. 174, 177–84.

42. Quoted in Iu. B. Soloviev, "Pravitelstvo i politika ukrepleniia klassovykh pozitsii dvorianstva v kontse XIX veka," in *Vnutrenniaia politika tsarizma (seredina XVI-nachalo XX v.)* (Leningrad, 1967), p. 279.

43. In the summer of 1897 Durnovo requested all *guberniia* marshals of nobility to submit their suggestions for the improvement of the first estate's corporate institutions, of the education of noble youths, and of the material well-being of noble landowners. Durnovo's circular is in TsGADA, f. 1254, op. 1, d. 83, ll. 1–2; the conference's agenda is in TsGIAL, f. 1283, op. 1, d. 4, ll. 195–96.

CHAPTER 4

1. Semenov, p. 74.

2. A. I. Elishev in *Russkoe obozrenie*, May 1898, pp. 311–13. See also Polivanov, *Mysli*, p. 108, and the fears expressed earlier by *Moskovskie vedomosti*, quoted in F. Danilov, "Obshchaia politika pravitelstva i gosudarstvennyi stroi k nachalu XX veka," in L. Martov, P. Maslov, A. Potresov, eds., *Obshchestvennoe dvizhenie v Rossii v nachale XX-go veka* (St. Petersburg, 1909–1914), 1:441.

3. Liaskovskii, pp. 566–67.

4. Blum, *End of the Old Order*, p. 419.

5. Elishev, *Dvorianskoe delo*, p. 118; N. Karyshev, "Mezhdusoslovnaia mobilizatsiia zemel v 45 guberniiakh v 1893-m g.," *Russkoe bogatstvo*, Jan. 1898, pt. 2, p. 16; S. S. Bekhteev, *Khoziaistvennye itogi istekshago sorokapiatiletiia i mery k khoziaistvennomu podëmu* (St. Petersburg, 1902–1911), 1:12.

6. Elishev, *Dvorianskoe delo*, p. 210. See also Semenov, pp. 59–61; N. E. Baratynskii, *Sbornik statei o dvorianskikh nedelimykh imeniiakh* (St. Petersburg,

208 · NOTES TO PAGES 68–71

1893), p. 124; D. V., "Gosudarstvennyi soslovnyi kredit," *Russkii vestnik*, June 1885, pp. 848–49, 859–60.

7. Pavlovsky, pp. 119–20, 129; Zaionchkovskii, *Rossiiskoe samoderzhavie*, pp. 200–203.

8. Semenov, pp. 70–72; Elishev, *Dvorianskoe delo*, p. 210, and in *Russkoe obozrenie*, May 1898, p. 313; TsGIAL, f. 1283, op. 1, d. 4, ll. 1–3; *Severnyi vestnik*, Dec. 1889, pp. 104–6.

9. TsGIAL, f. 593, op. 1, d. 101, l. 268; Soloviev, *Samoderzhavie i dvorianstvo v kontse XIX veka*, pp. 210–11.

10. *Russkaia mysl*, Apr. 1896, pt. 2, pp. 185–86; A. Smolenskii, "Dvorianskii vopros," *Novoe slovo*, Aug. 1897, pt. 2, pp. 134–35; TsGADA, f. 1254, op. 1, d. 86, ll. 3a–7a.

11. TsGADA, f. 1254, op. 1, d. 86, l. 7a; Soloviev, *Samoderzhavie i dvorianstvo v kontse XIX veka*, p. 350; idem, "Samoderzhavie i dvorianskii vopros," p. 202; TsGIAL, f. 1283, op. 1, d. 236, l. 66.

12. F. M. L. Thompson, *English Landed Society in the Nineteenth Century* (London, 1963), pp. 66–68. Along with other aspects of the land laws in England, entail was under attack by the advocates of free trade in land. Although their aims were not fully realized until 1925, there was a fundamental change in the nature of entail as a consequence of the Settled Land Act of 1882, which permitted the life-tenant of an entailed estate to sell part or all of it; the money realized from the sale, however, if it was not spent on the improvement of the estate, remained subject to the settlement. In other words, from 1882 it was the capital value of the land rather than the land per se that was the object of the entail. See Thompson, pp. 283–84 and David Spring, *The English Landed Estate in the Nineteenth Century: Its Administration* (Baltimore, 1963), p. 175.

13. Blum, *End of the Old Order*, pp. 428–29.

14. The 1909 figures are from Anfimov, *Krupnoe pomeshchiche khoziaistvo*, p. 42; by an error in addition, Anfimov gives the total as 991,000 *desiatiny*. The percentages have been calculated on the basis of 1905 data on total noble holdings and acreage from *Statistika zemlevladeniia 1905 g.*, p. 12, and would actually be slightly higher if based on 1909 data.

15. *PSZ*, 1st ser., vol. 5, no. 2789, Romanovich-Slavatinskii, pp. 248–52.

16. Anfimov, *Krupnoe pomeshchiche khoziaistvo*, p. 43, Romanovich-Slavatinskii, pp. 254–55. The law of July 16, 1845, is in Blosfeldt, *Sbornik zakonov*, pp. 252–64. Entails created under this law were officially designated *zapovednye nasledstvennye imeniia* (entailed hereditary estates) but were commonly referred to as *maioraty*, a term also used for Polish entails in the western *gubernii*, because they descended by primogeniture.

17. TsGIAL, f. 593, op. 1, d. 101, l. 307; Gosudarstvennyi sovet, *Vsepoddanneishii otchet predsedatelia za sessiiu 1898–1899 gg.*, pp. 18–19.

18. The number of landowners in 1877 qualifying for the establishment of *maioraty* is based on Ershov, p. 35; of landholdings qualifying in 1905, from *Statistika zemlevladeniia 1905 g.*, p. 78. Had the old minimum been retained, only 527 estates (0.5 percent) would have qualified in 1905. Between 1845 and 1870, seventeen *maioraty* were established (Romanovich-Slavatinskii, p. 256); between 1871 and 1888, thirteen (A. V. Meshcherskii, *Poiasnitelnaia zapiska No. 2-i po povodu khodataistva poltavskago dvorianstva o svobode zaveshchaniia zapovednykh imenii* [Moscow, 1888], p. 2); between 1889 and 1898, twenty-five (TsGIAL, f. 593, op. 1, d. 101, l. 271); and between 1899 and 1905, five (Terner, "Dvorianstvo," Aug. 1905, p. 489). The acreage encompassed by *maioraty* in 1914 is from Anfimov, *Krupnoe pomeshchiche khoziaistvo*, p. 46. Percentages were calculated on the basis of data in *Statistika zemlevladeniia 1905 g.*, pp. 12, 28, 36, 56, 58, 78,

yielding 22 percent and 10 percent, but there was a significant decrease in noble acreage after 1905.

19. V. P. Orlov-Davydov, "Zemledelie i zemlevladenie," *Vestnik Evropy*, June 1873, p. 856; *Russkaia mysl*, Apr. 1880, pt. 5, p. 64; N. E. Baratynskii, "O nedelimykh imeniiakh," *Russkii vestnik*, May 1892, p. 276. See also Leroy-Beaulieu, 1:360–61, 394.

20. N. E. Baratynskii, *Iz gubernii* (St. Petersburg, 1887), reprinted in his *Sbornik statei o dvorianskikh nedelimykh imeniiakh* (St. Petersburg, 1893), pp. 1–57. This collection also includes four other works by Baratynskii that had appeared between 1888 and 1892. Prince Meshcherskii published a memorandum on the Poltava nobility's petition (see above, n. 18) and two pamphlets, each entitled *O zapovednykh imeniiakh* (St. Petersburg, 1888, and Moscow, 1894).

21. TsGIAL, f. 593, op. 1, d. 101, l. 265; Baratynskii, "O nedelimykh imeniiakh," p. 277; *Vestnik Evropy*, Apr. 1892, p. 845. For the noble assemblies' petition campaign on entail, see Hamburg, "Land," chap. 5.

22. For the discussion of entail by the Abaza commission, see Soloviev, "Pravitelstvo i politika," pp. 243–50; by the special conference, TsGIAL, f. 593, op. 1, d. 101, ll. 265–82, 295–99; by the State Council, ibid., ll. 464–78, 498–505, and Gosudarstvennyi sovet, *Vsepoddanneishii otchet predsedatelia za sessiiu 1898–1899 gg.*, pp. 17–19.

23. The Homestead Act was cited as a model in Meshcherskii, *Poiasnitelnaia zapiska*, pp. 10–13, and *O zapovednykh imeniiakh* (1888), pp. 4, 14; Baratynskii, *Sbornik statei*, pp. 116–17 and "O nedelimykh imeniiakh," pp. 268–75; *Russkii vestnik*, May 1892, pp. 387–89; Zalomanov, pp. 36–37. Contrary to the claims made in these books and articles, homestead allotments were inalienable only during the five-year period during which a farmer was working the land and establishing his right to a definitive title to it. Once he received title at the end of five years of residence and cultivation, he could dispose of the land or mortgage it as he pleased. And only in the case of debts contracted prior to the award of title was the property exempt from forced sale to satisfy creditors. See *Revised Statutes of the United States, passed at the First Session of the Forty-Third Congress, 1873–74*, 2d ed. (Washington, D.C., 1878), title 32, chap. 5, sec. 2289, 2291, 2296. This is the edition cited by Meshcherskii.

24. Absenteeism among the noble landowners of Kazan *guberniia* in 1888 was highest among the owners of fewer than 200 *desiatiny* and more than 2,000. N. E. Baratynskii, "Nedelimye dvorianskie uchastki," *Russkii vestnik*, May 1888, pp. 74–76.

25. *Vestnik Evropy*, Apr. 1892, pp. 840–41, 853–54; N. E. Baratynskii, "Semeinye uchastki v bytovom otnoshenii," *Russkii vestnik*, May 1890, pp. 210–11; idem, "O nedelimykh imeniiakh," pp. 277–80; idem, *Sbornik statei*, pp. 48–49, 118, 121; idem, "Nedelimye dvorianskie uchastki," p. 83.

26. Meshcherskii, *Poiasnitelnaia zapiska*, p. 9; idem, *O zapovednykh imeniiakh* (1894), p. 15; D. V., "Gosudarstvennyi soslovnyi kredit," pp. 861–62; *Vestnik Evropy*, Apr. 1892, p. 844.

27. *Vestnik Evropy*, Mar. 1893, p. 377; *Sovremennye dvorianskie voprosy* (St. Petersburg, 1897), p. 30.

28. Approximately 18,000 estates met the minimum size in the thirty-seven *gubernii* with noble elections (see chap. 7 below), of which 500 were too large for term entail (see n. 18 above). In the nine western *gubernii* and in Viatka and Perm, where the minimum size was set in 1899 at 125–475 *desiatiny* (Blosfeldt, *Sbornik zakonov*, pp. 273–76), an additional 9,300 properties fell between the upper and lower limits for term entail.

29. *Vestnik Evropy*, Apr. 1892, p. 852, and Mar. 1893, p. 377; *Sovremennye*

dvorianskie voprosy, p. 32; Planson, *O dvorianstve v Rossii*, p. 45. In England property was entailed for three generations only, typically by a father for his eldest son and the latter's eldest son until the age of twenty-one. Normally the property was resettled in each generation at the time of the eldest son's marriage.

30. Meshcherskii, *Poiasnitelnaia zapiska*, p. 9; idem, *O zapovednykh imeniiakh* (1894), pp. 15-16.

31. V. A., "K dvorianskomu voprosu," *Russkoe bogatstvo*, Nov. 1897, pt. 2, pp. 15-16; Baratynskii, *Sbornik statei*, p. 47; A. A. Planson, "*Osoboe soveshchanie.*" *Zapiska* (St. Petersburg, 1897), p. 21.

32. Soloviev, *Samoderzhavie i dvorianstvo v kontse XIX veka*, pp. 316-17; idem, "Pravitelstvo i politika," pp. 249-50; idem, "Samoderzhavie i dvorianskii vopros," p. 187; TsGIAL, f. 593, op. 1, d. 101, l. 266; Gosudarstvennyi sovet, *Stenograficheskie otchety, 1911-12 gg.*, col. 1608.

33. *Russkaia mysl*, Apr. 1880, pt. 5, pp. 60-61; Baratynskii, "Nedelimye dvorianskie uchastki," pp. 76-77; D., *K voprosu o dvorianskom zemlevladenii* (Moscow, 1888); *Russkaia mysl*, Apr. 1896, p. 186; TsGIAL, f. 1283, op. 1, d. 4, ll. 1-3. See also Golovin, "Krupnoe zemlevladenie," May 1887, pp. 136-37, and Semenov, p. 74.

34. "Svod zakonov grazhdanskikh," 1900 ed., arts. 396-99, 1067-68, 1112, *SZ*, vol. 10, pt. 1. The nationwide conference of *guberniia* marshals in the late 1890s rejected a proposal to equalize the legal shares of sons and daughters. TsGADA, f. 1254, op. 1, d. 104, ll. 1a-1b.

35. TsGIAL, f. 593, op. 1, d. 101, ll. 268-69, 307-9.

36. TsGIAL, f. 593, op. 1, d. 101, l. 178; the various revisions of Trubetskoi's proposal are in TsGIAL, f. 1283, op. 1, d. 87, ll. 133, 200-205 and TsGADA, f. 1254, op. 1, dd. 97, 103, 104; TsGIAL, f. 1283, op. 1, dd. 187, 72b, 187a; "Svod zakonov grazhdanskikh," 1900 ed., art. 1068, as amended on June 3, 1912. See also William G. Wagner, "Legislative Reform of Inheritance in Russia, 1861-1914," in William E. Butler, ed., *Russian Law: Historical and Political Perspectives* (Leyden, 1977), pp. 167-75.

37. "Svod zakonov grazhdanskikh," 1900 ed., arts. 1346-73; Terner, "Dvorianstvo," Mar. 1903, pp. 23-24 and Aug. 1905, pp. 495-96.

38. TsGIAL, f. 1283, op. 1, d. 4, ll. 1-3; A. D. Zinoviev, *Zapiska o merakh k oblegcheniiu polozheniia zaemshchikov Gosudarstvennago dvorianskago zemelnago banka i po dr. voprosam* (St. Petersburg, 1899), pp. 91-99; TsGIAL, f. 593, op. 1, d. 101, ll. 309-14.

39. TsGIAL, f. 593, op. 1, d. 101, ll. 493-96; Blosfeldt, *Sbornik zakonov*, pp. 264-73.

40. "Zadolzhennost chastnago zemlevladeniia," *Otechestvennye zapiski*, Feb. 1880, pt. 2, p. 160.

41. V. Kabanov in *Russkii vestnik*, Aug. 1889, pp. 304-5; Elishev, *Dvorianskoe delo*, pp. 3, 53; Zalomanov, pp. 16-17; Soloviev, *Samoderzhavie i dvorianstvo v kontse XIX veka*, p. 206.

42. See, for example, Semenov, passim.

43. Veselovskii, "Dvizhenie zemlevladeltsev," 1:297; Soloviev, *Samoderzhavie i dvorianstvo v kontse XIX veka*, pp. 170, 172-74, 185. For the noble assemblies' petition campaign on credit, see Hamburg, "Land," chap. 4.

44. Quoted from Alexander III's April 21, 1885, rescript marking the centenary of Catherine's Charter to the Nobility, in which he first made public his decision to establish the bank. Blosfeldt, *Sbornik zakonov*, pp. 277-78.

45. Except where otherwise noted, the following account is drawn from the bank's charter as amended through 1900, in Blosfeldt, *Sbornik zakonov*, pp. 278-314, and from M. N. Pokrovskii, "Obshchaia politika pravitelstva

1866–1892 gg.," in *Istoriia Rossii v XIX veke* (St. Petersburg, 1907–1911), 5:49, 53.

46. *Vestnik Evropy*, Jan. 1886, p. 385.

47. Pavlovsky, p. 154; *Ezhegodnik Rossii 1908 g.*, p. xciii. In 1895 the Peasant Bank lowered the interest rate on its mortgages to 4.5 percent, and by 1905 the outstanding loan balance of the Noble Bank was less than twice as large as that of the Peasant Bank.

48. *Tsifrovyia dannyia*, pp. 42–43.

49. The figures for 1906–1913 are virtually identical. For 1902–1907 see *Ezhegodnik Rossii 1909 g.*, p. 403; for 1908–1913, *Ezhegodnik Rossii 1914 g.*, p. 43.

50. Terner, "Dvorianstvo," Mar. 1903, pp. 33. On Nov. 1, 1896, the bank held mortgages on 12,801 properties in thirty-nine *gubernii*. *Tsifrovyia dannyia*, pp. 42–43.

51. Soloviev, *Samoderzhavie i dvorianstvo v kontse XIX veka*, pp. 186–88; Semenov, pp. 37–38, 59.

52. TsGADA, f. 1254, op. 1, d. 80, ll. 4b–5b.

53. TsGIAL, f. 1283, op. 1, d. 4, ll. 1–3; "Upadok dvorianskogo zemlevladeniia v Saratovskoi gub.," *Mir bozhii*, Jan. 1897, pt. 2, p. 25; Paltov, p. 215; Zalomanov, pp. 36–37, 40–41; *Vestnik Evropy*, July 1897, p. 1897, p. 359; TsGADA, f. 1254, op. 1, d. 86, l. 10a; ibid., d. 80, l. 6a; Iarmonkin, *Zadacha*, pp. 28–29.

54. Soloviev, *Samoderzhavie i dvorianstvo v kontse XIX veka*, pp. 241–42; Gindin, p. 108; TsGADA, f. 1254, op. 1, d. 80, ll. 10–12; Planson, "Osoboe soveshchanie," pp. 22–23. See also Semenov, pp. 82–83.

55. Soloviev, *Samoderzhavie i dvorianstvo v kontse XIX veka*, pp. 234–37, 241–42; idem, "Pravitelstvo i politika," pp. 267–72.

56. Blosfeldt, *Sbornik zakonov*, pp. 278–314, 323; Soloviev, "Pravitelstvo i politika," pp. 270–73.

57. *Ezhegodnik Rossii 1904 g.*, pp. 396–97; *Ezhegodnik Rossii 1908 g.*, pp. 210–11. No estates were sold in 1897, so the annual average for 1891–1905 was thirty-two. As of Jan. 1, 1902, 22,758 estates were mortgaged to the bank (*Ezhegodnik Rossii 1904 g.*, p. 398).

58. Anfimov, *Krupnoe pomeshchiche khoziaistvo*, pp. 324–25.

59. TsGIAL, f. 593, op. 1, d. 101, ll. 404–11; TsGIAL, f. 1283, op. 1, d. 22, l. 263; Soloviev, "Samoderzhavie i dvorianskii vopros," pp. 198–99.

60. Gindin, pp. 333–34; TsGADA, f. 1254, op. 1, d. 80, ll. 6–8; Gindin and Gefter, pp. 148–50.

61. Gindin and Gefter, pp. 150–52. The estimated mortgage debt of the nobility at the beginning of 1896 was 875 million rubles, interpolated from the data in chap. 2 above.

62. *Severnyi vestnik*, Dec. 1889, p. 104; TsGIAL, f. 1283, op. 1, d. 4, l. 4; ibid., d. 87, ll. 123, 130–31.

63. Anfimov, *Krupnoe pomeshchiche khoziaistvo*, pp. 331–32; Gindin and Gefter, p. 150; Terner, "Dvorianstvo," Aug. 1905, pp. 476, 479–80.

64. N. Novoselskii, "Usilenie dvorianskago elementa v zemstve i kratkosrochnyi kredit dlia pomeshchikov," *Russkii vestnik*, Mar. 1885, pp. 225–28; *Moskovskoe gubernskoe dvorianskoe sobranie 18–25 fevralia 1890 g. Zhurnaly, otchety, doklady* (Moscow, 1890), ll. 21a–21b; TsGADA, f. 1254, op. 1, d. 86, ll. 19b–20b; Zinoviev, pp. 23–28.

65. Gos. sovet, *Otchet za 1901–1902*, p. 206.

66. TsGIAL, f. 1283, op. 1, d. 4, l. 188.

67. TsGADA, f. 1254, op. 1, d. 86, ll. 1a–2b; Semenov, pp. 67–69. See also *Doklad i. d. kazanskago gubernskago predvoditelia dvorianstva ocherednomu sobraniiu dvorianstva Kazanskoi gubernii o predstavlennykh Osobomu Soveshchaniiu po delam*

dvorianskago sosloviia svedeniiakh po trebovaniiu Predsedatelia Osobago Soveshchaniia Stats-Sekretaria Durnovo (Kazan, 1898), pp. 15–16.

68. Soloviev, "Samoderzhavie i dvorianskii vopros," pp. 203–7; TsGIAL, f. 593, op. 1, d. 101, ll. 800–3.

69. Soloviev, "Samoderzhavie i dvorianskii vopros," pp. 207–8; TsGIAL, f. 1283, op. 1, d. 72b, l. 1; Gos. sovet, *Otchet za 1901–1902*, pp. 203–7.

70. G. E. Blosfeldt, ed., *Noveishiia uzakoneniia o rossiiskom dvorianstve. 1901–1902 gg.* (St. Petersburg, 1903), pp. 14–26.

71. *Ezhegodnik Rossii 1904 g.*, pp. 396–97; *Ezhegodnik Rossii 1908 g.*, pp. 210–11.

72. Iarmonkin, *Zadacha*, pp. 29–31; Terner, "Dvorianstvo," Mar. 1903, pp. 33–36; Gindin and Gefter, pp. 139–41; TsGADA, f. 1254, op. 1, d. 80, ll. 4a–4b; Anfimov, *Krupnoe pomeshchiche khoziaistvo, pp. 257–58.

73. Zaionchkovskii, *Rossiiskoe samoderzhavie*, pp. 195–97; *Vestnik Evropy*, Nov. 1885, p. 405; V. A., pp. 5–6.

74. Maslov, *Agrarnyi vopros*, pp. 361–65; TsGADA, f. 1254, op. 1, d. 80, ll. 2b–3a; Paltov, pp. 241–42.

75. TsGIAL, f. 593, op. 1, d. 101, ll. 700–8; Soloviev, "Samoderzhavie i dvorianskii vopros," pp. 193–96. Pleve's proposal was rejected by the special conference.

76. Romanovich-Slavatinskii, p. 65, *Russkaia mysl*, Apr. 1895, pt. 2, pp. 141–42; Soloviev, "Samoderzhavie i dvorianskii vopros," p. 190; V. A. Stepynin, "Iz istorii popytok nasazhdeniia v Sibiri dvorianskogo zemlevladeniia," Krasnoiarskii gosudarstvennyi pedagogicheskii institut, *Uchenye zapiski* 4, No. 1 (1955):134–35; Anfimov, *Krupnoe pomeshchiche khoziaistvo*, pp. 357–58. During 1878–1882 the average selling price of a *desiatina* of land was 8.17 rubles in Ufa and 6.37 in Orenburg. A. P. Korelin, "Dvorianstvo v poreformennoi Rossii 1861–1904 gg.," *Istoricheskie zapiski* 87 (1971):163, states that during 1876–1881 in these two *gubernii* 461,300 *desiatiny* were sold for a total of 871,300 rubles—an average price of 1.89 rubles per *desiatina* and not 19, as Korelin has it.

77. Baratynskii, "Nedelimye dvorianskie uchastki," pp. 75–76; *Sovremennye dvorianskie voprosy*, pp. 34, 36; TsGIAL, f. 1283, op. 1, d. 87, ll. 123, 130–32; Paltov, pp. 205–6, 212, 215, 217, 219–23.

78. In 1897 in all of Siberia there were only 1,314 noble landholdings comprising 524,437 *desiatiny*, mostly uncultivated; Tobolsk *guberniia* alone contained 48 percent of the properties and 54 percent of the acreage belonging to nobles.

79. Stepynin, pp. 137, 139–44, 147–49; TsGIAL, f. 1283, op. 1, d. 4, ll. 1–3; ibid., d. 22, l. 299; *Russkaia mysl*, Apr. 1895, pt. 2, pp. 141–44; Soloviev, "Samoderzhavie i dvorianskii vopros," pp. 190–93; idem., *Samoderzhavie i dvorianstvo v kontse XIX veka*, pp. 331–33; Korelin, "Dvorianstvo," p. 154; Gosudarstvennyi sovet, *Vsepoddanneishii otchet predsedatelia za sessiiu 1900–1901 gg.*, pp. 59–62. The June 8, 1901, law is in Blosfeldt, *Noveishiia uzakoneniia*, pp. 32–36.

80. Blosfeldt, *Noveishiia uzakoneniia*, pp. 27–29.

81. Stepynin, pp. 151–60.

CHAPTER 5

1. TsGIAL, f. 1283, op. 1, d. 5, t. 1, supplement, p. 123; Ustimovich, p. 11.

2. Romanovich-Slavatinskii, pp. 44, 63; Dukes, pp. 146–51; Torke, "Continuity," pp. 464–66. For the 1722 Table of Ranks, see *PSZ*, 1st ser., vol. 6, no. 3890; for its final form, "Ustav o sluzhbe po opredeleniiu ot pravitelstva," 1896 ed., app. to art. 244, *SZ*, vol. 3. See also Z. I. Malkova and M. A. Pliukhina,

"Dokumenty vysshikh i tsentralnykh uchrezhdenii XIX-nachala XX v. kak istochnik biograficheskikh svedenii," in *Nekotorye voprosy izucheniia istoricheskikh dokumentov XIX-nachala XX veka* (Leningrad, 1967), pp. 206–9 and Romanovich-Slavatinskii, p. 420.

3. Malkova and Pliukhina, pp. 208–9, 212; Romanovich-Slavatinskii, pp. 27–28; *O sostave*, pp. 12, 15–16; Korelin, "Dvorianstvo," p. 98. Promotion from rank fourteen to rank five proceeded in the following manner: the holder of a given rank was eligible for appointment to offices of the same class and also of the next two higher classes; he could also be promoted one rank above the class of his current office. Thus promotion in rank for either meritorious service or simply length of service could lead to a higher office, and appointment to a higher office could hasten a promotion in rank. See Daniel T. Orlovsky, "High Officials in the Ministry of Internal Affairs, 1855–1881," in Walter M. Pintner and Don K. Rowney, eds., *Russian Officialdom* (Chapel Hill, 1980), p. 270, and Helju A. Bennett, "*Chiny, Ordena*, and Officialdom," in ibid., pp. 166–68.

4. TsGIAL, f. 1283, op. 1, d. 5, t. 1, l. 13; ibid., d. 148[a], l. 4.

5. TsGIAL, f. 1283, op. 1, d. 5, t. 1, l. 109. Staff officers were those in classes six through eight (colonel, lieutenant colonel, and major); junior commissioned officers were those in classes nine through fourteen (captain and below).

6. Malkova and Pliukhina, pp. 210–11; Korkunov, 1:290; P. A. Zaionchkovskii, *Samoderzhavie i russkaia armiia na rubezhe XIX-XX stoletii, 1881–1903* (Moscow, 1973), p. 206n.

7. Malkova and Pliukhina, pp. 210–11; "Uchrezhdenie ordenov i drugikh znakov otlichiia," 1892 ed., arts. 86, 90, 106, 143–44, 148, *SZ*, vol. 1, pt. 2; Blosfeldt, *Sbornik zakonov*, pp. 376, 379; Zaionchkovskii, *Samoderzhavie i russkaia armiia*, p. 206n.; Korkunov, 1:290. Class ranks awarded to private individuals not in state service in recognition of outstanding achievement did not confer hereditary noble status.

8. Ustimovich, pp. 14, 17.

9. TsGIAL, f. 1283, op. 1, d. 5, t. 1, supplement, pp. 121–22.

10. Annual average for 1825–1845 calculated from data in Korelin, "Rossiiskoe dvorianstvo," p. 60; for 1875–1884, from data in TsGIAL, f. 1283, op. 1, d. 5, t. 1, l. 13; for 1882–1896, from data in ibid., d. 148[a], l. 4; and for 1892–1896, from data in ibid., d. 5, t. 1, l. 32, and supplement, p. 127. The total for 1858–1874 is an estimate based on an interpolated annual average of 1,100. Korelin, "Rossiiskoe dvorianstvo," gives a figure of 37,000 for 1875–1896, based on his reading that the total of 20,889 for 1882–1896 refers to the number of dependents only, rather than heads of families plus their dependents (p. 60). Such a reading would yield an annual average of 1,899 persons ennobled during 1882–1891, a figure very much out of line with the averages for the preceding and succeeding periods.

11. For the method of projecting natural increase and for estimates of the total number of nobles, see app. B below.

12. See, for example, Baratynskii, *Sbornik statei*, p. 49; Ustimovich, pp. 12–13, 17; Elishev, *Dvorianskoe delo*, p. 202; Planson, *O dvorianstve v Rossii*, pp. 20–23.

13. *Russkii vestnik*, Mar. 1890, pp. 327–30.

14. *Vestnik Evropy*, Apr. 1885, pp. 812–16, and Mar. 1893, p. 374; *Russkaia mysl*, Mar. 1890, pt. 2, pp. 223–30. N. A. Rubakin (*Rossiia v tsifrakh* [St. Petersburg, 1912], pp. 58–59), on the other hand, exaggerated the statistical impact upon the first estate of the influx of commoners.

15. Fadeev, pp. 67, 76; editorial in *Moskovskie vedomosti*, no. 108 (1885), reprinted in M. N. Katkov, *O dvorianstve* (Moscow, 1905); Soloviev, *Samoderzhavie i*

dvorianstvo v kontse XIX veka, p. 176. Witte is quoted in Soloviev, "Samoderzhavie i dvorianskii vopros," p. 166.

16. TsGIAL, f. 1283, op. 1, d. 5, t. 1, ll. 13–15, 18; Soloviev, *Samoderzhavie i dvorianstvo v kontse XIX veka*, p. 176; A. A. Polovtsov, *Dnevnik gosudarstvennogo sekretaria A. A. Polovtsova, 1883–1892* (Moscow, 1966), 1:306–309, 466. Whelan, p. 136.

17. Korelin, "Dvorianstvo," p. 98; Paltov, p. 196.

18. TsGIAL, f. 1283, op. 1, d. 5, t. 1, ll. 1–7, and supplement, pp. 99–108; ibid., d. 4, ll. 5–6; *Russkii vestnik*, Mar. 1890, pp. 327–30; *Vestnik Evropy*, Mar. 1893, pp. 368–70; *Russkaia mysl*, Mar. 1890, pt. 2, pp. 223–30.

19. Vorontsov-Dashkov as quoted in Soloviev, "Samoderzhavie i dvorianskii vopros," p. 168.

20. TsGIAL, f. 1283, op. 1, d. 148ᵃ, ll. 1–9. Persons who were not in service and who held no class rank were no longer eligible for the third degree of the order of St. Vladimir.

21. Blosfeldt, *Sbornik zakonov*, pp. 379, 381; Korelin, "Dvorianstvo," p. 100.

22. TsGIAL, f. 1283, op. 1, d. 148ᵃ, ll. 9–10; Gos. sovet, *Otchet za 1899–1900*, 2:580, 590, 641; "Svod zakonov o sostoianiiakh," 1899 ed., art. 24, *SZ*, vol. 9. In families where three successive generations had held ranks conferring personal nobility, regardless of the time spent in such ranks, members of the fourth generation who entered service had been entitled to hereditary nobility. Korelin, "Dvorianstvo," p. 115, confuses the two provisions and claims the fourth generation could request hereditary nobility if three generations had each served twenty years in ranks conferring personal nobility.

23. The 1722 law establishing the Table of Ranks stipulated that the descendants of any commoner who was ennobled by reaching class eight rank in the civil service or class fourteen in the military were to be full members of the nobility, but that the children of commoners in civil service ranks in classes nine through fourteen "are not nobles." Two years later an *ukaz* expressly provided for the ennoblement of chancellery clerks of common birth upon their promotion to the lowest class rank but made no reference to their children. Catherine II's Charter of the Nobility regularized the status of this anomalous group of ennobled junior bureaucrats whose children were not nobles by recognizing them as "having only personal [*lichnoe*], not hereditary, nobility" (*PSZ*, 1st ser., vol. 6, no. 3890, arts. 11, 15; ibid., vol. 22, no. 16187, art. 92).

24. "Svod zakonov o sostoianiiakh," 1899 ed., arts. 46–48, 514–15. Merchants who were granted orders were thereby elevated only to the hereditary distinguished citizenry. From 1856, civil service ranks in classes ten through fourteen conferred personal distinguished citizenship.

25. *Statisticheskiia tablitsy Rossiiskoi imperii. Vyp. II* (1863), p. 267; *Obshchii svod rezultatov perepisi*, 1:160.

26. "Svod zakonov o sostoianiiakh," 1899 ed., arts. 111, 188, 963.

27. Gos. sovet, *Otchet za 1901–1902*, pp. 177–79; Korkunov, 1:293; Zaionchkovskii, *Rossiiskoe samoderzhavie*, p. 397; "Svod zakonov o sostoianiiakh," 1899 ed., arts. 350, 382.

28. Romanovich-Slavatinskii, pp. 21–22.

29. Kliuchevskii, 6:279.

30. Fadeev, p. 74; *Doklad kazanskago predvoditelia dvorianstva*, p. 7.

31. A. Ch., *Zhelatelnaia reforma* (St. Petersburg, 1881), pp. 20–26; Zinoviev, p. 38.

32. TsGIAL, f. 1283, op. 1, d. 4, ll. 185–93; ibid., d. 13, ll. 209, 211, 235; Gos. sovet, *Otchet za 1901–1902*, p. 155.

33. TsGIAL, f. 1283, op. 1, d. 13, ll. 282–83, 315–17; Gos. sovet, *Otchet za*

1901–1902, pp. 161, 181–84; idem, *Vsepoddanneishii otchet predsedatelia za sessiiu 1901–1902 gg.*, p. 24.

34. Gos. sovet, *Otchet za 1901–1902*, pp. 176–77, 179; TsGIAL, f. 1283, op. 1, d. 4, ll. 1–3; Blosfeldt, *Sbornik zakonov*, pp. 346–47.

35. TsGADA, f. 1254, op. 1, d. 86, ll. 7b–8a.

36. TsGIAL, f. 1283, op. 1, d. 13, ll. 13, 84, 204, 210, 234–35, 238–46, 277–81, 312–15; Gos. sovet, *Otchet za 1901–1902*, pp. 160–61, 173–81; idem, *Vsepoddanneishii otchet predsedatelia za sessiiu 1901–1902 gg.*, pp. 23–24; Blosfeldt, *Noveishiia uzakoneniia*, p. 7.

37. Gos. sovet, *Vsepoddanneishii otchet predsedatelia za sessiiu 1898–1899 gg.*, pp. 19–21; idem, *Otchet za 1901–1902*, p. 177; Blosfeldt, *Sbornik zakonov*, p. 347.

38. TsGIAL, f. 1283, op. 1, d. 5, t. 1, ll. 1–7, 13–15; ibid., d. 4, ll. 5–6; Korelin, "Rossiiskoe dvorianstvo," p. 65; *Russkii vestnik*, Mar. 1890, pp. 327–30; *Vestnik Evropy*, Mar. 1893, pp. 368–70. The minimum size proposed by the 1896 conference of marshals—ten times the minimum acreage required for a direct vote in the noble and *zemstvo* elections—was larger than 90 percent of the estates owned by the hereditary nobility at the end of the nineteenth century.

39. Pazukhin, p. 61; D. V., Aug. 1885, pp. 788–89; Liaskovskii, pp. 566–67. See also Fadeev, p. 77; G. A. Evreinov, *Proshloe i nastoiashchee znachenie russkago dvorianstva* (St. Petersburg, 1898), p. 91; Elishev, "Sliianie soslovii," p. 286.

40. TsGIAL, f. 1283, op. 1, d. 148ª, ll. 15–17.

41. Quoted in Korelin, "Rossiiskoe dvorianstvo," p. 65.

42. *Vestnik Evropy*, Mar. 1885, p. 385; Apr. 1885, pp. 812–16; Mar. 1893, pp. 370–73.

43. *Russkaia mysl*, Mar. 1890, pt. 2, pp. 223–30.

44. TsGIAL, f. 1283, op. 1, d. 4, ll. 5–6; ibid., d. 5, t. 1, ll. 1–7.

45. TsGIAL, f. 1283, op. 1, d. 148ª, ll. 11–14; ibid., d. 4, ll. 98–101; Soloviev, "Samoderzhavie i dvorianskii vopros," pp. 165–74, 176.

46. The journals of the State Council's sessions dealing with this issue are in TsGIAL, f. 1283, op. 1, d. 5, t. 2, ll. 420–87; for a summary, see Gos. sovet, *Otchet za 1899–1900*, 2:585–641.

47. TsGIAL, f. 1283, op. 1, d. 148ª, l. 25; Gos. sovet, *Otchet za 1899–1900*, 2:583. Thirty thousand rubles was twice the value of real estate other than agricultural land required for a direct vote in noble elections.

48. Blosfeldt, *Sbornik zakonov*, p. 225.

49. A. P. Korelin, *Dvorianstvo v poreformennoi Rossii 1861–1904 gg.* (Moscow, 1979), p. 152. See also section entitled "Local Government Reform" in chap. 8.

50. Terner, "Dvorianstvo," Sept. 1905, pp. 71–74. See also Terner's article of the same name in the same journal for Mar. 1903, pp. 11–12.

51. "Svod zakonov o sostoianiiakh," 1899 ed., art. 961.

52. "Svod zakonov o sostoianiiakh," 1876 ed., art. 148, and 1899 ed., art. 158; Korelin, "Rossiiskoe dvorianstvo," pp. 64–65; *Vestnik Evropy*, Mar. 1893, p. 375.

53. Korelin, "Rossiiskoe dvorianstvo," p. 65; Gos. sovet, *Otchet za 1899–1900*, 2:584–85, 596, 639.

54. Planson, *O dvorianstve*, pp. 14–16, 18; idem, *"Osoboe soveshchanie,"* p. 25; idem, *Sosloviia*, p. 64. Another highly desirable result in Planson's eyes would have been the Russification (1) of the *guberniia* societies in the western, southern, and eastern borderlands, where Great Russian nobles were often landowners but not members of the local societies, and (2) of Polish nobles who owned estates in Great Russia and the Ukraine but remained members of the noble societies in the western *gubernii* where their families' lands had formerly been located. An ardent chauvinist, Planson expected that the complete identification of the *guberniia* societies with the local landowners would enable the Great Russian nobility to

dominate the corporate life of the first estate in the borderlands and to assimilate the Polish landed nobles living in its midst. Largely as a result of punitive measures adopted after the 1863 revolt, 17 percent of the Polish nobles in European Russia in 1897 lived outside the region that had fallen to Russia in the eighteenth-century partitions of Poland (the nine western *gubernii* plus Courland). The Polish minority among the first estate was scattered so widely that only eight of the fifty *gubernii* contained fewer than 250 Polish nobles, and none fewer than 140. Outside of their historic homeland, Poles constituted between 12 and 21 percent of the first estate in Livonia, Pskov, Ekaterinoslav, Kherson, Bessarabia, Perm, Viatka, and Archangel and from 2 to 10 percent in thirty-one other *gubernii*. For the nobility's ethnic composition, see app. B below.

55. Korelin, "Rossiiskoe dvorianstvo," p. 64; "Svod zakonov o sostoianiiakh," 1876 ed., art. 267. See also Zinoviev, p. 40.

56. TsGIAL, f. 1283, op. 1, d. 148ª, ll. 26–31, 34; Gos. sovet, *Otchet za 1899–1900*, 2:596.

57. Gos. sovet, *Otchet za 1899–1900*, 2:593–95, 629–38.

58. Gos. sovet, *Otchet za 1903–1904*, pp. 306–10; G. E. Blosfeldt, ed., *Rossiiskoe dvorianstvo. Uzakoneniia i raziasneniia 1901–1910 gg.* (St. Petersburg, 1910), pp. 44–46. The national register covered the entire empire with the exception of the three Baltic *gubernii*, Poland, and Finland.

59. The following discussion is based on "Svod zakonov o sostoianiiakh," 1899 ed., arts. 762–63, 767–816, and *Evreiskaia entsiklopediia* (St. Petersburg, 1906–13), vol. 13, cols. 620–25.

60. *Obshchii svod rezultatov perepisi*, 2:378.

61. The civil servant and diplomat Petr Pavlovich Shafirov and the financier Ludwig Stieglitz were created barons by Peter I and Nicholas I, respectively; both were sons of Jews who had converted to Christianity. Among the Jews ennobled by Alexander II were Ia. S. and S. S. Poliakov, rewarded for their services in banking and railroad building, and the family of Baron Horatio Ginzburg, also a financier, whose title, received from the Grand Duke of Hesse-Darmstadt, was recognized by the emperor as valid in Russia.

62. *Evreiskaia entsiklopediia*, vol. 3, cols. 160–64, 167–70; Peter Kenez, "A Profile of the Prerevolutionary Officer Corps," *California Slavic Studies* 7 (1973):137, 148; "Ustav o sluzhbe po opredeleniiu ot pravitelstva," 1896 ed., arts. 9, 40, 48–49, 57–58, *SZ*, vol. 3.

63. Although there were no obviously Jewish names among the holders of ranks in classes two and three in 1900, there were several in class four. Typical were Iakov Markovich Galpern, an official of the Ministry of Justice, who had been ennobled through receipt of a Vladimir third degree in 1887 after eighteen years in service; Leonard Leopoldovich Girshman, professor of medicine at Kharkov University, who had achieved the rank of actual state councillor and noble status in 1889 after twenty-one years in service; and Boris Mikhailovich Shapirov, a doctor in the frontier guards, who also after twenty-one years in service had been promoted to actual state councillor in 1896. (*Spisok grazhdanskĭm chinam pervykh trëkh klassov, 1900; Spisok grazhdanskim chinam chetvertago klassa, 1900.*) Of a total of eighteen Jews employed in class ranks in the Ministry of Communications in 1904, two were the sons of hereditary nobles and ten had acquired personal nobility in service. Of these ten, one was in line for promotion to the rank of actual state councillor and hereditary noble status. See Erik Amburger, "Behördendienst und sozialer Aufstieg in Russland um 1900," *Jahrbücher für Geschichte Osteuropas*, n.s., 18 (1970):133.

64. L. M. Rogovin, ed., *Sistematicheskii sbornik deistvuiushchikh zakonov o evreiakh* (St. Petersburg, 1913), p. 336. For Grinkrug, see TsGIAL, f. 593, op. 1, d. 101,

ll. 687–88. Iakov Solomonovich Poliakov was one of those who had been refused membership but had not pursued the matter; see S. Iu. Witte, *Vospominaniia* (Moscow, 1960), 1:121. *Evreiskaia entsiklopediia*, vol. 7, col. 34, claims that until the end of the nineteenth century Jews usually were allowed to enroll in noble societies without objection. For Manasein's ruling see TsGIAL, f. 1283, op. 1, d. 87, l. 127.

65. TsGIAL, f. 1283, op. 1, d. 87, l. 127; ibid., d. 22, ll. 275–76.

66. TsGIAL, f. 1283, op. 1, d. 13, pp. 33–34, and ll. 17–18; TsGIAL, f. 593, op. 1, d. 101, ll. 687–91; Gos. sovet, *Otchet za 1899–1900*, 2:651–64.

CHAPTER 6

1. See Walter M. Pintner, "The Social Characteristics of the Early Nineteenth-Century Russian Bureaucracy," *Slavic Review* 29 (1970):435. The total number of civil servants in class ranks grew from 2,051 in 1755 (S. M. Troitskii, *Russkii Absoliutizm i dvorianstvo v XVIII v.* [Moscow, 1974], p. 173) to 86,066 in 1857 and an estimated 378,000 in 1903. See P. A. Zaionchkovskii, *Pravitelstvennyi apparat samoderzhavnoi Rossii v XIX v.* (Moscow, 1978), p. 71. For the growing professionalization of the bureaucracy, see Walter M. Pintner, "The Evolution of Civil Officialdom, 1755–1855," in Walter M. Pintner and Don K. Rowney, eds., *Russian Officialdom* (Chapel Hill, 1980), p. 224.

2. Zaionchkovskii, *Pravitelstvennyi apparat*, pp. 130–61 passim and 199–215 passim.

3. Whelan, pp. 147 and 152.

4. Troitskii, pp. 221–22.

5. Based on L. G. Beskrovnyi, *Russkaia armiia i flot v XIX veke* (Moscow, 1973), pp. 40, 44, 547–48. The officer corps grew from 34,790 in 1864 to 40,352 in 1897.

6. For the average length of service among officers, see Raymond L. Garthoff, "The Military as a Social Force," in Cyril E. Black, ed., *The Transformation of Russian Society* (Cambridge, Mass., 1960), p. 327.

7. Garthoff, pp. 325–26.

8. Derived from data in P. A. Zaionchkovskii, "Soslovnyi sostav ofitserskogo korpusa na rubezhe XIX–XX vekov," *Istoriia SSSR*, no. 1 (1973), p. 149.

9. Kenez, p. 143.

10. Percentages for 1755 are calculated from data in Troitskii, pp. 300–301; for 1853 and 1902, from data in Zaionchkovskii, *Pravitelstvennyi apparat*, pp. 91–93, 95–96. Pintner, "Evolution of Civil Officialdom," working with a somewhat smaller sample than Zaionchkovskii, produces data that yield exactly the same percentage of serfowners for the mid-nineteenth century (pp. 204–7). Korelin, *Dvorianstvo*, gives similar figures for the higher ranks in 1858 and 1902—54 percent and 27 percent, respectively (p. 98). Manning, *Crisis*, also cites Zaionchkovskii, *Pravitelstvennyi apparat*, pp. 90–97, but unaccountably comes up with the claim that "at Emancipation [noble landowners] constituted 81.3%" of civil servants in the top four classes (pp. 26–27).

11. Zaionchkovskii, *Pravitelstvennyi apparat*, p. 208.

12. Walter M. Pintner, "Civil Officialdom and the Nobility in the 1850s," in Walter M. Pintner and Don K. Rowney, eds., *Russian Officialdom* (Chapel Hill, 1980), p. 242.

13. Calculated from data in Zaionchkovskii, "Soslovnyi sostav," pp. 150–52. Zaionchkovskii's data cover 75 of the 130 generals who were not members of the Russian or foreign ruling houses, 255 of the 410 lieutenant generals, 185 of the 208 major generals on the general staff, and 283 of the 308 colonels on the general

staff. Of the generals in the sample, 97.5 percent were nobles by birth; of the lieutenant generals, 96.0 percent; of the major generals, 85.9 percent; and of the colonels, 74.2 percent.

14. Korelin, "Dvorianstvo," p. 162. This evidence belies Manning's insistence that "the professionalization of the civil service eventually eliminated the possibility of crossovers from military to civil service careers" (*Crisis*, p. 31).

15. For this and following estimates, see app. F.

16. Leroy-Beaulieu's claim in the 1880s that the majority of nobles who entered service retired after five or ten years was probably simply a repetition of Haxthausen's observation a generation earlier. See Leroy-Beaulieu, 1:382, and Haxthausen-Abbenburg, *Russian Empire*, 2:214–15.

17. Manning, *Crisis*, pp. 30–32.

18. In 1897 there were some 100,000–101,000 noble landowning families (interpolated from data in app. C) in European Russia, containing 111,000–112,000 noble landowners, of whom probably 15–20 percent were women—either as the only landowner in a family or as landowning wives of landowning noblemen. This leaves a total of 89,000–95,000 male noble landowners, of whom 44.6 percent (rate interpolated from data in chap. 2), or 40,000–42,000, owned properties containing more than one hundred *desiatiny* each, and the balance (49,000–53,000) owned holdings of one hundred *desiatiny* and under. Assuming that 60–80 percent of the intermediate and large proprietors, but only 20–40 percent of the smallholders, were full-time landowners, the total of such was 34,000–55,000, or 14–22 percent of the 250,000 adult male nobles in the fifty *gubernii*. I have also assumed that some 10 percent of the 40–42 percent of adult noblemen who were in state service were actually full-time landowners still following the traditional pattern of early retirement, and have reduced the proportion of noblemen in service to 36–38 percent so as to avoid counting the same individuals twice.

19. Nancy M. Frieden, *Russian Physicians in an Era of Reform and Revolution, 1856–1905* (Princeton, 1981), p. 204.

20. A. S. Nifontov, "Formirovanie klassov burzhuaznogo obshchestva v russkom gorode vtoroi poloviny XIX v. (Po materialam perepisei naseleniia g. Moskvy v 70-90-kh godakh XIX v.)," *Istoricheskie zapiski* 54 (1955):244.

21. L. N. Tolstoi, *Anna Karenina*, pt. 6, chap. 29.

22. Terpigorev, *Oskudenie*, 1:223; Tolstoi, pt. 7, chap. 17. Oblonskii's salary of 6,000 rubles was very handsome. According to Rubakin, p. 66, in 1906 only 2.6 percent of all civil servants in class ranks received over 5,000 rubles annually; 25.3 percent received 2,000–5,000; and 72.1 percent received only 1,000–2,000.

23. Iarmonkin, *Zadacha*, p. 29; Anfimov, *Krupnoe pomeshchiche khoziaistvo*, pp. 271–74, 278–79.

24. Rieber, pp. 135–37, 158–60, 251, 422.

25. Nifontov, "Formirovanie," pp. 243–44; L. M. Ivanov, "O soslovno-klassovoi strukture gorodov kapitalisticheskoi Rossii," in *Problemy sotsialno-ekonomicheskoi istorii Rossii* (Moscow, 1971), p. 338. The remaining nobles with independent incomes comprised those in the military and civil service (20–21 percent), pensioners (18.7 percent), and large landed proprietors (1.5 percent). Ivanov includes the last named among the industrial entrepreneurs. In St. Petersburg in 1869, 548 nobles were white-collar employees, 263 were blue-collar employees, and 355 were self-employed craftsmen. See Korelin, *Dvorianstvo*, p. 124.

26. Brower, p. 42.

27. *PSZ*, 1st ser., vol. 6, no. 3890, art. 11.

28. Pintner, "Evolution of Civil Officialdom," p. 192; Robert D. Givens,

"Eighteenth-Century Nobiliary Career Patterns and Provincial Government," in Walter M. Pintner and Don K. Rowney, eds., *Russian Officialdom* (Chapel Hill, 1980), pp. 109–10.

29. "Ustav o sluzhbe po opredeleniiu ot pravitelstva," 1896 ed., arts. 5, 7, 9, 40, *SZ*, vol. 3; Gradovskii, 7:351. Commercial councillor was an honorary status granted to merchants after twelve years as members of the first guild (V. M. Gribovskii, *Gosudarstvennoe ustroistvo i upravlenie Rossiiskoi imperii* [Odessa, 1912], p. 46).

30. Pintner, "Civil Officialdom," p. 236; "Ustav o sluzhbe," arts. 28–29, 57–58, 295, 305; Harold A. McFarlin, "The Extension of the Imperial Russian Civil Service to the Lowest Office Workers: The Creation of the Chancery Clerkship, 1827–1833," *Russian History* 1 (1974):16–17; *O sostave*, pp. 104–5; Romanovich-Slavatinskii, p. 226.

31. "Ustav o sluzhbe," art. 326. Promotion to class five upon retirement was automatic only for nobles who had served four years in class six, to class four only for those who had served five years in class five; promotion upon retirement to classes one through three was at the emperor's discretion (ibid., art. 792). From 1847, commoners also were promoted automatically upon retirement, but only up through class six (class five from 1856), the last class before the one conferring hereditary nobility, and only if at the time of retirement they had already served the full minimum period required for eligibility for such a promotion in active service (ibid., art. 794).

32. Zaionchkovskii, *Samoderzhavie i russkaia armiia*, pp. 240–45.

33. Fadeev, pp. 49–88 passim, 132; A. I. Elishev, *Sluzhebnyia prava dvorian* (Moscow, 1894), p. 55; idem, *Dvorianskoe delo*, pp. 123–27, 162, 165, 170–74; Planson, *O dvorianstve*, pp. 95–98; idem, "*Osoboe soveshchanie*," p. 27; Soloviev, *Samoderzhavie i dvorianstvo v kontse XIX veka*, p. 369.

34. Soloviev, *Samoderzhavie i dvorianstvo v kontse XIX veka*, pp. 362–65, 367; Elishev, *Dvorianskoe delo*, pp. 152–54.

35. Quoted in Soloviev, *Samoderzhavie i dvorianstvo v kontse XIX veka*, p. 371. See also Korelin, *Dvorianstvo*, p. 93.

36. *PSZ*, 3d ser., vol. 26, no. 28392.

37. Beskrovnyi, pp. 123–25; Patrick L. Alston, *Education and the State in Tsarist Russia* (Stanford, 1969), pp. 8–10; Romanovich-Slavatinskii, pp. 82–85, 217–19.

38. His Imperial Majesty's Page Corps groomed its students for officers' commissions in the elite guards regiments and was open, by imperial appointment only, to sons and grandsons of nobles holding military or civil ranks in the three highest classes—field marshals, generals, lieutenant generals, fleet admirals, admirals, vice admirals, chancellors, actual privy councillors, and privy councillors. See Blosfeldt, *Sbornik zakonov*, pp. 329–30.

39. *O sostave*, p. 122; Beskrovnyi, pp. 174–76; Kenez, p. 125.

40. Blosfeldt, *Sbornik zakonov*, pp. 329–31; Beskrovnyi, pp. 177–79, 182, 185; *O sostave*, pp. 122–23.

41. Beskrovnyi, p. 181; Zaionchkovskii, *Samoderzhavie i russkaia armiia*, pp. 311–12, 315–16; TsGIAL, f. 1283, op. 1, d. 167, l. 9. The four-year military progymnasia declined in number from ten in 1880/81 to only two a decade later. Manning, *Crisis*, wrongly claims that "increasingly the hereditary nobility did not avail themselves of these opportunities" for secondary and higher military education as they lost interest in army careers (p. 32).

42. TsGIAL, f. 1283, op. 1, d. 167, l. 9. For the *junker* schools, see Kenez, pp. 126–27 and TsGIAL, f. 593, op. 1, d. 101, l. 343. At the beginning of the 1890s the *junker* schools produced roughly half of all newly commissioned officers. See Korelin, *Dvorianstvo*, p. 83.

43. *Sovremennye dvorianskie voprosy* (St. Petersburg, 1897), pp. 39–43.
44. TsGIAL, f. 1283, op. 1, d. 4, ll. 4–6, 8–11. See also Provintsial, "Vragi pomestnogo dvorianstva," *Russkoe obozrenie*, Aug. 1897, p. 807.
45. TsGIAL, f. 1283, op. 1, d. 167, ll. 9, 66.
46. TsGIAL, f. 1283, op. 1, d. 167, l. 32; TsGADA, f. 1254, op. 1, d. 86, ll. 16–18.
47. TsGIAL, f. 1283, op. 1, d. 4, ll. 4–6, 8–11; ibid., f. 593, op. 1, d. 101, ll. 323, 329–44, 360–71. See also *Vestnik Evropy*, Mar. 1893, pp. 377–78; Planson, "*Osoboe soveshchanie*," pp. 15–16; idem, *Sosloviia*, p. 61.
48. To the eighteen corps in existence in 1881, two had been added in the reign of Alexander III (the Don and the Second Orenburg) and another in 1896 (the Iaroslavl) (Zaionchkovskii, *Samoderzhavie i russkaia armiia*, p. 312).
49. For the May 25, 1899, law, see Blosfeldt, *Sbornik zakonov*, pp. 332–34; for the discussion in the special conference, TsGIAL, f. 593, op. 1, d. 101, ll. 388–91.
50. Beskrovnyi, p. 181; Zaionchkovskii, *Samoderzhavie i russkaia armiia*, pp. 311–12.
51. TsGIAL, f. 593, op. 1, d. 101, ll. 606–9; Terner, "Dvorianstvo," Aug. 1905, pp. 484–87; Zaionchkovskii, "Soslovnyi sostav," p. 154. The law of April 2, 1903, is in Blosfeldt, *Rossiiskoe dvorianstvo*, pp. 15–16.
52. TsGIAL, f. 1283, op. 1, d. 167, ll. 9, 66. On the same date there were 10,600 daughters of hereditary nobles enrolled in girls' gymnasia and progymnasia.
53. TsGIAL, f. 1283, op. 1, d. 167, ll. 9, 66. In this document, a compilation of statistics on noble children in various types of schools as of January 1, 1897, presented to the Special Conference on the Affairs of the Noble Estate, the combined total student body for gymnasia and technical/vocational schools is printed as 69,418 but should read 96,418. From this misprint derives the incorrect figure of 25.6 percent (instead of 18.4 percent) for the proportion of hereditary nobles in both types of school which appears in the document and is cited without question in the conference's journal no. 5 (TsGIAL, f. 593, op. 1, d. 101, l. 333) and in Korelin, "Rossiiskoe dvorianstvo," p. 70.
54. V. R. Leikina-Svirskaia, *Intelligentsiia v Rossii vo vtoroi polovine XIX veka* (Moscow, 1971), p. 62; TsGIAL, f. 1283, op. 1, d. 167, l. 66. For 1880, see also Frieden, p. 202.
55. Nicholas Hans, *History of Russian Educational Policy (1701–1917)* (London, 1931), pp. 235, 238. Only during 1881–1894 did the expansion of university enrollments slow down, while the student body in boys' gymnasia and progymnasia actually decreased.
56. There were 1,885 hereditary nobles in the universities in 1880, and 3,578 in 1897 (Leikina-Svirskaia, p. 62; TsGIAL, f. 1283, op. 1, d. 167, l. 66). Between 1870 and 1897 the nobility increased in size by 54–63 percent; prorated for 1880–1897, the increase is 34–40 percent.
57. Based on data for the fifty *gubernii* of European Russia in *Obshchii svod rezultatov perepisi*, 1:198, 200. Of all males in this composite social group in 1897, hereditary nobles alone constituted 65.8 percent.
58. G. B. Sliozberg, *Dorevoliutsionnyi stroi Rossii* (Paris, 1933), p. 100.
59. Don K. Rowney, "Organizational Change and Social Adaptation: The Prerevolutionary Ministry of Internal Affairs," in Walter M. Pintner and Don K. Rowney, *Russian Officialdom* (Chapel Hill, 1980), pp. 310, 314–15.
60. In 1897 there were eleven times as many gymnasia and progymnasia as cadet corps, with a total of eight to nine times as many students (Beskrovnyi, pp. 180–81).

61. Alston, pp. 27–28, 35; Romanovich-Slavatinskii, pp. 85–86.
62. TsGIAL, f. 593, op. 1, d. 101, ll. 332–33; Korelin, "Rossiiskoe dvorianstvo," pp. 69–70.
63. Elishev, *Dvorianskoe delo*, pp. 233–34, 237–38. See also Provintsial, p. 800, and Semenov, p. 85.
64. Terner, "Dvorianstvo," Aug. 1905, p. 484.
65. Planson, *O dvorianstve*, pp. 79–81; idem, *"Osoboe soveshchanie,"* pp. 17–18.
66. Provintsial, pp. 801–2.
67. The Imperial Alexander Lycée in St. Petersburg had been established in 1811 for sons of nobles whose families were enrolled in sections five or six of the *guberniia* genealogical registers, i.e., titled families and those whose noble status dated from before 1685, as well as for sons of noble officers no lower than the rank of colonel and of noble *chinovniki* no lower than state councillor. The Alexander Lycée trained its students for careers in the civil service, especially the Ministry of Internal Affairs. The Imperial School of Jurisprudence in St. Petersburg, founded in 1838, had similar admissions restrictions and prepared its students for judicial careers. At the end of Alexander III's reign both institutions were opened to all hereditary nobles without distinction. See Blosfeldt, *Sbornik zakonov*, pp. 324, 326.
68. TsGADA, f. 1287, op. 1, d. 3878, l. 69.

CHAPTER 7

1. Fadeev, pp. 75, 85.
2. Zaionchkovskii, *Rossiiskoe samoderzhavie*, pp. 196, 227–28.
3. Zaionchkovskii, *Krizis*, pp. 431–34; idem, *Rossiiskoe samoderzhavie*, pp. 217–33; L. G. Zakharova, *Zemskaia kontrreforma 1890 g.* (Moscow, 1968), pp. 69, 73, 77–82; *Vestnik Evropy*, Mar. 1885, p. 386, and Jan. 1886, pp. 385–86.
4. Quoted in Zaionchkovskii, *Rossiiskoe samoderzhavie*, pp. 393–94. See also, ibid., pp. 366–96. Thomas S. Pearson, "The Origins of Alexander III's Land Captains: A Reinterpretation" (*Slavic Review* 40 [1981]: 384–403), while correctly emphasizing the "practical statist considerations," represented by Tolstoi, that figured in the drafting of the law on *zemskie nachalniki*, goes too far in depreciating Pazukhin's contribution. Whelan argues that it is a mistake to link Tolstoi's policies to the "gentry reaction"; his sympathetic attitude toward the gentry's needs was predicated on his view of "the gentry as the best qualified and most virtuous of state servitors. His support of its interests was thus linked to his perception that what could benefit the gentry would redound to the benefit of the state" (p. 67). Whelan here follows George Yaney's point of view, argued first in *The Systematization of Russian Government* (Urbana, 1973), pp. 375–76, and subsequently, in greater detail, in *Urge to Mobilize*. In the latter study, Yaney argues provocatively, but unconvincingly, that the post of *zemskii nachalnik* was created not in order to restore the influence of noble landowners over the peasantry, but rather as part of a quest by reforming administrators in St. Petersburg for "virtuous knight-servitors" who could extend into the villages modern notions of rational administration (pp. 52–54). Thus would be realized the reformers' aim "to mobilize the peasantry" (p. 78), i.e., to "force the rural population into conformity with 'modern' assumptions regarding human nature" in order to satisfy the "inner need" of those same Westernized reformers to impose their "belief in a systematic universe" upon "all the Russian people" (pp. 5–7). For Yaney's equally unconvincing attempt to present not only Tolstoi, but Pazukhin as well, as one of these modernizing reformers, see ibid., pp. 71–75, 90–92, 396; on this

point, at least, Whelan refuses to follow Yaney (see Whelan, pp. 175, 178, 184–85). Whelan and Yaney are creating a false dichotomy, for no traditionalist ever dreamed of distinguishing between the interests of the nobility and the true interests of the state, and it was a cardinal belief of the *soslovniki* that not only did nobles make the best servants of the autocracy, but that their privileges were closely linked to their role as state servants, a role the traditionalists were very concerned with strengthening (see chap. 6 above). There was no dichotomy between the interests of the state and those of the nobility (as interpreted by the *soslovniki*) in the case of the counterreforms, at least. Nor is any light shed on the 1880s by Yaney's claim that "Alexander III 'favored' his gentry in approximately the same way Lenin and Stalin would 'favor' their workers" *(Urge to Mobilize*, p. 79).

5. Yaney, *Urge to Mobilize*, pp. 85–86.

6. *O sostave*, pp. 55–59; Zaionchkovskii, *Rossiiskoe samoderzhavie*, pp. 396–401.

7. Reported in *Vestnik Evropy*, Mar. 1890, pp. 383–85.

8. *Vestnik Evropy*, Mar. 1885, pp. 378–82; Sh., "Dvorianstvo v Rossii," *Vestnik Evropy*, Mar. 1887, pp. 277–78, 282. See also *Vestnik Evropy*, May 1897, pp. 345–49, and Evreinov, pp. 42–43, 46–48, 97, 102–3.

9. F. D. Samarin, "Zametki po povodu zakona o zemskikh nachalnikov," undated ms. evidently written ca. 1889–90, GBL, f. 265, papka 117, ed. 1, l. 3.

10. Witte, 1:299.

11. Quoted in Yaney, *Systematization*, p. 375. Pazukhin had earlier argued for the abolition of the rural justice of the peace as an essential part of the proposal to establish the *zemskii nachalnik* but had been defeated by Minister of Justice Manasein. See Whelan, pp. 176–78.

12. Quoted in Danilov, 1:442. See also V. A., p. 15; Planson, "*Osoboe soveshchanie*," p. 15; and the views of S. S. Bekhteev, an *uezd* marshal in Orel *guberniia*, as presented in V. [P.] V[orontsov], "Nedochety soslovnykh programm," *Vestnik Evropy*, Jan. 1903, pp. 363–64. For data on the total number of *zemskie nachalniki* at the beginning of the century and their qualifications, see Gos. sovet, *Otchet za 1903–1904*, p. 124.

13. Zaionchkovskii, *Rossiiskoe samoderzhavie*, p. 398. Zaionchkovskii notes that the percentage of commoners among the *zemskie nachalniki* of the ten *gubernii* was undoubtedly higher than the national average.

14. Yaney, *Urge to Mobilize*, pp. 99–101.

15. Zinoviev, p. 129; Semenov, pp. 46–47, 84.

16. Paltov, pp. 226–29, 234–37.

17. Yaney, *Urge to Mobilize*, pp. 100, 103–4, 104n. For the 1906 *ukaz*, see chap. 6 above.

18. Fadeev, pp. 75, 85.

19. Whelan, p. 174. For a similar view see Yaney, *Systematization*, pp. 349, 373.

20. For Pazukhin's first draft, see Zaionchkovskii, *Rossiiskoe samoderzhavie*, pp. 401–4; Zakharova, *Zemskaia kontrreforma*, pp. 91, 101–2, 105–6; S. Ia. Tseitlin, "Zemskoe samoupravlenie i reforma 1890 g. (1865–1890)," in *Istoriia Rossii v XIX veke* (St. Petersburg, 1907–1911), 5: 130–31.

21. Under the 1864 *zemstvo* statute, the first curia consisted of all private individual owners of rural land; the second, of all private individual owners of urban property and corporate property owners other than peasant communes; and the third, of peasants in their capacity of holders of communal land allotments. The first and second curiae included members of all four estates—nobles, clergy, townsmen, and peasants; the third included peasants exclusively, but only because of the unique nature of communally owned allotment land. Rieber is there-

fore misleading in asserting that the 1864 electoral system "combined property qualifications and soslovie membership" and that the 1890 revisions in the statute "gave greater prominence to sosloviia" (pp. 95–96); in fact, the revised statute recognized social estates for the first time.

Whelan is mistaken in declaring that under the 1864 statute, "peasantry, townsfolk, and gentry . . . elected, at separate meetings, deputies to zemstvo assemblies at the district (uezd) level" (p. 172). This misconception is undoubtedly a major reason for her conclusion that changes in the electoral process were "of secondary importance" in the 1890 revision and that "a deepening division of social classes [sic] in the provinces . . . was in basic accord with the original statute of 1864" (pp. 189, 193).

22. Under the 1864 statute, each of the first two curiae was entitled to one representative in the uezd zemstvo assembly for every thirty units of land owned by its members, each unit equaling the minimum area necessary for a landowner to qualify for a personal vote in the first curia. The third curia was entitled to one representative for every three thousand male peasants. Pazukhin proposed to give the restructured first curia one representative in the uezd zemstvo assembly for every twenty units of land, the second curia one for every thirty units, and the third curia one for every four thousand male peasants.

23. Pazukhin's draft lowered the property qualification for a direct vote in the first curia from 200–800 desiatiny to 125–475 desiatiny, depending on the uezd.

24. Pazukhin proposed raising the minimum necessary for a vote in the assembly of small landowners from one-twentieth to one-tenth of the acreage required for a direct vote in the first curia.

25. To qualify for automatic membership landowners would have had to possess estates equal to thirty times the minimum size for a direct vote, i.e., 3,750–14,250 desiatiny; in the thirty-four gubernii with zemstvo elections there were more than 1,120 such magnates.

26. Zaionchkovskii, Rossiiskoe samoderzhavie, pp. 404, 406–7; Tseitlin, pp. 127–28, 132; Zakharova, Zemskaia kontrreforma, pp. 132, 136.

27. Tseitlin, pp. 135–38; Zaionchkovskii, Rossiiskoe samoderzhavie, p. 408; O sostave, p. 51; "Polozhenie o gubernskikh i uezdnykh zemskikh uchrezhdeniiakh," 1892 ed., SZ, vol. 2.

28. B. B. Veselovskii, Istoriia zemstva (St. Petersburg, 1909–1911), 3: 433–34, 680–81. Statistika Rossiiskoi imperii 9 (1890):50–51, gives the following percentages of hereditary and personal nobles alone for 1883–1886: 35 percent in the uezd assemblies, 70 percent in the guberniia assemblies, 44 percent on the uezd boards, and 74 percent on the guberniia boards.

29. Veselovskii, Istoriia zemstva, 3:352, 681.

30. "Svod zakonov o sostoianiiakh," 1876 ed., arts. 102, 119, 121, SZ, vol. 9; M. T. Iablochkov, Istoriia dvorianskago sosloviia v Rossii (St. Petersburg, 1876), pp. 675–76.

31. Percentages calculated from data in Ershov, pp. 34–35. When Ufa guberniia was carved out of Orenburg in 1865, it received its own noble society, bringing the number of such in European Russia to forty-six, but with elections and assemblies in only thirty-seven. In 1878 the first estate of Terek oblast was permitted to organize, raising to four the number of noble societies in the Caucasus (see Liubimov).

32. "Svod zakonov o sostoianiiakh," 1876 ed., art. 102.

33. O sostave, p. 79; "Svod zakonov o sostoianiiakh," 1876 ed., art. 96; PSZ, 2d ser., vol. 50, no. 55219. Manning, Crisis, asserts that "only those noble proprietors who possessed bureaucratic or military ranking at the officers' level (chin) could legally participate in the local noble assemblies" (p. 85). Manning both

ignores the 1875 change in the statute and confuses the requirements for voting with the requirements for merely participating in the assemblies.

34. "Svod zakonov o sostoianiiakh," 1876 ed., art. 188; *PSZ*, 2d ser., vol. 50, no. 55219; *O sostave*, p. 84.

35. Korelin, *Dvorianstvo*, p. 142; "Polozhenie o zemskikh uchrezhdeniiakh," 1892 ed., app. to art. 16, *SZ*, vol. 2; "Svod zakonov o sostoianiiakh," 1899 ed., arts. 118, 132. In a single *uezd* of Samara *guberniia* the minimum was fixed at 550 *desiatiny*. The numbers of properties qualifying their owners for direct and indirect votes have been calculated from data in *Statistika zemlevladeniia 1905 g.*, pp. 18–78, and are consistent with the estimate of 16,000 fully enfranchised noble landowners in the mid-1880s given in Baratynskii, *Sbornik statei*, p. 25.

36. Although the minimum property qualification actually ranged from 125 to 475 *desiatiny*, according to the *uezd*, for the exercise of a direct vote in the first curia in elections to the *zemstvos* (from 1890), the noble assemblies (from 1896), and the State Duma (from 1905), in the thirty-seven *gubernii* with noble elections, for convenience' sake I have used a minimum of 200 *desiatiny* for all fifty *gubernii* to arrive at the figure of 31,000. The figure of 34,107, derived from data in *Statistika zemlevladeniia 1905 g.*, p. 78, after adjustment for multiple holdings and personal nobles, reduces to 31,000 noble proprietors and 28,000 noble families, containing 126,000 persons or 12 percent of all hereditary nobles in 1905 (see app. C below). The estimate of 31,000 noble landowners, although arrived at by different means, is almost exactly identical to the figure of 30,000 noble landowners meeting the property qualification for a personal vote in the first curia used in Roberta T. Manning, "The Russian Provincial Gentry in Revolution and Counterrevolution, 1905–07" (Ph.D. diss., Columbia University, 1975), p. 623, and also by Leopold H. Haimson, "Introduction," p. 19 and n., and "Conclusion," pp. 292–93, in Leopold H. Haimson, ed., *The Politics of Rural Russia, 1905–1914* (Bloomington, 1979), pp. 19, 19n, 292–93. In *Crisis*, however, Manning reduces her previous estimate by one-third, claiming that "approximately 18,000–20,000 of the roughly 30,000 private landowners possessing the full property requirement to vote in the Duma elections were noblemen" (p. 325 and n.). Manning cites *Statistika zemlevladeniia 1905 g.*, p. 78, according to which source there were in the fifty *gubernii* in 1905, 18,102 properties of more than 500 *desiatiny* belonging to nobles, and 21,732 properties of more than 400 *desiatiny*. But the overwhelming majority of noble landowners lived in *uezdy* with minimum property qualifications *lower* than 400 *desiatiny*. Minima of 400 or more applied in 46 of 116 *uezdy* in thirteen *gubernii*, nine of which were located in the north or east and contained few nobles. See "Svod uchrezhdenii gosudarstvennykh," 1906 ed., app. to art. 28, *SZ*, vol. 1, pt. 2.

37. Derived from statistics in *Statistika zemlevladeniia 1905 g.*, p. 78. In 1905, noble landowners held 52 percent of all estates of more than one hundred *desiatiny* and 68 percent of the acreage included in them (see table 9).

38. Kornilov, 2:156, 221–23; Terence Emmons, *The Russian Landed Gentry and the Peasant Emancipation of 1861* (Cambridge, Eng., 1968), pp. 267–69, 284–98, 309–10, 378–80 and passim.

39. Emmons, *Russian Landed Gentry*, pp. 396–97, 408–11; "Svod zakonov o sostoianiiakh," 1857 ed., art. 135; ibid., 1876 ed., art. 142.

40. A. P. Korelin, "Dvorianstvo," pp. 106–7; Korkunov, 2:624–27. There were four noble assemblies in the Baltic *gubernii*, since in Estonia there was a separate *Landtag* for the island of Ösel.

41. In 1864 the noble societies formed only a decade and a half earlier in the five *gubernii* of the kingdom of Poland were abolished outright. In the *gubernii* acquired by Catherine II in the partitions of Poland, where Poles formed a

majority of all nobles in the 1860s except in Minsk and Mogilev and owned the overwhelming majority of the land, *guberniia* and *uezd* marshals and *uezd* deputies were henceforth appointed by the minister of internal affairs in Minsk, Mogilev, and Vitebsk and by the regional governors-general in the northwest (Kovno, Vilno, and Grodno) and southwest (Volynia, Podolia, and Kiev), preferably from among local landowners "of non-Polish descent" ("Svod zakonov o sostoianiiakh," 1899 ed., 1906 supp., arts. 179^1 and 179^2). Easily the most famous of the government's appointees was P. A. Stolypin, who served first as *uezd* and then *guberniia* marshal in Kovno from 1889 to 1902. Although the reinstitution of noble assemblies and elections in the western *gubernii* was discussed in the Committee of Ministers in March 1905, no action was ever taken (Korelin, "Dvorianstvo," p. 110). After the 1863 revolt Poles were banned from acquiring land other than by inheritance in the western *gubernii*, but at the end of the century they still owned 33–40 percent of all private holdings in Mogilev and Kiev, 47–54 percent in Vitebsk, Volynia, Podolia, Minsk, and Grodno, and 73–75 percent in Vilno and Kovno (A. I. Kastelianskii, ed., *Formy natsionalnago dvizheniia v sovremennykh gosudarstvakh* [St. Petersburg, 1910], p. 363; Korelin, "Dvorianstvo," p. 109).

42. Korelin, "Rossiiskoe dvorianstvo," pp. 68–69; Blosfeldt, *Sbornik zakonov*, pp. 365–72.

43. *Moskovskoe gubernskoe ocherednoe dvorianskoe sobranie (18–26 fevralia 1890 g.)* (Moscow, 1890), p. 78; Zinoviev, p. 88.

44. Zinoviev, pp. 80–81, 83–84, 87; *Moskovskoe dvorianskoe sobranie (1890 g.)*, p. 79; *Moskovskoe gubernskoe dvorianskoe sobranie, 1893* (Moscow, 1893); TsGAM, f. 4, d. 522, l. 15.

45. Percentages calculated by dividing the total vote on major motions (from Emmons, *Russian Landed Gentry*, pp. 268, 285, 292, 297, 340, 377, 379, 409n) by number of landowners with one hundred or more serfs in 1859 (from Troinitskii, p. 45). Actually, landowners with as few as five serfs were entitled to vote on the resolutions in question, although only owners of one hundred or more were fully enfranchised.

46. Koshelev, "O dvorianstve i zemlevladeltsakh," pp. 50–51; Korelin, "Rossiiskoe dvorianstvo," pp. 80–81. An identical proportion (21 percent) of eligible landowners participated in *zemstvo* elections during 1883–1886 (Tseitlin, p. 91).

47. Data on noble landownership in the four *gubernii* are from *Statistika zemlevladeniia 1905 g.*, pp. 36, 60, 76; property qualifications for a personal vote in elections are from "Polozhenie o zemskikh uchrezhdeniiakh," 1892 ed., app. to art. 16. The three Moscow votes are from *Moskovskoe dvorianskoe sobranie 1890 g. Zhurnaly*, ll. 26b–27a; TsGIAL, f. 1283, op. 1, d. 15, l. 6; ibid., d. 35, l. 9. The 1902 vote in Saratov is from ibid., d. 78 (1905), ll. 8–14; the 1896 vote is from "Upadok dvorianskogo zemlevladeniia v Saratovskoi gub.," *Mir bozhii*, Jan. 1897, pt. 2, p. 25. The Penza and Kherson votes are from *Vestnik Evropy*, Apr. 1892, p. 846.

48. Planson, *O dvorianstve*, p. 17.

49. Hamburg, "Land," pp. 41, 129. Korelin (*Dvorianstvo*, pp. 15, 260) correctly notes the lack of sympathy on the part of the majority of the first estate for most of the petitions from the noble assemblies.

50. "Svod zakonov o sostoianiiakh," 1857 ed., art. 135, which granted noble assemblies the right to petition the government not only on their own needs but also on local administrative problems affecting other groups as well, was dropped from the 1876 edition of the code but its essence was repeated in art. 169 of the 1899 edition. For the restoration of this right, see Leroy-Beaulieu, 2:155–56; *O sostave*, pp. 89–90; Korelin, "Rossiiskoe dvorianstvo," pp. 75–77; idem, *Dvorianstvo*, pp. 254, 259–60; *Vestnik Evropy*, Mar. 1890, pp. 386–87.

51. Quoted in *Vestnik Evropy*, Mar. 1890, p. 387. In fact the 1865 ban on the noble assemblies' discussing matters other than their own needs and interests and specifically on "touching upon questions relating to the alteration of the essential principles of Russia's state institutions," embodied in "Svod zakonov o sostoianiiakh," 1876 ed., art. 142, was not repealed in 1888. The 1876 article was retained without change as art. 152 of the 1899 edition of the code. Apprehensions similar to those expressed by *Moskovskie vedomosti* underlay the unanimous rejection by a subcommittee of the special conference on the nobility in May 1899 of suggestions for a nationwide organization of the first estate (Korelin, *Dvorianstvo*, p. 137).

52. TsGIAL, f. 1283, op. 1, d. 13, ll. 39, 42; Gos. sovet, *Otchet za 1901-1902*, pp. 159-60.

53. Gos. sovet, *Otchet za 1901-1902*, pp. 155-56, 165-66; Blosfeldt, *Noveishiia uzakoneniia*, p. 9.

54. TsGIAL, f. 1283, op. 1, d. 13, l. 34.

55. Manning nevertheless insists on "the revitalized noble assemblies" of the postreform era and the "new vogue in the eyes of the gentry" enjoyed by the noble assemblies as increasing numbers of nobles left their desks in government offices and joined the "turn to the land" (*Crisis*, pp. 38, 45).

56. TsGADA, f. 1254, op. 1, d. 86, l. 13a; Zinoviev, p. 41; TsGIAL, f. 1283, op. 1, d. 13, ll. 12-13; Blosfeldt, *Noveishiia uzakoneniia*, p. 7.

57. *Vestnik Evropy*, Mar. 1893, p. 378; TsGIAL, f. 1283, op. 1, d. 4, l. 6; ibid., d. 13, ll. 48-58, 211-16, 304-5; *Doklad kazanskago predvoditelia dvorianstva*, pp. 6-7; Zinoviev, pp. 41, 49-50; TsGADA, f. 1254, op. 1, d. 86, l. 13b; Gos. sovet, *Otchet za 1901-1902*, pp. 166-68; Blosfeldt, *Noveishiia uzakoneniia*, pp. 9-11.

58. Korf, "Predvoditel dvorianstva," p. 111; "Svod zakonov o sostoianiiakh," 1876 ed., art. 295; ibid., 1899 ed., art. 384; P. P. Trubetskoi, *Pamiatnaia kniga dlia uezdnago predvoditelia dvorianstva* (Odessa, 1887), pp. 38-40; *O sostave*, pp. 49-50, 65, 68-69, 72-73. Compare this description of the *uezd* marshal's responsibilities with Yaney's claim that the *guberniia* marshal especially, but the *uezd* marshal as well, "did not play a vital *administrative* role" (*Systematization*, p. 341).

59. Quoted in S. S. Tatishchev, *Imperator Aleksandr II* (St. Petersburg, 1903), 2:101-2.

60. Tseitlin, p. 104.

61. *O sostave*, p. 85; Leroy-Beaulieu, 2:165; Planson, *O dvorianstve*, pp. 25-26; Korf, "Predvoditel dvorianstva," p. 111. The quotation is from *Sovremennye dvorianskie voprosy*, p. 18. Before 1831 the office of *uezd* marshal had been rated class seven; the office of *guberniia* marshal was raised in 1831 from class five to class four (the same as the governor's office), where it remained (Korelin, *Dvorianstvo*, p. 221).

62. "Svod zakonov o sostoianiiakh," 1876 ed., art. 299. See also ibid., art. 294 and *O sostave*, pp. 48-50, 68-69, 72-73. On the ex officio duties of both *uezd* and *guberniia* marshals, see also Blosfeldt, *Sbornik zakonov*, pp. 145n, 383-405.

63. Romanovich-Slavatinskii, pp. 70, 456-62. See also Emmons, *Russian Landed Gentry*, p. 13.

64. Terpigorev, *Oskudenie*, 1:108.

65. Korf, "Predvoditel dvorianstva," p. 100; Korelin, *Dvorianstvo*, p. 225. Manning participates in this consensus, asserting that "tenure in such offices [as *uezd* marshal] was generally protracted, sometimes lasting as long as twenty years" (*Crisis*, p. 39).

66. All data in this section are from Liubimov, passim.

67. Hamburg's findings for marshals who held office between 1859 and 1916 are similar ("Land," pp. 19–22), but by including appointed marshals, who usually served longer than elected marshals, he obtains a somewhat lower rate of turnover in office.

68. Between 1777 and 1910 there were eighty cases in forty-one *gubernii* of the marshalship's being held by two or more members of a family; in thirty-five of these instances, a father was succeeded by his son, usually after an interval during which someone else had held the post.

69. The Bobrinskiis and the Kapnists were the most notable examples. V. A. Bobrinskii served as *guberniia* marshal in Tula from 1862 to 1863, his son in Moscow from 1875 to 1883, his nephew in St. Petersburg from 1869 to 1872, and the latter's son also in St. Petersburg from 1876 to 1888 and again from 1891 to 1895. And five members of the Kapnist family served a total of eleven terms as *guberniia* marshal between 1784 and 1901 in Kiev, Ekaterinoslav, Poltava, and Kharkov.

70. In Bogorodsk between 1869 and 1908 N. F. Samarin and his three nephews held the post continuously with two brief exceptions for the years 1872–1875 and 1896–1899. V. K. Shlippe, his brother, and his son served as marshals in Vereia without interruption from 1873 to 1912. A survey of *uezd* marshals in sixteen *gubernii* between 1885 and 1917 yielded results very similar to those for *guberniia* marshals (Hamburg, "Land," pp. 19–22).

71. The service records (*formuliarnye spiski*) in question are in TsGIAL, f. 1283, op. 1, various *delo* numbers.

72. Hamburg calculates an average age of forty-eight at first election for a sample of eighty-six *guberniia* marshals (period not specified) ("Land," p. 32); elsewhere he finds that eighteen out of forty *guberniia* marshals (45 percent) in 1903 had some higher education ("Portrait of an Elite: Russian Marshals of the Nobility, 1861–1917," *Slavic Review* 40 [1981]:595).

73. Among a sample of twenty-two *guberniia* marshals in 1895, the average landholding was somewhat over 5,500 *desiatiny* (Hamburg, "Portrait," p. 592). Manning finds that twenty-nine of thirty-one *guberniia* marshals sampled in 1905 owned an average of 5,552 *desiatiny* (*Crisis*, p. 377).

74. Manning, *Crisis*, p. 28. In the half century ending in 1911, Manning cites nineteen former marshals who were appointed "as governors, vice-governors, or heads of departments" in the Ministry of Internal Affairs (p. 28n). Nineteen is hardly a significant proportion of either the total number of marshals who held office during that period or the total number of governors, vice-governors, and heads of departments. It would also be pertinent to know how many of the nineteen were, like Stolypin, appointed marshals in the western *gubernii*.

75. Pazukhin, pp. 33–34. The traditionalists' idealization of the marshal of nobility was challenged by Senator G. A. Evreinov in a work published in 1888, which noted that in the previous two decades *uezd* marshals had constituted a higher percentage of embezzlers of *zemstvo* funds than had any other group of local officials. Evreinov's work is cited in Veselovskii, *Istoriia zemstva*, 3:333–34.

76. TsGIAL, f. 1283, op. 1, d. 13, l. 75. Planson (*O dvorianstve*, p. 28) also opposed salaries for *uezd* marshals. One anonymous publicist had proposed a minimum annual salary of 3,000 rubles—equal to the salary plus expense account of the chairman of the executive board of an *uezd zemstvo* (*Sovremennye dvorianskie voprosy*, pp. 18–20). Only the marshals appointed by the government in the nine western *gubernii* received salaries (Korelin, *Dvorianstvo*, p. 226).

77. TsGIAL, f. 1283, op. 1, d. 13, ll. 218–19, 222, 238–46; Planson, *O dvorianstve*, pp. 27–28.

78. TsGIAL, f. 1283, op. 1, d. 13, ll. 296, 299, 321–25; Gos. sovet, *Otchet za*

1901–1902, pp. 158, 163–64, 169, 190–99; idem, *Vsepoddanneishii otchet predsedatelia za sessiiu 1901–1902 gg.*, pp. 26–27; Korelin, *Dvorianstvo*, p. 225. The June 10, 1902, law is in Blosfeldt, *Noveishiia uzakoneniia*, pp. 11–13.

79. For the special conference's discussion of these questions, see the archival source cited in n. 77 above; for the State Council, n. 78. Manning is misleading in stating simply that "the marshalships conferred high service rank on their bearers" (*Crisis*, p. 74 and also p. 28).

80. A. I. Elishev in *Russkoe obozrenie*, May 1897, p. 479.

81. Quoted in Korelin, "Dvorianstvo," p. 173.

82. Korelin, "Rossiiskoe dvorianstvo," p. 79; idem, *Dvorianstvo*, p. 135; Soloviev, *Samoderzhavie i dvorianstvo v kontse XIX veka*, pp. 193, 219–20.

83. Soloviev, *Samoderzhavie i dvorianstvo v kontse XIX veka*, pp. 221–25, 227; idem, "Pravitelstvo," pp. 255–59.

84. See, for example, the letters of Prince P. N. Trubetskoi, Moscow *guberniia* marshal and chairman of the conferences through 1906, to Minister of Internal Affairs von Pleve of Oct. 16, 1902, and Oct. 13 and Nov. 17, 1903, TsGIAL, f. 1283, op. 1, d. 87, ll. 2, 262–63, 268. Memoranda produced by many of the conferences are in TsGIAL, f. 1283, op. 1, d. 87.

85. Pleve to Trubetskoi, Oct. 31, 1902, TsGIAL, f. 1283, op. 1, d. 87, ll. 6–7.

86. Two minor acts were still to come: the Apr. 2, 1903 law on the five-year cadet schools and the establishment in June 1904 of the national genealogical register for nobles not enrolled in *guberniia* societies (see chaps. 5 and 6 above).

87. *Moskovskie vedomosti* is cited in *Vestnik Evropy*, July 1897, p. 364; Nicholas II's rescript to Durnovo is in Blosfeldt, *Noveishiia uzakoneniia*, pp. 42–43.

88. V. I. Gurko, *Features and Figures of the Past: Government and Opinion in the Reign of Nicholas II* (Stanford, 1939), p. 84; "Dnevnik A. A. Polovtseva [1901–1903]," *Krasnyi arkhiv* 3 (1923):140–42, 146–48; Gos. sovet, *Otchet za 1901–1902*, pp. 110–21; idem, *Vsepoddanneishii otchet predsedatelia za sessiiu 1901–1902 gg.*, pp. 30–32; Blosfeldt, *Noveishiia uzakoneniia*, pp. 42–43.

89. Quoted in Korelin, "Rossiiskoe dvorianstvo," p. 78n.

90. Terner, "Dvorianstvo," Mar. 1903, p. 5.

CHAPTER 8

1. On the liberation movement, see George Fischer, *Russian Liberalism: From Gentry to Intelligentsia* (Cambridge, Mass., 1958), chaps. 4 and 5, and Shmuel Galai, *The Liberation Movement in Russia 1900–1905* (Cambridge, Eng., 1973). According to Emmons, *Formation of Political Parties*, three-quarters of the Constitutional Democratic Central Committee in 1905 were noblemen, and most were landowners, although only one-fifth devoted themselves solely to agriculture (pp. 63, 113).

2. Fischer, pp. 182–87; D. N. Shipov, *Vospominaniia i dumy o perezhitom* (Moscow, 1918), pp. 261–65. Fischer translates *soslovnyi* as "class" rather than "estate."

3. Manning, *Crisis*, pp. 83–84. See also Galai, p. 270. In even discussing the question of representative government, the noble assemblies were stretching to the limit their right to deal with local administrative shortcomings concerning the entire community and were in fact in violation of the ban on discussing fundamental changes in Russia's political structure. See chap. 7, n. 51 above.

4. Manning explains the noble assemblies' behavior in 1905 as the culmination of the "turn to the land" of nobles who (1) despised and resented their former

bureaucratic colleagues for their common birth and their ungentlemanlike professionalism and who (2) used the noble assemblies and zemstvos as surrogates for their thwarted bureaucratic careers, but her own analysis of the factors underlying the liberals' control of the zemstvos until the winter of 1906/1907 is applicable with but minor changes to the noble assemblies, where the sway of the liberals was of much briefer duration: "the traditional electoral absenteeism that prevailed among the landowning gentry . . . ; the political lethargy of the more traditional, and conservative landowners; and the liberals' administrative abilities and willingness to devote themselves wholeheartedly to zemstvo affairs" (Crisis, p. 274). See also Roberta T. Manning, "Zemstvo and Revolution: The Onset of the Gentry Reaction, 1905–1907," in Leopold H. Haimson, ed., The Politics of Rural Russia, 1905–1914 (Bloomington, 1979), pp. 42–43.

5. Quoted in Galai, pp. 242–43.

6. Quoted in Manning, Crisis, p. 109. The preceding paragraph draws on ibid., pp. 99, 111–12.

7. Ibid., pp. 113–14; Iu. B. Soloviev, Samoderzhavie i dvorianstvo v 1902–1907 gg. (Leningrad, 1981), p. 174.

8. S. M. Sidelnikov, Obrazovanie i deiatelnost pervoi gosudarstvennoi dumy (Moscow, 1962), p. 136. The property qualification for direct participation in the first curia generally ranged between 100 and 475 desiatiny; it was the same as that required for a personal vote in uezd zemstvo elections in the thirty-four original zemstvo gubernii, but in the six Belorussian and southwestern gubernii the property qualification for Duma elections was double that established for zemstvo elections when the latter were introduced in 1911. The minimum for a personal vote in the first curia was somewhat higher than 475 desiatiny in a few uezdy of four northern and eastern gubernii (Archangel, Vologda, Samara, Astrakhan) and in Minsk and Volynia. See "Svod uchrezhdenii gosudarstvennykh," 1906 ed., app. to art. 28, SZ, vol. 1, pt. 2; and "Polozhenie o zemskikh uchrezhdeniiakh," 1892 ed., app. to art. 16 and app. 2 to art. 3, sec. 2, SZ, vol. 2.

9. See chaps. 6 and 7. For the peasantry, see also Robinson, pp. 209–11.

10. For the electoral law governing the representative half of the State Council, see "Svod uchrezhdenii gosudarstvennykh," 1906 ed., and A. M. Davidovich, Samoderzhavie v epokhu imperializma (Moscow, 1975), pp. 240–44, 256–59, 265.

11. Alexandra S. Korros, "The Landed Nobility, the State Council, and P. A. Stolypin (1907–11)," in Leopold H. Haimson, ed., The Politics of Rural Russia, 1905–1914 (Bloomington, 1979), pp. 126–27.

12. Quoted in A. N. Naumov, Iz utselevshikh vospominanii, 1868–1917 (New York, 1954–1955), 2:4–5.

13. Soloviev, Samoderzhavie i dvorianstvo v 1902–1907 gg., pp. 199–200. On Chemodurov, see also chap. 7 above.

14. Nicholas wrote in the margin of Witte's Jan. 10, 1906, report to him incorporating Kutler's project: "I don't approve" and "private property must remain inviolable." On January 18 the emperor admonished a delegation of peasant representatives from Kursk guberniia to remember that "the right to property is sacred" and explained that this worked both ways: "what belongs to the pomeshchik is the pomeshchik's, and what belongs to the peasant is the peasant's" (quoted in Soloviev, Samoderzhavie i dvorianstvo v 1902–1907 gg., p. 197).

15. Geoffrey A. Hosking and Roberta T. Manning, "What Was the United Nobility?" in Leopold H. Haimson, ed., The Politics of Rural Russia, 1905–1914 (Bloomington, 1979), pp. 147–51; Naumov, 2:63–64.

16. Geoffrey A. Hosking, The Russian Constitutional Experiment (Cambridge, Eng., 1973), p. 19. This account of the events of 1906 relies heavily on Manning, Crisis. Neil B. Weissman, Reform in Tsarist Russia (New Brunswick, 1981), sees

Stolypin's agrarian program, as well as his electoral reform of 1907, as reflecting "a convergence of opinion" between "state policy and gentry demands" rather than "any causal connection" between the two (pp. 115–16).

17. Hosking and Manning, pp. 145–47, 151–55; Manning, *Crisis*, pp. 91–93, 113–14, 231.

18. Apparently oblivious to the discrepancy, Manning in *Crisis* gives the number of *gubernii* that elected their marshals as thirty-five (p. 231), thirty-nine (p. 233), and forty-nine (p. 76). For the United Nobility, see George W. Simmonds, "The Congress of Representatives of the Nobles' Associations, 1906–1916: A Case Study of Russian Conservatism" (Ph.D. diss., Columbia University, 1964) and Hosking and Manning.

19. Soloviev, *Samoderzhavie i dvorianstvo v 1902–1907 gg.*, p. 215; Manning, *Crisis*, pp. 232–33.

20. Rieber, pp. 335–36.

21. Naumov, 2:76–77; Simmonds, pp. 99n, 150.

22. Hosking and Manning, pp. 159–62, 181n; Korros, p. 126.

23. Manning, "Russian Provincial Gentry," pp. 362, 367, 514–17. Of 498 deputies in the first Duma, 101 were large or intermediate noble landowners; 79 additional noble deputies were distributed as follows: 51 in the professions, 8 industrialists, 4 owners of large or intermediate nonagricultural properties, 13 white-collar employees, and 3 clerics. See Sidelnikov, p. 190.

24. Manning, "Russian Provincial Gentry," pp. 501–3, 506–9.

25. In 1905, 68.2 percent of all noble properties were two hundred *desiatiny* or less in size (derived from statistics in *Statistika zemlevladeniia 1905 g.* [St. Petersburg, 1907], p. 78). For the use of two hundred *desiatiny* as the dividing line between smallholders and those entitled to participate personally in the first curia, see chap. 7, n. 36, above.

26. Manning, *Crisis*, erroneously states that the 1907 electoral law excluded from the first curia "peasant proprietors who held allotment land converted to private property or who had acquired their holdings through the Peasants' Land Bank" (p. 357). It was continued membership in a peasant commune, rather than the origin of the private property he owned, that barred a peasant from participating in the first curia. Manning cites, but misinterprets, Leopold H. Haimson, "Introduction," in Leopold H. Haimson, ed., *The Politics of Rural Russia, 1905–1914* (Bloomington, 1979), p. 18. Once a peasant proprietor had withdrawn from his commune, he was eligible to vote in the first curia.

27. Emmons, *Formation of Political Parties*, pp. 237–38, 372. The fifty-first *guberniia* was Stavropol in the North Caucasus.

28. Manning, *Crisis*, p. 326n, states that nobles accounted for 48.9 percent of all deputies in the third Duma and 47.5 percent in the fourth; of these, 87.0 percent and 81.2 percent, respectively, were landowners. Therefore, 42.5 percent and 38.6 percent of the deputies in the third and fourth Dumas, respectively, were noble landowners or "landed gentry"—not "close to half . . . (47–49%)" as Manning claims on p. 326.

29. Korf, "Predvoditel dvorianstva," pp. 112–16.

30. Weissman, *Reform in Tsarist Russia*, pp. 49, 74–76, 97, 129–44 passim; V. S. Diakin, "Stolypin i dvorianstvo (Proval mestnoi reformy)," in *Problemy krestianskogo zemlevladeniia i vnutrennei politiki Rossii. Dooktiabrskii period* (Leningrad, 1972), pp. 238–43; Hosking, p. 18; Korros, pp. 128–29. According to Manning, noble landowners paid no more than 11 percent of the *zemstvos'* total tax bill, in contrast to the peasants, who paid two-thirds (*Crisis*, p. 330).

31. Quoted in Diakin, "Stolypin i dvorianstvo," p. 241.

32. Hosking, p. 157. Weissman, *Reform in Tsarist Russia*, states flatly that "the

estate principle and the gentry institutions that were its embodiment were the primary target of the Stolypin ministry in its work toward local reform" (p. 118).

33. Quoted in Manning, "Russian Provincial Gentry," p. 559. The preceding paragraph is based on ibid., pp. 571–72, 637–38; Hosking, p. 156; Diakin, "Stolypin i dvorianstvo," pp. 244–46; Weissman, *Reform in Tsarist Russia*, pp. 160–61.

34. Neil B. Weissman, *Reform in Tsarist Russia*, pp. 169–75; idem, "State, Estate and Society in Tsarist Russia (Ph.D. diss., Princeton University, 1976), pp. 259–64. For the United Nobility's defense of the *uezd* marshal's role in local administration, see Manning, *Crisis*, pp. 330–46.

35. Quoted in V. S. Diakin, *Samoderzhavie, burzhuaziia i dvorianstvo v 1907–1911 gg.* (Leningrad, 1978), p. 130. See also idem, "Stolypin i dvorianstvo," pp. 255–57, and Hosking, pp. 158–59, 162.

36. Diakin, "Stolypin i dvorianstvo," pp. 240–43, 263–69; Hosking and Manning, pp. 164, 166–67; Hosking, pp. 162, 167–69; Weissman, *Reform in Tsarist Russia*, pp. 184–86, 196–97; idem, "State, Estate and Society," pp. 195–96, 203–4.

37. Quoted in Manning, "Russian Provincial Gentry," pp. 417–18. See also Simmonds, pp. 103–5, 109.

38. Manning, *Crisis*, pp. 362–65. Faithful to the notion of the nobility's inability to compete in a market economy, Manning refers to government spending on agriculture as "subsidies" and alleges that noble landowners "had come to depend" on them and that such assistance was a major factor in reducing the annual losses in noble acreage from 1909 on (ibid., pp. 364–66, 369). On the actual magnitude of this reduction, see table 3 above. One form of aid that the government did not grant, although requested to do so by the United Nobility's fifth congress, was the merger of the peasant and noble land banks. Manning errs in declaring that the government's response to this request was to place both banks under a common director in 1909 *(Crisis*, p. 362). In fact, the two banks had been managed by a single director de jure ever since Nov. 1895—and de facto even earlier. See Erik Amburger, *Geschichte der Behördenorganisation Russlands von Peter dem Grossen bis 1917* (Leiden, 1966), p. 213, and N. P. Eroshkin, *Istoriia gosudarstvennykh uchrezhdenii dorevoliutsionnoi Rossii*, 3d ed. (Moscow, 1983), p. 213.

39. Simmonds, p. 105; Hosking and Manning, p. 169.

CONCLUSION

1. Robert A. Feldmesser, "Social Classes and Political Structure," in Cyril E. Black, ed., *The Transformation of Russian Society* (Cambridge, Mass., 1960), p. 244.

2. Davidovich, p. 228. Less doctrinaire Soviet historians are left with the inexplicable paradox that the state, although it was the supposed agent of the ruling class, nevertheless refused to share its political power with that class and even pursued a policy of industrial development to the detriment of noble landowners. See Soloviev, *Samoderzhavie i dvorianstvo v kontse XIX veka*, pp. 133–34, 193; idem, "Samoderzhavie i dvorianskii vopros," pp. 150–51; Korelin, "Rossiiskoe dvorianstvo," pp. 78, 81.

3. Alexander Gerschenkron, "Soviet Marxism and Absolutism," *Slavic Review* 30 (1971):867–68.

4. Quoted in Hosking, pp. 201–2. There was some basis in law for Nicholas's view. Russia's 1906 Fundamental State Laws, while establishing a constitutional monarchy along the lines of the German Empire, nevertheless declared that "Supreme autocratic power belongs to the Emperor of all the Russias" ("Osnovnye

gosudarstvennye zakony," art. 4, *SZ*, vol. 1). At the final discussion of the draft of the Fundamental Laws in April 1906, Nicholas had unsuccessfully tried to restore the adjective "unlimited" to the description of the monarch's power. See Emmons, *Formation of Political Parties*, p. 17.
5. Soloviev, *Samoderzhavie i dvorianstvo v 1902–1907 gg.*, pp. 206, 250.
6. Manning, *Crisis*, p. 370.
7. Ibid., pp. 355–57.
8. Ibid., pp. 370–71.
9. Edelman, *Gentry Politics*, p. 1.
10. Ibid., pp. 6–7, 78.

APPENDIX A

1. Romanovich-Slavatinskii, p. 46.
2. Korelin, "Dvorianstvo," pp. 101–3. The following is based on ibid.; on Romanovich-Slavatinskii, pp. 36–40; and on Amburger, *Geschichte der Behörden-organisation*, p. 504.

APPENDIX B

1. *Obshchii svod rezultatov perepisi*, 1:160.
2. *Statisticheskiia tablitsy*, 2:267; *Statisticheskii vremennik Rossiiskoi imperii*, 1st ser., 1 (1866):40; idem, 2d ser., 10 (1875):22.
3. For the rates of natural increase, see A. G. Rashin, *Naselenie Rossii za 100 let (1811–1913 gg.)* (Moscow, 1956), p. 218; for the numbers of persons ennobled, see chap. 5, section on "Ennoblement via State Service" above. The formula was kindly suggested by Barbara Anderson.
4. Korelin, "Dvorianstvo," p. 125.
5. Rubakin, p. 60, attributes the numerical decline of the nobility in the 1860s to the negative impact of the great reforms, but Korelin, "Dvorianstvo," pp. 117–25, makes a much more convincing case for the influence of the Polish revolt.
6. Provincial percentages for 1858 are calculated from data in *Statisticheskiia tablitsy*, 2:267, 292–93, and for 1897 from data in *Obshchii svod rezultatov perepisi*, 1:164–65.
7. This group of nineteen was composed of five northern *gubernii* (Archangel, Olonets, Vologda, Viatka, and Perm), six Volga and trans-Volga *gubernii* (Kazan, Simbirsk, Saratov, Astrakhan, Samara, and Orenburg), five central industrial or non–Black Soil *gubernii* (Tver, Iaroslavl, Kostroma, Vladimir, and Nizhnii Novgorod), and the three easternmost of the central agricultural or Black Soil *gubernii* (Penza, Tambov, and Voronezh).
8. For the number of urban nobles by *guberniia*, see *Obshchii svod rezultatov perepisi*, 1:172. For the level of urbanization among the nobility as a whole in 1858 and 1897, see chap. 2 above.
9. The following analysis of the nobility's ethnic composition is based on data in *Obshchii svod rezultatov perepisi*, 2:2–5, 12, 374, 376, 378, and in the first fifty volumes of *Pervaia vseobshchaia perepis naseleniia Rossiiskoi imperii, 1897 g.* (St. Petersburg, 1899–1905).

APPENDIX C

1. The figure for the forty-four *gubernii* was reported in 1892 by the marshals of nobility to the Central Statistical Committee and is taken from TsGADA, f.

1287, op. 1, d. 3873, ll. 161–62. Estimates for Bessarabia and the Don Army Oblast are based on the number of serfowning landed proprietors in 1858, from Troinitskii, p. 45; estimates for the three Baltic *gubernii* are from Korelin, "Dvorianstvo," pp. 139–40. Before the separation of Ufa from Orenburg in 1865 there were forty-nine *gubernii* in European Russia.

2. Ershov, pp. x, 30.

3. *Tsifrovyia dannyia o pozemelnoi sobstvennosti v Evropeiskoi Rossii*, pp. 30–31.

4. *Statistika zemlevladeniia 1905 g.*, p. 12.

5. Anfimov, *Krupnoe pomeshchiche khoziaistvo*, p. 345. Anfimov (p. 356) suggests that after 1905, nobles who sold land usually tried to retain the minimum acreage necessary to qualify for a personal vote in the Duma, *zemstvo*, and noble elections.

6. Korelin, "Dvorianstvo," p. 140n.

APPENDIX F

1. From Zaionchkovskii, *Pravitelstvennyi apparat*, p. 71. See chap. 6, n. 1, above.

2. From Beskrovnyi, pp. 40, 44, 547–48. See chap. 6, n. 5, above. Korelin's samples ("Dvorianstvo," pp. 157, 160) are only 30 percent of Zaionchkovskii's estimated total for the civil service in 1897 and 56 percent of Beskrovnyi's total for the officer corps in 1864; for 1897, by counting different categories of military personnel, Korelin gets a total 6 percent higher than Beskrovnyi's.

3. See *Obshchii svod rezultatov perepisi*, 1:190.

4. The estimate of three thousand is based on data in Korelin, "Dvorianstvo," pp. 157 and 160, augmented to include those ennobled through receipt of orders.

5. See Beskrovnyi, pp. 44, 548.

GLOSSARY OF RUSSIAN TERMS

(plurals in parentheses)

chin (-y)	Rank (social, bureaucratic, or military)
chinovnik (-i)	Broadly, any holder of class rank in the civil service; narrowly, such a person belonging neither to the hereditary nor to the personal nobility; often pejorative
desiatina (-y)	Land measure equal to 2.7 acres
duma	Municipal council in a major city from 1870
Duma	Lower house of parliament from 1906
dvoriane	Nobles
dvorianstvo	Nobility
Gosudarstvennyi Sovet	State Council
guberniia (-ii)	Province
inorodets (-tsy)	Alien subject of the Russian state (a classification including nomadic peoples and Jews)
intelligent (-y)	Member of the intelligentsia

junker or iunker	Cadet; young nobleman serving as a noncommissioned officer
kulak	Prosperous peasant who exploited his peers
maiorat (-y)	Large entailed estate inherited by right of primogeniture
meshchane	Members of the unprivileged urban estate; artisans and laborers
meshchanstvo	The unprivileged urban estate as a whole
oblast	Frontier province
pomeste (-ia)	Land grant akin to a fief, awarded to military servitors by Muscovite tsars
raznochinets (-tsy)	Technically, a person who had left the social estate of his father but had not enrolled in another; loosely, an upwardly mobile commoner, especially a member of the professional intelligentsia; pejorative when used by traditionalists
ruble	Monetary unit equal to fifty-one cents in 1914
selskoe obshchestvo	Peasant commune
soslovie	Social estate
soslovnik (-i)	Defender of traditional system of social estates and legal privilege
uezd (-y)	District; subdivision of a *guberniia* or *oblast*
ukaz	Edict
uprava (-y)	Administrative board
volost	Peasant township; subdivision of an *uezd*
zemskii (-ie) nachalnik (-i)	Land captain from 1889
zemstvo	Rural organ of limited self-government from 1864

BIBLIOGRAPHY

ARCHIVES

Gosudarstvennaia Biblioteka SSSR imeni Lenina, Otdel Rukopisei, Moscow:
Fond 265, Samarin family
Tsentralnyi gosudarstvennyi arkhiv drevnikh aktov, Moscow:
Fond 1254, Arseniev, Iu.V.
Fond 1287, Sheremetev family
Tsentralnyi gosudarstvennyi arkhiv goroda Moskvy, Moscow:
Fond 4, Chancellery of the Moscow Noble Deputy Assembly
Tsentralnyi gosudarstvennyi istoricheskii arkhiv, Leningrad:
Fond 593, State Noble Land Bank
Fond 721, Sipiagin, D.S.
Fond 1283, Ministry of Internal Affairs, Chancellery on the Affairs of the Nobility

OFFICIAL AND UNOFFICIAL COLLECTIONS OF STATISTICS, STATUTES, INSTITUTIONAL PROCEEDINGS, DOCUMENTS, ETC.

Blosfeldt, G. E., ed. *Noveishiia uzakoneniia o rossiiskom dvorianstve. 1901–1902 gg.* St. Petersburg, 1903.
———. *Rossiiskoe dvorianstvo. Uzakoneniia i raziasneniia 1901–1910 gg.* St. Petersburg, 1910.
———. *Sbornik zakonov o rossiiskom dvorianstve.* St. Petersburg, 1901.
Ershov, G., ed., *Raspredelenie pozemelnoi sobstvennosti v 49-ti guberniiakh Evropeiskoi Rossii v 1877–78 gg. (Statisticheskii vremennik Rossiiskoi imperii.* 3d ser., vol. 10.) St. Petersburg, 1886.

Ezhegodnik Rossii. St. Petersburg, 1904–1914.

Gosudarstvennyi sovet, *Otchet po deloproizvodstvu za sessiiu 1899–1900 gg./1903–1904 gg.*

———. *Stenograficheskie otchety, 1911–12 gg.*

———. *Vsepoddanneishii otchet predsedatelia za sessiiu 1898–1899 gg./1902–1903 gg.*

Khrestomatiia po istorii SSSR, 1861–1917. Moscow, 1970.

Liubimov, S. *Predvoditeli dvorianstva vsekh namestnichestv, gubernii i oblastei Rossiiskoi imperii, 1777–1910 g.* St. Petersburg, 1911.

Materialy po statistike dvizheniia zemlevladeniia v Rossii. 25 vols. St. Petersburg, 1896–1917.

Moskovskoe dvorianstvo. Spiski sluzhivshikh po vyboram, 1782–1910. Moscow, 1910.

Moskovskoe gubernskoe dvorianskoe sobranie, 18–25 fevralia 1890 g. Zhurnaly, otchety, doklady. Moscow, 1890.

Moskovskoe gubernskoe dvorianskoe sobranie, 1893. Doklady i postanovleniia. Moscow, 1893.

Moskovskoe gubernskoe ocherednoe dvorianskoe sobranie (18–26 fevralia 1890 g.). Moscow, 1890.

Obshchii svod po imperii rezultatov razrabotki dannykh pervoi vseobshchei perepisi naseleniia, proizvedennoi 28 ianvaria 1897 goda. 2 vols. St. Petersburg, 1905.

O zadolzhennosti zemlevladeniia v sviazi s statisticheskimi dannymi o pritoke kapitalov k pomestnomu zemlevladeniiu so vremeni osvobozhdeniia krestian. (Vremennik tsentralnago statisticheskago komiteta, no. 2, [1888]).

Pervaia vseobshchaia perepis naseleniia Rossiiskoi imperii, 1897 g. 89 vols. St. Petersburg, 1899–1905.

Polnoe sobranie zakonov Rossiiskoi imperii. 1st ser. (1649–1825), 45 vols. St. Petersburg, 1830; 2d ser. (1825–1881), 55 vols. St. Petersburg, 1830–1884; 3d ser. (1881–1913), 33 vols. St. Petersburg, 1885–1916.

Revised Statutes of the United States, passed at the First Session of the Forty-third Congress, 1873–74. 2d ed. Washington, 1878.

Rogovin, L. M., ed. *Sistematicheskii sbornik deistvuiushchikh zakonov o evreiakh.* St. Petersburg, 1913.

Rubakin, N. A. *Rossiia v tsifrakh.* St. Petersburg, 1912.

Spisok grazhdanskim chinam chetvertago klassa, 1900.

Spisok grazhdanskim chinam pervykh trëkh klassov, 1900.

Statisticheskiia tablitsy Rossiiskoi imperii. No. 2. *Nalichnoe naselenie imperii za 1858 god.* St. Petersburg, 1863.

Statisticheskii vremennik Rossiiskoi imperii. 1st ser., vol. 1. St. Petersburg, 1866.

Statisticheskii vremennik Rossiiskoi imperii. 2d ser., vol. 10. St. Petersburg, 1875.

Statistika Rossiiskoi imperii. Vol. 10. 1890.

Statistika zemlevladeniia 1905 g. Svod dannykh po 50-ti guberniiam Evropeiskoi Rossii. St. Petersburg, 1907.
Svod statisticheskikh svedenii po selskomu khoziaistvu Rossii k kontsu XIX v. 3 vols. St. Petersburg, 1902–1906.
Svod zakonov Rossiiskoi imperii. 16 vols. Various editions. St. Petersburg, 1857–1916.
Troinitskii, A. G., ed. *Krepostnoe naselenie v Rossii, po 10-i narodnoi perepisi.* St. Petersburg, 1861.
Tsifrovyia dannyia o pozemelnoi sobstvennosti v Evropeiskoi Rossii. [St. Petersburg], 1897.

JOURNALS

Russkaia mysl. 1880–1896.
Russkii arkhiv. 1869.
Russkii vestnik. 1889–1893.
Russkoe obozrenie. 1897–1898.
Severnyi vestnik. 1889.
Vestnik Evropy. 1885–1897.

OTHER PRIMARY SOURCES

A. Ch. *Zhelatelnaia reforma. Chetyre stati o dvorianstve.* St. Petersburg, 1881.
Aksakov, I. S. "Dvorianskoe delo." In A. I. Koshelev, *Golos iz zemstva,* vol. 1, appendix, pp. 33–49. Moscow, 1869.
Baratynskii, N.E. "Nedelimye dvorianskie uchastki." *Russkii vestnik,* May 1888, pp. 71–86.
———. "O nedelimykh imeniiakh." *Russkii vestnik,* May 1892, pp. 268–82.
———. *Po voprosu o zapovednykh imeniiakh.* Kazan, 1890.
———. *Sbornik statei o dvorianskikh nedelimykh imeniiakh.* St. Petersburg, 1893.
———. "Semeinye uchastki v bytovom otnoshenii." *Russkii vestnik,* May 1890, pp. 194–211.
Bekhteev, S. S. *Khoziaistvennye itogi istekshago sorokapiatiletiia i mery k khoziaistvennomu podёmu.* 3 vols. St. Petersburg, 1902–1911.
Benckendorff, Count Constantine. *Half a Life: The Reminiscences of a Russian Gentleman.* London, 1954.
Chicherin, B. N. *Neskolko sovremennykh voprosov.* Moscow, 1862.
D. *K voprosu o dvorianskom zemlevladenii.* Moscow, 1888.
D. V. "Gosudarstvennyi soslovnyi kredit." *Russkii vestnik,* June 1885, pp. 847–73, and August 1885, pp. 777–801.

Doklad i. d. kazanskago gubernskago predvoditelia dvorianstva ocherednomu sobraniiu dvorianstva Kazanskoi gubernii o predstavlennykh Osobomu Soveshchaniiu po delam dvorianskago sosloviia svedeniiakh po trebovaniiu Predsedatelia Osobago Soveshchaniia Stats-Sekretaria Durnovo. Kazan, 1898.

Drutskoi-Sokolninskii, D. "Nashe selskoe khoziaistvo i ego budushchnost." *Vestnik Evropy*, January 1891, pp. 345–68; October 1891, pp. 698–734.

Elishev, A. I. *Dvorianskoe delo. Sbornik statei.* Moscow, 1898.

——. "Ocherki dvorianskago dela." *Russkoe obozrenie*, November 1897, pp. 271–98.

——. "Sliianie soslovii." *Russkoe obozrenie*, September 1897, pp. 279–95.

——. *Sluzhebnyia prava dvorian.* Moscow, 1894.

Emelianov, N. "Izbytok svobody." *Russkii vestnik*, February 1901, pp. 601–12.

Evreinov, G. A. *Proshloe i nastoiashchee znachenie russkago dvorianstva.* St. Petersburg, 1898.

Fadeev, R. A. *Russkoe obshchestvo v nastoiashchem i budushchem (Chem nam byt?).* In *Sobranie sochinenii*, vol. 3, pt. 1. St. Petersburg, 1889.

Gindin, I. F., and M. Ia. Gefter, eds. "Trebovaniia dvorianstva i finansovo-ekonomicheskaia politika tsarskogo pravitelstva v 1880–1890-kh godakh." *Istoricheskii arkhiv*, no. 4 (1957), pp. 122–55.

Golovin, K. F. "Krupnoe zemlevladenie v Zapadnoi Evrope i v Rossii." *Russkii vestnik*, February 1887, pp. 481–537; April 1887, pp. 433–79; May 1887, pp. 120–58.

——. *Moi vospominaniia.* 2 vols. St. Petersburg, 1908–1910.

Golubev, P. A. "K voprosu o prichinakh ekonomicheskogo upadka selskogo naseleniia i pomeshchichego khoziaistva." *Iuridicheskii vestnik*, October 1892, pp. 194–247.

Gradovskii, A. D. *Nachala russkago gosudarstvennago prava.* In *Sobranie sochinenii*, vols. 7–9. St. Petersburg, 1899–1908.

Gribovskii, V. M. *Gosudarstvennoe ustroistvo i upravlenie Rossiiskoi imperii.* Odessa, 1912.

Gurko, V. I. *Features and Figures of the Past; Government and Opinion in the Reign of Nicholas II.* Stanford, 1939.

Haxthausen-Abbenburg, Baron August, Freiherr von. *The Russian Empire, Its People, Institutions, and Resources.* 2 vols. London, 1856 (Originally published Hanover and Berlin, 1847–1852).

——. *Studies on the Interior of Russia.* Chicago, 1972 (A new translation of the same work).

Iablochkov, M. T. *Istoriia dvorianskago sosloviia v Rossii.* St. Petersburg, 1876.

Iarmonkin, V.V. *Pisma iz derevni.* St. Petersburg, 1896.

——. *Zadacha dvorianstva.* St. Petersburg, 1895.

Iasnopolskii, M. "Razvitie dvorianskago zemlevladeniia v sovremennoi Rossii." *Mir bozhii*, December 1903, pt. 1, pp. 212–28.

Ignatyev, Lt. Gen. Count A. A. *A Subaltern in Old Russia*. London, 1944.

Ionov, V. "Fakty i illiuzii v voprose dvizheniia chastnoi zemelnoi sobstvennosti." *Zhizn*, April 1900, pp. 193–213.

Kabanov, V. "Pisma iz gubernii." *Russkii vestnik*, August 1889, pp. 295–307.

Kalachov, N. V., ed. *Materialy dlia istorii russkago dvorianstva*. 3 vols. St. Petersburg, 1885–1886.

Karnovich, E. P. *Zamechatelnyia bogatstva chastnykh lits v Rossii. Ekonomichesko-istoricheskoe izsledovanie*. St. Petersburg, 1874.

Karyshev, N. "Mezhdusoslovnaia mobilizatsiia zemel v 45 guberniiakh, v 1893-m g." *Russkoe bogatstvo*, January 1898, pt. 2, pp. 1–33.

Kastelianskii, A. I., ed. *Formy natsionalnago dvizheniia v sovremennykh gosudarstvakh*. 2 vols. St. Petersburg, 1910.

Katkov, M. N. *O dvorianstve*. Moscow, 1905.

Kavelin, K. D. *Sobranie sochinenii*. 4 vols. St. Petersburg, 1897–1900.

Kliuchevskii, V. O. *Sochineniia*. 8 vols. Moscow, 1956–1959.

Korf, Baron S. A. *Dvorianstvo i ego soslovnoe upravlenie za stoletie 1762–1855*. St. Petersburg, 1906.

————. "Predvoditel dvorianstva, kak organ soslovnago i zemskago samoupravleniia." *Zhurnal ministerstva iustitsii*, March 1902, pt. 2, pp. 93–116.

Korkunov, N. M. *Russkoe gosudarstvennoe pravo*. 7th ed. 2 vols. St. Petersburg, 1909 (1st edition, 1893).

Koshelev, A. I. "Chto takoe russkoe dvorianstvo, i chem ono byt dolzhno?" In *Golos iz zemstva*, vol. 1, pp. 26–49. Moscow, 1869.

————. "O dvorianstve i zemlevladeltsakh." In *Golos iz zemstva*, vol. 1, pp. 50–71. Moscow, 1869.

————. *O sosloviiakh i sostoianiiakh v Rossii*. Moscow, 1881.

————. *Zapiski Aleksandra Ivanovicha Kosheleva (1812–1883 gody)*. Berlin, 1884.

Kovanko, P. L. "Osvobozhdenie krestian i obiazatelnyi vykup." *Russkaia mysl*, June 1912, pt. 2, pp. 1–37.

Kuznetsov, P. "Vykup dvorianskikh zemel v kaznu." *Severnyi vestnik*, October 1894, pt. 2, pp. 20–32.

"K voprosu o dvorianskom zemlevladenii." *Mir bozhii*, June 1901, pt. 2, pp. 32–34.

Leroy-Beaulieu, Anatole. *The Empire of the Tsars and the Russians*. 3 vols. New York, 1893–1896 (Originally published Paris, 1881–1889).

Liaskovskii, V. "Pomestnaia sluzhba." *Russkoe obozrenie*, June 1893, pp. 549–68.

Meshcherskii, A. V. *O zapovednykh imeniiakh*. St. Petersburg, 1888.

————. *O zapovednykh imeniiakh. Istoricheskii ocherk*. Moscow, 1894.

————. *Poiasnitelnaia zapiska No. 2-i po povodu khodataistva poltavskago dvorianstva o svobode zaveshchaniia zapovednykh imenii*. Moscow, 1888.

Meshcherskii, V. P. *Moi vospominaniia*. 3 vols. St. Petersburg, 1897–1912.

Miliukov, P. N. *Ocherki po istorii russkoi kultury*. 6th ed., pt. 1. St. Petersburg, 1909.

Minutko, S. "Ob uprazdnenii dvorianskogo zemlevladeniia pri posredstve Krestianskogo banka." *Russkoe obozrenie*, December 1896, pp. 948–86.

Naumov, A. N. *Iz utselevshikh vospominanii, 1868–1917*. 2 vols. New York, 1954–1955.

Nepliuev, N. N. *Istoricheskoe prizvanie russkago pomeshchika*. Moscow, 1880.

Novoselskii, N. "Usilenie dvorianskago elementa v zemstve i kratkosrochnyi kredit dlia pomeshchikov." *Russkii vestnik*, March 1885, pp. 219–33.

Orlov-Davydov, V. P. "Zemledelie i zemlevladenie." *Vestnik Evropy*, June 1873, pp. 814–60.

O sostave, pravakh i preimushchestvakh rossiiskago dvorianstva. St. Petersburg, 1897.

Palmer, Francis H. E. *Russian Life in Town and Country*. New York, 1901.

Paltov, V. "*Vzgliad i nechto*" *o dvorianstve*. Moscow, 1904.

Pazukhin, A. D. *Sovremennoe sostoianie Rossii i soslovnyi vopros*. Moscow, 1886.

"Perepiska Vitte i Pobedonostseva (1895–1905 gg.)." *Krasnyi arkhiv* 30 (1928):89–116.

Peshekhonov, A. V. "Sovremennye argonavty." *Russkoe bogatstvo*, March 1899, pt. 1, pp. 93–125.

"Pisma iz provintsii. Bankrotstvo khoziaev (Pismo iz Simbirskoi gubernii)." *Obrazovanie*, January 1905, pt. 2, pp. 54–69.

"Pisma iz provintsii. Iz Tambova. (Nashi agrarii)." *Novoe slovo*, July 1897, pt. 2, pp. 137–44.

Planson, A. A. *O dvorianstve v Rossii. Sovremennoe polozhenie voprosa*. St. Petersburg, 1893.

————. "*Osoboe soveshchanie*." *Zapiska*. St. Petersburg, 1897.

————. *Poslanie k dvorianam tsentralnoi Rossii*. St. Petersburg, 1897.

————. *Sosloviia v drevnei i sovremennoi Rossii, ikh polozhenie i nuzhdy (o tsentre)*. St. Petersburg, 1899.

Polivanov, M. K. *Mysli o pomestnom nachale v Rossii*. Vladimir, 1897.

————. *O znachenii i pravakh russkago dvorianstva (Mysli i zametki po povodu odnogo razgovora)*. Vladimir, 1881.

Polovtsov, A. A. "Dnevnik A. A. Polovtseva [1901–1903]." *Krasnyi arkhiv* 3 (1923):75–172.

————. *Dnevnik gosudarstvennogo sekretaria A. A. Polovtsova, 1883–1892*. 2 vols. Moscow, 1966.

————. "Iz dnevnika A. A. Polovtsova (1895–1900 gg.)." *Krasnyi arkhiv* 46 (1931):110–32.

Porai-Koshits, I. A. *Ocherk istorii russkago dvorianstva ot poloviny IX do kontsa XVIII veka, 862–1796*. St. Petersburg, 1874.

Provintsial. "Vragi pomestnogo dvorianstva." *Russkoe obozrenie*, August 1897, pp. 776–810.

Romanovich-Slavatinskii, A. *Dvorianstvo v Rossii ot nachala XVIII veka do otmeny krepostnago prava*. St. Petersburg, 1870.

Romer, F. E. "Padenie dvorianstva." *Russkii vestnik*, February 1900, pp. 733–49.

Semenov, N. P. *Nashe dvorianstvo*. St. Petersburg, 1898.

Sh. "Dvorianstvo v Rossii." *Vestnik Evropy*, March 1887, pp. 239–84; April 1887, pp. 531–71; May 1887, pp. 186–210; June 1887, pp. 421–52.

Shidlovskii, S. I. *Vospominaniia*. 2 vols. Berlin, 1923.

Shipov, D. N. *Vospominaniia i dumy o perezhitom*. Moscow, 1918.

Sliianie soslovii; ili dvorianstvo, drugiia sostoianiia i zemstvo. St. Petersburg, 1870.

Slonimskii, L. Z. "Ekonomicheskie zametki. Selskokhoziaistvennyi krizis i dvorianskoe zemlevladenie." *Vestnik Evropy*, July 1897, pp. 318–33.

————. "Pozemelnyia zadachi." *Vestnik Evropy*, August 1894, pp. 810–27; September 1894, pp. 328–47.

Smolenskii, A. "Pisma iz provintsii. Iz Riazani ('Dvorianskii vopros')." *Novoe slovo*, August 1897, pt. 2, pp. 130–39.

Sovremennye dvorianskie voprosy. St. Petersburg, 1897.

Terner, F. G. "Dvorianstvo i zemlevladenie." *Vestnik Evropy*, March 1903, pp. 5–55; August 1905, pp. 470–97; September 1905, pp. 67–94.

Terpigorev, S. N. [Sergei Atava, pseud.]. *Oskudenie*. 2 vols. Moscow, 1958.

————. *Potrevozhennye teni*. Moscow, 1959.

————. "Strizhennye zaitsy (Iz vospominanii tambovskogo pomeshchika)." *Russkoe bogatstvo*, August 1880, pp. 67–89.

Trubetskoi, P. P. *Pamiatnaia kniga dlia uezdnago predvoditelia dvorianstva*. Odessa, 1887.

"Upadok dvorianskogo zemlevladeniia v Saratovskoi gubernii." *Mir bozhii*, January 1897, pt. 2, pp. 24–26.

Ustimovich, P. A. *Mysli i vospominaniia pri chtenii zakonov o dvorianstve*. Moscow, 1886.

V. A. "K dvorianskomu voprosu." *Russkoe bogatstvo*, November 1897, pt. 2, pp. 1–16.

Volkov-Muromtsev, A. N. *Memoirs of Alexander Wolkoff-Mouromtzoff.* London, 1928.

V[orontsov], V. [P.]. "Dvorianskoe zemlevladenie posle reformy." *Russkaia mysl*, October 1898, pt. 2, pp. 69–98.

———. "Nedochety soslovnykh programm." *Vestnik Evropy*, January 1903, pp. 359–76.

Wallace, Sir Donald Mackenzie. *Russia.* 2d ed. 2 vols. London, 1905.

Witte [Vitte], S. Iu. *Vospominaniia.* 3 vols. Moscow, 1960.

Wrangel, N. E. *The Memoirs of Baron N. Wrangel 1847–1920.* London, 1927.

Z. "Sovremennye sofizmy. Novyia soslovnyia tendentsii v nashei pechati." *Vestnik Evropy*, July 1898, pp. 323–36.

"Zadolzhennost chastnago zemlevladeniia." *Otechestvennye zapiski*, February 1880, pt. 2, pp. 141–60.

Zalomanov, N. P. *Dvorianskoe zemlevladenie i mery k ego sokhraneniiu i razvitiiu (istoricheskaia spravka).* St. Petersburg, 1899.

Zinoviev, A. D. *Zapiska o merakh k oblegcheniiu polozheniia zaemshchikov Gosudarstvennago Dvorianskago Zemelnago Banka i po dr. voprosam.* St. Petersburg, 1899.

SECONDARY WORKS

Alston, Patrick L. *Education and the State in Tsarist Russia.* Stanford, 1969.

Amburger, Erik. "Behördendienst und sozialer Aufstieg in Russland um 1900." *Jahrbücher für Geschichte Osteuropas*, n.s. 18 (1970):127–34.

———. *Geschichte der Behördenorganisation Russlands von Peter dem Grossen bis 1917.* Leiden, 1966.

Anderson, Eugene N., and Pauline R. Anderson. *Political Institutions and Social Change in Continental Europe in the Nineteenth Century.* Berkeley, 1967.

Anfimov, A. M. "Karlovskoe imenie Meklenburg-Strelitskikh v kontse XIX-nachale XX v." *Materialy po istorii selskogo khoziaistva i krestianstva SSSR* 5 (1962):348–76.

———. *Krupnoe pomeshchiche khoziaistvo Evropeiskoi Rossii (Konets XIX-nachalo XX veka).* Moscow, 1969.

———. *Zemelnaia arenda v Rossii v nachale XX veka.* Moscow, 1961.

Anfimov, A. M., and I. F. Makarov. "Novye dannye o zemlevladenii Evropeiskoi Rossii." *Istoriia SSSR*, no. 1 (1974), pp. 82–89.

Augustine, Wilson R. "Notes toward a Portrait of the Eighteenth-Century Russian Nobility." *Canadian Slavic Studies* 4 (1970):373–425.

Behrens, C. B. A. *The Ancien Régime.* New York, 1967.

Beloff, Max. "Russia." In *The European Nobility in the Eighteenth Century.* Edited by Albert Goodwin, pp. 172–89. New York, 1967.

Bennett, Helju A. "*Chiny, Ordena*, and Officialdom." In *Russian Officialdom; The Bureaucratization of Russian Society from the Seventeenth to the Twentieth Century.* Edited by Walter M. Pintner and Don K. Rowney, pp. 162–89. Chapel Hill, 1980.

Beskrovnyi, L. G. *Russkaia armiia i flot v XIX veke.* Moscow, 1973.

Black, Cyril E. "The Modernization of Russian Society." In *The Transformation of Russian Society: Aspects of Social Change since 1861.* Edited by Cyril E. Black, pp. 661–80. Cambridge, Mass., 1960.

Blum, Jerome. *The End of the Old Order in Rural Europe.* Princeton, 1978.

———. *Lord and Peasant in Russia from the Ninth to the Nineteenth Century.* Princeton, 1961.

———. "Russia." In *European Landed Elites in the Nineteenth Century.* Edited by David Spring, pp. 68–97. Baltimore, 1977.

Borovoi, S. Ia. *Kredit i banki Rossii (seredina XVII v.-1861 g.)* Moscow, 1958.

———. "K voprosu o zadolzhennosti pomeshchichego zemlevladeniia v predreformennyi period." In *Ezhegodnik po agrarnoi istorii Vostochnoi Evropy 1968 g.*, pp. 197–203. Leningrad, 1972.

Brainerd, Michael C. "The Octobrists and the Gentry, 1905–1907: Leaders and Followers?" In *The Politics of Rural Russia, 1905–1914.* Edited by Leopold H. Haimson, pp. 67–93. Bloomington, 1979.

Brower, Daniel R. *Training the Nihilists: Education and Radicalism in Tsarist Russia.* Ithaca, 1975.

Byrnes, Robert F. *Pobedonostsev, His Life and Thought.* Bloomington, 1968.

Confino, Michael. "Histoire et psychologie: A propos de la noblesse russe au XVIIIᵉ siècle." *Annales: Economies-Sociétés-Civilisations* 22 (1967):1163–1205.

Danilov, F. "Obshchaia politika pravitelstva i gosudarstvennyi stroi k nachalu XX veka." In *Obshchestvennoe dvizhenie v Rossii v nachale XX-go veka.* Edited by L. Martov, P. Maslov, and A. Potresov. Vol. 1, pp. 422–82. St. Petersburg, 1909–1914.

Davidovich, A. M. *Samoderzhavie v epokhu imperializma.* Moscow, 1975.

Diakin, V. S. *Samoderzhavie, burzhuaziia i dvorianstvo v 1907–1911 gg.* Leningrad, 1978.

———. "Stolypin i dvorianstvo (Proval mestnoi reformy)." In *Problemy krestianskogo zemlevladeniia i vnutrennei politiki Rossii. Dooktiabrskii period*, pp. 231–74. Leningrad, 1972.

Drozdov, I. G. *Sudby dvorianskago zemlevladeniia v Rossii i tendentsii k ego mobilizatsii.* Petrograd, 1917.

Druzhinin, N. M. "Pomeshchiche khoziaistvo posle reformy 1861 g. (Po dannym Valuevskoi komissii 1872–1873 gg.)." *Istoricheskie zapiski* 89 (1972):187–230.

Dukes, Paul. *Catherine the Great and the Russian Nobility.* Cambridge, Eng., 1967.

Dzhanshiev, G. *Epokha velikikh reform. Istoricheskiia spravki*. 8th ed. Moscow, 1900.

Edeen, Alf. "The Civil Service: Its Composition and Status." In *The Transformation of Russian Society*. Edited by Cyril E. Black, pp. 274–92. Cambridge, Mass., 1960.

Edelman, Robert. "The Election to the Third Duma: The Roots of the Nationalist Party." In *The Politics of Rural Russia, 1905–1914*. Edited by Leopold H. Haimson, pp. 94–122. Bloomington, 1979.

———. *Gentry Politics on the Eve of the Russian Revolution: The Nationalist Party 1907–1917*. New Brunswick, 1980.

Egiazarova, N. A. *Agrarnyi krizis kontsa XIX veka v Rossii*. Moscow, 1959.

Emmons, Terence. "The Beseda Circle, 1899–1905." *Slavic Review* 32 (1973):461–90.

———. *The Formation of Political Parties and the First National Elections in Russia*. Cambridge, Mass., 1983.

———. *The Russian Landed Gentry and the Peasant Emancipation of 1861*. Cambridge, Eng., 1968.

Eroshkin, N. P. *Istoriia gosudarstvennykh uchrezhdenii dorevoliutsionnoi Rossii*. 3d ed. Moscow, 1983.

Evreiskaia entsiklopediia. 16 vols. St. Petersburg, 1906–1913.

Feldmesser, Robert A. "Social Classes and Political Structure." In *The Transformation of Russian Society*. Edited by Cyril E. Black, pp. 235–52. Cambridge, Mass., 1960.

Field, Daniel. *The End of Serfdom: Nobility and Bureaucracy in Russia, 1855–1861*. Cambridge, Mass., 1976.

Fischer, George. *Russian Liberalism: From Gentry to Intelligentsia*. Cambridge, Mass., 1958.

Ford, Franklin L. *Europe 1780–1830*. New York, 1970.

Frieden, Nancy M. *Russian Physicians in an Era of Reform and Revolution, 1856–1905*. Princeton, 1981.

Galai, Shmuel. *The Liberation Movement in Russia 1900–1905*. Cambridge, Eng., 1973.

Garthoff, Raymond L. "The Military as a Social Force." In *The Transformation of Russian Society*. Edited by Cyril E. Black, pp. 323–38. Cambridge, Mass., 1960.

Gerschenkron, Alexander. *Continuity in History and Other Essays*. Cambridge, Mass., 1968.

———. *Economic Backwardness in Historical Perspective. A Book of Essays*. Cambridge, Mass., 1962.

———. "Problems and Patterns of Russian Economic Development." In *The Transformation of Russian Society*. Edited by Cyril E. Black, pp. 42–72. Cambridge, Mass., 1960.

———. "Soviet Marxism and Absolutism." *Slavic Review* 30 (1971):853–69.

Gerth, H. H., and C. W. Mills, eds. *From Max Weber: Essays in Sociology*. New York, 1946.

Geyer, Dietrich. " 'Gesellschaft' als staatliche Veranstaltung; Bemerkungen zur Sozialgeschichte der russischen Staatsverwaltung im 18. Jahrhundert." *Jahrbücher für Geschichte Osteuropas*, n.s. 14 (1966):21–50.

Gindin, I. F. *Gosudarstvennyi bank i ekonomicheskaia politika tsarskogo pravitelstva (1861–1892 gody)*. Moscow, 1960.

Givens, Robert D. "Eighteenth-Century Nobiliary Career Patterns and Provincial Government." In *Russian Officialdom*. Edited by Walter M. Pintner and Don K. Rowney, pp. 106–29. Chapel Hill, 1980.

Hagen, Everett E. *On the Theory of Social Change: How Economic Growth Begins*. Homewood, Ill., 1962.

Haimson, Leopold H. "Conclusion: Observations on the Politics of the Russian Countryside (1905–14)." In *The Politics of Rural Russia, 1905–1914*. Edited by Leopold H. Haimson, pp. 261–300. Bloomington, 1979.

————. "Introduction: The Russian Landed Nobility and the System of the Third of June." In *The Politics of Rural Russia, 1905–1914*. Edited by Leopold H. Haimson, pp. 1–29. Bloomington, 1979.

Hamburg, Gary M. "Land, Economy, and Society in Tsarist Russia: Interest Politics of the Landed Gentry during the Agrarian Crisis of the Late Nineteenth Century." Ph.D. diss., Stanford University, 1978.

————. *Politics of the Russian Nobility: 1881–1905*. New Brunswick, 1984.

————. "Portrait of an Elite: Russian Marshals of the Nobility, 1861–1917." *Slavic Review* 40 (1981):585–602.

Hans, Nicholas. *History of Russian Educational Policy (1701–1917)*. London, 1931.

Hassell, James. "Implementation of the Russian Table of Ranks During the Eighteenth Century." *Slavic Review* 29 (1970):283–95.

Hosking, Geoffrey A. *The Russian Constitutional Experiment: Government and Duma, 1907–1914* (Cambridge, Eng., 1973).

Hosking, Geoffrey A., and Roberta T. Manning. "What Was the United Nobility?" In *The Politics of Rural Russia, 1905–1914*. Edited by Leopold H. Haimson, pp. 142–83. Bloomington, 1979.

Iatsunskii, V. K. "Izmeneniia v razmeshchenii naseleniia Evropeiskoi Rossii v 1724–1916 gg." *Istoriia SSSR*, no. 1 (1957), pp. 192–224.

————. *Sotsialno-ekonomicheskaia istoriia Rossii XVIII–XIX vv*. Moscow, 1973.

Ivanov, L. M. "O kapitalisticheskoi i otrabotochnoi sistemakh v selskom khoziaistve pomeshchikov na Ukraine v kontse XIX v." In *Voprosy istorii selskogo khoziaistva, krestianstva i revoliutsionnogo dvizheniia v Rossii*, pp. 312–37. Moscow, 1961.

————. "O soslovno-klassovoi strukture gorodov kapitalisticheskoi Rossii." In *Problemy sotsialno-ekonomicheskoi istorii Rossii. Sbornik statei*, pp. 312–40. Moscow, 1971.

Johnson, William H. E. *Russia's Educational Heritage*. Pittsburgh, 1950.

Jones, Robert E. *The Emancipation of the Russian Nobility, 1762–1785*. Princeton, 1973.

Kabuzan, V. M. *Narodonaselenie Rossii v XVIII-pervoi polovine XIX v*. Moscow, 1963.

Kabuzan, V. M., and S. M. Troitskii. "Izmeneniia v chislennosti, udelnom vese i razmeshchenii dvorianstva v Rossii v 1782–1858 gg." *Istoriia SSSR*, no. 4 (1971), pp. 153–69.

Kamosko, L. V. "Izmeneniia soslovnogo sostava uchashchikhsia srednei i vysshei shkoly Rossii (30-80-e gody XIX v.)." *Voprosy istorii*, no. 10 (1970), pp. 203–7.

Katz, Martin. *Mikhail N. Katkov: A Political Biography 1818–1887*. The Hague, 1966.

Kenez, Peter. "A Profile of the Prerevolutionary Officer Corps." *California Slavic Studies* 7 (1973):121–58.

Khromov, P. A. *Ekonomicheskoe razvitie Rossii. Ocherki ekonomiki Rossii s drevneishikh vremen do Velikoi Oktiabrskoi revoliutsii*. Moscow, 1967.

————. *Ekonomicheskoe razvitie Rossii v XIX–XX vekakh (1800–1917)*. Moscow, 1950.

————. *Ekonomika Rossii perioda promyshlennogo kapitalizma*. Moscow, 1963.

Kocharovskii, K. *Sotsialnyi stroi Rossii*. Prague, 1926.

Korelin, A. P. *Dvorianstvo v poreformennoi Rossii 1861–1904 gg*. Moscow, 1979.

————. "Dvorianstvo v poreformennoi Rossii (1861–1904 gg.)." *Istoricheskie zapiski* 87 (1971):91–173.

————. "Rossiiskoe dvorianstvo i ego soslovnaia organizatsiia (1861–1904 gg.)." *Istoriia SSSR*, no. 5 (1971), pp. 56–81.

Kornilov, A. A. *Kurs istorii Rossii XIX veka*. 2d ed. 3 vols. Moscow, 1918.

Korros, Alexandra S. "The Landed Nobility, the State Council, and P. A. Stolypin (1907–11)." In *The Politics of Rural Russia, 1905–1914*. Edited by Leopold H. Haimson, pp. 123–41. Bloomington, 1979.

Kovalchenko, I. D. "K voprosu o sostoianii pomeshchichego khoziaistva pered otmenoi krepostnogo prava v Rossii." In *Ezhegodnik po agrarnoi istorii Vostochnoi Evropy 1959 g.*, pp. 192–227. Moscow, 1961.

————. "Sootnoshenie krestianskogo i pomeshchichego khoziaistva v zemledelcheskom proizvodstve kapitalisticheskoi Rossii." In *Problemy sotsialno-ekonomicheskoi istorii Rossii. Sbornik statei*, pp. 171–94. Moscow, 1971.

Kovalchenko, I. D., and L. V. Milov. *Vserossiiskii agrarnyi rynok XVIII-nachalo XX veka. Opyt kolichestvennogo analiza*. Moscow, 1974.

Kovalchenko, I. D., N. B. Selunskaia, and B. M. Litvakov. *Sotsialno-ekonomicheskii stroi pomeshchichego khoziaistva Evropeiskoi Rossii v epokhu kapitalizma*. Moscow, 1982.

Kozin, M. I. "Kapitalisticheskaia evoliutsiia pomeshchichego khoziaistva Lifliandskoi gubernii vo vtoroi polovine XIX v." In *Ezhegodnik po agrarnoi istorii Vostochnoi Evropy 1959 g.*, pp. 261–73. Moscow, 1961.

Landes, David S. *The Unbound Prometheus*. Cambridge, Eng., 1969.

Laverychev, V. Ia. *Krupnaia burzhuaziia v poreformennoi Rossii 1861–1900*. Moscow, 1974.

Leikina-Svirskaia, V. R. *Intelligentsiia v Rossii vo vtoroi polovine XIX veka*. Moscow, 1971.

Litvak, B. G. *Russkaia derevnia v reforme 1861 goda. Chernozemnyi tsentr 1861–1895 gg*. Moscow, 1972.

Lyashchenko, Peter I. *History of the National Economy of Russia to the 1917 Revolution*. New York, 1949.

McFarlin, Harold A. "The Extension of the Imperial Russian Civil Service to the Lowest Office Workers: The Creation of the Chancery Clerkship, 1827–1833." *Russian History* 1 (1974):1–17.

McGrew, Roderick E. "The Politics of Absolutism: Paul I and the Bank of Assistance for the Nobility." *Canadian-American Slavic Studies* 7 (1973):15–38.

Malkova, Z. I., and M. A. Pliukhina. "Dokumenty vysshikh i tsentralnykh uchrezhdenii XIX-nachala XX v. kak istochnik biograficheskikh svedenii." In *Nekotorye voprosy izucheniia istoricheskikh dokumentov XIX-nachala XX veka. Sbornik statei*, pp. 204–28. Leningrad, 1967.

Manning, Roberta T. *The Crisis of the Old Order in Russia: Gentry and Government*. Princeton, 1982.

———. "The Russian Provincial Gentry in Revolution and Counter-revolution, 1905–07." Ph.D. diss., Columbia University, 1975.

———. "Zemstvo and Revolution: The Onset of the Gentry Reaction, 1905–1907." In *The Politics of Rural Russia, 1905–1914*. Edited by Leopold H. Haimson, pp. 30–66. Bloomington, 1979.

Marshall, T. H. *Class, Citizenship, and Social Development*. Garden City, N.Y., 1964.

Maslov, P. P. *Agrarnyi vopros v Rossii*. 6th ed. Moscow-Leningrad, 1926.

———. "Razvitie zemledeliia i polozhenie krestian do nachala XX veka." In *Obshchestvennoe dvizhenie v Rossii v nachale XX-go veka*. Edited by L. Martov, P. Maslov, and A. Potresov. Vol. 1, pp. 1–38. St. Petersburg, 1909–1914.

Mayer, Arno J. *The Persistence of the Old Regime: Europe to the Great War*. New York, 1981.

Minarik, L. P. "Kharakteristika krupneishikh zemlevladeltsev Rossii kontsa XIX-nachala XX v." In *Ezhegodnik po agrarnoi istorii Vostochnoi Evropy 1963 g.*, pp. 693–708. Vilnius, 1964.

————. "Ob urovne razvitiia kapitalisticheskogo zemledeliia v krupnom pomeshchichem khoziaistve Evropeiskoi Rossii kontsa XIX-nachala XX v." In *Ezhegodnik po agrarnoi istorii Vostochnoi Evropy 1964 god*, pp. 615–26. Kishinev, 1966.

————. "Proiskhozhdenie i sostav zemelnykh vladenii krupneishikh pomeshchikov Rossii kontsa XIX-nachala XX v." In *Materialy po istorii selskogo khoziaistva i krestianstva SSSR* 6 (1965):356–95.

————. "Sistema pomeshchichego khoziaistva v Rakitianskom imenii Iusupovykh (1900–1913 gg.)." In *Materialy po istorii selskogo khoziaistva i krestianstva SSSR* 5 (1962):377–97.

————. " 'Statistika zemlevladeniia 1905 goda' kak istochnik po izucheniiu krupnogo pomeshchichego zemlevladeniia Rossii v nachale XX veka." In *Maloissledovannye istochniki po istorii SSSR XIX–XX vv.*, pp. 56–73. Moscow, 1964.

Mosse, Werner E. "Russian Bureaucracy at the End of the Ancien Régime: The Imperial State Council, 1897–1915." *Slavic Review* 39 (1980):616–32.

Mousnier, Roland. *Les hiérarchies sociales de 1450 à nos jours*. Paris, 1969.

Nifontov, A. S. "Formirovanie klassov burzhuaznogo obshchestva v russkom gorode vtoroi poloviny XIX v. (Po materialam perepisei naseleniia g. Moskvy v 70-90-kh godakh XIX v.)." *Istoricheskie zapiski* 54 (1955):239–50.

————. *Zernovoe proizvodstvo Rossii vo vtoroi polovine XIX veka*. Moscow, 1974.

Orlovsky, Daniel T. "High Officials in the Ministry of Internal Affairs, 1855–1881." In *Russian Officialdom*. Edited by Walter M. Pintner and Don K. Rowney, pp. 250–82. Chapel Hill, 1980.

Parsons, Talcott. "Some Principal Characteristics of Industrial Societies." In *The Transformation of Russian Society*. Edited by Cyril E. Black, pp. 13–42. Cambridge, Mass., 1960.

Pavlenko, N. I. "K voprosu ob evoliutsii dvorianstva v XVII–XVIII vv." In *Voprosy genezisa kapitalizma v Rossii*, pp. 54–75. Leningrad, 1960.

Pavlovsky, George. *Agricultural Russia on the Eve of the Revolution*. London, 1930.

Pearson, Thomas S. "The Origins of Alexander III's Land Captains: A Reinterpretation." *Slavic Review* 40 (1981):384–403.

Pershin, N. P. *Agrarnaia revoliutsiia v Rossii*. 2 vols. Moscow, 1966.

Pintner, Walter M. "Civil Officialdom and the Nobility in the 1850s." In *Russian Officialdom*. Edited by Walter M. Pintner and Don K. Rowney, pp. 227–49. Chapel Hill, 1980.

————. "The Evolution of Civil Officialdom, 1755–1855." In *Russian Officialdom*. Edited by Walter M. Pintner and Don K. Rowney, pp. 190–226. Chapel Hill, 1980.

———. *Russian Economic Policy under Nicholas I*. Ithaca, 1967.

———. "The Social Characteristics of the Early Nineteenth-Century Russian Bureaucracy." *Slavic Review* 29 (1970):429–43.

Pipes, Richard. *Russia under the Old Regime*. London, 1974.

———. "Russian Conservatism in the Second Half of the Nineteenth Century." *Slavic Review* 30 (1971):121–28.

Pokrovskii, M. N. "Obshchaia politika pravitelstva 1866–1892 gg." In *Istoriia Rossii v XIX veke*, vol. 5, pp. 1–78. St. Petersburg, 1907–1911.

Proskuriakova, N. A. "Razmeshchenie i struktura dvorianskogo zemlevladeniia Evropeiskoi Rossii v kontse XIX-nachale XX veka." *Istoriia SSSR*, no. 1 (1973), pp. 55–75.

Raeff, Marc. *Origins of the Russian Intelligentsia: The Eighteenth-Century Nobility*. New York, 1966.

Rashin, A. G. *Naselenie Rossii za 100 let (1811–1913 gg.)*. Moscow, 1956.

Rieber, Alfred J. *Merchants and Entrepreneurs in Imperial Russia*. Chapel Hill, 1982.

Robinson, Geroid T. *Rural Russia under the Old Régime*. New York, 1932.

Rowney, Don K. "Higher Civil Servants in the Russian Ministry of Internal Affairs: Some Demographic and Career Characteristics, 1905–1916." *Slavic Review* 31 (1972):101–10.

———. "Organizational Change and Social Adaptation: The Prerevolutionary Ministry of Internal Affairs." In *Russian Officialdom*. Edited by Walter M. Pintner and Don K. Rowney, pp. 283–315. Chapel Hill, 1980.

Ruffmann, Karl-Heinz. "Russischer Adel als Sondertypus der europäischen Adelswelt." *Jahrbücher für Geschichte Osteuropas*, n.s. 9 (1961):161–78.

Russkii kostium 1750–1917. 5 vols. Moscow, 1960–1972.

Schapiro, Leonard. *Rationalism and Nationalism in Russian Nineteenth-Century Political Thought*. New Haven, 1967.

Sidelnikov, S. M. *Obrazovanie i deiatelnost pervoi gosudarstvennoi dumy*. Moscow, 1962.

Simmonds, George W. "The Congress of Representatives of the Nobles' Associations, 1906–1916: A Case Study of Russian Conservatism." Ph.D. diss., Columbia University, 1964.

Simonova, M. S. "Problema 'oskudeniia' tsentra i ee rol v formirovanii agrarnoi politiki samoderzhaviia v 90-kh godakh XIX-nachale XX v." In *Problemy sotsialno-ekonomicheskoi istorii Rossii. Sbornik statei*, pp. 236–63. Moscow, 1971.

Sinel, Allen. *The Classroom and the Chancellery: State Educational Reform in Russia under Count Dmitry Tolstoi*. Cambridge, Mass., 1973.

Sliozberg, G. B. *Dorevoliutsionnyi stroi Rossii*. Paris, 1933.

Soloviev, Iu. B. "Pechat o politicheskoi roli dvorianstva v kontse XIX v." In *Problemy krestianskogo zemlevladeniia i vnutrennei politiki Rossii. Dooktiabrskii period*, pp. 210–31. Leningrad, 1972.

———. "Pravitelstvo i politika ukrepleniia klassovykh pozitsii dvor-ianstva v kontse XIX veka." In *Vnutrenniaia politika tsarizma (seredina XVI-nachalo XX v.)*, pp. 239–80. Leningrad, 1967.

———. "Samoderzhavie i dvorianskii vopros v kontse XIX v." *Istoricheskie zapiski* 88 (1971):150–209.

———. *Samoderzhavie i dvorianstvo v kontse XIX veka.* Leningrad, 1973.

———. *Samoderzhavie i dvorianstvo v 1902–1907 gg.* Leningrad, 1981.

Spring, David. *The English Landed Estate in the Nineteenth Century: Its Administration.* Baltimore, 1963.

Stepynin, V. A. "Iz istorii popytok nasazhdeniia v Sibiri dvorianskogo zemlevladeniia." *Uchenye zapiski Krasnoiarskogo gosudarstvennogo pedagogicheskogo instituta* 4, no. 1 (1955):134–60.

Stökl, Günther. "Gab es im Moskauer Staat 'Stände'?" *Jahrbücher für Geschichte Osteuropas*, n.s. 11 (1963):321–42.

Strelsky, Nikander. *Saltykov and the Russian Squire.* New York, 1940.

Strumilin, S. G. *Ocherki ekonomicheskoi istorii Rossii i SSSR.* Moscow, 1966.

Sviatlovskii, V. V. *Mobilizatsiia zemelnoi sobstvennosti v Rossii (1861–1908 g.).* 2d ed. St. Petersburg, 1911.

Tarasiuk, D. A. "Iz istorii statistiki zemlevladeniia v Rossii (Perepis 1877–1878 gg.)." *Vestnik Moskovskogo universiteta*, ser. 9 (History), no. 3 (1973), pp. 47–61.

Tarnovskii, K. N. "Problemy agrarnoi istorii Rossii perioda imperializma v sovetskoi istoriografii (Diskusii nachala 1960-kh godov)." In *Problemy sotsialno-ekonomicheskoi istorii Rossii. Sbornik statei*, pp. 264–311. Moscow, 1971.

Tatishchev, S. S. *Imperator Aleksandr II.* 2 vols. St. Petersburg, 1901–1903.

Thaden, Edward C. *Conservative Nationalism in Nineteenth-Century Russia.* Seattle, 1964.

Thompson, F. M. L. *English Landed Society in the Nineteenth Century.* London, 1963.

Toennies, Ferdinand. "Estates and Classes." In *Class, Status, and Power*, 2d ed. Edited by Reinhard Bendix and Seymour M. Lipset, pp. 12–21. New York, 1966.

Torke, Hans J. "Continuity and Change in the Relations between Bureaucracy and Society in Russia, 1613–1861." *Canadian Slavic Studies* 5 (1971):457–76.

———. *Die Staatsbedingte Gesellschaft im Moskauer Reich; Zar und Zemlja in der Altrussischen Herrschaftsverfassung 1613–1689.* Leiden, 1974.

Troitskii, S. M. *Russkii absoliutizm i dvorianstvo v XVIII v.; formirovanie biurokratii.* Moscow, 1974.

Tseitlin, S. Ia. "Zemskoe samoupravlenie i reforma 1890 g. (1865–1890)." In *Istoriia Rossii v XIX veke*, vol. 5, pp. 79–139. St. Petersburg, 1907–1911.

Veselovskii, B. B. "Dvizhenie zemlevladeltsev." In *Obshchestvennoe dvizhenie v Rossii v nachale XX-go veka*. Edited by L. Martov, P. Maslov, and A. Potresov. Vol. 1, pp. 291–312; vol. 2, pt. 2, pp. 1–29. St. Petersburg, 1909–1914.

————. *Istoriia zemstva za 40 let*. 4 vols. St. Petersburg, 1909–1911.

Wagner, William G. "Legislative Reform of Inheritance in Russia, 1861–1914." In *Russian Law: Historical and Political Perspectives*. Edited by William E. Butler, pp. 143–78. Leiden, 1977.

Weber, Max. "The Development of Caste." In *Class, Status, and Power*, 2d ed. Edited by Reinhard Bendix and Seymour M. Lipset, pp. 28–36. New York, 1966.

Weissman, Neil B. *Reform in Tsarist Russia: The State Bureaucracy and Local Government, 1900–1914*. New Brunswick, 1981.

————. "State, Estate, and Society in Tsarist Russia: The Question of Local Government, 1900–1908." Ph.D. diss., Princeton University, 1976.

Whelan, Heide W. *Alexander III and the State Council: Bureaucracy and Counter-Reform in Late Imperial Russia*. New Brunswick, 1982.

Yaney, George L. *The Systematization of Russian Government: Social Evolution in the Domestic Administration of Imperial Russia, 1711–1905*. Urbana, 1973.

————. *The Urge to Mobilize: Agrarian Reform in Russia, 1861–1930*. Urbana, 1982.

Zaionchkovskii, P. A. *Krizis samoderzhaviia na rubezhe 1870–1880-kh godov*. Moscow, 1964.

————. *Otmena krepostnogo prava v Rossii*. 3d ed. Moscow, 1968.

————. *Pravitelstvennyi apparat samoderzhavnoi Rossii v XIX v*. Moscow, 1978.

————. *Provedenie v zhizn krestianskoi reformy 1861 g*. Moscow, 1958.

————. *Rossiiskoe samoderzhavie v kontse XIX stoletiia*. Moscow, 1970.

————. *Samoderzhavie i russkaia armiia na rubezhe XIX–XX stoletii, 1881–1903*. Moscow, 1973.

————. "Soslovnyi sostav ofitserskogo korpusa na rubezhe XIX–XX vekov." *Istoriia SSSR*, no. 1 (1973), pp. 148–54.

Zakharova, L. G. "Krizis samoderzhaviia nakanune revoliutsii 1905 goda." *Voprosy istorii*, no. 8 (1972), pp. 119–40.

————. *Zemskaia kontrreforma 1890 g*. Moscow, 1968.

INDEX

Land grants for nobles, 86–88, 133, 203n.51
Land prices, 43–45
Landowners, noble: voting rights of, in *guberniia* societies of nobility, 21, 23, 199n.63; number of, 28, 30, 186–88, 218n.18; traditional attitude of, toward land, 29–31; stratification of, by size of holdings, 36–40; methods of exploiting properties, 42–44; motives of, for selling properties, 45, 50, 53; use of capital realized from confiscation, sale, and mortgaging of land, 51–53; political role of, after 1905, 159, 163, 165–66, 168, 170; emergence of class consciousness among, 169, 173. *See also* Assemblies of nobility, *guberniia*; Congress of Representatives of Noble Societies; Mortgage debt of noble landowners
Landownership, noble: decline in acreage, 28, 31–33, 41, 44–45, 189; purchases, 33–35; aggregate value of acreage, 44, 49, 202n.34; capital sum realized from confiscation and sale of acreage, 46–47; proposals to ban sales to commoners, 68–69; in Siberia, 212n.78
Leontiev, M. N., 207n.39
Leroy-Beaulieu, Anatole, 29
Liaskovskii, V., 100
Lithuanian nobles, 184–85
Liven, A. A., 76, 82, 206n.38

Manasein, N. A., 106, 222n.11
Manning, Roberta T., 9–13, 32–34, 149, 176, 189, 196n.27, 197n.40, 201n.11, 217n.10, 218n.14, 219n.41, 223n.33, 224n.36, 226nn.55, 65, 227n.74, 228nn.79, 4, 230nn.18, 26, 28, 231n.38
Marshals and deputies, *guberniia* assembly of, 74, 143
Marshals of nobility: *guberniia* 20–23, 26, 145–51, 226nn.61, 65, 227nn.72, 73; national conferences of *guberniia*, 13, 64, 66, 69, 72, 76, 80–81, 83–84, 94, 99–100, 104, 106, 121–22, 127, 151–53, 157, 160, 162, 167–68, 210n.34; *uezd*, 20–22, 144–47, 149–51, 166–68, 227nn.70, 75, 76
Mayer, Arno, 4–5, 169, 196n.8
Meshcherskii, A. V., 71, 74

Meshcherskii, V. P., 63–65, 80, 86, 131
Miliutin, D. A., 120–21
Mortgage debt of noble landowners, 10, 47–51, 79–82, 84–85, 190–91, 211n.61
Moskovskie vedomosti, 64, 66, 119, 132, 142, 153
Muraviev, N. V., 101, 106, 206n.38
Muromtsov, L. M., 207n.39
Mutual Aid Funds, 82, 84–85

Naryshkin, A. A., 167
National genealogical register of nobility, 104–5
Nicholas I, 20, 91
Nicholas II, 60, 63–65, 71, 75, 81–82, 85–86, 88, 95, 98–99, 102, 104, 107, 118, 122–23, 135, 150–53, 157, 161, 168, 175, 229n.14, 231n.4
Nobility: demographic characteristics of, 17–18, 28, 181–85, 200n.1; civil rights and privileges of, 18–20, 25, 27; corporate organization and privileges of, 20–24, 26–27, 138–40, 143; new occupational roles of, 52–53, 114–15, 218n.25; social transformation of, 171–73; alleged political inflexibility of, 176–78; genealogical subdivisions of, 179–80. *See also* Assemblies of nobility, *guberniia*; Deputy assemblies, *guberniia* noble, Landowners, noble; Landownership, noble; Marshals of nobility
Noble Bank, 203n.42
Noble Land Bank. *See* State Noble Land Bank
Noble question, 57–60, 64, 154

Obolenskii, A. D., 76, 207n.38
Octobrists, 160, 167
Orlov-Davydov, A., 53
Oskudenie, 8
Overcoat, The (Gogol), 97

Page Corps, 120, 219n.38
Paltov, Vladimir, 133
Patriotic Union, 161
Paul I, 19, 22
Pavlov, N. A., 160
Pazukhin, A. D., 58, 60, 62, 68, 100, 130–32, 134–36, 149–50, 205n.12, 221n.4, 222nn.11, 20, 223nn.22, 23, 24
Pearson, Thomas S., 221n.4